10/10   10 —

Special Forces

Special Forces

The Changing Face of Warfare

Mark Lloyd

ARMS AND
ARMOUR

Arms and Armour Press
A Cassell Imprint
Wellington House, 125 Strand, London WC2R 0BB

Distributed in the USA by Sterling Publishing Co. Inc., 387 Park Avenue South, New York, NY 10016-8810.

Distributed in Australia by Capricorn Link (Australia) Pty. Ltd, 2/13 Carrington Road, Castle Hill, NSW 2154.

British Library Cataloguing-in-Publication Data: a catalogue record for this book is available from the British Library

ISBN 1-85409-170-0

Designed and edited by DAG Publications Ltd.
Designed by David Gibbons; edited by Gerald Napier;
Printed and Bound in Great Britain by
Hartnolls Ltd, Bodmin, Cornwall.

Contents

Contents

Contents

Preface

The concept of military elitism is far from new. From the earliest days of warfare commanders have gathered about them a nucleus of the best troops available, both for their personal protection and to give them an edge in battle. Whether these troops fought out of feudal loyalty or for money was largely irrelevant; the superior training, motivation and discipline on the battlefield often turned defeat into victory, stalemate into overwhelming success.

As new weapon systems were introduced and warfare became more complex, new and more specialist elites evolved. During the fifteenth and sixteenth centuries English archers and German Landsknechts prevailed against often larger, more conventional forces. Some 300 hundred years later Napoleonic Tirailleurs and the British Rifle Brigade forced the introduction of fire and movement to a previously static battlefield. During the early stages of the American Civil War the marksmen of Berdan's Rifles wrought havoc among the lines of the Confederate artillery which, until then, were deployed unprotected in the front line. Later Boer Commandos picked off British officers with impunity at ranges previously discounted as impractical by the general staffs of every European army.

As the twentieth century has progressed, elite units have become more specialist - and selective - in response to the growing size and sophistication of the battlefield. In recent years many such special units have come to regard terrorism as their major enemy, honing their skills in counter-insurgency and hostage rescue to meet the new threat.

So diverse are the demands made of today's special forces that a mere handful - perhaps only the SAS, Green Berets and Spetsnaz - have remained truly ubiquitous. Most have compromised generality for a specialisation, accepting that they can only realistically excel in one field. Thus has mushroomed a series of special purpose forces - paratroopers, marines, reconnaissance experts - all excellent troops in their own discipline but limited in others.

Used cohesively, special and special purpose forces can complement each other with devastating success. During the Falklands campaign, SAS and SBS teams paved the way for the advance along two axes of the Royal Marines and paratroopers of the much enhanced 3 Commando Brigade. The sheer discipline and iron resolve of these special purpose troops more than compensated for their lack of material support as they 'yomped' through the ferocity of a South Atlantic winter from one side of East Falkland to the other, stopping only to give occasional battle to the well dug in and numerically superior enemy.

Preface

Unlike special forces, who wherever possible operate covertly, special purpose forces can normally only expect to enjoy the benefit of surprise for a short period. Thereafter they must rely for survival on their discipline, training and resolve (words which occur frequently in their vocabulary). Ideally they should not be committed to conventional battle. The 1st British Airborne Division at Arnhem fought like lions but, without adequate anti-tank artillery, they stood no chance against the combined might of two German panzer divisions and were slaughtered.

The presumptions of four decades that the Third World War would be fought by massed armoured units in Europe, with the strong possibility of nuclear release, were shattered with the disintegration of the Soviet Union. At about the same time the Gulf War proved the necessity for mobility. The first major Coalition units to reach Saudi Arabia were special purpose combat units from the US Marine Corps. Although subsequently they took little part in the land battle their early presence ashore proved at once the United States' military commitment to Kuwait and possibly tempered Saddam Hussein's further territorial ambitions. Since then, special purpose forces have been deployed extensively in Grenada and Panama, while their very presence off the shores of Haiti made possible the subsequent peaceful occupation.

Given that the major military powers are moving towards, some would say returning to, the days of out-of-area bush warfare, the need for highly trained and well-motivated special purpose forces, supplemented by special forces where necessary, is now greater than ever.

1

An Introduction to Special Forces

An Historical Overview

The concept of the elite fighting unit is by no means a modern idea. Throughout history armies have contained units which by reason of superior training and equipment, or greater combat experience, were considered to be an elite. They have been dependable, able to repel the enemy's onslaughts and continue fighting even when cut off from the rest of the army. Occasionally they have been trained to fight away from the main army, harrying the enemy at his rear or flanks. More recently they have been expected to strike away from the main battle itself; targeting supply lines, headquarters, choke-points and communications centres in an attempt to disrupt their adversary's ability - and will - to fight.

During the second half of the twentieth century elite units have become more specialist - and secretive - to meet the demands of the increasingly sophisticated modern battlefield. They have also divided: into so-called special forces units capable of operating in any theatre in the world; special purpose forces designed and trained for a single type of warfare; and units of special designation (a peculiarly wartime phenomenon) trained and equipped for a single operation.

Many of the world's most famous elite forces are in fact special purpose, selected and trained for a specific type of warfare. These are the paratroopers, rangers, marines and commandos of all the major armed forces and the conscripted elements of the former-Soviet Spetsnaz. They are shock troops in the finest traditions of the historical elite. Unlike true special forces however, they are not trained to live off the land for long periods, and would expect to be relieved by conventional forces relatively quickly. Typically, former-Soviet paratroopers were equipped with light artillery, BM-14 rocket launchers and a limited number of BMD armoured personnel carriers (APCs) but, even so, were not expected to hold a position for more than 24 hours.

Occasionally one force has spawned another as circumstances have changed. Thus the SAS was born of the Long Range Desert Group (LRDG) and grew from a special purpose unit (raiding behind Rommel's lines) to arguably the finest special force in the world. Special forces and special purpose forces troops are invariably volunteers. However units of special designation are often pressed men, attached to units chosen at random to fulfil a particularly hazardous mission. Merrill's Marauders and Orde Wingate's First Chindits were volunteers but the Second Chindits were not, nor were the glider battalions which landed in support of the paratroopers on D Day and at Arnhem.

The three elites cannot always be differentiated by role. Elements of a special force may well find themselves working closely with special purpose forces, and even

1 An Introduction to Special Forces

forces of special designation. Prior to the disintegration of the Warsaw Pact, United States Green Berets and British SAS (both special forces) were trained to operate in the general reconnaissance/guerrilla role deep inside enemy territory; collecting intelligence, raiding or conducting a prolonged campaign of irregular warfare. Artillery spotters (special purpose forces chosen from the elite within the gunner regiments) were trained to 'stay behind' while the advancing enemy rolled over their covert positions, register targets for the heavy artillery and eventually retire through the enemy lines, using their skills in escape and evasion to reach the safety of their own positions. Infantry reconnaissance platoons (units of special designation drawn from the forward line battalions) were trained to patrol as far forward as possible, probing the forward line of the enemy's troops (FLET) in an attempt to establish his immediate intentions. All were involved in reconnaissance yet their training and selection were vastly different.

When not fulfilling their specialist roles the gunner stay behind observers and the infantry forward patrollers would have been expected to carry out the more mundane duties of the ordinary soldier. The special forces would not. Not only would they have been wasted in the front line but their personal battle skills would almost certainly have been inadequate for the task. During the final years of the Cold War the massive improvements in infantry firepower and mobility, exemplified by the introduction of new personal and anti-tank weaponry and the increased use of mechanised infantry combat vehicles (MICVs), led to a rethinking of basic tactics which would have been alien to a specialist divorced from the daily training routine of a conventional battalion. It is in training and selection (described in detail in Chapter Six) that the true division between the special forces, special purpose forces and forces of special designation - and indeed the division between elite and conventional forces - becomes most apparent.

The Royal Marines Commando

The British Royal Marines Commando is one of the finest special purpose forces in the world, with a proud history dating back to October 1664 when 250 men were raised as the 'Duke of York and Albany's Maritime Regiment of Foot.' The King of England, Charles II, was very much in favour of creating a standing force of men trained to fight on land and at sea, and foresaw in the creation of the Regiment, the need for professional servicemen to crew the King's ships, rather than the seamen who then signed on for one voyage at a time.

The soldiers who joined the 'Admiral's Regiment' (identified by name as a special purpose force even then) were lured by the promises of bounty and prize money, and rapidly proved their worth, not merely as shipborne infantry capable of fighting ashore, but also as trained ship's crew, discarding their heavy yellow coats and wide-brimmed hats in favour of seaman's dress.

The sea-soldiers of the Admiral's Regiment took the title 'Marines' in 1672, and became a strong backbone to the crews of many ships of the line, where vigorous Marine discipline was often much better than that of the seamen with whom they served. After seeing considerable action against the Dutch, the Marines were formed into a Corps in 1755, and took part in most of the major British campaigns over the next 150 years, fighting either as well-disciplined infantry reinforcing the Army, or as naval troops fighting from ships.

The Corps won its first VC at the Battle of Inkerman in 1854. During the First World War, the 4th Battalion Royal Marines took part in the amphibious raid at Zeebrugge on 23 April 1918, winning its eighth and ninth VCs, both of which were awarded by ballot.

During the Second World War, the Government formed a number of Commando units, the name and concept taken from the Afrikaner raiding parties who had carried out swift strikes across the Transvaal in the Boer War. These British Commando units (typical wartime units of special designation) were intended to be relatively small, highly mobile and capable of carrying out surgical attacks against tactical or strategic targets.

Commando units were raised from Army and Royal Navy personnel as well as from the Royal Marines, but at the end of a distinguished wartime service by the Commandos, the title and training standards were retained only within the Royal Marines. All Royal Marine personnel, save bandsmen, have been commando-trained since the end of World War II. The Royal Marines Commando, an excellent special purpose force within its own right, has spawned a number of 'elites within an elite', notably the Special Boat Service (SBS) and Mountain & Arctic Warfare Cadre (M & AW Cadre) which will be described in greater detail in later chapters.

The Parachute Regiment

Britain did not possess a capability to launch an airborne offensive at the beginning of the Second World War. Indeed such was the essentially defensive strategic thinking at the commencement of hostilities that no plans existed to raise such a unit, in spite of the considerable interest shown in airborne forces by such countries as the United States of America, Italy, the Soviet Union and Germany.

The spectacular successes of the German 'Blitzkrieg' offensive in 1939-40 forced a major rethink in British tactical and military planning, and the rapid seizure by German glider troops of the Eben Emael fortress in Belgium convinced the newly-elected Prime Minister, Winston Churchill, of the need for a similar British airborne force.

From the outset the role of the British airborne force was envisaged to be that of a highly mobile special purpose offensive capability, able to strike deep behind enemy lines. Such a force would seize tactical or strategic objectives and hold them until relieved by more heavily armed units.

In July 1940, authorisation was given to form a corps of 5,000 troops, and a recently formed commando unit was assigned to Major Rock of the Royal Engineers to begin training. From this late start the 1st Airborne Division was formed, and after an initial unsuccessful operation against the Tragino Aqueduct, carried out a successful commando-type raid on a radar station at Bruneval in north-west France.

In November 1942 the 1st Parachute Brigade was deployed to Tunisia, as part of the First Army, and was parachuted into the outskirts of Tunis with orders to capture three separate airfields. The 1st and 3rd Battalions were able to seize their objectives, but the 2nd Battalion was widely scattered and found itself stranded some 80km behind enemy lines. The Battalion fought its way back to join with an American column; the action was a foretaste of the most ambitious operation of the war, and emphasised the vulnerability of special purpose forces dropped behind enemy lines where reinforcement was essential to the success of the operation.

Despite heavy losses, the achievements of 1st Airborne Brigade in North Africa convinced the British High Command of the effectiveness of such a unit, and in May 1943, the 6th Airborne Division was formed. 6th Airborne was chosen to spearhead the British assault on D Day in June 1944, securing the left flank of the British landings north of Caen. Despite some battalions being widely scattered, 6th Airborne was able to seize its main objectives, and hold them until reinforced.

Operation 'Market Garden' was the largest airborne assault of all time, and has gone down in history as one of the most heroic, if ill-judged. 1st Airborne Division found on landing that IX and X SS-Panzer Divisions were regrouping in the area of Arnhem, and encountered ferocious opposition from heavily-armed, well-trained troops. Fighting with outstanding gallantry, the Division succeeded in holding its position for nine days, when reinforcement had been expected in two. Fewer than 3,000 from the total of 10,000 men involved in the operation escaped captivity or death.

The United States

Today's US Army Special Forces, the Green Berets, can trace their origins back to a combined Canadian and American unit formed during the Second World War, the First Special Service Force (SSF). The force was raised by General George C. Marshall following a visit by Lord Louis Mountbatten who had been one of the great advocates of the use of small raiding parties, and had been instrumental in the creation of the British Commando Forces.

Originally comprising three regiments of two battalions each, 1st SSF fought in the Aleutian Islands, North Africa, France and Southern Italy, acquitting itself well. This was partly a result of the considerable skills of the volunteers comprising the force, and partly as a result of its deployment and use in the special purpose role envisaged, that of light raiding.

At the end of hostilities, 1st SSF was disbanded, in common with so many of the highly specialist and successful irregular special purpose forces created during the Second World War. However the need for such a unit was re-examined in 1951, the 10th Special Forces Group (SFG) was raised in June 1952, and the 77th SFG in September 1953.

The US Marine Corps is the largest, and one of the oldest of its kind in the world. Formed by Act of Congress in 1798 it played a relatively minor role in the American Civil War. From then until the First World War the Marines were active in the defence of United States overseas interests, particularly in South America.

In the Second World War the reputation for toughness enjoyed by the Corps was enhanced by the bloody battles fought against the Japanese in the Pacific theatre. The style of amphibious warfare made necessary by the 'island hopping' strategy was ideally suited to the Marines training and the famous actions at Wake, Guadalcanal and Iwo Jima stand out as tributes to the bravery and resourcefulness of the officers and enlisted men. By the conclusion of the war there were nearly 500,000 servicemen in the Corps and their activities in the Pacific had ensured a role for them in the future.

Although not officially regarded as part of its Special Operations Forces by the US Government, the Marines nonetheless undergo rigorous selection and training and may truly be recognised as one of the most potent special purpose forces in the world.

The US Army Rangers are the oldest of America's special forces units and enjoy a considerable reputation. They have always operated as highly trained light infantry, without heavy support; ideally suited to quick-reaction, short-term deployment. They are at their best attacking high prestige targets, conducting specialist raids and gathering intelligence on enemy troop concentrations.

The history of the Rangers can be traced back to the seventeenth and eighteenth centuries when irregular troops were employed in America to fight against the Indians. The first group to be formally integrated into the Army (as an early special purpose force) was commanded by Captain Robert Rogers. Rangers fought for both sides in the American War of Independence and the Civil War, and also fought in the Mexican War. The creation of the modern Ranger units took place during the Second World War when it was realised that special assault formations could wreak damage out of all proportion to their size. The first Ranger unit was formed in 1942 at Carrickfergus, Northern Ireland, under the command of Major William Derby. Trained by, and closely emulating, the British Commandos, the Rangers took part in Operation 'Torch', the invasion of North Africa. Subsequently they participated in the battles for Sicily and Italy, during which they sustained terrible losses.

In all, six Ranger battalions were raised during the Second World War and these units were often to be found in the vanguard of Allied operations against the Axis powers. In 1942 and 1943 Rangers were used in raids on the coast of Europe and in the following year the skill and daring of these units was recognised by the major role assigned to the 2nd and 5th Battalions in the Normandy landings. It was not just in Europe that the Rangers played an active part, for they were also in the Pacific war. The 6th Rangers took part in the recapture of the Philippines and then performed a highly successful raid to liberate over 500 American prisoners of war held at the Cabanatuan camp on Luzon.

In India, the US Army established several Long Range Patrol units the most famous of which, the 5307th Composite Unit (Provisional), was formed on 3 October 1943 specifically for service in Indo-China, in which theatre it earned itself the nickname of 'Merrill's Marauders' in honour of its far-sighted and dashing commander, Major General Frank D. Merrill. Throughout the spring and summer of 1944, the 5307th operated behind Japanese lines in support of the Chinese 22nd and 38th Divisions, harrying supply lines and disrupting communications. The Marauders were recognised and redesignated the 475th Infantry Regiment on 10 August 1944, deactivated on 1 July 1945 and reformed as the 75th Infantry Regiment on 21 June 1954.

With the exception of units such as the SEALs and Delta Force, formed much later and discussed in Chapter Five, the 82nd Airborne (All American) and the 101st Airborne (Screaming Eagles) Divisions, the United States' present parachute and air assault formations, comprise the balance of her elite forces.

82nd Airborne Division was originally raised as an infantry division in 1917 for service on the Western Front, where it spent more consecutive days in the front line than any other American unit. Deactivated in 1919, the 82nd was reformed at Camp Clairborne, Louisiana, in 1942 and in August of that year declared an airborne unit. By the war's end the division had spent nearly two years overseas, including 442 days in combat. It participated in Operation 'Husky', the invasion of Sicily, and was subsequently tasked with the seizure of Nijmegen bridge as part of Operation Market Garden.

101st Airborne, also raised at Camp Clairborne in 1942, served in Europe and was awarded the Distinguished Unit Citation for its action at Bastogne, where it played an important part in blunting the German counter-attack in the Ardennes. It returned to the United States for deactivation in November 1945.

German Experiences

In Germany before the Second World War the attitude of the professional soldier to special forces was one of total abhorrence. True, the Army had gained a number of successes with its stormtroopers in 1918, but these men had proudly worn the uniform of the infantry and had remained firmly within the conventional command structure. Those wishing to fight in disguise were seen as misfits within the military system or as spies and agents.

Although this rejection was shared by the senior staff, the German counter-intelligence service, the Abwehr, formed a number of small commandos, later to be known as 'Brandenburg' units (see Chapter Four.) The SS, which shared none of the Army's Imperial traditions, recognised the practical advantages to be gained through the use of irregular forces fighting along orthodox lines. Many senior SS officers were veterans of the early Nazi street battles and fully appreciated the value of shock troops properly led.

The Security Service of the SS (the Sicherheitsdienst or SD) employed elite elements in the agents provocateurs role to foment political crisis prior to the invasion of Czechoslovakia. Later it engineered the mock attack on the radio station at Gleiwitz, the German pretext for the invasion of Poland.

German reticence did not extend to the uniformed elite. Germany was one of the first countries to recognise the usefulness of airborne troops in modern warfare and was the first successfully to employ paratroops in combat. In the early stages of the Second World War the Fallschirmjäger, then part of the Luftwaffe, played an important part in the initial German offensives, including the invasions of Czechoslovakia, Poland, Denmark, Norway and the Low Countries. It was not until the invasion of Crete in 1941 that the use of German airborne forces was restricted. Although the massive airborne invasion was successful, the casualties sustained by the Fallschirmjäger were so heavy (over 4,000 men) that they spent the remainder of the war employed as elite ground forces. As such they conducted a number of extremely well fought battles towards the latter stages of the Second World War, including the defence of Monte Cassino against ultimately hopeless odds.

The Soviet Experience

The term special designation is derived from the Russian 'spetsialnogo naznacheniya' and was first used by the Soviets to describe several types of formations, including special engineer formations, armoured trains, special radio-technical units and a number of experimental formations.

'Voiska spetsialnogo naznacheniya' (VSN), known universally as Spetsnaz within NATO, and the best known of Soviet elites, had no peer in the West. In the eyes of the Soviet Union (and now Russia) it has always been a force of special designation rather than a NATO-style special purpose force. At its peak in the 1980s a staggering 90 per cent of its members were conscripts among whom standards varied greatly.

Until 1989, references in the Soviet military press to VSN were rare and usually couched in historical terms. Units were described in the context of 'special reconnaissance' (spetsialnaya razvadka) or 'diversionary reconnaissance' (diversiya razvadka,) and never as units or subunits 'of special designation' (podrazdelenie spetsial'nogo naznacheniya.)

The very existence of a multitalented elite within the Soviet Army was discounted as Western propaganda. Troops specialising in reconnaissance were designated 'razvadchiki.' Long Range Reconnaissance Patrol (LRRP) operators became 'iskatelia' (those who seek); High Altitude Low Opening/High Altitude High Opening (HALO/HAHO) specialists were known as 'vysotniki' and prisoner snatch squads as 'okhotniki' or 'capture.'

In 1989 the Kremlin partly lifted its veil of secrecy and allowed a series of articles to appear in the Soviet military and civilian press referring in detail and performance to units of special designation.

The first recorded use of forces of special designation by the Soviets occurred soon after the Revolution. In the spring of 1918 the 'chasti osobogo naznacheniya' (ChON), comprising detachments of procommunist workers, was moved into the major industrial complexes to ensure their total adherence to the new regime. A year later the force was expanded by the Cheka (the precursor of the KGB) into a paramilitary territorial unit within the Red Army. As such it saw considerable action against the Moslem 'basmachi' (bandits) in the south, until it was itself disbanded in 1925.

The Soviets pioneered the use of airborne special forces as early as 1927. Reconnaissance teams ('razvadchiki') were used to devastating effect against Afghan insurgents in 1929 and against the basmachi in Central Asia until the latter's virtual suppression in 1931. By 1932 the embryonic regular airborne forces had become almost completely dedicated to deep reconnaissance ('spetsialnaya razvadka') and to the destruction of the enemy's command and control facilities.

By the early 1930s Soviet special operations units had successfully suppressed the majority of domestic dissent and felt ready to concentrate on the suppression of anti-Soviet activity abroad. In 1936 the Cheka created an Administration for Special Tasks to kill or kidnap enemies outside the USSR and set about the ruthless elimination of its enemies. During the Spanish Civil War (1936-39) the newly formed NKVD (the Peaple's Commissariat of Internal Affairs) and GRU (Military Intelligence) undertook terrorist, sabotage and guerrilla activities behind Nationalist and Republican lines on a scale never before envisaged.

During the early stages of the Great Patriotic War (the Second World War) the Soviets introduced a wide variety of elite, if initially ad hoc, Chekist, GRU, assault combat engineer and naval special reconnaissance units. Few were truly elite and many were composed of conscripts. Nonetheless they played a crucial part in the ultimate Soviet victory. Incorporating the lessons of the earlier airborne 'Razvadchiki' with the experience of the Cheka agents, they created recce-diversionary brigades, NKVD special groups, guards battalions and headquarters reconnaissance detachments, and as such may be regarded as the true antecedents of the modern Spetsnaz.

Soviet naval special forces played a crucial part in the Great Patriotic War. In three years of fighting they spearheaded many of the 110 tactical and four operational beach landings undertaken by the conventional Naval Infantry. More fundamentally they were the first naval forces to pioneer agent penetration and deep reconnaissance behind enemy lines.

In late 1941, in a desperate attempt to gain intelligence on German strengths in the Murmansk area, the Northern Fleet formed the Fourth Special Volunteer Detachment of Sailors. Ultimately renamed the 181st Special Reconnaissance Detachment, or 'osobogo razvadyvatel'nogo otriada,' this force comprised the true antecedents of Soviet Naval Spetsnaz. Tasked directly by the fleet commander, Admiral Golovko, the clandestine agents and commandos of the Detachment operated often hundreds of kilometres from their home base in Poliarnyi. Whilst some undertook aggressive search and destroy missions against established shore installations others concentrated on covert reconnaissance, target acquisition, coast-watching, prisoner snatching and field interrogation. Many were accomplished linguists, a few even pro-communist foreign sympathisers.

Great Patriotic War special purpose operations were of course in no way limited to the Navy. In particular the Soviets employed large scale engineering forces behind the enemy lines in an attempt to disrupt his logistics and communications. A Guards battalion of miners, designated 'otdelnyy gvardeyskiy batal'on' or OGBM, was attached to each operational Front with a brigade in reserve. Working closely with the various partisan groups they either crossed the front line at night in small groups or were inserted by parachute, landing some 15km from their objective. In the winter of 1943-44 the OGBM alone derailed 576 trains and five armoured trains, blew up approximately 300 tanks and self-propelled guns, 650 wheeled vehicles and armoured cars and 300 rail and road bridges, killing and wounding thousands of enemy soldiers in the process. As with all Soviet forces of special designation, OGBM troops were selected on the basis of their political loyalty, moral courage, resilience and stamina. Most were Party members, aged 18 to 30 years and, in many cases, were experienced sportsmen and hunters.

Operational training for the OGBM was highly specialised. Once selected and designated the miners were segregated from other units. Much of their initial field training related to conventional platoon and company drills much loved by the higher echelons of the Red Army. Thereafter training became more arduous. The miners were taught LRRP procedures, demolitions, terrain and night navigation, escape and evasion, Arctic and swamp survival. High losses, both in training and operationally, were regarded as acceptable. Nothing was allowed to interfere with the successful attainment of an objective. Injured or exhausted soldiers were simply left to their own devices to fend for themselves as best they could.

Immediately after the Great Patriotic War the Soviets disbanded their forces of special designation, delegating the execution of primary rear area missions to conventional airborne units. During the late 1950s however they recreated their specialist units, structuring them within the new KGB and GRU frameworks.

The French Foreign Legion

The French Foreign Legion came into being on 10 March 1831, and in over 160 years of warfare has earned itself a reputation for elitism second to none. The mass of its earliest recruits were Europeans driven into its ranks by economic privation and political turmoil. There were also a number of Frenchmen, some tempted by the chance of battle, adventure and booty, others keen to put some distance between themselves and the law. Many of its officers were veterans of Napoleon's Grande Armée, rotting on half pay since 1815.

The Old Legion comprised five battalions, initially under the command of Colonel Stoffel, a Swiss officer and veteran of the Napoleonic Peninsula campaign. By October 1832 it had been joined by the 6th (Belgian) and 7th (Polish) battalions and numbered 5,538 officers and men. The Legion was committed to the Spanish Civil War in 1835, and was virtually annihilated in a disastrous series of pyrrhic victories.

The 'New' Legion was formed in 1837, initially with two battalions but with a third added a year later. The numbers increased steadily until, in 1841, the Legion had expanded sufficiently to be divided into two regiments, the 1er and 2eme Régiments Etrangers. For the next 70 years the Legion played a major part in France's foreign campaigns; in the Crimea, in Italy, Mexico, North and Equatorial Africa and Indo-China.

In 1914 the Legion was overwhelmed by volunteers from more than 50 nationalities. Four regiments were constituted; the II/1st RE and II/2nd RE supplemented by veterans from North Africa, the III/1st, formed in Paris to include drafts from the police and fire brigade, and the IV/1st, entirely composed of Italians and commanded by a grandson of the great Garibaldi. The II/1st RE was the first to see action, at Artois in May 1915. In bloody and largely futile fighting, from a strength of 2,900 it lost its commander, Colonel Cot, all its battalion commanders, over 50 officers and 1,889 men.

The regiment was brought up to strength and sent back to the battle at Givenchy on 16 June, when it lost a further 624 men dead, wounded or missing. In September 1915 it was again in action, at Navarin Farm in Champagne, east of Berry-au-Bac. On this occasion its losses were so great that it was disbanded.

In the meantime the II/2nd RE, the sister regiment, had also been committed to Champagne, in the Rheims and Paissy sectors and later at Souain and Navarin Farm. The remnants of both regiments were collected together and reformed into the Régiment de Marche de Légion Etrangère, the Foreign Legion Marching Regiment (RMLE). In exactly three years from its inception on 11 November 1915 to the Armistice on 11 November 1918, the RMLE became the most decorated regiment in the French Army. The price of this privilege however was horrific; 139 officers, 349 sous-officers and 3,628 légionnaires killed or missing.

2
Mythology to Fact
The Evolution of the Classical Specialist

The Age of the Heroic Elite

Since the beginnings of recorded history, and the earliest organised societies, there have been elite military forces. As ancient civilisations prospered and developed they spawned complex social hierarchies; fiefdoms, monarchies, empires and even primitive republics. Rulers successful in battle turned to their scribes to preserve often highly subjective accounts of their triumphs for the benefit of history. In so doing they created the first written myths, and a clearer indication of the earliest elite military forces.

The mythological societies of Ancient Greece depended on the archetypical elite figure, the individual military superman - Ajax or Achilles - or the warrior-traveller such as Odysseus or Aeneas. Many assumed the mantle of demi-gods, accounts of whose deeds in overcoming their enemies form a potent cocktail of fact, traditional folklore and pure myth. The tradition spread to other societies and adopted new forms.

Plato's imaginary 'Guardians' assumed military as well as civic responsibilities in his idealised *Republic*. Classical Greece and Rome adopted Ares and Mars as their gods of war. Later warrior-societies adopted their own individualistic models, such as the Norse gods Thor and Odin, or the berserker heroes of the sagas. As Roman Britain disintegrated into chaos the knightly heroes of King Arthur's Round Table rode forth in their forlorn attempt to stem the tide of Anglo-Saxon conquest. More than a thousand years later the fictitious Sir Percy Blakeney, the Scarlet Pimpernel, risked his life for the aristocracy of revolutionary France when no mere mortal could be found to fulfil the hopeless task. Even modern society has its cult figures; its, Richard Hannays, James Bonds and John Rambos. Although their patent lack of chivalry, innate aggression and unbridled ferocity tend to devalue them in the eyes of many, they are in essence the direct descendants of the knights of old.

From Myth to Reality

The dawn of the historic era saw the emergence of the first truly organised and identifiable military elites. Tasked with the physical protection of their ruler and the subjugation of his enemies, they quickly assumed a social status far in excess of that of the farmer or artisan. In approximately 1100BC the Jewish commander Gideon, in the course of defeating the Midianites, used highly effective selection methods to form a temporary corps d'élite for a special night operation against the enemy's camp.

The Persian Emperors, Darius the Great (521-486BC) and Xerxes, had their bodyguards of 'Immortals', 10,000 strong with many times that in reserve, Xerxes threw them against the Spartans and their Peloponnesian allies at Thermopylae in one of the first true elite versus elite engagements. The core of the Immortals comprised an elite regiment, known as the King's 'Spearbearers' or 'Arstibara', selected from the cream of Persian society serving within the Amrtaka.

Military service was compulsory for all Persians, and it is probable that the rump of the Immortals comprised the pick of the conscripts.

Often their duties to their sovereign carried the elite from this life to the next. The inner tomb of the boy Pharaoh Tutankhamen (c. 1350BC) was found to be guarded by statues of his Nubian guards. The first Chinese Emperor, Qin Shi Huang, had terracotta replicas of his warriors buried in vast pits in Shaanxi Province (c. 209BC), of which some 7,000 examples have since been discovered and excavated.

The Scythians

On several occasions in early history warrior states emerged to stamp their authority on their neighbours. Many were barbaric, even by the harsh yardsticks of the day, despising that which they failed to understand and destroying that which they despised. Others were willing to compromise adopting, or at the very least exploiting, the more useful attributes of their vassals.

The Scythians lived in the Early Iron Age and inhabited the northern areas of the Black Sea. The 'Scythian period' in the history of Eastern Europe lasted little more than 400 years, from the seventh to the third centuries BC; yet their horsemen made such an impression that for a thousand years after the demise of the Scythians as a sovereign power, their heartland and the core of the territories dominated by them continued to be known as Greater Scythia.

Little has been ascertained about their mode of campaign. It is not known whether they sought out their enemies as disorganised bands of nomad plunderers, or as a unified people with a disciplined army. What is certain is that from the very beginnings of their emergence on the world scene the Scythians took part in the greatest campaigns of their times, defeating such mighty contemporaries as Assyria, Urartu, Babylonia, Media and Persia.

As befitted a nomadic people, the bulk of the Scythian Army was mounted, with infantry support offered by poorer Scythians and pressed levies conscripted from the vassal tribes. Although defensive armour was introduced in the later campaigns, Scythian warriors remained offensive in their outlook. Most horsemen were lightly armed, protected by no more than fur or hide jackets and headgear. For long range fighting they used bows and arrows, often fired at full gallop; at intermediate ranges they employed spears and javelins; and for hand-to-hand combat, swords, axes, maces and daggers. The Scythian corps d'élite was its heavy cavalry. Well protected and heavily armed it fought in disciplined and closely packed formations, delivering its main blow against the centre of the enemy position. Capable of manoeuvring en masse, it was trained to break through the enemy ranks, regroup in the thick of the action, locate the enemy's weak point and exploit it. When the enemy had been thrown into disarray the lightly-armed mass of the Scythian horse attacked to complete the rout.

No one, not even the Scythian leaders, knew the precise size of their armies, although they have been assessed at more than 150,000 warriors at their peak. Almost the entire adult population, including a large number of women, fought on campaign. Scythia was the first truly successful military state to subordinate her entire social structure to the art of war.

Alexander the Great

Alexander the Great (reigned 336-323BC) inherited from his father, Philip II, an elite escort of 'Companions'. Originally under 100 strong and drawn from the ranks of the Macedonian aristocracy, it was later expanded to a maximum of 3,300 by the inclusion of carefully selected paladins from allied Greek states. The Companions formed their 'ilai', or squadrons, into 'embolos', delta-shaped wedge-formations invented by the Scythians and adopted by Philip II. This formation permitted rapid wheeling and withdrawal and was ideal for penetrating other cavalry formations. Armed with the sarissa, a spear at least 4.5m in length, the Companions were able to penetrate formations of infantry armed with the conventional 2-2.5m hoplite spear.

The iron core of the Macedonian army was its phalanx. The ordinary Macedonians served as infantrymen, the elite of whom formed the 'Pezhetairoi', the 'Foot Companions', so called to stress their relationship to the king as a tactical and political counter to the aristocratic Companions. By the spring of 334BC, immediately prior to Alexander's invasion of Persia, his infantry numbered 24,000, of whom 12,000 were left behind in Macedonia (together with 1,500 Companions) under the command of Alexander's Regent, Antipater.

Of the 12,000 who formed part of Alexander's expeditionary force, 9,000 were organised, on a territorial basis, in six 'taxeis' (brigades) of Pezhetairoi, while the remaining 3,000 formed an elite Guard, the Hypaspists or 'Shield-bearers.' After the Battle of Issus (333BC) three taxeis were honoured with the title 'Asthetairoi' or 'Best Companions.' Three years later a seventh taxeis was added to the force.

The Hypaspists were organised into three chiliarchies of 1,000 men of which one, the elite 'Agema', paralleled the 'ile' among the Companions. The conventional taxeis were themselves divided into smaller units of 'dekad', originally ten men strong but later expanded to sixteen. Each dekad formed a file of the taxeis drawn up in deep battle order or a double-file in the eight-deep battle order which Alexander preferred.

In the attack each member of the taxeis occupied a space less than 1m in width, but when receiving an enemy attack the phalanx closed up even further into 'synaspismos' or 'locked-shield order', in which each phalangite presented a front of less than 0.5m. The first five ranks extended their 6-7m pikes, or sarissas, beyond the bodies of the men in the front rank, holding their weapons progressively higher in each rank, thus presenting the enemy with an impenetrable hedge of spear points.

The Roman Empire

Early rulers had to be sure that they kept the loyalty of their military elite. Excellent pay and conditions were not always enough. The elite Praetorian Guard were allowed to involve themselves deeply in Roman politics, to the extent that they occasionally took it upon themselves to depose the very emperors whom they were sworn (and paid) to protect. In 68AD the Praetorian Guard felt so confident in itself that it actually auctioned off the Empire to the highest bidder. A few years later the same formation assassinated the insane Gaius Caesar Caligula, replacing him with his unwilling uncle, Tiberius Claudius.

The origins of the Roman military system are lost in pre-history. During the sixth century BC the Roman Army was divided into seven distinct groups, according to wealth. The richest citizens, the equites, were grouped into eighteen centuries (of 100 men each) and formed the cavalry, providing their own horses. The first class, the next wealthiest, were formed into 80 centuries of spearmen fully armed with helmet, cuirass, greaves and round shield. The second, third and fourth classes each provided twenty centuries of spearmen with diminishing layers of protection; the fifth class twenty centuries armed with slings and javelins. The 'capite censi', literally the head count, were composed of the residue with little or no land or money. As such they were felt to have no incentive to protect the state and were thus not considered fit to serve in its army. However during the next three centuries this group grew in importance as the army expanded and Rome struggled to keep pace with its insatiable demand for manpower.

In 390BC Rome was sacked by the Senones, a Celtic tribe from north of the Appenine mountains. The Latins were compelled to hold an inquest. Their traditional defensive phalanx, adopted from the Greeks, was abandoned; new tactics, involving frontal assault, were introduced. The well armoured second-class ('hastati') were rearmed with heavy javelins and placed out ahead of the heavily armed spearmen of the first-class. Once the hastati had broken the force of the Celtic assault they withdrew through prepared gaps in the line of spearmen behind them, leaving the main Roman defensive line intact. By 340BC Roman tactics had moved to the offensive. Now the hastati, instead of running away once they had thrown their javelins, drew their swords and charged the enemy at close quarters, exploiting the confusion caused by their missiles. If they failed to defeat their foe they withdrew through the lines of the first-class, who then charged the by now disrupted lines of the enemy.

Roman tactics worked well. The forces of Hannibal were defeated in 202BC, those of Philip V of Macedonia in 197BC and the armies of Antiochus the Great of Syria in 190BC. In 168BC the Roman legions met and defeated the Macedonian phalanxes for the last time, at Pydna beneath Mount Olympus.

Rome was the first great military power to introduce large scale engineering to the field of warfare. In 58BC Caesar employed his one available legion to fortify the bank of the River Rhône for a distance of nearly 30km 'by means of a wall 16ft high with a ditch'. Once constructed he placed forts at intervals along the wall, successfully frustrating the proposed movement of the migrating Helvetii.

The Roman Empire, which followed the Republic in 31BC, introduced a number of innovations which led to the creation of a truly elite professional army. The Emperor Augustus, perhaps the greatest of the Roman military leaders, consolidated his legions with those of Mark Anthony when he assumed power. Thereafter legions were no longer disbanded at the end of a campaign, save when disgraced or wiped out. Nor were they immediately replaced when they met with disaster, notably the three legions annihilated in the Teutoburg Forest, in Germany, in 9AD. For the next 200 years the number of legions never fell below 25 nor rose above 30, allowing each to draw upon its own traditions and esprit de corps.

More fundamentally, terms of service were increased from six to sixteen (and later twenty) years, creating in less than a decade a truly professional, battle hardened nucleus of fighting men. Each legion comprised a single cohort of five double centuries and nine cohorts of six centuries each, the established strength of a century being 80 men. Although a cavalry element of 120 men was added for reconnaissance duties, the strength of the legion remained in its heavily armed infantry; each equipped with helmet, body armour and large shield for protection and javelin and sword for attack.

The officer structure was also changed, introducing a far higher degree of professionalism among the senior echelons. Permanent command of each legion passed to a legate, appointed directly by the Emperor. He was supported by six tribunes, the senior of whom (the 'tribunus laticlavius') wore a broad stripe on his tunic denoting his candidature for the Senate. There was no cohort commander, the presumption being that command would devolve upon either the senior centurion or a junior tribune. The centurions remained the backbone of the legion, the most senior being appointed to the new post of Prefect of the Camp; effectively an early quartermaster with general responsibility for equipment and rear area administration.

In theory all legionaries were Roman citizens. In reality however the harsh terms of service, much of it spent far from Italy, made military service unpopular with most Italians who preferred to enlist in the cohorts in Rome. The burden of recruitment was increasingly borne by the provinces, particularly those in which the legions were stationed. Young men were granted citizenship on enlistment, increasing considerably the number of sons who followed their fathers into the service.

Attila the Hun

During the years before Attila's reign the Huns jostled with the Goths, Vandals and other Germanic peoples in the so-called Great Migration, which was ultimately destined to bring about the downfall of Rome. Around 445AD Attila assumed the leadership of the confederacy of Hun tribes, which grew from being a barbarian nuisance to become a deadly peril. Attila preferred diplomacy to warfare. Despite Roman assertions to the contrary he was no mere ogre; nor was he a divine leader of his people, simply a brilliant soldier whom they chose to follow. Many of the stories of Hun atrocities, and indeed of their acts of superhuman military prowess, were spread by their defeated foes by way of explanation for their humiliation and as such cannot be taken as accurate.

The Huns had a devastating effect not just on Rome but on the Middle East. They were basically divided into two groups, the Hephthalite or 'White' Huns who invaded Persia and the 'Black' Huns who attacked Europe. Little concrete is known of the Hephthalites who may have been more Mongol than Turkish in appearance. As their invasions of Transoxiana, Afghanistan and Iran, and their sorties into India show they were a powerful nation by the fifth and early sixth centuries. Their language was a form of Turkish and they fought with long-hilted, long-bladed swords and composite bows, but strangely they had no stirrups on their saddles.

The Black Huns who conquered the Russian Steppes around 370AD seem to have sprung from nowhere. While in Russia the Huns seemed to have lived a typical nomadic existence. But everything seems to have changed once they moved west into the Hungarian Plain. They lost their nomad logistical base and became raiders. They no longer fled from battle on horseback but retired in good order to their fortified bases. Although their reliance on cavalry virtually ceased they remained excellent archers, retaining a well armoured mounted elite which fought with long spears as well as bows. Most warriors however now dismounted to fight as infantrymen or archers. Campaigns were supported by a siege train, possibly manned by Roman renegades.

By 450AD the greater part of Attila's army was almost certainly of Germanic origin having assimilated a large number of local warriors. It had lost most of its nomadic traditions, and with them its military edge. It is said the Attila had even contemplated conversion to Christianity. It owed its victories against Rome more to the inefficiencies of the dying Latin state rather than to its own military prowess. By 453AD however Attila was dead, his armies had been shattered by an abortive invasion of northern France, and his people were weakened by internecine quarrels. The army was destined to disintegrate, its surviving warriors to be driven back to the Steppes, where ironically they resumed their nomadic existence after the death of their leader.

The Early Armies of Islam

The growth of Islam as a military elite can be traced back to 661 and the establishment of the Umayyad caliphate as a dynastic state. The early Muslims were frustrated by an acute lack of horses. The bulk of the army fought dismounted, in close ranks for moral support. The cavalry, where it did exist, was husbanded on the flanks, its horses led to the battlefield and only then mounted to preserve their stamina.

When Yemen and Oman were wrested from nominal Persian rule, the horses and camels demanded in tribute enabled the Muslims to assume a limited offensive. Rarely strong enough to lay formal siege to hostile outposts, they survived by adopting the specifically Arab tactic of bypassing enemy strongpoints. Their superior strategy, based upon the widespread use of the camel, enabled their mounted infantry to outmanoeuvre their foes, giving battle at times and places of their own choosing.

As the area under Muslim control widened so an increasing number of horse-raising territories were acquired, until by the mid-seventh century Islam possessed the finest cavalry mount available; the Syrian-Arab crossbreed. By the eighth century the cavalry was divided into two types; the armoured, who fought as a small elite of shock troops, and the unarmoured who were limited to reconnaissance. Most armoured cavalry fought with lance, mace, sword and a large Khanjar dagger. A few may have carried bows, although they would have discarded these early in the battle, and all would have been capable of fighting on foot.

The early ninth century saw the introduction of the 'ghulams,' freed slaves who acted like the Praetorian guard of Imperial Rome. Initially the ghulams were recruited as captives from beyond the Muslim frontier in Transoxiana. Later they were purchased as children to be trained and then freed as Muslims. They were formed into a new corps, theoretically owing loyalty to the Caliph in Baghdad, but in reality focusing their fealty on their own commanders. The ghulams rarely took part in external operations, but were instrumental in maintaining order at home.

They were exceptionally good horse-archers, carrying a lasso and two or three bows which they were able to fire forward or to the rear, at the gallop. Although slower than the more lightly armoured Arabs they were equally competent with the lance.

2 Mythology to Fact

Post-Roman Europe

The so-called Dark Ages which succeeded the withdrawal of the Roman legions from western Europe led to periods of great confusion, with rulers requiring the services of spécial guards for their own protection. Charlemagne, crowned Holy Roman Emperor in 800, was served by elite cavalry forces - ancestors of the feudal knights of the Middle Ages - who, commanded by such paladins as Roland and Oliver, proved redoubtable in battles against the Moors and other adversaries. The Anglo-Saxon monarchs of England had special escorts of thegns and huscarles - such as those who formed the famous 'shield-wall' and fought to the death in defence of Harold Godwinson at Hastings in 1066.

When the Roman government of Britain collapsed in the fifth century, the Romanised native population struggled for a time to preserve its Roman, and by now largely Christian, way of life. Gradually this was submerged by invaders from the Continent. Although known collectively as Anglo-Saxons, the invaders were in fact drawn from three distinct Germanic nations: Saxons from northern Germany and Holland; Angles from the south of the Danish peninsula; and Jutes from Jutland. At the time there were similar tribal movements taking place throughout Europe, causing the invaders to intermarry and ultimately merge into one amorphous people.

The earliest Anglo-Saxons to reach Britain came by invitation, possibly even before the Roman Government had collapsed. They came as organised mercenaries, under their own chiefs, to protect the demoralised Britons against attacks from the Picts, Scots and southern continentals. These small groups slowly combined into larger units and ultimately into colonies.

Large scale invasions followed as the mercenary-settlers sent word to their homelands of the easy pickings, and the native population began to resist the expansionist tendencies of their by-now unwelcome former allies. Legendary leaders such as Ambrosius Aurelanius and Arthur fought valiantly against the advancing hordes of the like of Hengist and Horsa but to no avail. Gradually, over a century and a half, the native peoples were forced into submission as a dozen rival Anglo-Saxon kingdoms were formed.

By 650 the Northumbrian kings had established themselves as supreme in England. However a revolt by the Mercians in 658 ended all hopes of unity and led to a gradual realignment of power in the south, with East Anglia, Essex, Sussex and Wessex incorporated into the Mercian kingdom by 670. A series of campaigns by the kings of Wessex, beginning in 821, led to yet another transfer of power. From then until 1066, apart from a short interlude of 26 years when the land fell under Danish sovereignty, England remained at least nominally under the control of the House of Wessex.

In 1051 the family of the Earl of Godwin rebelled against the rule of Edward the Confessor and were banished. They returned in the following year, driving out much of the Norman influence then pervading the country. When Earl Godwin died in 1053 de facto control of England passed to his son, Harold Godwinson.

Edward the Confessor died on 5 January 1066, leaving three contenders for the throne of England: William, Duke of Normandy; King Harold Hardraada of Norway; and Earl Harold Godwinson. Godwinson moved south to counter the threat from Normandy while the kings of Mercia and Northumbria took up battle positions in the north in anticipation of a Norse invasion.

The Evolution of the Classical Specialist

Hardraada struck first, and in a set-piece battle at Fulford, on the outskirts of York, defeated the combined armies of Mercia and Northumbria. Hearing the news Godwinson at once marched north in support, to be met en route by emissaries of Mercia and Northumbria offering him their total fealty. Godwinson met and destroyed the disorganised Norse army at Stamford Bridge. As undisputed king of England he then turned his exhausted army and marched south to meet the Norman forces which had taken advantage of the distraction in the north to land an invasion force along the coast of Sussex.

On Sunday, 14 October 1066 the by-now exhausted and depleted forces of King Harold met Duke William on Senlac Ridge with disastrous results for the Anglo-Saxons. Harold was killed in battle and his army scattered.

The English army which Harold Godwinson led to defeat had a number of elite elements born of the Anglo-Saxon feudal system. At the top of the social apex were the 'athelings', princes of the blood who shared many of the privileges and responsibilities of the king, including military service and command in the field. Athelings were supported by the 'eoldormen' (later earls), the ruling nobility drawn from the ranks of the under-kings of formerly independent peoples. Each was responsible for the administration and justice within a shire, and for calling out the military reserve, or 'Fyrd', when required.

The king, and many of his higher nobility, gathered around them a 'thegn' or personal bodyguard. Loyal service by a thegn could result in the accumulation of vast riches and even elevation to an earldom. Below the thegns were the 'ceorls', simple freemen or yeoman farmers who formed the backbone of Anglo-Saxon society. The ceorls were further subdivided into three classes: the 'geneatas,' the peasant aristocracy who paid rent to their landlord; the 'kotsetla,' who paid for their land in the form of duties; and the 'gebur', who paid no rent but whose lives were totally dominated by the labour services contractually due to their landlords. Ceorls could win elevation to the thegn through wealth or military service. A ceorl could not, however, rise to be an earl.

At the very bottom of the social heap came the serfs or bondsmen, little better than slaves, with few privileges or obligations to military service.

During the early ninth century England came under increasing threat from the Vikings. In response the kings formed 'Hirds' or Hearth troops, corps of elite warriors whom they were able to dispatch at short notice to areas under particular likelihood of attack. However the Hearth troops could not always respond in time, leaving the onus for immediate defence on the earls, their thegns and the bands of local able-bodied males whom they were able to press into service. These groups of lightly armed farmers provided little protection against the Vikings and were soon replaced by groups of semi-professional soldiers recruited on a regional basis. The richer earls supplemented their full time cadre of thegns with mercenaries, often Scandinavians themselves, backed up by the Select Fyrd. This was raised by selective recruitment rather than general levy and comprised one man for every five hides of land. Many of the Select Fyrd were themselves thegns, but when insufficient thegns were available ceorls were substituted. Towns were assessed on their wealth and also obliged to send representatives to the Select Fyrd, although those wishing to opt out could elect to pay the crown twenty shillings in lieu of each warrior, the exact sum to hire a replacement.

2 Mythology to Fact

The Select Fyrds were well armed and equipped, and after a few skirmishes with the Vikings, battle-hardened. The Select Fyrd could be called out at any time and active service depended entirely upon need. When mobilised, each hide was charged four shillings towards the maintenance and payment of its selected representative. Each soldier could thus expect to earn in the region of four pence per day, a sum roughly comparable to the wages of a Norman knight and ample to ensure that membership of the Select Fyrd became highly competitive.

In addition to the Select Fyrd there was the Great Fyrd, a general levy of all able-bodied freemen summoned in emergencies to defend their shires. The role of these untrained men, most of whom were farmers who simply picked up a spear and perhaps shield in response to their master's summons, must have been extremely limited. They could not be asked to serve more than half a day's march from their homes without pay and could not be kept in the field for more than a few days. Nonetheless they proved extremely useful defensively, releasing the mounted Select Fyrd for service further from home.

Housecarls, professional mercenaries with their own set of rules and paid in cash rather than kind, were introduced in the early eleventh century. They formed a small but highly efficient standing army, well disciplined and heavily armed. By 1050 these paid but landless warriors, together with the earls, their thegns and the Select Fyrd provided the Saxon kings with a highly professional nucleus; mobile, loyal and a match for any army it was likely to encounter.

By 1066 the royal housecarls probably numbered some 3,000. At Hastings the Saxon army had been weakened by its northern campaigns and by the sheer speed of its march south. It was short of the quota for both the Select and Greater Fyrd, yet successfully withstood the Norman army for several hours. Had the Saxon army been at full strength the result of the Battle of Hastings, and the subsequent history of England, might have been very different.

The Vikings

From the narrow, British perspective the Viking era may be defined as beginning with the murder of the king's reeve, Beaduheard, and the first great raid on Lindisfarne in 793 and ending on the bloody fields of Stamford Bridge in 1066. More broadly, the Vikings began to seek new settlements abroad in the mid-eighth century, after an earlier population explosion had rendered their existing farm lands inadequate for their needs.

There was never a true Viking nation; indeed for a long time there were no nations of any kind in Scandinavia. There were groupings, mostly tribal, dominated by leaders who arose, ruled and were struck down in a constant confusion of warfare, regicide, rebellion and catastrophe. Unified by language and religion the Viking peoples remained a northern, pagan bloc two centuries after the Saxons had succumbed to Christianity.

The way in which society was organised was recognisably the same in all the lands from which the Vikings sailed. Their areas were divided into districts, each with its 'thing' or assembly of free householders, responsible for upholding the law, making decisions and agreeing issues. Initially disputes were often settled by trials of combat. As the societies grew in sophistication however, written laws were introduced and wise men, or even judges employed to bring continuity.

The Norwegians began the raids, but the Danes and Swedes soon followed suit. Sweden, facing east, thrust across the Baltic, using the complex of lakes and waterways to drive far into the Russian steppes. From there they spread south and east, down the Volga and Dnieper to threaten Constantinople itself. The Byzantine emperors were so impressed by the fighting abilities of the Vikings that they recruited a special corps - the Varangian Guard - for their army. For more than two centuries the Vikings served the Byzantine empire as shock troops or imperial bodyguards, fighting with distinction on many occasions.

The Danes and Norwegians tended to sail south; the Norwegians to the Orkneys, Shetlands, Hebrides and on to Ireland; the Danes down the North Sea to England, the Lowlands, Normandy and France. From 834 the Danish Vikings appeared annually along both sides of the English Channel. In 859 62 ships sailed southwards from the Loire. They pillaged the Spanish coast, sacked Algeçiras and entered the Mediterranean to ravage the North African coast. They wintered in the Rhône delta, looting Arles, Nîmes and other cities before sailing on to sack Pisa.

In England only Alfred of Wessex succeeded in putting up a successful resistance. He defeated the Danes in the south, but could not save the north-east which was systematically ransacked. By the early eleventh century Viking power was on the wane. Ireland was lost in 1014 and soon thereafter Iceland declared its independence. King Knut, who had earlier welded England, Denmark, Norway and parts of southern Sweden into a loose confederation, died in 1035 leaving a void. The Anglo-Saxons wrested England from Norse control in 1042 and Harold Hardraada died trying to reclaim it in 1066.

The Vikings were not barbarians, nor were they invincible. The small size of the vast majority of their war parties left them vulnerable to the larger Frankish and Anglo-Saxon forces by whom they were often defeated. Losses were high, often as much as two-thirds in a single expedition, but these were accepted.

The Normans

A large Danish raiding party under Hrolf arrived along the coast of France in 911 to pillage the lower Seine valley. His attempts to besiege Chartres proved abortive, yet his threat to the Seine valley was considered so great that Charles, King of the Franks, ceded the area of Upper Normandy to him as part of a negotiated peace. By 924 the Danish enclave had expanded to incorporate the districts of Bayeux, Exmes and Sees, and in 933 the Cotentin and Avranchin. Hrolf was baptised in 912 and adopted the name of Rollo. Within two generations he and his Danes had become wholly assimilated, adopting the Frankish language, religion, customs and laws.

The Normans' maritime traditions, coupled with their dynamic energy made them so commercially successful that by the late eleventh century theirs was one of the most powerful states in the Christian world. They travelled to Spain to fight the Moors, to Byzantium to fight the Turks and to England to conquer the Anglo-Saxons. In 1015 Normans were recruited as mercenaries to fight for the rebels against the Byzantine empire and were wiped out a year later by the Byzantine army - which included detachments from the Varangian Guard. Later the Normans allied themselves to the Byzantines, but in 1040 turned against their employers seizing large tracts of southern Italy in the process.

At its greatest the Norman empire was never large. Yet for over a century it was the greatest in the Christian world. By 1066 William controlled a highly organised feudal state, yet the army owing him direct allegiance remained small. Of the 7,000 men who followed him to England less than half were Normans. The residue were mercenaries from Flanders, Brittany, Picardy and even Sicily and southern Italy.

Unlike their Danish predecessors, or indeed the Anglo-Saxons who rode to war but fought on foot, the Normans had an experienced cavalry able to fight from the saddle. The estimated 2,000 horsemen at Hastings however fought as individuals, having no concept of the massed cavalry charge, nor any inclination to do battle with a well organised shield wall. The Normans made excellent use of archers and slingers at Hastings, although seemingly preferred to employ mercenaries from Flanders in this still specialist role.

Elites in the Age of the European Monarchies

The feudal period which followed from the eleventh to the fifteenth centuries did not produce elites as such, as most military service was based on land tenure and sub-contracting. However certain classes of troops earned special reputations as the Middle Ages progressed. The Swiss cantons became famous for their pikemen, Genoa produced reputedly the best crossbowmen, whilst Cheshire and Welsh longbowmen became the terrors of the French mounted nobility as the Hundred Years War continued. At the outset of the age of gunpowder, German 'landsknechts' were much admired and emulated, but not until the mid-twentieth century would elitism again be associated with whole categories of specialised troops such as paratroops.

As the power of the European monarchs increased throughout the sixteenth century, and once over-powerful subjects were forced to disband their private armies, the full concept of Royal Guards as a corps d'élite began to emerge. They performed various functions, both decorative and utilitarian, political and military, and were invariably clothed and housed in conditions of comparative splendour. They guarded their monarch and benefactor, providing sentries and royal escorts, occasionally enhancing their duties with ornate ceremonial. In the days before standing armies elite guards often represented a force of last resort, the ultimate basis of regal power. In time of war they were expected to provide an example to lesser troops both in and out of action.

Royal Guards could also represent sources of considerable peril for their masters, especially those of an autocratic persuasion. They could become dominated by aristocratic cliques of officers, who might seek to impose their own particularist views on their monarch. To minimise this peril, many rulers added foreign contingents - Scots or Swiss were particularly favoured on the Continent.

The Swiss Guards

The warriors of the lakeside communities of Schwyz, Uri and Unterwalden (the 'Waldstätte') gathered together on 1 August 1291 to swear an eternal oath of mutual defence against their Hapsburg overlords, and as such are generally credited with the formation of the first Swiss Army. During the centuries which followed, the Swiss gained their independence from the Hapsburgs, at the Battle of Mortgarten in 1315; and thereafter won for themselves a reputation for ferocity, ruthlessness and at times cruelty in the service of the highest paymaster.

Swiss mercenaries fought for, and at times against, the foundling armies of England, Spain and the Italian city states, but above all they fought in France. By the eighteenth century the Bourbon dynasty had come to rely more heavily upon their Swiss levies than upon their fellow Frenchmen for protection, and it is no surprise that it was Swiss mercenaries who died in their hundreds in defence of the doomed Louis XVI during the final days of the monarchy.

Swiss proficiency in arms was no coincidence. From the mid-sixteenth century all fit men between the ages of 16 and 60 were expected to practice the art of pike drill and were frequently tested to ensure that the uncompromisingly high standards demanded were maintained. The introduction of conscription allowed the Swiss to field huge armies at short notice. Generally the numbers to be conscripted were determined by the cantonal and local councils of elders.

The Swiss relied upon three categories of soldier: the 'Auszug', an elite corps comprising younger, usually unmarried men aged between 18 and 30; the 'Landwehr', formed of older men willing to serve abroad if required; and the 'Landstrum', the mass levy only resorted to in times of emergency. Each soldier was obliged to buy his own armour and weapons, although their repair was the responsibility of the parent canton or community which was also obliged to finance its own contingents. A roll call, or 'Mannschaftsrodel', set out in detail the number of men to be supplied by each community, their weapons and equipment. Officers were elected at the musters, with supreme command usually passing to the canton which had originally called for the mobilisation. Training was an individual canton responsibility, but once the troops were mobilised discipline and control were both centralised and rigid. Soldiers were ordered to report with from four to six days supplies and were thus able to move at once, a luxury enjoyed by few other armies of the day.

The Mercenary Tradition

In theory all post-medieval monarchs could call upon large bodies of infantry and cavalry, but with few exceptions neither force could be relied upon. Nationalism was an unknown factor. Many failed to heed the call to arms, preferring to remain at home to exploit the void caused by the absent head of state and his army. Those who did mobilise often fought among themselves, looking to their earls and barons rather than their king for leadership, even if in so doing they destroyed the army as a cohesive fighting force in the process.

As early as the twelfth century military leaders recognised that no efficient army could be raised entirely from the feudal system and began to employ bands of mercenaries. By 1400 it had become standard practice to pay all soldiers whether pressed or volunteer to ensure their loyalty and to stiffen their numbers with troops of imported professionals.

By the late thirteenth century the city states of northern Italy, exhausted by internal squabbling, began to relinquish their authority to a number of ruling families.

2 Mythology to Fact

The families soon came to realise that they could not hope to retain their power and influence without a solid military base, and began to import bands of foreign mercenaries. Such 'compagnie di Ventura', or companies of fortune, usually comprised between 50 and 100 poorly armed men. Few were trustworthy and many reverted to brigandry at the end of the campaign. Larger, better disciplined and equipped mercenary bands such as Werner von Urslingen's Great Company of Germans and Swiss and Fra Moriale's 7,000 mounted men at arms and 2,000 crossbowmen followed. By the 1450s the Italians began to form their own bands of mercenaries until by the end of the century whole armies were being raised.

The Landsknechts

The Landsknechts, literally 'the servants of the country,' first appeared around 1487. Mercenaries from the German states of Alsace, Baden, Württemberg and the Austrian Tyrol, they provided a force of 12,000 foot and 1,200 horse in the service of the Holy Roman Empire. After the storming of the fortress of Stuhlweissenberg in Bohemia in 1490 the force was ordered to swear an oath of allegiance to Maximilian and then began to adopt a number of the disciplinary and administrative measures of the Swiss.

Thereafter, in the manner of Swiss tradition, when a lord required an army to settle a dispute he contracted an 'obrist' or gentleman of war by means of a 'bestellungsbrief' or letter of appointment. This contained a recruiting commission and the 'artikelsbriefe', the letter of articles defining the terms of the contract. Once satisfied the Obrist would appoint his Second in Command and the captains in charge of his 'fahnlein' or companies.

Selection was undertaken at the muster parade, a practice adopted from the Swiss and essential in determining the efficiency of the unit to be raised. Each recruit had to possess his own weapons. He had then to pass through two columns of his fellow recruits and beneath an arch comprising two halberds and a pike. If during this process the Paymaster was able to satisfy himself that the recruit was sound of mind and limb he would be accepted.

A regiment normally comprised ten fahnlein of 400 men each, 100 of whom (the 'doppelsoldner') would be veterans on double pay. The fahnleins were further divided into the 'rotten' or platoons, of ten ordinary landsknechts or six doppelsoldner which elected their own 'Rottmeister.' Should the Obrist have overall charge of several regiments during a campaign, the task of leading his own regiment fell to his 'Locotenent' (lieutenant colonel;) his Second in Command who would otherwise hold the rank of captain.

Rigid discipline was maintained by a full complement of military police and judges supported by the Provost, who remained unimpeachable during a campaign, a bailiff and an executioner. A regimental sergeant major (the 'Oberster-Feldwebel') was responsible for battle formation, the sergeants ('weibel') for discipline and the 'gemeinweibel,' elected from the ranks on a monthly basis, for liaison between the officers and men. Pay was set by decree (400 guilders per month for a colonel to four guilders per month for an ordinary soldier) and was paid regularly to avoid disquiet and possible mutiny.

English Elite Foundations

While mercenary armies were ravaging central and southern Europe the kings of England were laying the foundations of a primitive standing army. Edward I (1272-1307) attempted to increase the size of the cavalry by making landowners with a wealth in excess of £20 a year render the service of a knight, but he met with stiff baronial resistance. Subsequently Edward III attempted to defray the cost of maintaining a well equipped infantry from shire levies but met with no greater success. Mercenaries were therefore employed on an increasing scale during the Scottish and Welsh border wars and later in France. However Magna Carta prevented an English king from employing large numbers of foreigners and therefore these mercenaries were for the most part English - laying the foundation for a small but elite standing army. The longbowmen were selected from volunteers at village archery contests, one of the first recorded instances of competition for places in a military elite.

In 1341 Edward III introduced a system of written indentured contract which was destined to spread throughout north-western Europe. Captains were contracted to provide given numbers of trained and equipped troops for a stated period of service at the king's behest. Most were retained by the captain in times of peace and paid a bounty when mobilised, repayable by the king as soon as practical.

Many of the battles of the Hundred Years War were fought by mercenaries, groups of whom occasionally refused to disband at the end of the engagement preferring to revert to brigandage on their own behalf. In an attempt to rid France of these bands the Marquis of Montferrato hired a number of trustworthy French, English and German companies in 1361 and attempted to seize the duchy of Milan. Enguerrand de Courcy took a large band, known as the Guglers, to Switzerland; only to be almost totally annihilated by the Bernese. John Hawkwood's White Company rampaged through northern Italy until its leader's death in 1394 while Bertrand du Guesclin's Great Company held the Pope to ransom in Avignon.

At the end of the Hundred Years War, France and England were bankrupt, their administrations in chaos. The nobles deserted the king and his laws, preferring to rely on their own might to settle their growing quarrels. England was polarised between the Houses of York and Lancaster making the civil War of the Roses (1455-85) inevitable. Many veteran soldiers of the French wars found employment in the armies of the nobles. The king, lacking a standing army, could only counter the disloyalty of certain nobles by buying the loyalty of others.

Yeomen, farmers and the lesser gentry, no longer able to look to the king's law for protection, turned to the great families. They entered into contracts of Livery and Maintenance whereby they offered to adopt the family livery and badge and to fight for it when required in exchange for its protection.

On 22 August 1485 Henry, Earl of Richmond, won the last great battle of the War of the Roses near the Leicestershire town of Market Bosworth. The earl assumed the throne as Henry VII and set about restoring stability to his shattered country. He raised the Yeoman of the Guard and the Gentleman Pensioners as a personal bodyguard. Later, his more parsimonious granddaughter, Elizabeth I, preferred to entrust her personal safety to the skills of the faithful spymaster Walsingham than to an expensive standing army. After her soldiers and sailors destroyed the Spanish Armada in

1588 she stood the force down at once rather than continue its payment, leaving many of its veterans to revert to begging to survive.

Charles II retained many of his father's veterans, adding a number of elite Regiments of Household Cavalry and Foot Guards to his embryonic standing army. Later the Swedish Vasas introduced the Drabants and the Austrian Hapsburgs the Trabants, who remained loyal to their Emperor until the disintegration of Austria-Hungary in 1919. Frederick William I of Prussia raised the multi-national 'Giant Grenadiers' (every one of them over 1.83m tall), although Frederick the Great immediately disbanded them on his accession in favour of the older Gardes du Corps who successors served the Kaiser until 1918.

Less successfully the Czars of Russia raised fine regiments of Imperial Guards, notably the Semenovsky and Preobrazhensky Grenadiers, who failed them in their hour of greatest need in 1917.

The Household Troops of Louis XIV

The 'Maison' or Household Troops of Louis XIV typified the cream of the military elite in the service of the European monarchies. They comprised both horse and foot. The mounted escort was found by one company of Mounted Grenadiers, up to four companies of 'Gardes du Corps', a company of Guard Gendarmes and two companies of Musketeers (named 'gris' and 'noir' on account of the colour of their horses.) The Maison was invariably brigaded with the four squadrons of the Gendarmerie - itself an elite regiment of line cavalry of which the king himself was nominally captain.

The privileges of these formations reflected their proximity to the monarch's person. From 1719, the officers of the 'Gardes de Corps', for example, enjoyed considerable advantages of rank. Their lieutenants and ensigns held equivalent 'army rank' of full colonels of line cavalry, while their 'exempts' were regarded as captains of horse. The gentlemen-guards enjoyed no such precise advantage, although it was the custom to appoint them to the command of a troop as lieutenants with seniority calculated from the date of their entry into the Maison.

The greater part of the French Household Troops was formed by the infantry element. The 'Régiment des Gardes Françaises' in 1691 comprised six battalions, and totalled 3,684 officers and men. The equally prestigious 'Régiment des Gardes Suisses' consisted of only one formation, but with large company establishments so that it totalled (in 1720) 2,468 officers and men. Their colonels-proprietor were appointed from the very highest in the land, including princes of the blood and marshals of France. Privileges of pay and rank were also enjoyed; but these did not prevent the Gardes Françaises from joining the proletariat of Paris in storming the Bastille on 4 July 1789, thus inaugurating the French Revolution and the eclipse of the Bourbons.

The Napoleonic Imperial Guard

Probably the most celebrated corps d'élite of all time was the Napoleonic Imperial Guard. From its humble beginnings in the Guard of the Convention, the Directory and Bonaparte's 'Guides' of the North Italian Campaign of 1796, 'la Garde Imperiale' ultimately burgeoned from a few hundred men into a self-contained miniature army, with its own headquarters complex, artillery and service units as well as infantry and cavalry. Only 800 strong at Marengo (1800), the Imperial Guard had grown to 5,000 by the time of Austerlitz (1805.) Seven years later as many as 50,000 members of the guard crossed the River Niemen into Russia. By 1814 some 114,000 officers and men could claim membership and by 1815, the year of the Guard's disbandment after Waterloo and the second restoration of the Bourbons, successive enlargements and elaborations had expanded the organisation to a staggering 80 Guard units. Not all survived until 1815. The less than popular 'Gendarmes d'Ordonnance', for example, were disbanded in October 1807 after only thirteen months, while many other units were merged in successive reorganisations. Thus the 'Tirailleurs-Chasseurs' became the 'Voltiguers', and the 'Tartares Lithuaniens', one of the several foreign elements within the Guard, became the 'Scouts-Lancers'.

The distinctive uniform, superior pay and considerable privileges made Guard membership a coveted privilege; yet, above all, it was the proximity to the Emperor's being that was most prized. Service near 'le Tondu' (the 'shorn-one' as the Guard irreverently dubbed Napoleon after he had adopted short hair in the classical style) was never easy, but the bond of intense personal loyalty and affection which he inspired was unique.

Napoleon was a past-master of man-management, and if many of the methods he used to bind his men to his service were deliberately theatrical they were nonetheless effective for that. The Emperor had few favourites among his officers, many of whom he never fully trusted and from whom he remained aloof. But he permitted the common soldiery, and particularly the Guard, a considerable degree of familiarity, moving comfortably among them to praise or chide as the situation might demand.

The needs of the growing empire and the long years of war led to a rapid expansion within the Imperial Guard. The Old Guard - horse and foot - was joined in January 1809 by the embryonic Young Guard, created by Imperial decree. The initial strength of its first formations, the Tirailleurs-Grenadiers and Tirailleurs-Chasseurs, was only 3,200 officers and men in all, with strict regulations laid down demanding a minimum of six years service prior to transfer to the Old Guard. By 1814, however, the Young Guard had been vastly expanded to a strength of several full divisions.

Its baptism of fire came on 22 May 1809, during the second day of the battle of Aspern-Essling when the Guard was ordered to recapture the crucial village of Essling from the Austrians. The Young Guard succeeded in its objective, but at the expense of over a quarter of its number, including six lieutenant colonels, killed or wounded.

During the following years Napoleon seemed far more willing to commit his Young Guard to the carnage of formal battle than the veterans of the Old Guard. Despite his generals' frequent requests for their participation Napoleon preferred to husband them as a tactical reserve. The Guard Cavalry saw limited action on the Pratzen Heights at Austerlitz, but not the Foot Grenadiers or Chasseurs of the Guard. At Jena (1806), Friedland (1807) and Borodino (1812) the story was much the same.

However the Consular Guard did intervene with good effect at Marengo (1800), when Grenadier Brabant was awarded the 'fusil d'honneur' for literally single-handedly serving a four-pounder cannon for 30 minutes (his other hand having been lost in action!). Equally, at Eylau in February 1807, a battalion of the Old Guard successfully cleared a village of a Russian column threatening their Emperor's command post, using nothing but the bayonet in the process! During the same battle the Guard Cavalry successfully engaged Benningsen's battle line. Again, at Wagram in July 1809, volunteers manned an improvised battery of heavy guns brought forward to plug a dangerous gap in the French front line.

The services of the Old Guard were more readily sought during the latter stages of the Empire. During the retreat from Moscow in 1812, Napoleon found his route blocked at Krasnoe, near Smolensk. Undeterred by their privations, his faithful veterans so completely cleared the obstacle that they were likened by an observer to 'a ship-of-the-line [cutting] through a fleet of fishing smacks.'

From then until their final defeat at Waterloo there was no shortage of hard action for any Guard formation, Old, Middle or Young. A round-shot killed Marshal Bessières, Commander in Chief of the Imperial Guard, just before Lützen (1813.) At Dresden (the same year), the Grenadiers were called upon to lead the critical attack; and at Leipzig they performed acts of prodigious valour around the villages of Probstheida and Kohlgarten.

During the Campaign in France (1814), the Guard fought valiantly and without question on at least twelve occasions. During the dying days of the Empire it was left to the Old Guard to drive the Prussians from the village of Plancenoit at the point of the bayonet in pouring rain. As a final act of defiance, on 18 June 1815, it covered the flight of the broken Armée du Nord from the field of Waterloo, following the abortive attack by the Middle Guard against Wellington's right-centre line at Mont St Jean.

The last French square to be overwhelmed during the entire campaign was formed by the Old Guard. Its annihilation fittingly epitomised the proud motto, 'The Guard dies but never surrenders.'

The American Civil War - Citizen Elites

The second half of the nineteenth century saw the introduction of unlimited warfare in which small standing armies were supplemented by tens or even hundreds of thousands of conscripts and volunteers. Initially, as in the American Civil War (1861-65), men volunteered for limited periods (as little as 90 days in 1861). Later it became necessary to extend these periods of service until, by the First World War (1914-18), volunteers were expected to enlist for the duration of hostilities.

The United States had few truly elite units at the outbreak of the Civil War. Contrary to public misconception, its cavalry element was minute, comprising no more than six lightly armed regiments. A few of its elite units survived the early stages of the war by refusing to lower their entry standards, a mistake subsequently made by a number of special forces units in later conflicts. The US Marine Corps, which stayed loyal to the Union remained relatively small throughout the Civil War. At no time did it number more than 4,167 officers and men, of whom 148 were killed in action. The Corps was too lightly armed and equipped to take a major part in the land war, although it did see action at the First Battle of Manassas (Bull Run) on 21 July 1861, and fought with conspicuous gallantry in the successful siege of Fort Fisher (6-15 January 1865). More conventionally, detachments fought with all but the smallest ships, frequently giving a good account of themselves in the numerous bloody naval engagements of the war.

The Evolution of the Classical Specialist

Occasionally volunteer units were formed around a nucleus of veterans of previous wars. The 79th New York (Highlanders) were formed in 1861 from Scottish immigrants, many of whom had seen service with the British Army during the Crimean War. Dour, hardy and deeply religious, they encompassed completely the traditions and discipline of a European regular army. Even when they were expanded from four to ten companies by the introduction of Irish and English expatriates they refused to compromise their heritage, continuing to parade in the full dress uniform of the 79th Cameron Highlanders from whom they took their traditions.

Occasionally units were formed from specialists whose civilian rather than military skills carried them into the realms of the elite. Hiram Berdan's Sharpshooters, formed on 30 November 1861 to fight for the Union, was one such unit. Every volunteer had to prove his ability to fire ten consecutive rounds into the ten inch diameter of a bull's eye at 200 yards and produce excellent references as to his character. 1,392 officers and men were accepted into the ranks of the 1st Regiment. A further 1,178 all ranks enlisted into the 2nd Regiment when it was formed under the command of Colonel Henry Post soon after.

The Sharpshooters were invariably deployed as skirmishers, usually in company strength and were never trained to fight conventionally. Although both regiments were eventually issued with Sharps rifles, the best massed produced rifle then available, many sharpshooters preferred to retain their own hunting rifles.

The 1st Regiment, which lost 546 killed and wounded in four years of fighting, acquitted itself well at the Battle of Mine Run, despite losing its new commander, Lieutenant Colonel Caspar Trepp, who had only recently succeeded Colonel Berdan. It was active throughout the Peninsula campaign, particularly in the battle for Yorktown when its members used their rifles with particular effect to neutralise Confederate gun batteries.

The 2nd Sharpshooters served with the ill-fated McDowell's Corps during the Peninsula campaign but were held in reserve. They were unusually, and wastefully, deployed as line infantry within Phelps' Brigade at Antietam (17 September 1862), where they lost 66 men in what is generally considered the most bloody day of the war. Thereafter the regiment served successfully with I, III and II Corps, usually as part of Birney's Division and alongside its sister regiment, the 1st Sharpshooters. Its heaviest losses occurred during the Wilderness campaign and at Spotsylvania where it sustained, respectively, 76 and 53 casualties. In all, the regiment lost 462 killed and wounded before being disbanded.

Occasionally a volunteer unit, although drawn from perfectly conventional raw material, was so well trained and led that it assumed the status of an elite unit. Such was the Iron Brigade of the West, formed and led by a retired railroad engineer, Rufus King, until his promotion to major general in March 1862. Brigadier John Gibbon, who succeeded King, was without doubt one of the finest tacticians of the war. A veteran of the Seminole War and a former West Point artillery instructor, Gibbon denied his family heritage in 1861, turning his back on his three brothers then fighting for the Confederacy to throw in his lot with the North.

Originally the brigade comprised the 19th Indiana, 2nd, 6th and 7th Wisconsin Regiments, although it was later joined by the 24th Michigan. The brigade recruited exclusively from the Midwest. Over half of its membership consisted of native Americans, 40 per cent were Scandinavian or Irish, the residue being of German or English extraction.

The brigade saw action at the First and Second Battles of Manassas (Bull Run), sustaining one-third casualties; and throughout the Maryland campaign, where during three weeks of bitter fighting it lost 58 per cent of its remaining strength. At Antietam (Sharpsburg), a war correspondent, sickened by the carnage yet mindful of the considerable part played by these Midwestern troops in the North's first victory, christened the brigade the 'Iron Brigade', in ignorance of the fact that this title had already been bestowed on a New York unit. After fighting at Fredericksburg and Chancellorsville, the Iron Brigade threw itself unreservedly into the Gettysburg campaign, losing two-thirds of the 1,800 who fought on Seminary Ridge. The soul if not the body of the Iron Brigade died at Gettysburg. It continued to function as an independent unit, but took no further major part in the war.

The South was not without its own elite forces. Stuart's cavalry were ragged, ill-disciplined, badly armed, and at times half starved; yet they were nonetheless arguably the finest fighting force of the Civil War. They consisted exclusively of experienced horsemen (all of whom had brought their own mounts when they volunteered), the majority of whom were drawn from rural backgrounds and, as such, had learned to shoot at a young age. Most Confederate cavalrymen were fiercely independent and did not take well to the regimentation of army life, yet this mattered little in a force which valued individualism highly. The Southern horsemen were rarely drawn into set-piece battle, and when they were, the mêlée was invariably short, ending conclusively in their favour.

The Confederate cavalry was without peer when acting in the role of hunter. Few of its officers, let alone the enlisted men, carried sabres and early experiments with the lance proved a failure. They were at their best when operating as mounted infantry, able to advance silently and at speed against an enemy, yet endowed with sufficient fire power to destroy the enemy once contact was made.

The Confederacy also raised a number of raiding forces under the command of men such as John Mosby and Nathan Bedford Forrest. These mounted units were lightly equipped and operated away from the main Southern armies, striking at will into the neutral States and against vulnerable points along the North's extensive supply and communications network.

The Boer War
The lessons of the American Civil War were not readily taken to heart by the various European Chiefs of Staff. They regarded the huge volunteer armies as amateur, ill-disciplined and badly led. Such attitudes ignored the devastating effect of musket fire against massed infantry ranks, discounted the role of elite units on both sides and failed to notice the chaos which a few skilled marksmen could cause in the ranks of the enemy command.

By the end of the nineteenth century European tactics had changed little from the days of Napoleon. However, wartime experience, particularly for the British, was to prompt radical reappraisals of established doctrine. The Second Boer War (1899-

1902) exemplified Britain's towering imperial status and at the same time exposed potentially crippling weaknesses in her military machine. It saw her army outmanoeuvred and outshot by Afrikaans-speaking farmers whom its leaders had earlier discounted as an irrelevant rabble. Columns of unacclimatised British and Commonwealth infantry and cavalry (some of them kilted despite the boiling sun) slogged across the open veldt after an elusive enemy who, in action, fought from trenches and used accurate, aimed shots to cut down rank after rank. Losses, particularly during Black Week (December 1899) when the British lost three battles in succession, caused a national outcry and forced a radical rethink of British tactics.

In response the British adopted the tactics of Stuart's Confederate cavalry. Abandoning their contempt for mounted infantry they deployed Imperial Yeomanry units, predominantly from Australia, New Zealand and Canada. Mounted and relatively lightly equipped, their ranks were filled by hardy and skilled frontiersmen who were superior to the Boers in the saddle and often their equals in marksmanship. The yeomanry chased and harried the Boers as never before, occasionally with a ferocity which the British commanders found untenable.

The Great War

The experience of the Boer War was of great importance to the British Army, and the use of camouflage and the idea of rapid but aimed rifle fire stood the British Expeditionary Force (BEF) in good stead during the opening months of the First World War. It was the Imperial German Army in the latter stages of the war, however, which created the first modern truly elite units.

Operation 'Michael', the last-ditch attempt to cut through the Allied lines in the Amiens sector in May-June 1918, saw the large-scale use of stormtroopers for the first time. These units, filled with veterans, enjoyed better food, pay, training and equipment. Troopers went into action in small, tightly-knit groups, carrying plentiful supplies of grenades. They were trained to probe the enemy for weaknesses, exploiting these in any way possible. Having captured a trench system they continued into the enemy rear to spread confusion, leaving the mopping up of strongpoints to the regular infantry.

On 27 May 1918, during the Second Battle of the Aisne, German stormtroopers infiltrated the boundary between the British 50th and 21st Divisions by moving at night through the marshes on either side of the Miette River. After a short bombardment they attacked the British from within their own lines causing the raw troops, many of whom were fresh from depot, to withdraw in confusion. The British reserve brigade to the rear held, but at terrible cost to itself. This action allowed the Allies to regroup and deny the Germans their breakthrough. Nonetheless the concept of blitzkrieg, destined to become a favoured tactic of later elite units, had been proved effective.

Mining, the science of piercing enemy fixed defences by driving tunnels beneath them, is almost as old as war itself. It was practised by the Israelites against the walls of Jericho and later in a number of Medieval sieges. However it was not until the Great War that tunnelling became a preserve of the elite. On 20 December 1914 German Engineers detonated ten mines along an 800m (half-mile) sector of the British trenches near Festubert. The hapless Indian Sirhind Brigade holding the line, already demoralised by the intensity of the winter cold and the German bombardment, broke and fled.

By and large the Germans retained the initiative in the tunnel war throughout 1915. Eventually Major John Norton Griffiths MP, a politician and tunnelling contractor, persuaded Lord Kitchener to approve the formation of a special mining unit recruited from civilian tunnel workers. The nucleus of this unit consisted of men employed by Griffith's peacetime company to dig sewer tunnels under the city of Manchester. They used the 'clay-kicking' technique, lying at an angle of 45 degrees on wooden frames, and using both feet to drive a spade into the clay at the tunnel face. As the loosened clay was removed, the clay kicker moved forward on his frame to extend the tunnel.

It was appallingly exhausting work, usually carried out in foul air which crude ventilating bellows could do little to freshen. Added to this was the ever-present risk of being killed by underground enemy tunnellers. The first British success came on the Ypres Salient in January 1915 when Hill 60 was blown. Thereafter a series of mines were dug, culminating in the blowing of nineteen mines at Messines Ridge on 7 June 1917. Shortly after the battle of Passchendaele which followed, the Germans withdrew to prepared defensive positions along the Hindenburg Line thus removing the realistic possibility of further mining. Thereafter tunnelling as a form of elite warfare lay dormant for nearly 50 years, to be resurrected by the United States tunnel rats in Vietnam.

Rogue Elites

Elite Guards units continued to protect the monarchs and presidents of many nations well into the twentieth century, although their often pampered presence did not always have the desired effect. The Russian Imperial Guard played an important part in suppressing the attempted Revolution in 1905, but proved far less effective twelve years later. Many Guards units proved disaffected, deserting Tsar Nicholas and his family in their hour of greatest need. Some elements defended the Winter Palace in St Petersburg against the revolutionary crowds giving their lives in the process, but many did not. 'My sailors, my own sailors - I can't believe it! They are all our personal friends!' was the incredulous reaction of the Tsarina Alexandra Feodorovna to the news that her favourites, the 'Garde Equipage,' had deserted the Romanov cause.

More recently Presidential Guards have paid a fundamental part in a number of palace coups. In 1964 King Sa'ud of Saudi Arabia was forced into exile when the Royal Guard switched its allegiance to Crown Prince Feisal; in 1970 the deposition of the Sultan of Oman in favour of his more westernised son was made possible by the (British inspired) inactivity of the Omani Royal Guard. More brutally the assassination of Mrs Indira Gandhi in 1986 was engineered by trusted Sikhs within her bodyguard.

The great enlargement in the scope and effects of warfare since August 1914 has created new military elites to meet new challenges. These have affected all armed forces - not just armies. Submarine warfare has led to the creation of a new kind of sailor, the submariner. Although in the eyes of some little more than pirates, submariners nonetheless engender connotations of sang froid and ruthlessness increasingly associated with the modern special forces.

Covert raiding from the sea is not a new phenomenon. It was undertaken successfully by the Italians during the First World War and by all the major combatants during the Second World War. The first recorded use of so-called human torpedoes took place in the Northern Adriatic on the night of 31 October/1 November 1918. On that night two Italians, Rossetti and Paolucci, negotiated their way through the Pola defences on an S-1 craft of their own design and placed mines against the hulls of the Austrian flagship *Viribus Unitis* and the liner *Wien*. Although the war was virtually at an end, and ironically the battleship was in the hands of mutineers at the time of the attack, this demonstrated the ease with which capital ships could be destroyed cheaply and with virtually no risk to life and had a profound effect on Italian naval thinking.

Despite his prevarications it is now clear that Mussolini realised as early as 1935 that his fleet would be no match for the Royal Navy in any future war in the Mediterranean. Accordingly, and mindful of the success of the S-1 craft, he ordered the creation of a dedicated mini-submarine squadron with a view to attacking the British capital ships in their home bases. The SLC boats with which the squadron was equipped were without peer. Despite their nickname of 'Maiale', or Swine, given them by their designer who nearly drowned when a prototype sank, they were highly manoeuvrable. Capable of carrying a 300kg detachable warhead they were equipped to operate at depths in excess of 30 metres, making them invisible to the most sensitive acoustic detectors of the time.

Typically, the special forces who operated the SLCs were not trusted by the Italian naval hierarchy. The squadron, which was initially formed in October 1935, was disbanded within months and not reformed until Italy entered the war in 1940. Even then it was held in reserve for a full year until German air power had wrested control of the Mediterranean from the British. It was not until 19 September 1941 that the squadron was allowed to prove its worth. In one night it sank two tankers and a 10,900 ton cargo vessel sheltering within the outer defences of Gibraltar harbour. Three months later, on 21 December, six brave men from the squadron scored Italy's greatest naval victory of the war when they breached the Alexandria harbour defences, sank a destroyer and tanker and crippled the 30,000 ton battleships *Valiant* and *Queen Elizabeth*.

War in the Air

The Great War brought about an escalation in aerial warfare, and with it the birth of the air ace. The concept of strategic bombing - the attack on factories and civilian populations from the air - posed great technological challenges. The German Zeppelin commanders and crews who opened the first bombing offensive against Britain in January 1915 were a new elite. They were castigated as 'baby-killers' by those whom they bombed, but this should be seen as a reflection on the ruthless impact of twentieth century warfare rather than as an attack on the crews themselves.

The need to cope with the menace of the Zeppelins created a new counter-elite among the fighter pilots. The press seized upon the new heroes - the 'air aces' - with enthusiasm, for it was particularly hard to find any other glamorous aspect of an increasingly horrendous war. On 3 September 1916 the Royal Flying Corps brought down its first Zeppelin over England. Air aces began to proliferate in all air forces. The

'Red Baron', Manfred von Richthofen, was credited with 80 kills before succumbing to small arms fire from ground troops in 1918; his brother Lothar shot down 40 aircraft; and the American pilot, Edward Rickenbacker, 26 between March and November 1918.

A number of truly remarkable pilots did not serve in primarily fighter squadrons, and thus did not come to the attention of a press corps looking for immediate and tangible signs of success. They were nonetheless an elite. The pilots of 3 Squadron, RFC quickly mastered the art of aerial photography, flying straight and low over the enemy lines to bring back useful intelligence on his trench systems. Their losses were high from the outset, and their efforts were initially discounted by a sceptical high command, but by 1915 they were producing photographic imagery of immeasurable value. During the prolonged Battle of the Somme, between 1 July 1916 and 17 November 1916, the Royal Flying Corps took more than 19,000 aerial photographs from which some 430,000 prints were made. The recognition and lionising of the individual aerial warrior continued into the Second World War, when the bravery of the individual Spitfire and Hurricane pilot in the skies over Southern England was apparent for all to see. Seventeen pilots serving with the RAF achieved ten or more kills in 1940. The most distinguished Luftwaffe aces were Wick, Molders and Galland, credited with 56, 54 and 52 kills respectively up to the end of the Battle of Britain. Later, elite status was earned by a number of bomber units; notably Guy Gibson's 617 Squadron (the 'Dambusters'), Curtis LeMay's 20th Bomber Command in the Far East, and 379th Bombardment Group of the Eighth US Army Air Force over Western Europe. However questionable their suicidal ethos, the Japanese Kamikaze pilots of 1945 must also merit inclusion.

Land forces also spawned new elites between 1914 and 1945. The Great War saw the introduction of the tank, and the crews of the British Tank Corps and their French and American equivalents earn special recognition. The Germans developed their specialist trench infiltration teams of 1918 into the blitzkrieg formations of 1939. During the Second World War Rommel's 7th 'Ghost' Division earned the particular respect of the Allies, as did the Waffen SS armoured formations on the Eastern Front. The British 7th Armoured Division, the Desert Rats, earned equal acclaim in the Western Desert, and later in the Italian and Northwest European campaigns.

The airborne forces, both paratrooper and glider-borne, came of age during the Second World War. The capture of Fort Eben Emael in Belgium in May 1940 by German glider-borne assault engineers (described in detail in Chapter Four) heralded the coup-de-main tactics to be adopted by the 6th Airborne Division in the capture of Pegasus Bridge in 1944. Not all airborne operations were successful. General Student's paratroopers never recovered from their costly victory in Crete, while Operation 'Market Garden' in Holland three years later proved the limitations as well as the possibilities of airborne assault.

The proliferation of special operations and raiding parties in the early 1940s led to the creation of a number of truly special forces groups such as the German Brandenburgers, the British LRDG, SAS and Commandos (Army as well as Royal Marines) and the American Rangers. A number of special purpose forces; Wingate's Chindits and Merrill's Marauders in Burma, and Popski's Private Army in North Africa, were

The Evolution of the Classical Specialist

raised for an occasion but, being useful for none other, were disbanded once their objective had been attained.

Between 1939 and 1945 a new concept of elitism came into being. After the war many of the finest units were disbanded at the behest of nervous politicians incited by jealous conventional soldiers. Most have since been reformed, although not all have retained their original names, as if to signify the crucial part that elitism has to play in modern warfare.

Armies with shorter histories and fewer traditions have learned to regard military excellence as a force multiplier when faced with a numerically superior enemy and have had no compunction in creating elite units. The reliance of the Israel Defence Force on the 'Hatzanhanihm' (the Paratroopers), the Golani and Giva'ati Brigades, and a host of secret ultra specialist units will be discussed in greater detail at a later stage.

3
Rebels, Renegades and Reactionaries
The Pioneers of Special Purpose Warfare

It is impossible in one short chapter to concentrate on more than a few pioneers of elite or irregular warfare. Some of the greatest exponents of novel or irregular warfare were generals in command of massed armies capable of altering the course of world history; others were mere men and women able to do no more than influence those immediately about them. This chapter attempts to draw on both.

There can be no realistic and agreed hierarchy of 'greats'. For every individual chosen in the following pages several others might have appeared in his or her place with equal, some would argue greater, justification. An attempt has been made to cover the great timespan of military history, with a bias in favour of the early, truly innovative, commanders and the more recent military leaders whose thoughts still greatly influence the modern battlefield.

Sun Tzu

Little is known of the early life of Sun Tzu save that he was a probable contemporary of Confucius. He was born around 500BC at Le'an, in the state of Qi, a part of Shangdong Province in modern day China. Sun Tzu followed his father, Sun Ping, into the military and quickly became an expert on the political, economic, cultural, diplomatic and military activities of the area. While in the service of the state of Qi he published his thirteen chapters on *The Art of War* which were destined to influence military thinking for centuries to come.

When Qi was thrown into internal disorder, Sun Tzu moved to the state of Wu, in modern Jiangsu Province. He was quickly appointed a general in the Wu army and subsequently assisted in the defeat of Chu, the annihilation of the state of Yue, and the extension of the borders of Wu to Sucheng, Luian, Qianshan and Cao County. After a three year period of rest and recuperation, Sun Tzu again defeated the armies of Chu at the Battle of Poju, occupying the enemy capital in the process. Sun Tzu made the state of Wu a great power in its day. He was not only a brilliant military theoretician, but also a great commander with a profound capability for organising campaigns.

Sun Tzu regarded war as more than a mere competition between military forces. He saw it as a comprehensive struggle embracing politics, economics, military force and diplomacy which would allow the victor to survive, while condemning the vanquished to ruin. Sun Tzu argued that the outcome of a war was dependant on five fundamental factors; politics, weather, terrain, the commander and doctrine. Each factor was assessed by asking a series of seven questions or 'elements': which of the opposing sovereigns was more sagacious, which commander was wiser and more able, which army had the advantage of nature and terrain, which side was better disciplined, which army was stronger, which had the better trained officers and men and which awarded punishments and rewards in the more enlightened a manner. Sun Tzu was among the first commanders to recognise the potential of what he defined as 'extraordinary' forces, emphasising their importance in his chapter on the 'Posture of Army'. He saw war as a matter of deception in which the enemy had to be thrown into a state of confusion by the sudden introduction of special troops using unusual tactics. Extraordinary forces had to be disguised as ordinary troops, and could only be committed once the enemy's weaknesses had been established.

Sun Tzu's principles of surprise were used to excellent effect by Tian Dan, a general of the Qi state, in 279BC. When besieged in the city of Jimo he collected more than 1,000 oxen and covered each with a colourful cloth. He then tied daggers on their horns and dried reeds dipped in oil to their tails. He assembled 5,000 of his best soldiers all disguised as monsters, and when night fell lit the reeds on the oxens' tails. The oxen stampeded towards the enemy camp followed by the 5,000 'extraordinary' soldiers. The enemy, taken by surprise, were thrown into utter chaos and annihilated.

Sun Tzu's *Art of War* is now considered too simplistic for the prosecution of modern war. However it was studied to great effect by Mao Tse Tung during the war against the Nationalists, and remains an important influence on today's Peoples' Liberation Army.

Alexander the Great

Alexander the Great is considered by many to be the greatest of all military commanders. A legend in his own short lifetime, after his death he became the subject of a full-scale legend of god-like proportions.

Alexander was born in 356BC at Pella, the capital of Macedonia, the son of Philip II and Olympias. From the age of 13 to 16 he was schooled by Aristotle, from whom he gained a deep understanding of the arts, medicine and philosophy. Acting as regent during his father's attack on Byzantium, he defeated the Thracian Maedi in 340BC, and two years later, while still only 18 years old, commanded the Macedonian left flank during Philip's crucial victory over the Greek city states at the Battle of Chaeronea.

Alexander was capable of exhibiting uncompromising cruelty towards those whom he regarded as a threat. When his father was assassinated in 336BC he assumed command of the army, and in a period of short but intense blood-letting summarily executed all those opposed to him. A year later, in an attempt to secure his northern borders, Alexander took his army across the Danube, and in a series of bloody battles he crushed an Illyrian tribal coalition planning an invasion of Macedonia. While Alexander was fighting in the north, the Greek city-state of Thebes, erroneously informed of his death, rose against the Macedonian leadership. In fourteen days Alexander force-marched his army 240 miles south from Pelion, in modern Albania, to Thebes. When that city refused to surrender he forced an entry, and in an orgy of blood-letting executed 6,000 of its citizens, selling the survivors into slavery. Cowed by this act of savagery Thebes' would-be allies among the other Greek city-states quickly succumbed, giving Alexander a stable home base from which to pursue his greatest aim, the subsequent invasion of Persia.

In the spring of 334BC Alexander crossed the Dardanelles at the head of an army of 30,000 foot soldiers and 5,000 cavalry. Earlier limited campaigns by Greek soldiers of fortune had revealed a series of potentially serious shortcomings in the huge but ponderous Persian army; these Alexander was determined to exploit. His own force was revolutionary; not only for its combative balance of lightly armed Cretan and Macedonian archers, Agrianian javelin throwers, cavalry and massed infantry phalanxes but for the inclusion of a massive logistics tail which allowed previously unheard of mobility and an almost unlimited operational scope.

Alexander encountered his first Persian army at the Granicus River, near the Sea of Marmara. In a sudden and wholly unexpected twilight attack against the enemy's strongest point, Alexander took the Persians and their Greek mercenary allies by complete surprise. The Persian line broke, and Alexander's victory was complete. Some 2,000 Greek mercenaries in the pay of Persia were sent home in chains; thousands of others were put to the sword in a further, savage object-lesson to those who would oppose the new regime. The Macedonians spent the next few months consolidating their hold over western Asia Minor, denying the hugely powerful Persian fleet access to the coastal cities. In the winter of 334-333BC Alexander moved east, subduing the hill tribes of Lycia and Pisidia before advancing along the coastal road to Perga. At Gordium tradition states that he cut the Gordian knot, which could only be loosened by the man destined to rule Asia. Although apocryphal and certainly distorted, this story served to accentuate the growing mystique which by then surrounded the young king.

From Gordium Alexander advanced to Ankara, and thence south through Cappadocia to the Cilician Gates. He engaged a massive enemy army at the Pinarus River and won an overwhelming victory, forcing the Persian King Darius to flee, abandoning his family to captivity. Alexander shunned Persian peace overtures and moved south into Syria and Phoenicia; his object once again being to isolate the Persian fleet from its bases and in so doing to destroy it as a fighting force. Damascus was secured, and with it Darius' war chest, as was Byblos and Sidon. Tyre put up a spirited defence, but was taken after a seven month siege attended by yet another instance of great carnage and the selling of the women and children into slavery.

In November 332BC Alexander entered Egypt, founded Alexandria on the western arm of the Nile and visited the celebrated oracle of the god Amon at Siwah. On reaching the oracle, Alexander was greeted as the son of Amon; an incident which later led to the story that Alexander was in fact the son of Zeus, and thus to his deification.

In July 331BC Alexander moved to Thapsacus on the Euphrates from whence he cut across northern Mesopotamia toward the Tigris. He met Darius again, at the Battle of Gaugamela, and for a second time defeated him decisively. In the summer of 330BC Darius was deposed and murdered, leaving Alexander the undisputed lord of the former Persian empire.

Despite his by-now wholly unassailable military position Alexander became increasingly distrustful of his subordinates. A series of often unwarranted executions excited widespread horror within the Macedonian ranks yet did much to cement the king's position relative to his critics. When Bessus raised a national revolt in the eastern satrapies Alexander had him flogged, mutilated and publicly executed as an object lesson. He later murdered Cleitus, one of his most trusted lieutenants, in a drunken brawl; he was only saved from retribution by his now restive army after an excessive, and almost certainly suspect, display of remorse.

In 327BC Alexander invaded India at the head of an army of 35,000 troops supported by perhaps 80,000 auxiliaries and camp followers. Dividing his forces in two, half the army with the baggage was sent south from what is now Afghanistan through the Khyber Pass while the king himself led the rest, including the siege train, through the hills to the north. He fought and won his last great battle by the Hydaspes before his by now exhausted army mutinied and refused to soldier on.

Alexander was obliged to retire and consolidate. While doing so he built a harbour and docks on the Indus delta and explored both arms of the Indus. In a final punitive expedition he set out along the coast through Baluchistan but was soon forced inland. The march proved both bloody and disastrous. Waterless desert and shortage of food caused great suffering, especially among the accompanying women and children who died in large numbers.

As Alexander withdrew into the heart of his new empire he exacted terrible revenge on any whom he felt had failed him. Between 326 and 324BC over a third of his district governors were superseded and six were executed, as were three generals accused of extortion. In the spring of 324BC Alexander returned to Susa, the capital of Elam and the administrative centre of the Persian empire. In an attempt to fuse Macedonians and Persians into his very personal ideal of a master race, he and 80 of his officers now took Persian wives while 10,000 of his soldiers were given large dowries to marry local women. This did much to alienate many native Macedonians who had no sympathy with Alexander's determination to introduce Persians on equal terms into the army and administration. The flame of discontent was fanned when Alexander attempted to introduce Persian nobles into the royal cavalry bodyguard while sending large numbers of Macedonian veterans home to an uncertain future. Alexander's desire to be elevated to the status of a god did nothing to placate his people. Although its status gave the possessor no particular rights in Graeco-Macedonian society, the very demand was seen by many as a growing sign of the king's instability and paranoia.

Alexander's reign ended suddenly in June 323BC when, after a sustained bout of eating and drinking he suddenly collapsed and died. Few of Alexander's aims survived him. Had he lived he might well have completed the conquest of Asia Minor and have furthered the integration of Macedonian-Persian society. As it was his successors were too weak, or too incapable to hold his empire together. As a general, Alexander was both skilful and imaginative. Certain in his aims, he nonetheless knew when to consolidate or even withdraw. Cruel, even sadistic towards his enemies, he was a generous friend to his allies; that is until he began to perceive them as a threat. Above all Alexander showed versatility, both in his use of a combination of different arms and in his adaption of enemy arms and tactics. His use of cavalry, and of elite units of archers and spearmen was so devastating that he rarely had to fall back upon the mass of his conventional infantry.

3 Rebels, Renegades and Reactionaries

Hannibal

Hannibal was born in 247BC, the son of the famous Carthaginian general, Hamilcar Barca. According to classical tradition he was taken to Spain as a boy and made to swear eternal hostility to Rome. True to his word, from the death of his father in 228BC until his own death in approximately 183BC, Hannibal dedicated his life to the overthrow of the Roman Empire.

Hannibal received his first command from Hasdrubal, the son-in-law and successor of Hamilcar, while serving in Spain. Although his duties were comparatively minor, he so impressed the army that it appointed him field Commander in Chief on the assassination of Hasdrubal in 221BC. A politician as well as a soldier, Hannibal realised the necessity for consolidating his hold over Spain. He married the Spanish princess, Imilce, and at once began the systematic conquest of one Iberian peninsular tribe after another. Rome was troubled, but did nothing until Hannibal attacked the independent city of Saguntum in 219BC. Saguntum had a friendship accord, if not a formal treaty, with Rome, which sent envoys to Carthage in protest at the attack. When the city fell Rome demanded Hannibal's arrest, and when this was refused declared war on Carthage.

Hannibal spent the winter of 219-218BC at Cartagena, actively preparing to carry the war into Italy. He appreciated that the Roman fleet controlled the Mediterranean and that, if allowed to, Rome would dictate the field of battle. He therefore elected to lead a pre-emptive attack across the Pyrenees into the soft underbelly of southern Gaul. His army of some 40,000 foot soldiers, 4,000 cavalry and a number of elephants suffered badly in the mountains, but once into Gaul they advanced quickly to the Rhône.

The Roman general Publius Cornelius Scipio crossed with his army by sea to Marseilles, and from there moved northward along the right bank of the Rhône to confront the Carthaginian. When he discovered that Hannibal had already crossed the river and was marching northward on the left bank, Scipio at last realised that Hannibal intended to cross the Alps and, rather than do battle in the unfamiliar mountains, he returned to Italy to await his enemy's arrival.

Hannibal's crossing of the Rhône was in itself a magnificent act of military planning. It is likely that the crossing took place at Fourques, opposite Arles, some four days march from the sea. He used locally commandeered boats and coracles for the troops, horses were embarked on large boats or made to swim, and the elephants were transported on earth-covered rafts. To compound Hannibal's difficulties the crossing was opposed by hostile Gauls on the opposite bank, and he was obliged to dispatch a force under Hanno to cross further upstream and engage the enemy from the rear.

Having safely crossed the Rhône, Hannibal sought the friendship of the northern Italian tribes, particularly the Boii, whose intimate knowledge of the Alpine passes was destined to prove invaluable. Before advancing further he intervened decisively in a local internecine civil war to insure the victory of one brother over his sibling in exchange for replenishment for his by now exhausted army.

Hannibal's army approached the Alps either by the Col de Grimone or the Col de Cabre, and then either through the basin of the Durance or into the upper Po Valley by the Genèvre or Mont Cenis passes. Throughout the crossing Hannibal had to contend not only with the vagaries of nature but with the hostility of the local tribes. Initially he took countermeasures, but when these began to involve him in heavy losses he reverted to a more defensive posture, bolstering his vulnerable rear echelons and providing as much close protection as he could for his baggage train. On the third day he captured a Gallic town and was able to provide his army with rations for two to three days, but even so supplies remained critical throughout the fifteen day epic.

Finally, after a journey of five months from Cartagena, Hannibal descended into Italy at the head of an army of 20,000 infantry, 6,000 cavalry and a few remaining elephants. His army as it stood was far too weak to threaten the might of Rome. Yet the very presence of Hannibal on the shores of the River Po bears testament to his brilliance as a general. His army had surmounted the difficulties of climate and hostile terrain, of thirst and deprivation, of the guerrilla tactics of numerous hostiles and the hit and run attacks of the Alpine tribes. Despite its diversity in temperament, race and language it had remained a potent force.

Scipio, who had rushed to the River Po to protect the newly founded Roman colonies in the area, met Hannibal in battle on the plains west of the Ticino River. Hannibal's Numidian cavalry prevailed and, not for the last time, the might of Imperial Rome was put to flight. Scipio was severely wounded, and the Roman army withdrew to Placentia. Later the combined armies of Semponius Longus and Scipio met Hannibal on the banks of the Trebia River south of Placentia. Again Rome was soundly defeated.

Encouraged by the patent fallibility of Rome, Gauls, Celts and Ligurians flocked to Hannibal's army. After a severe winter Hannibal proceeded in the spring of 217BC to the Arno River. Despite Roman superiority in numbers, Hannibal completely outflanked his enemy in the spring of that year; entrapping and destroying the army of Gaius Flaminius on the shores of Lake Trasimene.

Rome was now left undefended, but Hannibal was too exhausted to exploit his opportunity. Instead he spent the summer of 217BC resting, in the hope that Rome's allies would defect and cause civil war. The Italian tribes however were slow to join the Carthaginian cause. As Hannibal began to foray south a new Roman army, under the command of Fabius Maximus ('Cunctator'), began to dog his steps. It would never join in battle, nor would it allow Hannibal to stop and rest.

When the two armies did join in battle, in 216BC, Rome suffered one of the greatest defeats in its history. On a level plain near Cannae, chosen by Hannibal as his battlefield, an estimated 80,000 Roman legionaries delivered their attack against the centre of the Carthaginian convex formation. Gradually Hannibal withdrew his centre as if in defeat until the mass of the Roman infantry had crowded together in anticipation of victory. When they were too crushed and disorganised to act as a coherent force Hannibal's trap was sprung. The flanks and rear of the Roman infantry were attacked and turned by the vastly superior Carthaginian cavalry and the lightly armed Roman cavalry was driven from the field. Surrounded and confused the Romans were massacred, until fewer than 15,000 scattered fugitives were left alive.

The psychological effect of the battle was tremendous. The fable of Roman superiority was temporarily destroyed in southern Italy, reinforcements were sent from Carthage and several influential states prepared to throw their lot behind Carthage.

Hannibal once again failed to march on Rome and spent the winter of 216-215BC resting in Capua. As he did so the Carthaginian strength weakened. The Greek coastal towns remained loyal to Rome as did numerous Latin colonies. Carthaginian supplies and reinforcements were interrupted and eventually halted.

Denied the means of conducting offensive war, Hannibal was gradually forced onto the defensive. He had to surrender his gains in southern Italy and withdraw north towards the Alps. In 208BC Hannibal's brother Hasdrubal crossed the Alps with a relief army but was defeated at Metaurus, in northern Italy. Denied the possibility of external assistance Hannibal was forced to concentrate his remaining troops at Bruttium, where he was able to resist Roman pressure for four more years.

As Hannibal fretted in Italy, Rome attacked the Carthaginian outposts of Spain and Numidia. In order to go to the help of his country Hannibal abandoned Italy in 203BC. Hannibal and Scipio met for the last time on the banks of the Bagradas River. Hannibal was deficient in cavalry and had only enough veterans troops to man his third echelon. Inevitably his forces were annihilated with some 20,000 killed or captured.

Hannibal escaped, and for a few years was allowed to remain at liberty in Carthage. However internal factions jealous of his prestige conspired against him and he was ultimately forced to flee into exile. Hounded by Rome to the end Hannibal eventually poisoned himself, possibly in the year 183BC.

Saladin

Saladin, probably the most famous of Muslim heroes, was born in 1137 in Takrit, Mesopotamia. The Sultan of Egypt, Syria, Yemen and Palestine and founder of the Ayyubid dynasty, he captured Jerusalem from the Franks in 1187, and thereafter fought the Christian armies of the Third Crusade to a stalemate.

Saladin was born into a prominent Kurdish family in the service of the Turkish governor of northern Syria. As a boy he seemed more interested in religious studies than military training, yet he willingly joined the staff of his uncle, the military commander Asad ad-Din Shirkuh, when invited to do so. Saladin gained his military spurs at the side of his uncle during the First Crusade, when Shirkuh successfully frustrated Frankish attempts to wrest Egypt from Muslim control.

After Shirkuh's death in 1169, Saladin was appointed both commander of the Syrian army and Vizier of Egypt. Two years later he assumed total control in Egypt, and began to use that country's wealth to bring about a previously undreamt of union, under his own standard, of the Muslim territories of Syria, northern Mesopotamia, Palestine and Egypt. Where possible he used diplomacy to establish his aim, but was always willing to back reason with force when necessary. Gradually the Muslims rearmed physically and spiritually. Saladin encouraged the growth of religious institutions, courted scholars and clerics, and founded colleges and mosques in an attempt to create a moral renaissance upon which to build a revitalised military power base. He united the disparate military forces coming under his growing command into a single, disciplined army capable, at last, of challenging the all-pervading threat from Christian Europe.

In 1187 Saladin at last felt strong enough to declare a 'jihad', or holy war, against the crusader kings. In July of that year he trapped and destroyed a thirst-crazed crusader army at Hattin, near Tiberias. Within three months he had taken Acre, Beirut, Sidon, Nazareth, Nabalus and Jaffa. In October Jerusalem, holy to Christian and Muslim alike, fell leaving the crusaders in occupation of only three cities including the near impregnable coastal fortress of Tyre.

Saladin failed to anticipate the ferocity of the European reaction to the loss of Jerusalem. Responding to the appeal by Pope Clement III for a new crusade the three most powerful rulers of Europe; Emperor Frederick I of Germany, King Philip II of France and Richard the Lionheart, King of England joined in a loose, and often ill-tempered, alliance to recapture the Holy Lands for Christendom.

The crusade was long and exhausting, and resulted in almost complete stalemate. Saladin was unable to retain control of Acre, which fell to the Crusaders on 12 July 1191, but thereafter was able to frustrate Richard's attempts to recapture Jerusalem. During August and September 1191 Richard attempted to advance with a force of 50,000 Crusaders along the coast towards Ascalon. The English king's planning and logistics were superb and his tactical and strategic abilities were without peer, yet Saladin was able to harry the Christian force throughout, attacking the flanks and encouraging his cavalry to cut off stragglers at every opportunity.

Saladin's army, much of it comprising part-time levies, was unable to match the Crusaders in set-piece battle, but in irregular warfare it was more than a match. In 1192 Saladin executed a masterful withdrawal towards Jerusalem, destroying all crops, grazing land and wells in a devastating scorched-earth policy as he retired. The lack of water, absence of fodder for the horses and internal dissention within his multinational army forced Richard to the conclusion that he was simply too weak to take Jerusalem, and he was thus compelled to withdraw to the coast. Numerous minor engagements followed until Richard at last concluded a treaty with Saladin, leaving Jerusalem firmly in Muslim hands.

Saladin withdrew to his capital at Damascus, but within a year was dead, the exhausted victim of long years of campaigning and countless hours in the saddle. After his death it was found that Saladin had invested so much of his personal fortune in the Jihad that he had not left enough money to pay for a grave.

Arthur Wellesley, Duke of Wellington

Arthur Wellesley was born in Dublin in 1769, the fifth son of the First Earl of Mornington. A retiring boy, despite his later representations, he appears to have prospered little from his school days at Eton. He was sent to a military academy in France by his disappointed mother, but again seems to have failed to shine. Notwithstanding his unpromising start, Wellesley took a commission in the army at the age of 18 and was appointed Aide de Camp (ADC) to the Irish Viceroy.

In 1790 the young man entered the Irish Parliament as member for the family seat of Trim, and in 1794, as lieutenant colonel by purchase of the 33rd Foot, saw his first active service in Flanders. Wellesley was posted to India in 1796 where a new-found maturity, coupled with the timely arrival of his elder brother Richard, as Viceroy, enabled him to begin the exploitation of his hitherto latent military talents.

As a divisional commander against Tipu Sultan of Mysore, and later as Commander in Chief of the force sent to suppress the Marathas, Wellesley steadily learned the qualities that were later to prove so devastating on the battlefields of Europe. The characteristics of common sense, an eye for detail, compassion for the rank and file under command and political astuteness were rare assets in the general officers of the day, but Wellesley began to demonstrate them all in abundance.

When Wellesley returned to England in 1805 he was knighted for his services in India but was otherwise largely ignored. He participated in an abortive expedition to Hanover, and on his return was relegated to command of a home brigade stationed in Hastings. He married the ageing Kitty Pakenham, by whom he had been spurned twelve years earlier, and returned to Parliament. Wellesley spent two years in Ireland as Tory Chief Secretary, much of it defending his brother's record in India from radical Whig attacks. In 1807 however he was able to demonstrate that he had lost none of his military mettle by conducting a successful, albeit small, sortie into hostile Copenhagen.

When the Portuguese rose against Napoleon in 1808 Wellesley was ordered to support them. He led the British infantry to what was then a rare victory over the French at Vimeiro. He was frustrated in his attempts to pursue the defeated General Junot by the arrival of two more senior officers who, against his advice, sued for peace on terms favourable to the French. Such was the public outcry at home that a military tribunal was convened to examine the facts. Wellesley was fully exonerated. However he was replaced in Portugal by Sir John Moore who, despite being outnumbered ten to one, successfully harried the French communications until killed while evacuating his men from Corunna in January 1809.

Wellesley, who had returned to the Irish Parliament as Chief Secretary, persuaded the government to allow him to renew hostilities from Portugal. He arrived in Lisbon in April 1809 and at once took command of all British and Portuguese troops in the area. Guaranteed almost total military and political autonomy for the first time in his career, he was at last able to put into practice his revolutionary theories of warfare. Wellesley believed in the value of highly disciplined firepower and trained his infantrymen for hours in the basics of musketry. He chose his battlefields well, ensuring whenever possible that his flanks were secured by either natural or artificial features. He used his light infantry to great advantage, neutralising the French tirailleurs, decimating their forward troops and picking off their officers. He established an efficient supply system which allowed his forces to choose their ground according to the military situation without recourse to the need for forage. Finally, he developed a highly sophisticated staff system, employing intelligence officers, covert agents and cartographers to give him as complete an overview as possible of the tactical situation.

Wellesley's 1809 campaign began well. He surprised Marshal Soult, captured Oporto, and chased the French back into Spain which by then was in open rebellion against Napoleon. In July Wellesley was rewarded with a peerage (Viscount Wellington) for success on the battlefield of Talavera, but by early 1810 he was back in Portugal under preesure from heavily reinforced French forces. These he defeated in the autumn at the defensive battle of Busaco before retiring behind the line of fortifications he had had built at Torres Vedras during the preceding year.

Wellington applied a successful scorched earth policy. The British-Portuguese forces gradually grew in strength as reinforcements and provisions arrived via Lisbon and the River Tagus, while the French, who were forced to live off the land, slowly starved. In the spring of 1811 Wellington returned to the offensive. He recaptured the frontier fortress of Almeida after defeating Masséna at Fuentes d'Oñoro. In 1812 he captured the fortresses of Ciudad Rodrigo and Badajoz in brilliantly engineered, if bloody, sieges and in July defeated Soult at the head of 40,000 Frenchmen at Salamanca.

Wellington entered Madrid in August 1812, but ran into strong French resistance as he tried to capture Burgos, and was once more forced to withdraw to winter quarters in Portugal. In May 1813 Wellington conducted his third and final sortie into Spain. Throughout the winter the French had been harried and weakened by bands of Spanish-Portuguese guerrillas. Ferocious, ill-disciplined, but totally dedicated to their disparate causes; these irregulars had conducted a war of uncompromising cruelty. They had blocked the roads, intercepted couriers and murdered collaborators. In so doing they had forced Marshal Soult to deploy massive resources badly needed at the front. The French were thus exhausted when Wellington renewed his offensive, and their ability to fight had been badly compromised by their shattered morale.

After meeting little resistance Wellington comprehensively defeated the French near the Basque town of Vitoria, plundering their baggage train in the process and capturing their considerable haul of booty intact. Unusually, Wellington lost control of his men and, in the orgy of looting which followed, the British allowed the rump of the French army to escape into the Pyrenees. Later Wellington took San Sebastian and Pamplona and began an invasion of southern France. By the end of 1813 he was threatening Bayonne and in February captured Bordeaux. Crossing the rivers one by one he entered Toulouse on 10 April 1814, four days after Napoleon had abdicated. Already a Marquess and Field Marshal, Wellington was now created a Duke, awarded £500,000 and presented with the estate of Stratfield Saye by a grateful nation.

On 26 February 1815, however, Napoleon escaped from the island of Elba to which he had been exiled. He entered Paris in triumph on 20 March and at once set about creating an army from the veterans of his earlier campaigns. His enemies formed a coalition and planned to put five armies into the field against him. Wellington was given command of an Anglo-Dutch army of 90,000 men, and in conjunction with Blücher's 120,000 Prussians, was ordered to advance from Brussels into France.

Napoleon was determined to take the offensive before the coalition was able to group. He regarded the Anglo-Dutch and Prussians as the greatest immediate threat and marched with the Army of the North to do battle. He found Wellington at Waterloo, the Anglo-Dutch army drawn up in a series of well planned defensive positions. The French attacked Wellington's squares but were repulsed. Wellington advanced on the French in the evening and linked up with the Prussians who were hurrying to his aid. The French army disintegrated, and Napoleon was forced to abdicate four days later.

From 1816 until his death in 1852 Wellington devoted himself to the pursuit of politics. An unyielding Tory, he was nonetheless acutely aware of the need for compromise, particularly over the vexatious matters of Catholic Emancipation and the Irish question. Posthumously nicknamed the Iron Duke, Wellington was in reality neither cold nor hardhearted. His attitude towards his men, his perception of tactics and his understanding of the political implications of war placed him without peer. Unfortunately for the British Army, they were not to see his equal for well over half a century.

Robert E. Lee

Born the son of 'Light Horse Harry ' Lee, a veteran cavalry leader of the Revolutionary War, Lee could trace his ancestry through many of the great original families of America, including that of George Washington. Although Lee had married well, and despite his social background, he was not a rich man. Unable to afford a university education, he obtained a place at West Point from which he graduated second in his class, having been appointed corps adjutant, the highest honour available to an officer cadet. Commissioned into the elite Engineer corps in 1829, Lee later transferred to the cavalry in search of promotion but found little to inspire him in the peacetime army.

Lee's true military potential first became apparent during the Mexican War (1846-48) during which he served as a captain on the staff of General Winfield Scott. Lee concluded the war with one wound, three brevets for gallantry, and a mushrooming reputation which prompted General Scott to describe him as 'the very best soldier I ever saw in the field.'

As Superintendent of West Point between 1852 and 1855, Lee steadily continued to enhance his reputation. In October 1859, while on compassionate leave at his home in Arlington, Virginia, he was ordered to Harper's Ferry to suppress a pro-abolitionist insurrection led by the tempestuous John Brown. The latter's ill-conceived capture of the Federal arsenal had been contained by the time that Lee, at the head of a company of Marines, reached the area. Nonetheless the very insurrection itself led Lee to realise that open confrontation could not be delayed for long. Avidly anti-secessionist, and a non-slave owner himself, this placed Lee on the horns of a dilemma.

Lee had returned to his command in Texas when, on 1 February 1861, that state became the seventh to secede and the state government ordered all Federal troops to vacate its land forthwith. Now devoid of a command, Lee returned to Arlington to await events. On 18 April, at the instigation of General Scott and although still only a Colonel, Lee was ordered to Washington and offered command of an army then being formed to bring the seceded states back into the Union. Bitterly opposed to civil war, Lee declined to 'raise my hand against my native state, my relatives, my children and my home.' However, when Virginia joined the secession, Lee resigned from the army which he had served faithfully for 35 years and at once offered his services to the defence of his homeland.

Surprisingly Lee was not given immediate command, but was obliged to remain in Richmond as military adviser to President Davis. Working in unison with Thomas (later 'Stonewall') Jackson, Lee spent the early part of 1862 putting together a strike force from a number of static garrisons in northern Virginia, using it to excellent effect in an audacious attack along the Shenandoah Valley. Fearful of an attack on Washington, the North was forced to retain a large reserve corps for the defence of the capital thus denying its Army of the Potomac sufficient forces to effect an encircling movement around Richmond.

On 31 May 1862, General Joseph Johnston, in command of the Confederate field forces, was seriously wounded. Lee was appointed in his place and at once set about rebuilding the Army of Northern Virginia into one of the most potent fighting units of the war. Discipline and command were tightened, morale improved and control returned to headquarters. Unwilling to surrender the initiative, Lee linked up with Jackson to the north, and in a series of bloody skirmishes known collectively as the Seven Days' Battles, inflicted a humiliating defeat on the Union forces.

Ever a realist, Lee knew that he could never hope to defeat the North in a conventional war. Equally he knew that his army had to do more than merely defend. Always proactive in his attitude towards the enemy, in his planning he invariably weighed the risk of action against the positive loss of inaction and elected for battle. He had the knack of forcing the enemy to attack him on ground of his own choosing, and it was usually a strong defensive position which allowed him to detach a large force to carry out an audacious flanking movement.

Twice expelling the Federals from his beloved Virginia, Lee won notable victories at the Second Battle of Manassas (Bull Run) on 29-30 August 1862, at Fredericksburg on 13 December 1862, and at Chancellorsville on 1-6 May 1863 when, outnumbered by two to one, he split his forces and encircled the enemy.

In the summer of 1863 Lee was forced to embark upon the greatest gamble of his career. Conscious of the stalemate in Virginia, and unable to influence a series of Confederate reverses in the west, he took his army north into Pennsylvania in a last desperate attempt to carry the war to the enemy. Starved of supplies and reinforcements, his veteran troops were exhausted and many of his finest subordinates - Stonewall Jackson included - were dead. He suffered inevitable defeat at Gettysburg (1-3 July 1863) and was forced to retire once more behind his own defensive lines.

In May 1864 the Union began a two-pronged attack into the Confederacy which Lee was too weak to counter. Overwhelmed by superior forces, he could do little but fight a series of delaying actions to stave off inevitable defeat. His Confederates fought valiantly during the Wilderness Campaign, at Spotsylvania, and at Cold Harbor, but to no avail. Lee was forced to deploy the remnants of his exhausted troops in defensive positions of his own designing outside the remaining strongholds of Richmond and Petersburg. For over a year Lee's brilliantly engineered defences frustrated every attempt to storm them.

The end came on 2 April 1865 when the defensive lines around Richmond broke. On 9 April Lee accepted the inevitable and surrendered his army to General Grant at Appomattox Courthouse. For four bloody years Lee had demonstrated a bold and imaginative concept of warfare, combined with an ability to take advantage of an opponents' mistakes while making few himself. He had husbanded his resources brilliantly, creating from nothing one of the most potent fighting forces of the nineteenth century. Lee was respected by soldier and politician alike, often taking the advice of his subordinates yet never blaming them if their advice proved wrong. He died, aged 64, in 1870.

James Ewell Brown Stuart

James ('Jeb') Stuart was only 28 years old when the Confederacy seceded, but by then he had already seen considerable service on the frontier, had been seriously wounded in the Indian wars, and had served in Kansas during the bitter prewar border disturbances. While on leave of absence he had served voluntarily as Lee's ADC during John

Brown's raid on Harper's Ferry. He was among the first Virginian officers to resign his commission after secession.

As Colonel of the 1st Virginia Cavalry, Stuart saw action at the First Battle of Manassas (Bull Run.) He was promoted Brigadier General on 24 September 1861 after which he led first a brigade, then a division and ultimately a corps on a series of brilliantly executed raids deep into enemy territory. His bravery, endurance, dedication and sheer good humour in the face of adversity made this deeply religious man popular with all who served under him, and more than compensated for his vanity and extroversion. Blessed with an excellent staff, Stuart trained his subordinates with a calculated professionalism which made his the best cavalry in the world at that time. His death during the Battle of Yellow Tavern on 11 May 1864 (accidentally shot by his own side) left the South with a void which it found impossible to fill.

Stuart made several great raids, the first during the Second Manassas (Bull Run) campaign. On 22 August 1862 he crossed the Rappahannock River at the head of two guns and 1,500 troops. Moving quickly, and as covertly as a force of that size would allow, he attacked a Federal camp near Catlett's Station before sacking General Pope's baggage train. Under cover of a feint by the 1st and 5th Cavalry, Stuart then escaped with 300 prisoners and a considerable quantity of invaluable intelligence.

On two occasions in 1862 Stuart completely circumnavigated the lines of Union General McClellan, causing havoc in the Federal rear. Stuart was never happy in defence. While forming part of the Fredericksburg garrison he executed no less than four sorties behind the enemy lines, capturing large quantities of supplies and ammunition for the hard-pressed garrison.

Not all of Stuart's operations were wholly successful. In late June 1863 the Confederate cavalry was ordered to scout and harass the enemy in front of Lee's Army of North Virginia which had just advanced to Gettysburg. Stuart's orders were generous in their breadth and ambiguity, but even so he abused them. He moved three brigades eastward from the Confederate position, straight into the approaching Union Army of the Potomac. Lacking the firepower to fight his way through Stuart realised that he must either retire to safety, in which case he would have preserved his corps but failed in his intelligence mission, or attempt to ride around the enemy. Characteristically, he chose the more daring course, taking his command first south then east before turning north. In doing so, he put two mountain ranges and 75,000 enemy troops between himself and Lee. Committed to this new venture, Stuart completely lost sight of his original task, turning a crucial deep-reconnaissance mission into a needless full-blown raid.

When Stuart did eventually return to the Confederate lines, spurred on by the urgent representations of one of the eight couriers sent by Lee to scour the Pennsylvania countryside for him, he was roundly admonished for his actions. Whether Stuart's raid before Gettysburg was brilliant or foolhardy remains a matter of opinion. What is certain is that Stuart, and the troopers who rode with him, were without peer in the war. Their tenacity, resilience, and sheer élan were second to none.

Alfred von Schlieffen

Alfred von Schlieffen was born in Berlin in 1833 and died in the same city in 1913, eighteen months before the plan bearing his name was destined to bring Imperial Germany close to spectacular victory over the combined armies of France and Britain. The son of a Prussian general, von Schlieffen joined the army in 1854 and was quickly appointed to the general staff. His experiences during the war against Austria in 1866 and the Franco-Prussian War of 1870-71, together with a period of six years spent as head of the general staff military history section gave him a unique insight into the highest and lowest extremes of nineteenth century military tactics. His experiences led him to become a disciple of the 'strategy of annihilation', the concentration of overwhelming force into a single unstoppable assault against the very heart of an enemy.

When he was appointed Chief of the General Staff in 1891, von Schlieffen found himself preparing for the possibility of war on two fronts, against France in the west and Russia in the east. Unlike his predecessors, all of whom had regarded Russia as the weaker enemy and their prime target, von Schlieffen elected to conduct a lightning attack against the heart of France before dealing with Russia at his leisure. Accepting that a frontal attack would be too costly and had no certainty of success, he planned a flank assault through neutral Belgium.

By the time of his retirement in 1905, von Schlieffen had developed a plan of such massive complexity that it would have involved 90 per cent of the German troops allocated to the western front. His armies would have had to advance in a great wheeling movement through Belgium and the southern Netherlands (avoiding the fortresses of Liège and Namur) with their right wing entering France near the industrial heartland of Lille. Thereafter the armies would have had to continue to wheel anti-clockwise, severing the French armies' line of retreat while cutting off Paris from reinforcements in the south.

No one will ever know whether this most audacious of plans would have worked. Even von Schlieffen had some doubts as to Germany's ability to find sufficient manpower to execute so vast an enterprise, and immediately prior to his retirement he suggested a number of major modifications. His successor, Helmuth von Moltke, who was nervous of the immensity of the plan gratefully acceded to von Schlieffen's suggestions. He strengthened the German left flank while arranging for the right flank to turn southeast towards Paris from the north rather than west. Critically, von Moltke refused to regard the fortresses of Liège and Namur as impregnable, and moved the entire axis of advance south so as to preserve Dutch neutrality.

The Schlieffen plan as implemented in the autumn of 1914 failed to win Germany the intended immediate and decisive victory. However Schlieffen's theories were destined to have a wide impact elsewhere. They were used to devastating effect against the Russians at Tannenburg in August 1914 and were taught by the staff colleges of Britain and the United States in the inter-war years.

Sir Henry Hughes Wilson

Field Marshal Sir Henry Hughes Wilson was born near Edgeworthstown, County Longford, in what is now the Republic of Ireland. Ireland, however, was then a part of the United Kingdom, and Wilson grew up a fervent and unrelenting Unionist. A soldier from the 1880s, he rose to command the Staff College at Camberley, Surrey from 1907 to 1910.

3 Rebels, Renegades and Reactionaries

During this period he cultivated the friendship of his French opposite number, General (later Marshal) Ferdinand Foch, with whom he shared a deep distrust of the Germans. While serving in the War Office as Director of Military Operations between 1910 and 1914, Wilson maintained a close liaison with Foch. Convinced that war in Europe was imminent, he felt certain that the place of the British Expeditionary Force (BEF) would be alongside, and on the left flank of, the French. To this end he spent his annual leaves cycling quietly through the villages and countryside of northern France, planning future brigade and battalion deployments in the greatest detail.

When war came in August 1914 Wilson was largely responsible for the smooth mobilisation of the standing army, and its rapid movement to its predesignated locations in France. Wilson was a keen advocate of conscription, but for once was unable to convince the government of his point of view, and it was not until 1916 that the first drafted soldiers were called upon to fight.

Wilson himself went to France as Assistant Chief of the General Staff. Despite his deep understanding of the soldier in the field he was not given field command until December 1915 when he assumed command of IV Corps on the Arras front. As General Officer Commanding the Eastern Command from September 1917, and later as Chief of the Imperial General Staff from February 1918, he gained Prime Minister Lloyd George's ear and was instrumental in gaining Foch the appointment of Supreme Commander of the Allied armies on the Western Front.

Wilson was created a baronet and promoted to field marshal in 1919, but was refused reappointment as Chief of Staff by Lloyd George, with whom he had argued over the issue of Irish independence. Although a brilliant soldier, Wilson proved less successful as a statesman. He was briefly posted to Ireland during the Troubles, but was removed soon after he made a speech seemingly defending the shooting, by the Royal Irish Constabulary and Auxiliaries, of innocent people in the fight against the Nationalists.

Wilson left the army shortly thereafter, and entered the House of Commons as Conservative member for an Ulster constituency. His outbursts on behalf of Anglo-Irish Unionism, coupled with his comments made while serving in Ireland, evoked the hatred of his nationalist countrymen in general and of Michael Collins in particular. In June 1922 he was assassinated at the front door of his London home by two members of the Irish Republican Army.

T. E. Lawrence

T. E. Lawrence was an archaeology scholar, a military strategist and an author. However he is best known for his legendary war activities in the Middle East, for which he earned the world-renowned accolade Lawrence of Arabia.

Lawrence was born the illegitimate son of Sir Thomas Chapman and his long time companion, Sara Maden. Lawrence was well educated, first at Oxford High School and later at Jesus College, from which he gained a first class honours degree in history. His deep love of Arabia was nurtured when, in 1911, he was invited to join an expedition excavating a Hittite settlement in Carchemish on the Euphrates. Utilising his spare time to the full he travelled on his own, getting to know the language and establishing a deep understanding of, and profound respect for, the people. In early

1914 Lawrence joined a small team to explore northern Sinai, on the then Turkish frontier east of Suez. Although the expedition had a scientific basis it was in essence a map-making reconnaissance from Gaza to Aqaba, destined to be of almost immediate strategic value.

In August 1914 Lawrence became a civilian employee of the Map Department of the War Office in London, charged with the preparation of military maps of Sinai. Later that year he was commissioned and posted to Cairo, where his first-hand knowledge of Turkish-held Arab lands earned him a position on the intelligence staff. For a year he was content to process prisoners, filter information from covert agents and prepare maps, and even produced a handbook on the Turkish Army.

However the death in action of his brothers Will and Frank in France in mid-1915 concentrated his mind on the more active front in the West. Convinced of a method of undermining Germany's Turkish ally, Lawrence was given permission, in October 1916, to accompany the diplomat Sir Ronald Storrs on a mission to Arabia. The Amir of Mecca, Husayn ibn 'Ali, had earlier risen in revolt against the Turks and had placed his son, Faisal, at the head of an Arab force south-west of Medina. Realising the potential of these irregulars if properly led and motivated, Lawrence persuaded the authorities in Cairo to support the Arab aspirations for independence, and joined Faisal's army as political and liaison officer.

At the head of a small but, to the Turks intensely irritating, band of guerrillas Lawrence set up a second front behind the enemy lines. Bridges were mined and supply trains ambushed, unsuspecting military outposts were overwhelmed and reinforcements, badly needed on the major fronts, were tied down. More importantly the Damascus-to-Medina railway, the main artery for the Turkish army in the area, was rendered almost inoperable.

Although Lawrence was not the only British officer to become involved in the Arab rising, he was without doubt the most successful. He infected the fickle and cynical sheikhs with the enthusiasm of his very personal vision of an Arab nation, knowing precisely when to lead by example and when to offer bribery as an incentive. His taking of the port of Aqaba in July 1917, after a two-month march, mostly across desert, must rank as one of the greatest ever victories of the twentieth century for an irregular force over conventional troops.

Ironically Lawrence's very success almost brought about his downfall. Politically naive, he continued to accept Government promises of an independent Arabia long after the more astute Arab leaders had come to realise that Anglo-French aspirations in the region were not the same as theirs. In November 1917 Lawrence was captured at Dar'a while reconnoitring the area in Arab dress. Recognised, he was homosexually brutalised before he was able to escape. Although this experience left Lawrence with mental scars which were destined to haunt him for the rest of his life, it did not prevent him from taking part in the victory parade in Jerusalem in December, nor did it prevent him from leading a further series of audacious raids north towards Damascus.

Lawrence returned to Britain, physically and emotionally exhausted, shortly before the Armistice. He accepted promotion to local Acting Colonel to facilitate his journey home, but refused the Order of the Bath and the DSO when presented with them at Buckingham Palace, leaving a shocked King George V literally 'holding the box in my hand'. Promoted to substantive lieutenant colonel at 30, Lawrence was a private at 34. Having left the army and lobbied vainly for Arab rights, he enlisted into the Royal Air Force in August 1922 under the assumed name of John Hume Ross. Unable to settle and with his true identity compromised by the press, he later transferred to the Royal Tank Regiment.

Lawrence found despair as potent as success. Shunning luxury, he lived a life of austerity verging on the masochistic. Constantly seeking an identity and never willing to accept the value of his own being he died an unfulfilled man, the victim of a motorcycling accident, on 13 May 1935.

Nancy Wake

Nancy Wake was an SOE agent, and as such would not normally warrant an entry in a chapter such as this. However such was her influence over the Maquis of southern France that at one time she controlled an irregular army in excess of 20,000 partisans.

Nancy Wake was born, and still resides, in Australia. In her youth she worked as a journalist in Sydney, and as a nurse in a country mental hospital. In her early twenties she undertook a world tour, supporting herself by occasional freelance journalism but more often drawing on her exuberance and zest for living to overcome the daily difficulties besetting a woman travelling alone.

Immediately before the outbreak of war she moved to Marseilles, where she met and subsequently married Henri Fiocca, a wealthy industrialist fourteen years her senior. With the outbreak of hostilities she volunteered her services as an ambulance driver, but returned to Marseilles in anger and frustration when France fell. Soon after Henri had been repatriated from the Army, Nancy was approached by an escaping British prisoner of war and she soon became deeply involved in the covert movement of Allied combatants from Vichy France into the comparative safety of neutral Spain. She travelled regularly between Marseilles and Cannes to organise escape routes, financing herself from the Fiocca fortunes while using the family flat as a safe house for escapers.

The Fioccas became a vital part of the PAT escape line (named after Albert Guerisse, a Belgian also known as Pat O'Leary). Nancy was arrested by the French security police, but handled the situation so professionally that she was released. However, she was now considered too compromised to remain in France much longer, and when Guerisse himself was captured she was forced to flee across the Pyrenees. She succeeded in crossing the Spanish frontier at the fifth attempt, and, after a long delay, reached Britain in 1943. It would be a further two years before she would learn the tragic news that soon after her escape her husband had been arrested, tortured and shot.

Nancy Wake was almost immediately recruited by SOE and embarked upon a period of training as a courier, during which she succeeded in thoroughly exasperating her instructors. She was parachuted into the Auvergne late in February 1944. Under the command of John Farmer, a regular army officer parachuted with her, she set about assisting in the training and arming of the 22,000 potential resistants in the area. Although the local leader, Gaspart, was happy to accept SOE arms he was less willing to tolerate interference in the daily running of his organisation. Indeed, when Nancy and Farmer first landed they found themselves actually arguing for their lives. It was only when they were joined by their radio operator, the highly experienced Denis Rake, that their personal situation improved.

With the establishment of a dedicated radio link the agents were able to organise supervised parachute drops, ensuring that supplies only reached those groups which were willing to accept orders, as well as arms, from Britain. Nancy began to cycle from group to group taking their orders, assessing their needs, finding drop zones and arranging reception committees.

Tragically, when the Maquis rose in open revolt against the Germans, prior to the delayed Allied landings in southern France, they invited savage retaliation. Over 22,000 mainly front-line troops were sent into the Corrèze and Haute-Loire supported by armour and artillery. Throughout the brief but bloody engagement which followed, Nancy drove back and forth across the battlefield carrying ammunition forward and evacuating the wounded to the comparative safety of the rear. A lull in the battle brought her no rest when it was discovered that Denis Rake's radio codes had been destroyed in the fighting. Fearless of the consequences of being caught on the open road, she set out on an epic cycle ride, of 36 hours' duration across the mountains to the nearest working radio. Having delivered her messages and placed her orders for resupply with London she at once turned for home, reaching her base, tired, bleeding and sick, another 36 hours later.

After the war Nancy returned to Marseilles, where she learned the tragic news of her husband's violent death. She moved to England in the early 1950s from whence she returned to Australia. She subsequently stood for Parliament, becoming something of a celebrity. She later married John Forward, with whom she now lives as quietly as such a woman as she is capable. Nancy Wake was invested with the George Medal by Britain, and with two Croix de Guerre with Palm and a Croix de Guerre with Star by the French. She also received the Resistance Medal, a honour granted sparingly to French citizens and hardly ever to foreigners. For its part the United States Government invested her with the Medal of Freedom with Bronze Palm, again a rare honour hardly ever awarded to foreigners.

Wing Commander Forest Frederick Yeo-Thomas

Wing Commander Yeo-Thomas was 38 when the Second World War broke out. He was a veteran of the First World War, and of the Polish-Russian War when he had been captured by the Bolsheviks and sentenced to death, escaping only the night before the sentence was due to be carried out. Yeo-Thomas spoke perfect French, his family having settled in France in the mid-nineteenth century. When his adopted country fell he returned to England and enlisted in the RAF. Too old to fly, he gravitated naturally towards the world of espionage and was accepted into the RF (Free French) section of the SOE.

Early in 1943 Yeo-Thomas returned to France in the company of André Dewarvrin, head of RF section, and Pierre Brossolette, a left-wing broadcaster and journalist. On his return to London, Yeo-Thomas was able to advise de Gaulle that the spirit of resistance within France was growing, fuelled by the German policy of conscripting active young men for forced labour. The young men were escaping to the mountains and woods of the French interior where they were forming themselves into armed, but otherwise disorganised, special purpose groups. For his services to France de Gaulle awarded Yeo-Thomas the Croix de Guerre with Palm, but typically the RAF ordered him not to wear it as the Frenchman had not then been recognised as Head of State!

During a second covert visit to France, Brossolette and Yeo-Thomas spent eight weeks in the Arras area, assessing the weaknesses and potential of the local réseaux. When ordered to fly home by Lysander he travelled to the landing site hidden under flowers in a funeral hearse, gripping a Sten gun to defend the secrets he was carrying with him.

Obsessed by the RAF's refusal to release more aircraft in support of the Maquis, Yeo-Thomas elected to petition Churchill direct. In a meeting lasting less than an hour he convinced the Prime Minister of his case, and the RAF were ordered to increase substantially the number of aircraft for dropping supplies to France.

When Yeo-Thomas heard that Brossolette, who had remained in France, had been captured he decided to return to rescue him. Adopting the identity of Squadron-Leader Dodkin, shot down over France, he hatched an ingenious plan involving a number of colleagues disguised as German guards. However the plan never materialised, and Brossolette eventually committed suicide in Gestapo headquarters in the Avenue Foch.

Yeo-Thomas was eventually betrayed and arrested. He escaped first from Buchenwald and then, after recapture and posing as an escaped French Air Force prisoner, from a POW camp. During captivity he was subjected to appalling tortures, which precipitated his early death in 1964.

Colonel General Heinz Guderian

Born in Kulm, Prussia, in June 1888, Heinz Guderian was the architect of Germany's Panzer victories in France in May 1940, and in the Soviet Union in June 1941. He had served as a regular officer on the staff throughout most of the First World War, and despite the savage cuts in the armed forces dictated by the Treaty of Versailles, succeeded in retaining his commission thereafter.

During the interwar years Guderian found himself a visionary in an otherwise conservative army, and as such earned the distrust of the High Command. Nonetheless his revolutionary ideas on tank warfare, most of which were based on the as yet unproven theories of the British tactician J F C Fuller, were accepted by Hitler. In 1937 Guderian produced a widely acclaimed textbook, *Achtung! Panzer!*, in which he advocated the creation of independent armoured formations with strong air and mechanised infantry support, to increase mobility on the battlefield. He argued that special purpose forces, highly trained and capable of using their own initiative, could penetrate the enemy lines with minimal loss, trapping vast bodies of men and weapons in a series of encircling movements.

Guderian was selected to command XIX Panzer Corps, the vanguard of Field Marshal Kleist's Panzer Army. At the very time that France was planning a defensive campaign based on static positions and the might of the Maginot Line, Germany was organising its finest troops into a single cohesive force capable of smashing its way through any conventional army.

Guderian gave a perfect practical demonstration of his theories in the Polish campaign of September 1939. In June 1940 he unleashed his Panzers against the unprepared Franco-British armies, crossing the Meuse and travelling so fast that the German High Command felt it necessary to put a brake on him. In June 1941 Guderian led the Second Panzer Army deep into the Soviet Union, encircling the Red Armies defending Kiev and Umanen on the route to Moscow.

An excellent field commander, Guderian proved an unwilling subordinate. He persistently ignored orders and directives from his superior, Kluge, and when he withdrew his troops from the outskirts of Moscow in the face of a massive Russian counteroffensive, he was sacked by Hitler. He was recalled in February 1943, given the honorary title of Inspector General of the Armoured Troops, and tasked with the restoration of morale within the Panzer units.

Guderian established the priorities in the production of armoured vehicles and the deployment of armoured units, but saw his considerable efforts squandered during the tank battle of Kursk in July 1943. The day after Stauffenberg's failed attempt on Hitler's life on 20 July 1944, Guderian was appointed acting Chief of the General Staff. He placed unremitting pressure on Hitler to withdraw his forces to a line of steel around Germany, but was utterly frustrated by his leader's intransigence and unwillingness to accept military reality. Fortunately for the Allies Hitler never fully recognised Guderian's great gifts as a military commander and theorist. Guderian resigned in March 1945. He wrote the much acclaimed *Panzer Leader* in 1952, and died two years later.

Major General Orde Wingate

Orde Wingate was the very epitome of an irregular forces commander. An introvert and something of a mystic who rarely rested and who shunned bathing in favour of a vigorous scrub down with a toothbrush, he inspired the imagination of his troops and of the general public alike. Educated at Charterhouse and the Royal Military Academy, Woolwich he was commissioned into the Royal Artillery in 1923, serving in the Sudan where he was tasked with the exploration of the Libyan desert.

Wingate served as an intelligence officer in Palestine between 1936 and 1939 during which time he organised 'Special Night Squads', irregular light infantry units specially trained to repel Arab raids against Jewish communities along the Mosul-Haifa oil pipeline. From January to May 1941, at the head of 'Gideon Force', a group of Ethiopian-Sudanese irregulars, he again proved the worth of specially trained unconventional troops by capturing a number of Italian forts before returning the Emperor Haile Selassie to his capital of Addis Ababa.

Shunned by the more conventionally-minded military hierarchy, Wingate was then returned to England to a desk-job. There the tedium, heightened by a bout of malaria, drove him to attempt suicide. While recovering he was summoned to the Far East by General Wavell who offered him the opportunity to organise a series of 'Long Range Penetration Groups'. These were effectively brigade-sized units trained to operate behind the Japanese lines. They were to be supplied by air, to receive their orders by radio and to attack the enemy in strength where he least expected it; behind his lines and along his main supply routes. Wingate named his special purpose force the Chindits, after 'Chinthe', a mythical beast of the jungle.

The Chindits entered Japanese-held Burma from the west, crossing the Chindwin River in February 1943. They crossed the Irrawaddy a month later, but by then the Japanese were fully alerted to the presence of the Chindits and, more importantly, to their mode of replenishment. Wingate was forced to withdraw his troops circuitously to India, having lost a third of his troops and most of his equipment.

Despite his limited success Wingate became a popular hero and a favourite of Winston Churchill. Wingate prepared a far more ambitious raid, this time by six brigades to be supplied by its own air unit, 'Cochran's Circus'. The expedition was airdropped into Burma in February 1944 and almost immediately ran into difficulties. Wingate was killed in a jungle air crash on 24 March 1944. Thereafter the Chindits came under United States command with disastrous results.

Marshal of the Soviet Union Georgy Zhukov

Georgy Konstantinovich Zhukov was born in the Kaluga province of Russia in 1896. He was conscripted into the Imperial Army during The First World War, joined the Red Army in 1918 and served as a cavalry commander during the Russian Civil War. Graduating from the Frunze Military Academy in 1931, Zhukov first came to prominence during a successful operation against the Japanese in Mongolia in 1939, during which his deployment of the limited Soviet armour available proved decisive.

Zhukov was appointed Chief of Staff of the Red Army during the disastrous Russo-Finnish Winter War of 1939-40. During four months of vicious fighting conducted in the near-Arctic conditions of the Scandinavian winter, a small group of Finnish partisans held the might of the Red Army at bay, inflicting on it an estimated 250,000 casualties. Only when the spring thaw allowed the Soviets to deploy their massive assets fully were they able to overcome the lightly armed Finns. Zhukov avoided censure for this catastrophe, but at the same time learned a salutary lesson. Never again did he allow his armour to become entrapped, but ensured that it had, at all times, the scope to range freely; engaging the enemy at will over as wide a front as possible.

Zhukov was transferred to command the Kiev Military District, and in January 1941 was appointed Chief of the General Staff. After Germany invaded the Soviet Union in June 1941 he served briefly as Director of the Soviet High Command, serving well in the abortive defence of Smolensk in August 1941. In October he replaced Voroshilov as commander of the northern sector with direct responsibility for the defence of Leningrad. He was subsequently appointed Commander in Chief of the Western Front, successfully defending Moscow against two German offensives and planning the December 1941 counter-attack.

Zhukov master-minded the defence of Stalingrad in 1942, causing the ultimate encirclement and surrender of Paulus's Sixth Army in January 1943. Created a Marshal of the Soviet Union in the same month, he was subsequently appointed supremo of Stalin's personal headquarters, and as such took part in the planning and execution of every major engagement from then until the fall of Berlin.

Zhukov was closely involved in the Battle of Kursk in July 1943, the largest tank battle in history, during which the Soviet armour fought the German Panzers to a standstill. Having effected a full scale German retreat, Zhukov directed the Soviet sweep across the Ukraine, advancing the front at the rate of thirty miles per day until halted by a lack of supplies. He then took overall command of the Central Front in Belorussia, advancing to the outskirts of Warsaw by June 1944. When the offensive resumed in January 1945 he advanced at a rate of 100 miles per week deep into Prussia, until he was again forced to stop due to supply problems.

In April 1945 Zhukov took personal command of the final assault on Berlin, and then remained in Germany as commander of the Soviet forces of occupation and Soviet representative on the Allied Control Commission for Germany. A fascinating and popular personality and a close friend of Eisenhower, Zhukov was regarded by Stalin as a potential threat and, on his return to Moscow, he was posted to a series of relatively obscure regional commands.

On Stalin's death in 1953 Zhukov was appointed Deputy Minister of Defence. Having supported Khrushchev against Malenkov, his chairman of the Council of Ministers, Zhukov replaced Bulganin as Minister of Defence in 1955, and began slowly to improve the professional calibre of the armed forces. Inevitably his attempts to reduce the role of the Communist Party's political advisers in the Army met with fierce resistance from Khrushchev. However his spirited defence of his political master in the face of an attempted coup in June 1957 ensured his continued influence, and indeed earned him promotion to full membership of the Presidium.

In October 1957 Khrushchev's patience was at last exhausted, and Zhukov was dismissed as Minister of Defence and sacked from his political posts. He remained in comparative obscurity until Khrushchev fell from power in October 1964. In 1966 Zhukov was awarded the Order of Lenin, and two years later published his autobiography.

Vo Nguyen Giap

Vo Nguyen Giap was born in An Xa in 1912, the son of an ardent anti-colonialist scholar and mandarin of the second class. He attended the same high school as Ho Chi Minh, the future Communist leader, and while still a student joined the Tan Viet Cach Menh Dang, the Revolutionary Party of Young Vietnam. Giap was expelled from one lycée for subversion, but was allowed to complete his education at the Lycée Albert-Sarraut in Hanoi, where in 1937 he was awarded a law degree.

Giap was arrested by the French Sûrêté in 1930, convicted of supporting student strikes and was sentenced to three years in prison, but he was paroled after serving only a few months. In 1938 he married Minh Thai, and thereafter worked closely with her and her family in support of the Indochinese Communist Party. When the Party was proscribed a year later, Giap escaped to China to join Ho Chi Minh. His wife and sister-in-law however were less fortunate. Both were captured by the French police. His sister-in-law was guillotined; his wife received a life sentence, later commuted to fifteen years, but she died in prison after three years.

Giap studied Maoist communist military doctrine while in China, before joining the Viet Minh as a founder member and returning to Vietnam in 1942. Funded by the Office of Strategic Studies (OSS), aided by Japanese deserters and armed through Thailand, Hong Kong and by the Chinese communists, the Vietminh grew in three years from an original band of 34 to an army of 50,000. In August 1945, Ho Chi Minh took advantage of the military vacuum occasioned by the Japanese collapse to occupy

3 Rebels, Renegades and Reactionaries

Hanoi. Giap was placed in command of the army and of all police and internal security forces, and in a reign of terror as violent as any in modern history, he at once set about the systematic annihilation of his political enemies.

In a rare lapse of judgement Giap became complacent and allowed his forces to become over-extended; in 1951 he suffered a series of defeats at the hands of the French general, Jean de Lattre de Tassigny. Giap learned from his defeats, and when de Lattre died in January 1952, he resumed the offensive in a brilliantly conceived campaign which culminated in the French defeat at Dien Bien Phu on 7 May 1954. On the partition of the country in July 1954, Giap became Deputy Prime Minister, Minister of Defence and commander of the armed forces. As such he led the North Vietnamese Army to victory in the second Indo-China war, driving the Americans from the country in 1973 and bringing about the downfall of the Saigon government in 1975.

Giap set out his principles for waging war in 1961 in a classic exposition entitled *People's War, People's Army*. Although the hand of ideological correctness rests heavily throughout its pages the book is still regarded by the political left as an excellent manual on guerrilla warfare.

Inevitably Giap has his detractors. It has been argued that he was no match for de Lattre, who defeated him on no less than three occasions in as many months, and some would argue that had the French general not died so prematurely the fate of Indo-China might have been very different. Others would argue that the Americans, in their turn, made things easy for Giap. Had they unleashed their formidable aerial technology against Haiphong and the marshalling yards on the Chinese border the external supplies which enabled Giap to prosecute the war in the south so relentlessly would not have been forthcoming. Instead the Americans chose to pursue a land war on Giap's terms, condemning their poorly-trained, and often unwilling conscripts to a form of guerrilla warfare for which they were patently ill-equipped.

Giap will be remembered as a dedicated politician and brilliant technocrat; he will also be remembered as a general to whom casualty figures were meaningless. He seemed to care little for the men (and women) under his command, driving them relentlessly - and often cruelly - to victory. Had matters ended differently, Giap may well have been called to account before the equivalent of a Nuremberg Tribunal. As it is history will record him as a man who led a peasant army to victory against the forces of the most powerful and technologically advanced country in the world.

4
The Second World War
The Conception of a Modern Elite

In the Second World War elites were often formed more out of desperation than inspiration. Most began as special purpose forces, brought together for a particular, usually highly aggressive type of warfare. Others were forces of special designation, introduced for single missions or campaigns and then disbanded.

The German Challenge

The swiftness of the fall of France in 1940 was in significant measure due to the swift successes of a handful of elite units. The glider-borne landing on the Belgian fortress of Eben Emael by a highly trained band of paratroopers was a textbook operation; as was the seizure of a railway bridge over the River Gennep in Holland by Brandenburger troops disguised as Dutch military police.

Later in the war, German units were to become involved in other classic examples of elite force exploitation: the freeing of Mussolini from his mountain-top prison at Gran Sasso in the Italian Alps (September 1943); the use of English-speaking Brandenburger sabotage units during the Battle of the Bulge (December 1944); and the last desperate attempts of the Werewolf teams on the Eastern Front.

The war against the Anglo-French Allies opened while German forces were still fighting in Norway. Operation 'Gelb' began at 5.35am on the morning of 10 May 1940, when 135 German divisions struck across the borders of Holland, Belgium and France against a superior Allied force. Belgium and Holland were neutral at the time. When Britain and France had declared war on Nazi Germany on 3 September 1939, Belgium had refused to join the old Alliance, preferring to join the Netherlands in a policy of strict neutrality. Both combatants had mobilised their forces, placing the majority along the German border. At the same time they had strictly forbidden the Anglo-French to enter their countries to make effective preparations for their defence.

Britain had been forced to construct a series of wholly inadequate anti-tank ditches along the Franco-Belgian border during 1939. It was accepted that this created a dangerous gap of some 80km between the southern flank of the temporary British defences and the start of the near-impregnable French Maginot Line but this was discounted. The French felt that the Ardennes, which occupied the bulk of this area, were impassable to large modern armies and declined to place more than nine divisions, only two of which were up to strength, in the sector.

Only von Manstein and the German OKH realised the true folly of this complacency. He believed that the terrain, despite its lack of roads, presented no insurmountable obstacles. He appreciated that the keys to success lay in fast movement by Panzer formations driving deep into the Allied rear, supported by Stuka dive-bombers acting as long range artillery.

Brandenburger Successes

Von Manstein realised that Sixth Army in particular would have to pass through Belgium quickly, and to do so it would have to secure a series of bridges intact. Four companies of Brandenburgers were given the tasks of capturing the most crucial bridges. Prior to the campaign Brandenburg detachments, fluent in the languages of the countries which they were to attack, had been preparing themselves in the frontier areas. Reconnaissance patrols had slipped across the borders to report on the number of sentries and the location and strengths of local garrisons. From February onwards the number of incursions had increased until a complete intelligence picture had been gained.

The 400m Gennep railway bridge across the River Meuse was considered the major prize. It stood 3km within the Dutch border and had to be taken before the Dutch could destroy it in order to enable two heavily-laden troop trains, scheduled to cross the border at zero hour, to proceed west towards the main Dutch defences. At 11.30pm on the night of 9 May a small section of Brandenburgers disguised as Dutch military policemen slipped across the border. The group leader, a corporal who spoke fluent Dutch, led his party to a laying up point between the River Niers and the railway.

Just before dawn the Brandenburgers approached the sentries on the eastern approach to the bridge and overpowered them without a struggle. They then telephoned the guards on the far end advising them, in fluent Dutch, that two military policemen would be escorting four German prisoners across. The 'prisoners and escort' then set out, leaving a second party of Brandenburgers holding the eastern approaches. At the bridge's middle section the soldiers disguised as military policemen handed over their prisoners to the Dutch and returned to the eastern end. The Dutch, by now thoroughly alarmed, escorted the prisoners to their command post, leaving a single sentry to guard the demolitions. When the first troop train approached a few minutes later the sentry hesitated, just long enough to allow the Germans on board to jump off and overpower him. The original German 'prisoners' then overpowered their confused captors, thus the bridge fell into German hands intact allowing the trains to proceed westward.

The Koch Storm Detachment

The fortress at Eben Emael, considered impregnable, was built of granite and set upon a ridge some 50m above the surrounding countryside. Over 900m long and 700m wide, it was in essence a complex of interrelated infantry and artillery strong points coordinated to provide mutual defences and linked by kilometres of deep subterranean passages. It was protected to the north by a sheer drop to the Albert Canal. To the north-west the flood plain of the River Jeker had been raised to frustrate armoured attack. Anti-tank ditches with 4m walls had been dug to the south and west. With its own generators, telecommunications and over-pressure filtered ventilation system it had been designed to withstand any form of attack experienced in the previous war.

Eben Emael, the barrier to the advance of the Sixth Army into Belgium, became the objective of the Koch Storm Detachment. Formed amid great secrecy in Hildesheim in November 1939 and commanded by Captain Koch, the unit comprised the 1st Company of the 1st Parachute Regiment, the Parachute Sapper Detachment of the 7th Flying Division, the Freight Glider Unit, a beacon and searchlight detachment and airfield ground staff.

It quickly became apparent that landing by parachute offered scant chance of success. The task of neutralising the fortress fell to the glider-borne sapper unit. This detachment was unique. Consisting entirely of engineers who had volunteered for hazardous duties, it incorporated within its ranks some of the finest glider pilots of prewar Germany. Under the command of Lieutenant Witzig it had grown into a close-knit, confident and above all self-reliant unit. Its training had been top secret and specific, and had taken place in a number of widely dispersed locations so as not to draw undue attention.

The engineers were kept segregated from the rest of the army and given little indication of their mission until the very last minute. At 4.30am on the morning of 10 June the detachment took off in eleven gliders, each holding a section of seven or eight men. At precisely 5.25am nine of the gliders successfully landed in a tight configuration on the roof of the fortress. The teams left their aircraft within seconds of landing and moved at once to their objectives. Within ten minutes the engineers were in virtual control of the upper surfaces of the fortress rendering the garrison below impotent.

Exploiting the element of surprise to the full, specially designed 50kg hemispherical shaped cavity charges were then placed on seven of the reinforced artillery domes. Five of the emplacements were completely destroyed, and with them nine of the fortress's massive 7.5cm guns. By 8.30am Eben-Emael had been rendered ineffective. The engineers were forced to hold their position alone until relieved by elements of the 51st Sapper Battalion at 7.00am on the next morning. In 24 hours of sporadic fighting the Belgians lost 23 dead and 59 wounded, the Germans six dead and fifteen wounded.

The capture of the fortress was testament to the potency of special forces used properly. Witzig had relied on a brilliant plan, comprehensive training and excellent soldiering to suppress the will to fight of a numerically vastly superior enemy and ultimately to win.

The storming of Eben Emael, the first engineers' assault ever to be made from the air, became a blue-print for later special forces actions.

Otto Skorzeny

Major Otto Skorzeny was a dedicated SS officer. He lacked the intelligence and finesse of the earlier Brandenburgers, but more than made up for this in leadership ability and in an undisputed mastery of counter-insurgency warfare. When the

King of Italy removed Mussolini from the post of Prime Minister on 25 July 1943 and placed him under arrest, Hitler chose Skorzeny to effect his rescue.

Mussolini was moved frequently, from one prison to another, to frustrate German attempts at a rescue. In August the former Duce was taken to the area of the Gran Sasso Massif. German wireless-operators monitoring signals between Italian units picked up a message which indicated unusual activity in the Gran Sasso. Discreet inquiries established the presence of a very important personage in the Albergo Rifugio on the peak of a mountain. It could only be Mussolini and plans were made to rescue him from his prison.

The only conventional means of access were by hours of climbing or by using the cable-car system. The guards were under orders to shoot their prisoner (if an escape attempt were mounted) making a highly visible foot march or an assault from the cable car impractical. The unusual wind conditions prevailing in the area made a parachute drop, even from the lowest altitude of 60m, equally impossible leaving a glider-borne rescue the only option.

The operation was arranged in such secrecy that even the Commander in Chief of the Luftwaffe was not informed. The nearest glider group, in Grosseto, was ordered to fly into Practica di Mare airfield on the morning of 12 September. There they were joined by twenty Luftwaffe fallschirmjäger from Major Mors' Paratroop Training Battalion and 50 of Skorzeny's own SS commandos.

The party embarked in twelve fully-manned DFS 230 gliders, four of which dropped out en route and failed to reach the target area. The remaining gliders landing without incident close to the hotel. Skorzeny's glider halted only fifteen to twenty metres from the hotel's main door. In less than four minutes the highly skilled elite entered the building, destroyed the radio and found and liberated the Italian leader.

It has never been established why Skorzeny did not use the cable car down into the valley whence a fast convoy could have been organised to the airport. Instead he flew Mussolini from the Gran Sasso in a Fieseler Storch light aircraft. The operation had been a brilliant airborne success. Yet Skorzeny claimed the glory for his own SS. He was awarded the Knights Cross of the Iron Cross while the fallschirmjäger operation, skilfully planned and carried out, went unacknowledged. Skorzeny became the undisputed mentor of the German special forces. His influence was to be crucial in the later stages of the war.

The Ardennes Offensive

By the end of 1944 the tide of war was running against Germany. On the Eastern Front the Red Army had crossed the border and was exacting terrible revenge against the civilian population. In Italy the Allies were along the Rome-Rimini line, ready to resume their advance when the weather improved. In the west they were closing up to the Rhine and had already taken Aachen.

Hitler saw a last desperate chance for victory. The Allied armies, massed in the north-west were being supplied through the port of Antwerp. If an attack could be launched through the Ardennes, as it had been in 1940, the Panzers could cross the Maas and reach Antwerp in very little time. The Anglo-American armies would be split and forced to retreat. The winter offensive came to be known as the Battle of the Bulge and involved four armies; the Fifteenth, Sixth SS Panzer, Fifth Panzer and Seventh, and three special units; the Brandenburgers, the Fallschirmjäger, and Skorzeny's own commandos recruited in great secrecy for the mission.

The operation had been planned for the late autumn, but had to be postponed several times due to a chronic lack of supplies. D Day was eventually scheduled for 5.30am on 16 December.

The special forces were to be employed as shock troops, to rupture the enemy line on D Day. The Meuse was to be crossed within 24 hours, using the bridges at Englis, Amay and Huy which were to be captured intact by Skorzeny's commandos, supported on the flank by the Fallschirmjäger. It was estimated that the infiltration of commando troops dressed as Americans (some in the uniforms of military police) would not only spread panic among the enemy but ensure that the roads were kept open for the advancing panzers.

Skorzeny recruited two battalions for the purpose of this subterfuge. Volunteers had to be fit, mentally alert with strong personalities. They had to be trained in hand to hand combat, speak English and have a working knowledge of an American dialect. Ultimately Skorzeny selected ten volunteers with perfect mastery of American-English including idioms, over 30 with a good knowledge of English, 150 who could understand the language and some 200 with command of a few phrases.

Skorzeny massed the bulk of his special forces into 'Panzer Brigade 150', comprising an armoured battle group and the English-speaking commando force, which he eventually reduced to 160 men. The commandos were subdivided into sets of agents carrying out one of three types of duty. 'Saboteur' detachments, each of five or six men, were tasked with the destruction of enemy supply dumps and lines of communication. 'Reconnaissance' groups, comprising four or five men, were ordered to infiltrate the areas north and south of the Meuse, identify the enemy's armoured and artillery units and spread as much confusion as possible by changing road signs, removing minefield indicators, relaying false information and issuing conflicting orders. The third group, the Lead commandos, were to operate ahead of the advancing divisions, intercepting enemy radio signals and issuing conflicting counter-orders.

The armoured battle group was designed to add to the American confusion. Equipped as far as possible with captured or disguised enemy equipment, it was to act like a US armoured group fleeing in disorder from the advancing Germans. The battle group was in every respect a hotchpot, comprising two battalions of Fallschirmjäger, a company of Skorzeny's own 'Jagdverdband Mitte', two companies of SS paratroopers, two panzer and two panzer grenadier companies and an assortment of support troops.

Ultimately the special forces played little part in the Battle of the Bulge, although their presence undoubtedly unnerved some of the less experienced American troops. Skorzeny's Panzer Brigade was denied the element of surprise essential to all special forces operations. Eventually the American front line held. The German armoured columns, attempting to deploy along wholly unsuitable winter roads, began to coagulate. Unable to exploit the non-existent breakthrough in the American lines as intended, Skorzeny was forced to commit his panzer elite to the more conventional ground fighting role around Baughez, Stavelot and Malmédy where their additional training counted for little and their diverse and unusual weaponry was a positive disadvantage.

The special language commandos met with a little more success. An American tank battalion was sent in the wrong direction and an infantry unit was bluffed into withdrawing from a village which it held. Telephone lines were cut and an ammunition dump blown. Of the nine teams deployed, seven were able to infiltrate successfully and one reached the Meuse. Commandos from one of the captured units, the Einhert Steilau, were court martialled and shot.

Command of the 1,200 strong airborne elite was delegated to Oberst Baron von der Heydte, a man of immense experience, a veteran of Crete and the commander of the Fallschirmjäger School at Alten. The paras were ordered to prevent the arrival of American reinforcements from the north. Battle Group von der Heydte took off in an armada of 150 Junkers aircraft shortly after midnight on the morning of 16 December. However a combination of head winds, heavy flak and inexperience caused many of the young pilots to lose their way so that when they dropped their troops few of them came down near the target. Two hundred troopers landed in or near Bonn in Germany. Others fell into Holland. Only ten aircraft from the entire armada, including that carrying the commander, succeeded in dropping their loads accurately.

By daylight less than 150 troopers had rallied on the drop zone. They had no heavy weapons or equipment and little food, neither of the two radios in their possession worked and all ideas of fulfilling their mission had to be abandoned. Yet, in the finest traditions of the special forces they were not deterred. The depleted force struck out towards Malmédy in the hopes of linking with the SS spearhead units. When none was met the paratroops withdrew north-east to the woods where they made contact with a further 150 men survivors from the scattered battle group.

When a subsequent attempted breakout in force met with failure von der Heydte ordered his men to split into small teams to attempt individual escapes. He himself was badly wounded and ultimately captured. Although the Fallschirmjäger failed in their original role their sheer tenacity paid unexpected dividends. The Americans realised from the outset that the Fallschirmjäger were there but utterly overestimated their numbers. Whole divisions which might otherwise have been committed to the front were diverted to counter what was in essence little more than half a battalion of lightly armed men.

Werewolf

By early 1945 it had become clear to all but the most fanatical of Nazis that Germany faced total defeat. In desperation the Werewolf organisation, a special purpose force of the old and young not already fully committed to the fighting was formed to operate behind the Allied lines. It was inspired and planned by the Nazi Party, but administered by the OKW to give it a degree of legality.

Werewolf partisans were to allow themselves to be overrun. They were to go to ground and later emerge to harry the enemy supply lines and communications. German civilians in the occupied areas were to be kept loyal to Hitler by threat. Collaborators were to be shot and fly-posted placards and leaflets distributed to remind the populace where its duty lay. To the end Werewolf was an all-volunteer organisation. The first recruits were obtained by verbal invitation or personal recommendation. Once a nucleus of reliable men and women had been obtained the trawl was widened to incorporate others whom it was felt could keep a secret.

Training centres were established at Hulcenrath, a castle in the Rheinland, and later at Lubbecke, Waidhofen in Austria, Neustrelitz and Quenzee. Initially training was uncompromisingly harsh. As soon as the recruits entered camp there was no going back, those few, usually very young, volunteers who subsequently refused to join the partisans were shot as traitors by the SD. As soon as they entered camp trainees were stripped of all personal possessions which would act as a traceable link with home and possibly weaken their ultimate resolve to fight. Hours of political indoctrination turned loyal Nazis into cold-blooded fanatics. Field training was harsh, often brutal, with beatings from the instructors the punishment for those who failed to attain the highest standards. As the Allies closed in however training was of necessity curtailed, until the last students received little more than a few basic lessons in fieldcraft.

Trained in weapon skills, sabotage and communications the agents returned home to await the orders which would take them underground into the partisan organisation. Groups were organised into platoons of about 30 although they invariably operated in much smaller teams of four or five. Partisans, who fought in civilian clothes and who risked execution if caught, were supplied with false documents, while hideouts all over Germany and Austria were equipped with sufficient food, clothing and ammunition to keep them operational for years if necessary.

Little is known of the successes, or otherwise, of the 5,000 or so Werewolf partisans, although they are not regarded as significant and played no part in the final outcome of the war. Initially their activities were largely ignored by the advancing Allies, even when one of Field Marshal Montgomery's liaison officers, Major John Poston, was killed in an ambush. However when the American-appointed Mayor of Aachen was executed on 24 March, and the commander of 3rd Armoured Division, Major-General Maurice Rose, was murdered by the Werewolf in Paderborn on 8 April, attitudes hardened. Any fire aimed at the Americans was considered Werewolf activity and met by savage ferocity. On 5 June two Hitler Youth, one aged 16 and the other 17, accused of sniping on the occupation forces in Aachen were executed by firing squad.

No special force, however well motivated, can operate in a political void. The Werewolf was unpopular with the German people as a whole who had no desire to antagonise the occupation forces. It had already been weakened by daily arrests in the Franco-British sectors of Occupied Germany, by random searches in the American sector, and by the mass execution or deportation of suspects by the Russians. With the end of the war Werewolf died.

4 The Second World War

The British Response

The potential for guerrilla warfare in a future conflict was discussed by the British War Office as early as 1938. Radical ideas for sabotage, deception and escape and evasion were developed, but shelved until the spring of 1940 when the ultra-conservative War Office was at last persuaded to put some of these ideas into practice.

Three independent companies were formed to act as guerrillas and sent to Norway, but a golden opportunity was squandered when they were used as line infantry rather than deployed to harass enemy communications. In June 1940, with the tattered remnants of the BEF safely home and the Continent firmly in Nazi hands, Churchill determined to 'set Europe ablaze.' He ordered 'a vigorous, enterprising and ceaseless offensive against the whole German-occupied coastline.' He demanded that deep raids be made inland from the coast, cutting enemy communications and 'leaving a trail of German corpses behind them'.

The Striking Companies were increased from three to ten and were later redesignated Commandos. A proper system of espionage and intelligence along the occupied coast was introduced, proposals for transporting and landing tanks on the beaches was prepared and a proposal for the development of a paratrooper force of 5,000 men was mooted.

The first raid against the enemy coast was mounted near Boulogne, by a group of 120 commandos on 23 June 1940. Although the raid achieved little in itself it was an omen of things to come. The Combined Operations Command was set up in July 1940, and a few months later the Joint Planning Staff was instructed to study the feasibility of offensive operations in Europe.

More commando raids followed, including two against the Norwegian coast which prompted Hitler to reinforce his naval forces there with the battleships *Scharnhorst* and *Gneisenau* and the cruiser *Prinz Eugen*. Later the Commandos were joined by the Special Boat Squadron (SBS), the Special Air Service (SAS), two airborne divisions and a host of irregular units, providing Britain with arguably the finest elite forces of the war.

Early Days of the SAS

The origins of the Special Air Service lie in the Western Desert. At the time of its formation the Germans controlled most of western Europe and had recently captured Yugoslavia, Greece and Crete. Rommel's Afrika Korps had won a number of successful battles in North Africa, and together with the Italians posed a grave threat to British forces. The SAS was the brainchild of one man, a young Scots Guards subaltern by the name of David Stirling; then serving with Laycock's No 8 Commando in the Middle East. Tiring of a period of inactivity during which 'Layforce' was being run down, Stirling devised a plan to disrupt German communications and troop movements by making lightning hit-and-run raids against strategic targets well behind the German lines.

Stirling had first to present his ideas to the relevant authorities. Fearing that his plan would not reach the Commander in Chief, Sir Claude Auchinleck, if presented through the normal channels, he elected for a more direct approach. Despite being incapacitated by a parachuting injury sustained two months earlier Stirling succeeded in climbing over a security fence into the headquarters' building. Unable to find Auchinleck, he was nonetheless able to give his plan to Lieutenant General Neil Ritchie before being caught and ejected.

The Commander in Chief was so impressed by the plan, and its unique method of delivery, that he promoted Stirling to the rank of Captain. More importantly he authorised the formation of 'L Detachment', a force of 66 men who would be trained along lines similar to the vaunted Long Range Desert Group then operating successfully in North Africa. Stirling was uncompromising in the selection of the men he recruited, many of whom were to have a lasting influence on the character of the SAS. They were to include Blaire (Paddy) Maine, an Irish rugby international and accomplished boxer who was later destined to command the Regiment when Stirling was captured, Fitzroy Maclean and Anders Lassen.

L Detachment's first raid was a disaster. Aircraft became lost in the adverse weather and many of the men who parachuted in were swept away. It has also been suggested, though never substantiated, that the raid was compromised by loose talk in Cairo. Security was tightened, and the volunteers warned of the consequences of unguarded speech in the future. Subsequent raids were executed from ground vehicles. Initially rides to the targets were hitched with the Long Range Desert Group but later the force received a limited number of Willys jeeps, specially equipped with extra water and fuel tanks and armed with an array of Vickers K and Browning machine-guns.

Some spectacular successes were to follow in which L Detachment destroyed over 100 aircraft and horrified the German by their speed and surprise. This convinced British Army Command that the unit was worth nurturing, and in October 1942, L Detachment was redesignated 1st Special Air Service Regiment (1 SAS.) The title was chosen deliberately to give the impression of an airborne assault force of considerable size, though 1 SAS comprised at the time only 390 officers and men including a number of French paratroops.

The Regiment was to prove a disruption to German operations which totally belied its size, and many thousands of German troops were forced to guard installations, when they might have been usefully employed fighting the Allied forces. When David Stirling was captured, command of 1 SAS passed to Paddy Maine. In the meantime David's brother, Bill Stirling, was placed in command of the recently formed 2 SAS which conducted its initial raids in Sicily and along the Italian coastline.

In January 1944, an SAS brigade was formed in Scotland, consisting of two British regiments (1 and 2 SAS), two French regiments (3 and 4 SAS) and a Belgian independent parachute squadron (later 5 SAS). Support was provided by F Squadron GHQ Reconnaissance Regiment (Phantom) which acted as the Brigade's signal squadron. As D Day approached many influential opponents of irregular warfare began to question the usefulness of the SAS in the north-west European theatre. Initially it was decided to ignore the obvious expertise of the SAS in small-unit warfare, and to deploy it in a conventional airborne role. Fortunately wiser counsel prevailed, and it was eventually agreed to deploy the brigade strategically, reporting directly to Montgomery's 21st Army Headquarters when established.

As a sop to those who regarded the SAS as subordinate to the Airborne Division, eighteen parties were dropped in Brittany on D Day minus 1 (5 June 1944.) They assisted the Resistance in attacking lines of communication, so hindering the movement of enemy reserves towards Normandy. Such raids, however, were unpopular with the brigade as they frequently resulted in savage reprisals against the local civilian population. Subsequent raids were of a longer-term nature, designed primarily to establish semi-permanent operational bases.

Between D Day and the end of November, the SAS mounted some 780 air sorties of which 600 were successful. Two six-pounder anti-tank guns, 9,820 containers and 75 armoured jeeps were dropped in support. Of the 2,000 SAS participants, 330 became casualties. Enemy killed or severely wounded numbered 7,753; 4,764 were taken prisoner and 18,000 cut off. 7,600 vehicles were destroyed, as were 29 locomotives and 89 railway goods wagons. The railways were cut in 164 places.

It is perhaps easier to assess the full impact of the SAS in France by studying in detail one of the more successful raids. A massive drop, codenamed 'Houndsworth', took place in the Dijon area. Initially an advance party was dropped on D Day minus 1. Supported by a local 'Jedburgh' team comprising guides and local liaison officers under command of Headquarters Special Forces the team quickly swelled to a total of 153 officers and men supported by fourteen jeeps. The force was intended to be larger, but tragically an aircraft carrying a reinforcement team of eighteen troopers crashed killing all on board.

Early attempts to control a massive area of some 13,000km^2 was soon abandoned as over optimistic. Nonetheless Houndsworth accounted for an estimated 220 German dead, including a general killed when his vehicle ran over a landmine, for the loss of one officer killed and four troopers wounded. The railway was cut no less than 22 times between Dijon, Lyons and Paris with six trains destroyed. Sixteen allied aircrew and a female Resistance agent dropped into France by SOE were rescued, a Gestapo agent posing as a Belgian was uncovered, and 3,000 local Maquis were armed by the team.

Not all operations were so successful. 'Bulbasket' took place between 6 June and 7 July in the Châteauroux area. In all 55 troops from 1 SAS, supported by elements of the Phantom Regiment were dropped into the area. Initially all went well. They were able to cut the railway line a dozen times besides inflicting twenty casualties on the enemy. Success turned to tragedy when the SAS base was treacherously compromised by unknown elements of the local population. The base was attacked, resulting in 37 casualties of whom 33 were captured and executed. It has since been alleged that some of those shot had given themselves up when surrounded. Ignorant of Hitler's Commando Directive which ordered the summary execution of all captured special forces, they had assumed that they would be treated according to the terms of the Geneva Convention. The fate of the Bulbasket SAS represents one of the worst atrocities of the post-invasion war and exemplifies the attitude of a defeated enemy to a captured elite.

On the cessation of hostilities in Europe, the British Army dispensed with as many of the so-called private armies as possible, and units which had given sterling service during wartime were disbanded. The SAS was among the first to go, though its 'foreign daughters', the 3rd, 4th and 5th SAS Regiments were handed over to the French and Belgian armies with due ceremony.

The Commandos

During the Second World War the first Commando units were formed to conduct raids on the German-occupied coasts of Europe. The British Army initially formed three and later ten commandos; these were merged with the Royal Marines Commandos in 1943. These newly formed Royal Marines commandos served with distinction for the remainder of the war, both in the European and Far Eastern theatres.

Royal Marines Gunners were in action aboard HMS *Exeter*, *Ajax* and *Achilles* during the Battle of the River Plate in December 1939, and manned at least one turret in every capital ship throughout the war. Their guns were in action escorting convoys, and in the invasion bombardments of North Africa, Sicily, the Salerno beachhead, the landings in Normandy and actions throughout the Pacific. Royal Marines anti-aircraft Gunners helped to defend Britain during the Blitz, and in 1944 found 3,000 personnel for an anti-aircraft brigade.

The Royal Marines (Amphibious) Brigade, formed in 1939 and held for special operations is the true predecessor of today's Royal Marines Commando Brigade. It was sent to Dakar, French West Africa, in the summer of 1940 and was later expanded to provide men for the Royal Marines commandos and ultimately the three brigades of the Royal Marines Division. A total of nine commandos were formed, each of 450 officers and marines: five fought in north-west Europe, two in Italy and Dalmatia aiding the partisans and two in the Far East. Engineers serving with the Royal Marines reconnoitred invasion beaches prior to major landings and assisted in the clearance of captured installations. Volunteers served with the Special Boat Squadron and with the 'Cockleshell Heroes' of the Royal Marines Boom Patrol Detachment. Others served with a number of anonymous units with deliberately misleading titles; such as 'Detachment 385' whose canoeists were landed by flying boat for clandestine missions in occupied Malaya.

No single operation completely epitomises the unique contribution to the war effort of the Commando special forces. However the raids on Vaagso and St Nazaire, which were wholly different in their inception, give some idea of the versatility of these units.

During the summer of 1940 it became apparent that a successful morale-raising operation was needed to maintain the enthusiasm of the newly formed Commandos. Vaagso, in the Norwegian fjords, was chosen. It was argued that a successful attack would force the Germans to commit a large number of troops to that remote area instead of sending them to Europe or Africa. The attackers comprised five assault groups from Lieutenant Colonel Durnford Slater's No 3 Commando, two platoons from No 2 Commando, a detachment of Royal Engineers and a small group of Free Norwegians. Air support was provided by a squadron of Hampden bombers tasked with dropping smoke during the actual landing, and Blenheims and Beaufighters to neutralise the Luftwaffe response from the three neighbouring airfields. The entire ground force of 51 officers and 525 men was carried in the light cruiser *Kenya* and four destroyers supported by a submarine and two infantry assault ships.

The raid was mounted at 8.42am, shortly before dawn on the morning of 27 December 1941. Air-naval coordination was perfect and surprise was complete. During the ensuing few hours of Arctic daylight the Commandos succeeded in destroying virtually every military installation in the area before retiring in good order. Over 100 Germans were killed and about the same number taken prisoner. Some 16,000 tons of enemy shipping was sunk and 77 volunteers for the Free Norwegian forces were taken to Scotland. The Commandos lost 20 dead and 57 wounded, most of them in a single incident when a bomber was hit and crashed into a landing craft. The cruiser *Kenya* was damaged and eight aircraft lost but the mission was nonetheless declared an unqualified success.

March 1942 saw what was probably the greatest commando raid mounted by Combined Operations during the course of the entire war, and one which had an enormous effect on its outcome. St Nazaire, at the mouth of the River Loire, possessed a massive dry dock capable of holding any capital ship in the German Navy. It was also a central base for the U-boat 'wolf packs' then operating with considerable success in the Atlantic.

The dry dock was an obvious target, and as such had been rendered as near impregnable as possible by the defenders. Plans to raid the harbour were abandoned as impractical until it was realised that the river's mud flats, originally considered too shallow for shipping were in fact navigable during the high spring tides. A plan was devised to get lightly laden ships over the flats. There was no boom protecting the gate of the dock, nor any other defensive construction, since the Germans remained convinced that this approach was impossible.

It was planned that the old Lend-Lease destroyer *Campbeltown* should be filled with explosives and made to ram the dock gates. She was to be escorted by two Hunt-class destroyers, *Atherstone* and *Tynedale*, while sixteen Fairmile motor launches, a motor gunboat and a motor torpedo-boat were to carry the all-volunteer Commando force of 44 officers and 224 other ranks. The naval force was to be commanded by the former Antarctic explorer, Commander Robert Ryder, and the land force by Lieutenant Colonel Charles Newman of No 2 Commando.

Two of *Campbeltown*'s four funnels were removed and her superstructure altered to give her more of a German appearance. Her crew was reduced to 75 and nearly five tons of explosives were placed in her bows to blow the dock gates apart after she had been abandoned. The raid was planned in conditions of the utmost secrecy. The flotilla was spotted by a U-boat en route to St Nazaire but the submarine was forced to crash-dive before it could signal the force's location. Two French trawlers were intercepted and sunk, after their crews had been taken on board the destroyers.

As with so many successful special forces raids boldness was compounded by initiative to provide total surprise. As *Campbeltown* entered the Loire she was routinely challenged by a shore battery. Leading Seaman Pike, a fluent German speaker and familiar with German Navy signals, flashed a message with his Aldis lamp, identifying the flotilla as being German, and asking permission to enter harbour. The ensuing minutes of uncertainty bought Lieutenant Commander Sam Beattie and the crew of *Campbeltown* a precious breathing space before the enemy realised the ruse and opened up withering fire on the ship.

Campbeltown rammed the outer dock gates at 20 knots, her bow crumpling like a tin can. Minutes later the Commandos ran ashore from their motor launches, located their designated targets and began to neutralise the German defences. Inevitably, as the German defenders recovered from their shock and began to organise a coherent counter-attack, the Commandos were overwhelmed. A few men managed to escape. Two launches succeeded in disengaging themselves from the battle and successfully returned to England. Other survivors were found by the French underground and reached safety in Spain.

Losses were heavy. Some 169 men were killed and 200 taken prisoner. But the reward was great. During the course of the morning *Campbeltown* disintegrated in a giant ball of flame as her explosive charge detonated. Several hundred Germans on or near the ship, many of them high ranking officers, were killed. More importantly, the dock gates were damaged beyond repair denying the enemy an important facility for the rest of the war.

Airborne Forces

On 22 June 1940 Prime Minister Winston Churchill sent a memo to General Sir Hastings Ismay, head of the Military Wing of the War Cabinet Secretariat, which led directly to the formation of the British airborne forces: 'We ought to have a corps of at least 5,000 parachute troops, including a proportion of Australians, New Zealanders and Canadians, together with some trustworthy people from Norway and France. . . . advantage of the summer must be taken to train these troops, who can nonetheless play their part meanwhile as shock troops in home defence. Pray let me have a note from the War Office on the subject.'

In fact, the foundation stone for the training of airborne forces had already been laid by the Royal Air Force, who earlier that month had taken the decision to set up a parachute training centre at Ringway, near Manchester. This was the Central Landing School, commanded by Squadron Leader Louis Strange; with the task of 'organising the British airborne forces' delegated to his Second in Command, Major John Rock of the Royal Engineers.

While the school was being set up, a search was made for volunteers to train as parachutists. It was eventually decided to convert No 2 Commando to the parachute role. The unit was moved to Knutsford, not far from Ringwood, and placed under the command of Lieutenant Colonel Jackson of the Royal Tank Regiment. In November 1940 No 2 Commando was redesignated 11th Special Air Service Battalion and was reorganised into a headquarters, a parachute wing and a glider wing. By the end of the year it consisted of a total of 22 sub-sections, each with ten men.

Despite its lack of experience Britain's fledgling airborne unit was soon put to the test. A team of 38 men, consisting of seven officers and 31 men, was selected for a raid against the Tragino aqueduct in southern Italy. Although the operation was only partly successful the role of the airborne soldier was accepted and steps were taken to expand 11th SAS Battalion. In July 1941 authorisation was granted for the formation of a brigade headquarters, four parachute battalions and an airborne troop of Sappers. In early September 1941, Headquarters 1st Parachute Brigade was formed at Hardwick Hall, in Derbyshire, under the command of Brigadier Richard Gale. The 11th SAS Battalion was transferred en masse to become 1st Parachute Battalion while 2nd, 3rd (and later 4th) Battalions were formed from the trawl of recent volunteers.

In October 1941 the War office decided that an airlanding brigade of gliderborne troops would be formed in addition to 1st Parachute Brigade. The 31st Independent Infantry Brigade was selected for conversion to the role, and subsequently redesignated 1st Airlanding Brigade. Simultaneously 1st Parachute Brigade, 1st Airlanding Brigade and the glider units were formed into 1st Airborne Division. On 24 February 1942 the glider units were merged into the Glider Pilot Regiment, and a few weeks later 2nd Parachute Brigade was formed to bring the Division up to strength.

The 4th Parachute Battalion was transferred to the new brigade and 7th Battalion The Queen's Own Cameron Highlanders and 10th Battalion The Royal Welch Fusiliers redesignated 5th (Scottish) and 6th (Royal Welsh) Parachute Battalions. Those officers and men not wishing to qualify were transferred to other units, their places being taken by volunteers who had successfully passed through the Airborne Forces Depot. In the middle of 1942 the airborne forces received their most enduring recognition symbol, the red beret. This has since been adopted by airborne forces around the world and is universally accepted as a sign of military excellence.

In December 1941 a sharp eyed physicist, Dr Charles Frank, and an enthusiastic pilot, Flight Lieutenant Tony Hill, combined to launch one of the most famous - and skilfully executed - combined operations of the war. While studying some routine aerial photographs of the Bruneval area, Frank noticed what he thought to be the command post of a top secret German Würzburg radar complex. Low-level photographs later taken by Hill proved him to be correct, and a combined arms raid was ordered to steal vital technical components of the radar from under the German's noses.

On the night of 27 February 1942, 119 officers and men drawn from C Company 2nd Parachute Regiment and 1st Parachute Squadron Royal Engineers parachuted from No 51 Squadron's Whitley bombers into the skies around Bruneval on the French coast. The radar command post was located, its guards neutralised and the fragile equipment dismantled and made ready for shipment back to England. The party then fought its way down to the beach from where it was taken off by Captain Cook of the Royal Australian Navy and his small task force of landing craft and motor gunboats.

At the cost of two airborne soldiers dead, six wounded and six missing the mission exactly fulfilled its planners' intentions. The intelligence gained from the Bruneval Würzburg radar had far-reaching effects on British radar developments and on electronic warfare counter-measures. More immediately, it yet again proved to Hitler that nowhere was immune to the attentions of the British special forces.

In September 1942 it was decided to include an airborne unit amongst the Allied forces to take part in the forthcoming campaign in North Africa. Originally 2nd Battalion 503rd US Parachute Infantry was chosen. However it was later decided to commit 1st Airborne Brigade in support. The brigade fought a number of engagements in the Tunisian Campaign and, in 1943, joined the Air Landing Brigade in the invasion of Sicily. Subsequently it joined the newly formed 3rd and 4th Brigades in the landings in Italy, experiencing much hard fighting before returning to Britain. The 2nd Brigade was renamed 2nd Independent Parachute Brigade, and remained in Italy until committed to the invasion of southern France and, ultimately the suppression of the communist insurrection in Greece.

A second airborne division, 6th, was formed in anticipation of the invasion of Europe. 6th Airborne Division spearheaded the invasion into Normandy while 1st Airborne Division was held in reserve. The role of the Air Landing Brigade was particularly crucial during the first few hours of the invasion.

Nowhere was the mettle of these gliderborne troops more rigorously tested than in, the fight to secure the bridges over the Orne and Caen canal. The task of taking the two bridges, situated a few kilometres inland from Sword Beach fell to 2nd Battalion Oxfordshire and Buckinghamshire Light Infantry (Ox and Bucks) under the command of Major John Howard. The raid was executed by elements of B and D Companies supported by 30 Sappers drawn from 249 Airborne Field Company, Royal Engineers. Silence, surprise and speed were to be the essence of the operation. Two landing zones (LZs) were allocated and the 171 officers and men destined to take part were divided between the six Horsa gliders available.

At 00.16am on the morning of 6 June 1944 Staff Sergeant Jim Wallwork landed his glider within 40 metres of the canal bridge, an excellent feat considering the conditions of total darkness. The 29 men of A Platoon immediately disgorged to become the first invasion troops to set foot on occupied Europe on D-Day. In less than fifteen minutes they and their colleagues secured both bridges and began to dig-in in anticipation of a counter-attack.

The 8th Heavy Grenadier Battalion mounted several attacks all of which were repelled. As the pressure of the attacks increased the situation became more tense until, at 1.30pm that afternoon, the pipes of Lord Lovat's 1st Special Service Commando were heard above the noise of battle. Within minutes the green berets relieved the red berets to enable the invasion forces to sweep inland. By order of the French Government the bridge across the canal was renamed 'Pegasus Bridge' and the approach road 'Esplanade Major John Howard'. The cost to the Ox and Bucks was two men killed and fourteen wounded.

Arnhem is undoubtedly the best known name in airborne history. Operation Market Garden was an attempt involving three airborne divisions to secure a Rhine crossing by seizing and holding the town of Arnhem, simultaneously capturing the bridges across the Lower Rhine, Maas and Waal rivers. This would have allowed the British 2nd Army to punch a hole into the very centre of Germany's industrial heartland, the Ruhr. Initially the plan went well and the US 101st Airborne Division dropped between Veghel and Eindhoven capturing two of the bridges over which the 2nd Army was to cross. However as the British moved up to the bridges at Nijmegen and Grave, captured by the US 82nd Airborne Division, things at Arnhem began to go badly wrong.

Arnhem was at the extreme end of the corridor secured by the United States airborne forces and the lead elements of Horrocks' XXX Corps. In the eyes of many it was 'a bridge too far'. Due to the lack of available aircraft the entire British 1st Airborne Division had been unable to drop at one time and had been forced by geographical circumstance to employ DZs several kilometres from the objective. To compound their problems, when they landed they found that they were not facing the rabble of second line troops that they had anticipated, but two battle-hardened SS Panzer divisions refitting before joining battle in Normandy.

Although Lieutenant Colonel John Frost's 2nd Battalion and some divisional troops managed to reach the bridge they were quickly cut off from the remainder of the division, which was forced into a defensive position near Oosterbeek to the west. Second Army and the 82nd Airborne Division eventually broke the German hold on the Nijmegen bridge but their advance to Arnhem was considerably slowed. The Guards Armoured Division which was in the lead, was forced to fight its way along a single raised roadway which made it easy prey for the German anti-tank guns.

As the Arnhem perimeter shrank into an area known to the Germans as the cauldron it came under increasing fire from tanks, snipers and self-propelled artillery. On 23 September the glider troops of the Border Regiment were forced off the high ground overlooking Heveadorp ferry. Sosabowski's 1st Polish Independent Parachute Brigade, which had been due to join the battle days earlier but which had been delayed by adverse weather over Britain, was dropped to the south of the Rhine that afternoon, but was unable to cross to the support of its British allies. A number tried to swim across the river under cover of darkness but most were drowned. Only 50 finally made it to the British positions.

During the course of the next day the Dorset Regiment, spearheading the XXX Corps advance, reached the Rhine and attempted a crossing. Most were cut to pieces in their assault boats. Those who survived were swept down river to be taken prisoner. The evacuation of 1st Airborne Division began on the night of 25 September, eight days after the first landings and six days after its commander, Major General Urquhart, had been told that he might expect relief. Initially the Germans were taken unawares and did not react. When they discovered what was happening however, they began to bring down concentrated fire on the crossing points adding to the carnage. Over 1,200 airborne and glider-borne troops were killed at Arnhem and another 3,000 were taken prisoner. In spite of this, Operation Market Garden was not a total failure. Bridges across the Maas and Waal had been secured and the Allies had a base from which to launch an attack into Germany.

The final and largest single airborne operation of the war was executed by the British 6th and United States 17th Airborne Divisions in March 1945. Operation 'Varsity' involved a single lift daylight drop across the Rhine. The 6th Airborne Division achieved its primary objective and seized the high ground overlooking the town of Wesel before capturing its secondary objectives, the road and rail bridges across the Issel. After this assault the 6th Airborne Division advanced across Germany and were among the first troops to link up with the Soviets.

Wingate's Chindit Raiders

By the summer of 1942 the British position in the Far East was critical. Her ill-equipped and poorly trained army had been forced out of Burma by the much maligned Imperial Japanese Army. HMS *Repulse* and *Prince of Wales*, sent to the area to demonstrate the impregnability of the Royal Navy, lay at the bottom of the sea. Singapore and Hong Kong were in enemy hands and the National Congress Party was threatening Britain's sovereignty in India.

The British were eager to recapture Burma but it seemed an almost impossible dream. The near impenetrable border terrain with its 320kms of jungle covered mountains and numerous swift flowing and often deep rivers not only prevented a full-scale Japanese incursion into India, but also frustrated General Irwin's Eastern Army in its attempts to mount a counter-attack.

Lieutenant General Shorjiro Iada in command of the Japanese forces in the area withdrew the bulk of his divisions from the border and elected to wait, watch and consolidate. Inevitably lethargy soon pervaded the Allies and Japanese alike, and might have continued were it not for the intervention of Orde Wingate.

At the age of 38 Orde Wingate was already a legend. Blessed with boundless energy, if somewhat eccentric ways, he was an outstanding exponent of unconventional warfare. Wingate joined General Wavell's staff in March 1942, the two men having met a year earlier. At that time, as GOC Middle East, Wavell had come close to court-martialling his junior but instead had learned to tolerate his insubordination. He had listened attentively to Wingate's tales of successful guerrilla raids in Abyssinia and Palestine and now wished to investigate the possibility of translating these to the jungles of Burma.

Wingate was promoted to Colonel and placed in overall command of all guerrilla operations in Burma. He established his headquarters at Maymyo, where the Jungle Warfare School was located. Its commandant, Major Michael Calvert, also a superb soldier, quickly gained Wingate's confidence. Working in close conjunction the two men argued that a specially trained force, continually supplied from the air, could operate behind enemy lines almost indefinitely. Wingate considered that covert operations in the enemy rear by elite formations, large enough to inflict serious injury to the enemy yet small enough to escape when outnumbered, would pay enormous dividends.

Enthused by Wingate's arguments Wavell authorised the formation of the 77th Indian Infantry Brigade comprising the 13th King's Liverpool Regiment, the 3/2nd Gurkha Rifles, 142 Commando and a long-range signals support element from the RAF. Wingate named his new command the Chindits after a mythical creature which guards Burmese temples. In July 1942 the Chindits began a period of long and intensive training which was destined to turn them into one of the most famous special purpose forces in modern military history.

The force was divided into a number of strong company columns, each commanded by a major, self-contained to survive deep in enemy territory, and supported by a mule-train to carry the heavy loads. The Chindits first mission was to infiltrate deep into Burma. The force was divided into two groups, a larger northern group under Wingate's command, comprising the headquarters and four columns with 2,200 men and 850 mules, and a smaller southern group of two columns, with 1,000 men and 250 mules under command of Lieutenant Colonel Alexander.

The epic marches began without incident. The force crossed the River Chindwin at two points without interference and successfully received its initial air drop. The first brush with the enemy occurred on 18 February, when the southern group encountered an enemy outpost near Mainyaung, but they managed to disengage avoiding further contact by making a wide detour. Wingate's party was more fortunate, succeeding in reaching his intended bivouac site 8km to the west of Pinbon on schedule.

Once established, Wingate dispatched two columns to the railway where they succeeded in demolishing three bridges and dynamiting a gorge, causing hundreds of tons of debris to block the line. A third column under command of Major Bromhead met with less success. It encountered a large Japanese force near Pinlebu and was forced to disperse. True to their training however many of its soldiers succeeded in making their way back to the comparative safety of the Chindwin. Mindless of the hornets nest which he had now stirred up, Wingate refused to consolidate after his initial success but instead continued east across the Irrawaddy.

Suddenly things began to go terribly wrong. In the south Column 2 was ambushed and dispersed while in the north Wingate lost most of his mules while trying to cross the two-kilometre wide Irrawaddy. More crucially the Japanese discovered the secret of the Chindits' resupply when an air drop was witnessed by a rear area patrol. They immediately swamped the area of Wingate's proposed activity making movement difficult. To compound the Chindits' problems Wingate discovered that the area east of the Irrawaddy comprised dense virgin jungle, impenetrable save for the established roads and tracks which intersected it; quite unsuitable for hit-and-run warfare.

Wary of the enemy now massed to his rear Wingate ordered a staged return. Two columns under command of Majors Calvert and Fergusson were ordered to act as rearguard for the entire group. Fergusson's Column 5 suffered catastrophically when it was tricked by an unsympathetic boatman and marooned on a sandbank in midstream while negotiating a crossing of the River Shweli. The exhausted men were forced to wade the fast-flowing river in the certain knowledge that those who lost their footing would undoubtedly be swept away. Some men drowned, others sank into quicksand and disappeared, a few too weak to attempt the crossing were left behind to be taken prisoner. In all Fergusson lost 46 men, either dead or marooned, in this single incident. Those who survived were divided into ten small teams, most of which eventually reached the British base at Imphal safely - but in many cases too ill to soldier again.

Wingate's column made an unopposed crossing of the Irrawaddy and then swam over the River Chindwin, having abandoned most of its mules. Of the 3,000 men who entered the jungle with Wingate only 2,182 returned, of whom no more than 600 were adjudged fit for further front-line service. Although the railway was quickly repaired the expedition had not been a failure. A small elite force of specially trained troops had proved that the Japanese were not invincible in the jungle, and the first step along the path of ultimate victory in the Far East had been taken.

United States Special Forces

The Rangers

The US Army's 1st Ranger (Infantry) Battalion was formed when morale was low. The Allies had suffered a series of humiliating defeats and badly needed a force capable of striking back at the enemy. The Ranger ethos was based very much on that of the British Commandos with whom they enjoyed a close relationship throughout the war. The initial idea was the brain child of Brigadier General Lucien Truscott, head of the United States mission to Britain's Combined Operations. He convinced US Army Chief of Staff, General George C Marshall, of the need to raise an elite formation and was given permission to authorise Major William Darby, ADC to the GOC 34th Infantry Division in Northern Ireland, to begin recruiting.

Darby was painstaking in his selection. After carefully choosing a cadre of reliable officers he set about interviewing and selecting the first volunteers from within his division. Unlike Wingate, who encouraged older soldiers (whom he regarded as more reliable) to join the Chindits, Darby emphasised youth. Volunteers had to be fit and athletic, good swimmers and capable of maintaining a 30in pace on long speed marches. Skills such as mountain climbing, fieldcraft and the ability to navigate across country were also considered in selecting men for further training.

Those who passed initial selection were sent to Carrickfergus where they underwent a further two weeks of arduous physical testing. The successful 500 formed the basis for the 1st Ranger Battalion and were moved under the umbrella of the British Special Service Brigade to the Commando training centre at Achnacarry in the north-east highlands of Scotland. The next month was spent under the tutelage of the Commando instructors, learning a variety of skills including rock climbing and unarmed combat. Training was carried out under field conditions with full packs and live ammunition. Casualties were expected and accepted; this stood the survivors in excellent stead for the rigours of the amphibious training which followed.

After Achnacarry a detachment of six officers and 44 men was selected to participate in the raid on the heavily defended French port of Dieppe. The actual assault proved very costly in terms of men and material but provided a number of invaluable lessons for future operations. Although the role of the Rangers, who were integrated into Nos 3 and 4 Commandos, was relatively insignificant, the small force gave an excellent account of itself. Corporal Koons became the first United States soldier to kill an enemy in Europe, and was awarded the Silver Star and Military Medal for his bravery while fighting with No 4 Commando.

4 The Second World War

In October 1942 Darby was promoted to lieutenant colonel and the battalion ordered to the Mediterranean to spearhead Operation 'Torch', the invasion of North Africa. The Rangers landed ahead of the US 1st Division, and on 8 November secured the Algerian coastal town of Arzew against minimal Vichy resistance. Thereafter they embarked on several weeks of intensive training during which a number of volunteers, frustrated by the lack of combat, requested transfers to more 'active' units. However the maxim 'train hard fight easy' proved its worth when the Rangers moved up to Gafsa, 115km to the north, and were ordered to make a night assault on the 10th Bersaglieri Regiment dug into the mountains around El Guettar.

The operation against the Italians was a resounding success, but the Rangers were soon to find themselves facing a far more determined enemy in the Afrika Korps. The battalion was forced to fight a number of successful rearguard actions as the Germans counter-attacked and the Americans were pushed back to defensive positions near the coast. However the tide of war changed in favour of the Americans when General George S Patton assumed command of II Corps which included the 1st Armored and 34th Infantry Divisions, and immediately went on the offensive.

Darby's men were ordered to act as a spearhead for the 1st Armored Division. On 21 March 1943 the Rangers, supported by a divisional engineer mortar company, executed one of the most daring night assaults of the war when they scaled the Guettar Pass taking the well-placed Italian defenders in the rear. Field interrogation of some of the 1,400 Italian prisoners taken indicated the strong likelihood of an imminent German counter-attack in strength. The Battle of El Guettar which followed was a major Allied victory. The three German panzer grenadier and two Italian infantry divisions committed to the counter-attack were mauled and eventually forced to retreat. The battle lasted 21 days. Although the Rangers were withdrawn to be employed as reserve troops on day six, by their initial aggressive reconnaissances of the enemy positions and their subsequent scaling of the heights in the Italian rear they had been instrumental in the American success.

After the battle the battalion moved back to Oran to refit. Darby was offered promotion to colonel, but rather than take over command of an infantry regiment turned it down to stay with the Rangers. His loyalty was rewarded when Supreme Allied Commander, General Dwight D Eisenhower, realising the Rangers' potential, ordered the formation of an additional four battalions. Using the 1st Battalion as a nucleus for the others, two battalions were formed and trained in Oran while two more were raised in the United States.

The newly formed Ranger battalions were to prove as effective as the 1st Battalion. From mid-1943 the 1st, 2nd and 3rd Battalions were involved in the Allied invasions of Sicily and Italy. Ever acting as spearhead, they were the first ashore in the amphibious landings and thereafter in the vanguard of the advances inland. They saw action at Salerno and Monte Cassino, and at the bloody Battle of Cisterna where the 1st and 3rd Battalions virtually ceased to exist.

The 2nd and 5th Ranger Battalions went on to take part in the Allied landings in Normandy. As a prelude to the invasion the 2nd Battalion, under command of Lieutenant Colonel James E Rudder, was tasked with the neutralisation of a battery of six 155mm guns at Pointe du Hoc. This well-sited battery was in a commanding position with a field of fire covering both Omaha Beach to the east and Utah Beach to the north-west. It was sited on top of a large rock with cliffs in three directions, seaward, east and west and was considered near impregnable.

Three companies comprising 230 men were assigned to the assault. The rest of the battalion, together with Lieutenant Colonel Max Schneider's 5th Rangers, were scheduled to land with the 29th Infantry Division on Omaha Beach. If Rudder failed in his mission and the guns were to continue firing Schneider was to fight his way inland and go for the guns from the rear - an almost impossible task taking into account the depth and density of the surrounding defences.

The attackers reached the base of the cliff with little incident and at once began to scramble ashore. The Rangers had been well prepared for their mission. Eight of their landing craft had been specially fitted with three pairs of rockets capable of carrying ropes attached to grapnels up the cliffs. Others carried tubular ladders in sections, and two were even equipped with 30m turntable ladders donated by the London Fire Brigade, their hoses replaced by twin Lewis guns.

Machine-gunners in the assault boats kept the German infantry on the top of the rock occupied while the Rangers began their dogged climb. When a number of the rockets malfunctioned, their ropes sodden with seawater and too heavy to lift, many of the Rangers improvised with personal grappling hooks. Others reverted to their basic training and, seeking finger and toe holds in the nine storey high rock, climbed independently. As the Rangers reached the peak they came face to face with German machine-guns dug into the rock and were forced to lob grenades into the weapon pits to silence the guns.

Suddenly the naval gunfire, which had been pounding the rock in support, ceased. With loud battle cries the Rangers advanced to the gun emplacements, only to find them empty. Contrary to sound intelligence reports there were no guns mounted, nor had there ever been! A battery of unmanned and unprotected guns was located and captured a few kilometres inland. It can only be assumed that these guns had been intended for the Pointe du Hoc but had never been installed.

Losses were horrific, particularly taking into account the ultimately low value of the target. Of the 230 Rangers who scrambled ashore that morning only 90 avoided death or injury. Totally exhausted the survivors had to fight off a series of German counter-attacks until relieved by the 5th Rangers. Even then the battle was not over. The Rangers joined with the 116th US Infantry Regiment and pushed inland, fighting among the lanes and hedgerows of Normandy until they broke out into Central France several months later.

United States Airborne
The United States took her first step towards airborne warfare in July 1940 when the 50-strong Parachute Test Platoon was renamed the 1st Parachute Platoon and became the cadre for the 501st Parachute Battalion (PIB). Motivated by German successes in airborne operations on the Western Front the programme advanced steadily until, by the time of America's entry into the war in December 1941, four

battalions had been raised - the 501st, 502nd, 503rd and 504th. In early 1942 the battalions were raised to regimental strength and joined by the 505th, 506th, 507th, 508th and 511th Parachute Regiments (PIRs). In August of that year the 82nd and 101st Airborne Divisions were formed, to include integral airborne artillery and engineer elements, as well as glider and other specialist units.

The expansion of The US Army's airborne forces continued into 1943 when three further regiments - the 513th, 515th and 517th - were raised and three new divisions - the 11th, 13th and 17th - formed. United States airborne forces received their baptism of fire in November 1942 when the 509th PIB jumped into North Africa as part of Operation Torch. The 82nd Airborne Division arrived in North Africa in May 1943 and proceeded to train for further combat jumps. The 504th and 505th PIBs played a prominent role in the invasion of Sicily in July 1943, and in September were joined by the 82nd Division's 509th PIB in a combat jump into southern Italy.

After the landings in Italy the 82nd and 101st Airborne Divisions returned to Britain to begin intensive training for D Day. On the night of 5-6 June 1944 elements of both divisions jumped into Normandy prior to the amphibious landings to secure a number of key areas behind the invasion beaches. A month later the 509th and 551st PIBs, and 517 PIR were committed to the Allied landing in southern France. Over 10,000 men of General Frederick's 1st Airborne Division were parachuted and airlanded behind the German defences in the Muy area. The operation was a complete success. Less than 200 American lives were lost and the approach to the Argen valley was secured, denying the German defenders the opportunity to counter-attack the bridgehead before it had been consolidated.

After their successes in Normandy the 82nd and 101st Airborne Divisions were withdrawn to Britain in anticipation of their participation in Operation Market Garden. Final planning for the operation was completed in only six days. The 101st Airborne Division was allotted the task of landing close to Eindhoven, capturing the town and securing a series of road and railway bridges; across the Aa River and Willems Vaart Canal at Veghel, the Dommel River at St Oedenrode and over the Wilhelmina Canal at Son. The 82nd Airborne was to capture the bridges over the Maas at Grave and the Waal at Nijmegen. As already described, by far the most difficult exercise, the taking of the bridge at Arnhem, was allocated to the British 1st Airborne Division.

Priority in aircraft was given to the Americans on the basis that, were they to fail, British success at Arnhem would be irrelevant. The operation began on the morning of Sunday 17 September. Visibility was good, winds were light and cloud coverage high as the first of 1,545 aircraft and 478 gliders of 38 Group RAF and 9th United States Troop Carrier Command lifted off from eight RAF and 14 USAF airfields in Britain.

Nothing was left to chance. The routes were marked by beacons and coded lights aboard ships in mid-Channel and by ground strips, coloured smoke and beacons on the dropping and landing zones. Major General Maxwell Taylor's 101st Division landed without incident having survived relatively heavy fire on the approach to Eindhoven. The bridges across the Zuid Willems Vaart Canal at Veghel were captured intact but unfortunately the bridge across the Wilhelmina Canal at Son was partially damaged by retreating Sappers . While it was being repaired that night an airborne regiment crossed the canal to secure the road into Eindhoven in readiness for the British advance. Horrocks' XXX Corps did not let its Allies down and by nightfall the tanks of the Irish Guards Armoured Group, spearheading the Guards Armoured Division, had passed through Valkenswaard and Eindhoven and were on their way north.

Major General Gavin's 82nd Airborne landed with equal ease in the area of Grave and Nijmegen. One battalion, by landing astride the bridge over the Maas at Grave was able to secure it within an hour, registering the first Allied success. Six hours later the bridge across the Maas-Waal fell, allowing the Division to continue its advance towards Nijmegen.

Suddenly things began to go wrong as the timetable, always uncompromisingly tight, began to fall apart. Resistance in the Nijmegen area was found to be tougher than expected, making the early capture of the bridge over the Waal impossible. Throughout the Monday the Germans brought increasing numbers of troops into the counter-attack until, at one stage, it seemed that the American forward units would be overwhelmed. Indeed when the Grenadier Guards Armoured Group, now on point, reached the 82nd's positions Gavin was only able to spare one of his three regiments to assist in the taking of the bridge; the remainder of his troops were required simply to hold the perimeter.

On the morning of Wednesday 20 September a daring, if desperate, plan was hatched to enable the Nijmegen bridge to be assaulted from both ends simultaneously. British assault boats were brought up and men of the 504th PIR were ordered to cross the river 1.5km downstream of the town. The crossing represents one of the bravest actions in airborne forces history. The boats were launched into a strong current, under heavy fire and in broad daylight. Less than half the first wave reached the far bank over 400m away. Those who did managed to establish a small bridgehead, making it easier for the second and subsequent waves to cross. By late afternoon the Americans had broken out of the bridgehead and were flying the Stars and Stripes from the northern end of the railway bridge. Inspired by the sight of the flag the British Guards Armoured Division launched a further, and final assault from the south. Supported by Gavin's remaining regiments they successfully forced their way across to the waiting men of the 504th PIR, leaving the road to Arnhem open. Later that year both divisions were to play a crucial part in the destruction of the German counter-offensive in the Ardennes.

In March 1945 the 17th Airborne Division, newly arrived from the United States, joined with the British in Operation Varsity, in which the Allies crossed the Rhine into the German heartland.

While the 82nd, 101st and 17th Airborne Divisions were engaged in Europe, and the 13th was under training in the United States, the 11th Airborne Division was in action in the Pacific. In September 1943 the 503rd PIR carried out the first major parachute assault in the theatre with a jump into New Guinea. In July 1944 the 503rd PIR was again called upon to jump, this time on to Noemfoor Island. In February 1945 the 511th jumped in over Luzon while the 503rd went into action for the third and final time over Corregidor. The latter was a classic parachute deployment, and the last to involve American troops until Korea some five years later.

US Marine Corps

On 8 December 1941, less than 24 hours after the Japanese raid on Pearl Harbor, the tiny Marine garrison on Wake Island was overwhelmed by vastly superior forces. On the same day Guam was attacked by an invasion force of 6,000 men, and the 130 Marines protecting it were killed or captured. In the ensuing months the Japanese consolidated their hold on the South Pacific. Most of New Guinea fell to them, as did several of the Solomon Islands including Guadalcanal. Australia and New Zealand, conscious of their vulnerability, made plans to withdraw their troops from North Africa.

Two massive victories turned the fortunes of war in favour of the Americans and set the stage for a Marine offensive in the Pacific. A United States task force intercepted a Japanese fleet headed for Port Moresby, and in a four-day carrier aircraft battle succeeded in blocking the enemy push to the south-west. Shortly thereafter a second United States carrier task force intercepted a Japanese invasion fleet off Midway, and in two days of air-to-air and air-to-ship engagement sank four enemy carriers along with most of their aircraft.

The US Marine Corps began the war with 18,000 men. Its numbers were immediately swollen to 25,000, to whom were added a further 5,000 reserves a few months later. It was decided to spearhead the return to the offensive by creating an elite within an elite from this number. Raider battalions, a direct counterpart of the British Commandos, were formed and put through rigorous specialist training. They received their baptism of fire in August 1942 with landings on Guadalcanal and the surrounding islands. Prior to the main landings Lieutenant Colonel Merritt Edson's 1st Raider Battalion stormed ashore on Tulagi, killing 500 of its defenders. As the 1st Marine Division established a beachhead on Guadalcanal and drove inland two companies of the 2nd Raider Battalion landed by submarine on Makin Island.

Thereafter, as so often happens when the true value of an elite is not recognised, both battalions were squandered in conventional actions. However in November 1942 the 2nd Battalion was allowed to leave the frustrations of the Guadalcanal defensive perimeter to mount a 250km deep-penetration fighting patrol. In four weeks of sustained fighting, much of it against the Japanese 228th Infantry Regiment, it killed an estimated 500 enemy for the loss of sixteen Marines dead and eighteen wounded.

Despite opposition from the regular Marine hierarchy, two further Raider battalions and a Raider regiment were formed. The 2nd and 3rd Raider Battalions took part in the amphibious landings on Bougainville, a large island in the northern Solomons defended by a huge force of 35,000 Japanese. The island fell after a month of bitter fighting at the cost of 1,841 Marine casualties. By then the Raiders had been relegated to the role of conventional Marine units. Soon thereafter the survivors of the four Raider battalions were incorporated into the 4th Marine Regiment to replace its losses; plans to form a 5th and 6th battalion were shelved. An excellent opportunity to exploit a proven elite was squandered.

Merrill's Marauders

The 5307th Composite Unit (Provisional), better known as Merrill's Marauders, was a true force of special designation, raised exclusively for irregular warfare in the jungles of northern Burma. In August 1943 the war in the Far East was not going the way of the Allies. Spurred on by the formation of the Chindits the United States War Office determined to send special forces to the area to bolster, if not eclipse, the British effort.

Lieutenant General ('Vinegar Joe') Stilwell, commander of the Chinese forces in the China-Burma-India Theatre of Operations and in overall control of all American combat forces in the theatre, was given leave to mount a winter offensive in 1943. It had been agreed that the British would advance into southern and central Burma by way of Arakan and Tiddim. Simultaneously Stilwell's Chinese Army in India (CAI), comprising the Chinese 38th and 22nd Divisions which had earlier escaped westward from Burma, were to invade northern Burma to link up with the bulk of the Chinese forces pushing west. During the course of the summer, Stilwell's CAI was placed under the command of Lord Louis Mountbatten's newly established South-East Asia Command (SEAC) and the scope of the impending attack was severely curtailed.

Nonetheless the initial attack went well. The leading elements of the Chinese 38th Division encountered little resistance and moved slowly down the Hukawng Valley towards Shinbwiyang. However the Japanese had been thoroughly prepared for the advance and suddenly counter-attacked, quickly regaining the lost ground. Stalemate ensued and the campaign died among the encroaching monsoon rains.

Merrill's Marauders now arrived in theatre to provide Stilwell with his only American combat unit. Known locally by its codename 'Galahad' but officially designated the 5307th Composite Unit Provisional, this unique and somewhat macabre unit would only later gain the nickname 'Merrill's Marauders' in honour of its commanding officer, Brigadier General Frank Merrill.

Stilwell had requested hardened jungle fighters. Instead General Marshall sent him a mixture of the bored, the restless and the indifferent. Some were excellently motivated, others suffered from psychiatric disorders. A few yearned for adventure, many saw the assignment as a stepping stone back to the United States. Some 300 of the volunteers came from the South-West Pacific, 700 from the South Pacific and 1,000 from the Caribbean Defense Command and the United States itself.

The new force was organised into three battalions, each comprising two regimental combat teams, a headquarters and a support element. Initially training took place under the auspices of Wingate's Chindits. However as the weeks progressed the Americans' brashness began to upset the British veterans who soon began to hold them in open contempt. Unlike the Chindits, who had been schooled to avoid contact with larger enemy forces where possible, the inexperienced Marauders argued that aggression was of paramount importance. They made it clear that they would carry the fight to the enemy whenever and wherever they found him, regardless of the consequences. Merrill assumed command on 8 January 1944 and began to instil a degree of discipline and élan into the unit, but regretfully did little to ensure that it was fully balanced for the rigours ahead.

During the spring and summer of 1944 the Marauders were employed as a spearhead in the drive to recover northern Burma and clear the way for the construction of a road from India to China. Conditions during the campaign were appalling. The Chinese advancing in support of Merrill moved too slowly, at one stage allowing the Japanese to throw their formidable weight against his lightly equipped men. When the Chinese eventually counter-attacked the already exhausted Americans were ordered on a strength-sapping 800km trek through the jungles of North Burma to cut the Japanese trail.

By now the Marauders had been through two arduous jungle campaigns. They were underweight through constant marching and poor diet and in their weakened state were rapidly falling victim to disease. Merrill himself suffered two heart attacks and had to be evacuated. Galahad had been put into the field without adequate medical support or evacuation procedures. The most severely wounded were taken out in the aircraft bringing reinforcements, but eventually even these flights were cut when transports of the US 10th Air Force were reassigned to higher priority missions elsewhere. Conditions on the ground were so appalling that half the raw reinforcements became psychiatric casualties within 24 hours of their arrival.

On 28 April the Marauders accompanied by elements of the Chinese 30th Division - 7,000 men in all - were ordered eastwards over the Kuman Mountains to the Irrawaddy River. They reached Myitkyina, taking the strategically important neighbouring airfield on 17 May. Things then began to go wrong. The Japanese garrison in the town was far larger than anticipated. Worse, the exhausted force had been depleted to 3,000 semi-fit men by the long march and was shrinking at the rate of 75 to 100 a day as disease and exhaustion took its toll.

After the death of Wingate the Chindits had come under Stilwell's command. Although in an even worse state than the Marauders after four months in the jungle Stilwell had refused to allow the British to withdraw and did not believe that he could now offer the Americans the same option. Myitkyina eventually fell to the Chinese-American remnants on 3 August 1944, but only after the Japanese garrison commander had ordered a disastrously unsuccessful withdrawal. The siege of the town cost 3,000 Japanese lives, although 600 managed to escape. The Chinese lost 972 killed and 3,184 wounded, the Americans 272 killed and 955 wounded. In all 188 Chinese and 980 Americans were evacuated sick, of whom 570 were Marauders.

In late summer the remnants of Merrill's Marauders were withdrawn from the line. They had been kept in battle far beyond the limits of their effectiveness. They had expected to fight for no more than three months and had fallen apart when ordered to do so. Yet the 38th and 22nd Chinese Divisions had spent seven months in the jungle without complaining. For their part the Japanese had fought for years suffering far greater casualties. Whatever the cause of the collapse it had nothing to do with the apparent inability of the Occidental soldier to withstand hardships. Later the British 36th Division would spend nearly eight months of almost constant action in the jungle without flinching. When the Marauders had been formed they had lacked a number of vital constituents of a successful special force: selection, training, discipline, clear direction and motivation. They had also failed to learn from the earlier mistakes of the Chindits. In hindsight their fate was sealed from the outset.

Naval Elites
Italian Beginnings
From well before the beginning of hostilities the Italians knew that they would be no match for the Royal Navy in conventional warfare. The Underwater Division of the 10th MAS Flotilla, the Gamma Group, was therefore raised at La Spezia with a view to taking the battle to the British via unconventional means. When several Italian capital ships were sunk by Fleet Air Arm torpedo bombers at Taranto, 10th MAS swore revenge and began a number of daring and highly successful raids against British shipping and coastal installations.

On 26 March 1941, just before dawn, an Explosive Motor Boat commanded by Lieutenant Luigi Faggioni slipped undetected into the British naval base at Suda Bay in northern Crete. Seeing the cruiser *York* lying at anchor Faggioni approached his target at full speed, released his deadly load into her hull and sank her.

Human torpedo attacks began soon thereafter. The first attack came to Gibraltar, which abounded with merchant shipping en route to the war zones in North Africa. Charges were placed under three British ships, two tankers and a cargo vessel, the detonations being delayed to allow the men to make good their escape. The crews used a form of breathing apparatus that was light in weight, self-contained, and closed circuit so as not to give off any tell-tale exhaust bubbles. The explosions were not spectacular, little more than dull thuds, but their consequences were spectacular. All three ships sank and their precious cargoes were lost to the war effort.

A series of abortive raids on the Grand Harbour of Valetta in Malta followed. However on 17 December 1941, the 10th MAS Flotilla scored its most outstanding success. That night the converted submarine *Scire* left its base on the Dodecanese island of Leros. Three large containers were mounted on her deck, each containing a human torpedo or 'Pig'. The submarine sped south across the eastern Mediterranean to the Nile Delta which was then in full flood. Surfacing some 15km from the harbour of Alexandria, *Scire* released her cargo of two-man human torpedoes which at once began their slow and dangerous journey up river. Their targets were the battleships *Valiant* and *Queen Elizabeth* which Italian intelligence had vouched would be berthed in Alexandria.

For two freezing hours the Pigs moved silently towards the harbour with their hulls chained together and only the heads of their crews above water. Avoiding the unwanted attentions of a harbour patrol boat, the three attack craft approached the anti-submarine nets which barred the port's entrance. As the nets were opened to allow the passage of three British destroyers the submersibles entered. Once inside the group split up, each team going for its allotted target.

The group leader, Captain de la Penne, and his crewman, Emilio Bianchi, successfully negotiated their way under the hull of the *Valiant* before setting their explosive charges. Simultaneously Marceglia and his crewman, Schergat, set their explosives under the *Queen Elizabeth*, leaving the third craft to attack a near-by tanker. By the time the British were alerted to the Italians' actions it was too late. All three sets of explosives detonated with devastating effect; the tanker was sunk, *Valiant* was immobilised for a year and *Queen Elizabeth* was so badly damaged that she had to be towed to the United States for repairs.

The Italian special forces were captured, interrogated and eventually sent to a prison camp in Palestine, where they were held in considerable esteem by their British captors.

The British Response

The Admiralty had been shaken by the initial attack on Gibraltar. It had no idea that the Italians had developed human torpedoes and had no obvious counter. An Underwater Working Party, under the command of Lieutenant Lionel (Buster) Crabb, was introduced at Gibraltar to inspect the hulls of all ships entering and leaving the harbour, but little else was done to protect them from the unwelcome attention of the Italian special forces.

Prior to the Italian attacks in Alexandria harbour, Captain 'Blondie' Hasler of the Royal Marines had been trying to convince the authorities of the viability of a canoe-borne raiding force capable of covert infiltration into enemy harbours. The Admiralty had rejected the idea until spurred by Churchill to take retaliatory action for the loss of the battleships. Suddenly they concurred with the idea, and authorised Hasler to form a unit capable of translating his theories into fact.

Formed in Portsmouth in June 1942, the new unit bore the name of Royal Marine Boom Patrol Detachment to disguise its true purpose. The all-volunteer organisation was equipped with thin, close-fitting, flexible diving suits, specially designed by the Dunlop Rubber Company to allow the wearer to move freely in and out of confined spaces. An optional separate hood was provided which could be worn with or without underwater breathing apparatus; also provided were fins and face masks, both inventions recently developed in California.

The first attack, immortalised in the film *Cockleshell Heroes*, took place against enemy shipping in the port of Bordeaux, which lies some 100km up the River Gironde. Five two-man canoes were launched from a submarine on the night of 7 December 1942, close to the river's entrance. Paddling by night and hiding by day the party made its way upstream into the heart of the crowded harbour. The raid was a success. Several limpets were placed and a number of merchant ships sunk or damaged. However the cost in lives was high. Hasler and his partner, Marine Bill Sparks, escaped overland to Spain. The other eight Royal Marines were captured and executed, following Hitler's directive that special forces were to be treated as saboteurs and shot.

The Conception of a Modern Elite

In late 1942 the Admiralty ordered the formation of a Human Torpedo Unit. Using the captured remains of Italian Human Torpedoes Britain set about the task of developing similar craft. Under Commander Fell the unit called for 'special duties' volunteers, and after initial selection began training with underwater diving equipment in Portsmouth. After completion of diving training and the delivery of the first production models, or chariots as they came to be known, the unit moved to Loch Corrie in Scotland.

The chariots themselves were cylindrical, with a rudder, hydroplanes and propeller at the tapered tail. The fore end held the warhead and the design allowed the craft to run under water without it. Two seats were fitted astride the torpedo in the early models, although a primitive cockpit was subsequently fitted to enhance streamlining. The diving controls, luminous depth and pressure gauges and compass were fitted ahead of the front seat, the battery, electric motor, air tanks and ballast pump were within the main body. The craft had an operational speed of two to three knots. The 'number one' sat in the forward seat and controlled the craft, allowing the 'number two' behind him to fix the charge to the bottom of the enemy ship.

The chariots differed operationally from their Italian equivalents. The British used powerful magnets to hold the craft against the side of the ship. By moving the magnets down they were trained to guide the torpedo into position. Once the magnets were secured to the warhead the craft was disengaged to make its silent way to safety. By contrast the Italians manoeuvred their torpedoes under the target, released ballast until they came to the ship's bottom secured clamps on either side of her keel, ran a line between the clamps and secured the warhead to the line.

In June 1942 the Special Operations Executive (SOE) sought the assistance of the charioteers in the execution of a daring attack on the German battleship *Tirpitz*, then lying at anchor at Trondheim Fjord in Norway. After several weeks of planning it was decided to transport two chariots to within striking distance of the *Tirpitz* before releasing them for the final attack. On 26 October the motor fishing vessel *Arthur*, under the command of the resistance leader Leif Larson, set sail from the Shetlands. As the *Arthur* approached the Norwegian shore it lowered its cargo of two chariots overboard and continued on its voyage. It passed the scrutiny of a German patrol boat but then hit bad weather during which the two chariots slipped their chains and were lost. There was nothing for it but to escape to neutral Sweden, which both the crew and charioteers succeeded in doing.

The Royal Navy then decided to attack the battleship using their new X-craft. These were four-man midget submarines capable of remaining submerged, albeit under the most uncomfortable conditions, for up to 23 hours. The new craft packed a tremendous punch in the form of two external, crescent shaped charges containing two tons of explosives. The concept of the X-craft was not new. The principle had been discussed during the First World War and plans drawn up in the 1930s. However it was not until the first prototypes succeeded in carrying out a mock attack against shipping in Loch Cairnbawn that the concept was taken seriously.

It was planned that six of the midgets would each be towed by a submarine to the entrance of Alterfjord where they would be cast off to make their own way, submerged, to *Tirpitz*. To reach the anchorage in the isolated fjord of Kaafjord required the penetration of a minefield and a passage of 80km up the fjord. As the six midget submarines, *X-5* to *X-10*, entered the anchorage they had to penetrate the anti-submarine and torpedo nets. One of the submarines ran aground on an uncharted sand bank. Two of the craft were never seen or heard of again, and must be assumed to have got into difficulties while pressing ahead with the attack. Lieutenant Donald Cameron and the crew of *X-6* succeeded in placing their charges under the hull of the battleship before being forced to surface. Lieutenant Godfrey Place and the crew of *X-7* managed to approach *Tirpitz* unobserved and lay their charges close to those of *X-6*. However their escape was frustrated when they became entangled with the battleship's enclosing net and were forced violently to the surface by an ensuing explosion.

By now the Germans were fully alerted to the British attack but could do nothing the prevent it. The explosion which followed heavily damaged *Tirpitz*, breaking her back and forcing her to list heavily to port. She remained at her moorings until November 1944 when 617 Squadron, the Dambusters, eventually sent her to the bottom with 'Tallboy' bombs.

As D Day approached specialist underwater swimmers from the Combined Operations Pilotage Parties undertook a series of covert reconnaissance missions to establish the precise nature of the invasion beaches. Tanks attempting to land at Dieppe had become bogged down in the soft sand and the Allies were determined to ensure that no such fate befell the heavy equipment coming ashore at Normandy. When the swimmers reported that the Germans had sown masses of obstacles, many of them mined, below the high water mark, steps were taken to form a team of volunteers to clear the obstructions.

Few of the 120 men who volunteered for the Landing Craft Obstruction Clearance Unit (LCOCU) were regular servicemen and many had little or no underwater swimming experience. Yet the task which they performed on the morning of D Day doubtless saved the lives of hundreds, perhaps thousands of the first wave of invading troops. During the hours of darkness the ten teams of frogmen, four from the Royal Navy and six from the Royal Marines, approached the beaches in rubber boats, diving at the last minute to negotiate the submerged obstacles. Explosives were placed and detonated to create cleared lanes immediately before the arrival of the first landing craft.

As the first wave of troops stormed ashore the swimmers were waiting for them. During the course of the day they successfully cleared 900m of beach and removed over 2,500 obstacles, most of them mined. During the days that followed they remained to clear the flotsam of the initial battle freeing more of the bridgehead for the thousands of tons of equipment landing in support. The LCOCU was a true force of special designation. Once it had fulfilled its vital role it was disbanded.

German Endeavours

The German Navy had little need of special forces during the early stages of the war. Its surface fleet had fought well, a few armed raiders had sunk British ships and a number of blockade runners had successfully broken through the Royal

Navy's screen to bring home otherwise unobtainable goods. More importantly the U-boats were winning the Battle of the Atlantic, threatening to starve Britain into submission. There were early attempts to emulate the British Commandos but these were badly served and soon abandoned.

By mid-1943 however the tide of the war at sea was beginning to flow in favour of the Allies. By improved convoy tactics and the skilful decoding of Enigma they had succeeded in countering the U-boat threat and were now winning the war in the Atlantic. The German capital ships were either sunk or incapacitated, and those remaining operational had been ordered by Hitler not to be risked in open conflict with the Royal Navy.

In desperation the Germans turned to the Italians for inspiration. Doenitz ordered the formation of small specialist units (Klein Kampf Verbände) to carry the war to the enemy in the manner of the earlier Italian human torpedoes. An initial cadre of 30 volunteers was selected for the new K units. Captured British files were studied, prisoners interrogated and a captured X-craft evaluated.

In late 1943 the unit was transferred to the Baltic port of Heiligenhafen, redesignated Marine Einsatz Abteilung (Naval Assault Detachment) and expanded to four officers, four ensigns and 150 other ranks. After a period of intensive training undertaken in the utmost secrecy the Abteilung was divided into a number of Kommandos and declared operational.

The first of the several types of specialist vessel used by the K units, the Neger, floated just below the surface of the water. Prone to flooding, slow and with a very limited range of only 70km it was effectively a single-seater minisubmarine armed with a torpedo which it was capable of firing at ranges of up to 400m. The Neger's first mission, an attack on Anzio, was less than satisfactory. Of the 37 Negers brought to the water for the mission, fourteen failed to launch successfully. Those craft that succeeded in entering Anzio harbour found it virtually deserted. They managed to sink two small warships, but in so doing compromised their own secrecy when a Neger fell into Allied hands intact, its crewman dead from carbon monoxide poisoning.

A second Neger attack was launched three months later, this time against the massive fleet of merchantmen supporting the Normandy landings. A frigate and minesweeper were sunk for the loss of all but seven of the submersibles. A subsequent operation, launched on the night of 7/8 July, met with total disaster. The Allies were anticipating an attack and were fully alert. Most of the Negers fell victim to attack from swooping squadrons of Mustangs and Thunderbolts, others simply ran aground or broke down. Not a single crewman involved avoided death or capture.

Other attacks were carried out by the K Flotilla using both human torpedoes and Linsens. These were small, radio-controlled motor boats powered by standard Ford V-8 engines developing 90hp. Theirs was not a new concept. They had been used successfully by the Italians in the Mediterranean and by the Brandenburgers in Russia. However they were not suited to the choppy waters of the North Sea. Two Linsen attacks were launched in August without success and at the expense of a considerable number of K-men's lives.

4 The Second World War

As the Allies advanced into Europe and Germany began to find it almost impossible to release raw materials for experimental warfare, the OKM turned in desperation to frogmen commandos. Thirty volunteers considered fit and resolute enough for the almost suicidal mission ahead were trained to tow or push explosive warheads up river to their targets. The first two groups of K-frogmen were sent into action only two weeks after the Normandy landings, to attack the River Orne bridges carrying the British supply lines. The approach to the Orne took fourteen hours, but the frogmen reached and destroyed their targets.

The number of future raids was severely curtailed by the acute lack of volunteers embodying the requisite physical strength, mental resolve and determination. However a subsequent raid against the road and railway bridges at Arnhem proved successful with both bridges severely damaged for the loss of ten of the twelve K-frogmen participating.

A Special Courage: The SOE

In July 1940 Winston Churchill created the Special Operations Executive (SOE) to 'set Europe ablaze.' through the medium of economic sabotage. The term 'economic sabotage' was left deliberately vague and its scope broadened as the war progressed. SOE was empowered to extract staff from any government department at its absolute discretion and without recourse to higher authority.

In November 1940 Major General Sir Colin Gubbins, a larger than life veteran of the Royal Flying Corps, became effective director of operations and training. Wholly without experience in the field of espionage Gubbins suffered indifference and occasional hostility from the Establishment, particularly the Foreign Office and MI6.

SOE did not have a conventional headquarters but rather spread itself over a number of buildings. It moved in October 1940 to 64, Baker Street, a large complex of offices close enough to the hub of events to be convenient yet divorced enough to be discreet. As the war progressed its offices mushroomed until, by the winter of 1943-44, it had taken over most of the western side of Baker Street including the new head offices of Marks and Spencer.

As a secret organisation, SOE had to recruit its agents by stealth, relying on word of mouth and gentle subterfuge in sympathetic official channels. SOE had informal arrangements with HM Customs, the immigration services and the RAF to pass on information of personnel with connections to occupied countries. Vaguely worded appeals or advertisements were also placed asking people who spoke foreign languages to contact the War Office.

Few potential recruits for SOE knew the significance of their initial interview. Most had received rather uninformative letters, asking them to present themselves for a preliminary interview in connection with possible war work. Even those who had been introduced through personal contacts had no more than a vague idea that they were being interviewed for high security, and very dangerous, work. More than a few were women. Indeed, as the Germans in occupied Europe began to rely increasingly on slave labour to maintain their war effort, the sight of a fit young man on the streets was sufficient cause for suspicion in itself, and women came to be preferred.

The Conception of a Modern Elite

Potential agents were assessed over two or perhaps three interviews. Their present and past lives were analysed in depth to establish their 'worldliness', strength of character and potential for covert operations. Agents had to pass as locals in their operational country so a markedly British appearance was a drawback, as was a markedly Jewish appearance for those destined to work in Europe. A sound knowledge of the language of the target country was essential, although a strong dialect could occasionally be explained away by a clever cover story.

From June 1943 SOE adopted a new recruiting system. Candidates were no longer interviewed on a one-to-one basis but were instead assessed over several days by a board composed largely of psychiatrists. Failures were politely returned to the parent unit or to their civilian lives without ever learning the true purpose of the board.

Initially it was considered improper to employ women in active operations. They were expressly banned from carrying arms in the conventional forces and it was felt that this prohibition might extend to irregular warfare. Churchill was asked to adjudicate and deferred on the side or reality. Of the 52 female agents sent by SOE into France, seventeen were arrested of whom twelve died in concentration camps. Many women were recruited from the First Aid Nursing Yeomanry (FANY), one of the least known, and most socially exclusive yet effective of the services.

Unlike MI5 and MI6, SOE recruited foreigners when it felt it expedient. Many of its best agents enjoyed dual nationality, a few were even citizens of enemy states. Preliminary selection for SOE was but the first stage of acceptance. Training (described in detail in Chapter Six) was tough and only the very best went on to operational duties.

The exact size of SOE has never been revealed. However in its heyday in the summer of 1944 it is likely to have peaked at just under 10,000 men and 3,200 women of whom some 5,000 in total were trained, or under training, as agents. The rest, some retired veterans of earlier field work, were involved in planning, intelligence, operations, signals, transport and administration.

5
The Post-War Years
The Demise of Empire

The Birth of the Peasant Elite.
In 1945 Britain, France and to a lesser degree the Netherlands began an unequal struggle to retain the vestiges of empire in Africa and the Far East. In South-East Asia they found themselves facing growing armies of communist nationalists, convinced that western armies were far from invincible and hardened by over four years of unrelenting guerrilla warfare against the Japanese.

Indo-China Beginnings
Nowhere was the threat to empire stronger than in the French colony of Indo-China. French mastery of Tonkin, the northern province of modern Vietnam, had never been absolute. Localised guerrilla actions, and even rebellions, had been common and had always been suppressed with uncompromising brutality. An unsuccessful uprising at Yen Bay in 1929, however, had served to establish a pattern of resistance which had led a year later to the creation of the Indo-Chinese Communist Party (ICCP).

For ten years the ICCP bided its time; its founder, Ho Chi Minh, shunning open confrontation. Instead he established a network of clandestine cells throughout the provinces of Tonkin, and Annan to the south, to be activated should French influence in the area wane. In 1941, shortly after Indo-China had come under the control of the collaborationist Vichy Government, he formed the Viet Nam Doc Lap Dong Minh Hoi, soon to be recognised universally as the Viet Minh. French units in the region, including the 5th REI (5e Régiment Etranger d'Infanterie) - the only Legion unit in the area and by far the most impressive fighting force - were spared early bloodshed when Admiral Decoux, the French Commander in Chief, signed an uneasy protocol with the Japanese.

Towards the end of the war personnel from the American OSS jumped into the area to orchestrate resistance against the Japanese. Action groups made contact with the French generals in a successful attempt to persuade them to change their allegiance and mount a quick coup against the Japanese. However the Japanese struck first. On the evening of 9 March 1945 they launched a series of surprise attacks all over the peninsula, obliterating in a matter of hours the entire French presence.

The Legionnaires at Ha Giang were massacred when they refused to surrender. Lieutenant Duronsoy's motorised platoon was wiped out and General Lemonnier and the French resident, Camille Auphalle, were executed when they refused to surrender. At Tong, the captured Legionnaires were beheaded with swords. Three battalions of the 5th REI were able to consolidate and, with the aid of native units, fought a bloody and costly withdrawal into China, leaving Indo-China without a French military presence for the first time in 60 years.

When the Japanese seized control from the French the Viet Minh, recognising another window of opportunity, seized the power vacuum in the countryside, expanded Communist control and made ready to assume political power. On 2 September 1945 Ho Chi Minh celebrated the unexpectedly rapid surrender of the Japanese by entering Hanoi and declaring the establishment of a Democratic Republic of Vietnam. However his celebrations were curtailed when the British landed at Saigon, driving the Communists from the south, while the Chinese Nationalists advanced from the north. In February 1946 he was forced to approach the French for assistance in expelling the Chinese, in exchange for which he was forced to relinquish total independence accepting instead a unified Vietnam within a greater French-controlled Indo-Chinese Federation.

In March 1946 the French replaced Chinese troops in Hanoi and at once set about engineering a series of provocative incidents. In November the Viet Minh were ordered to quit the major port of Haiphong and in December were expelled from Hanoi. Embittered, Ho Chi Minh retreated to the safety of the countryside from which he undertook a series of guerrilla operations. Simultaneously France drafted a number of elite regiments to the area. The 5th REI, exhausted by the fighting of 1945, was replaced by the 2nd REI which was itself soon reinforced by the 13e Demi-Brigade de la Légion Etrangère (DBLE) and later by the 1st, 3rd and the reconstituted 5th REIs. Each regiment fielded from two to five battalions, enhanced at one stage by one or two locally recruited battalions formed under French command in an attempt to build the nucleus of an elite within the embryonic Vietnamese Army. The 1er Bataillon Etranger des Parachutistes (1st BEP) - the Legion's first parachute unit - was formed in 1948 and posted to Indo-China where it was quickly joined by the 2nd BEP.

In April 1949 the Viet Minh, now under the control of the brilliant Vo Nguyen Giap, went on to the offensive, successfully attacking elements of 3 REI in their series of outposts constructed to the north of Hanoi. In February 1950, strengthened by the defeat of Chiang Kai-shek's Chinese Nationalist forces in the north, Giap attacked the garrison at Lao Khe, close to the border. Despite the intervention of crack French paratroopers the garrison fell and with it the town of Dong Khe. Within months the French were forced to evacuate the border area, losing over 6,000 troops in the process.

Subsequent attempts by Giap to organise his troops into regular units for an attack on Hanoi failed. Although provided with ample weapons and equipment by the new Chinese Communist Government, his peasant army lacked the training and structure to combat elite French troops in open battle. Quick to recover, the French constructed a series of impregnable defended positions, the 'de Lattre Line' around Hanoi, and with the city secured returned to the offensive. In a series of set-piece attacks the Viet Minh lost heavily. Giap was defeated three times: at Mao Khe by the Legionnaires of the 5th REI supported by armour; on the Dhe River by the 13th DBLE; and at Nghia Lo, in October 1951, where he encountered the paratroopers of 2nd BEP.

In 1952 the war took a bloodier turn when the French withdrew from their most isolated bases leaving the northern countryside firmly in Communist hands. Giap at once postponed his ambition to take Hanoi and instead concentrated southwards, taking the Nghia Lo ridge between the Red and Black Rivers. Made overconfident by this victory, he committed one of his regular divisions against elements of the 3rd REI holding an isolated air strip at Na San. In three days of heavy fighting Giap saw his men slaughtered.

Chastened by this defeat, and aware that his men were still not capable of defeating the French by conventional means, Giap invaded northern Laos, forcing the French to commit their limited reserves to the Plain of Jars to protect the Laotian capital. Fearful of over-extending their fully-stretched resources the Viet Minh, having secured the annual opium crop, withdrew to the comparative safety of their northern strongholds.

Completely misinterpreting Giap's blatant act of regrouping as a sign of weakness the French decided to entice the Viet Minh into battle by creating an artificial target against which they might pound themselves to oblivion. They chose the village of Dien Bien Phu, close to the Laotian border, as an ideal killing ground, and in so doing condemned the bulk of the French colonial army, with its several elite units, to certain annihilation.

The Road to Destruction

Despite its being held by two companies of Viet Minh (who were quickly ejected), Dien Bien Phu had a number of advantages as a site for a set-piece battle. It straddled a Viet Minh supply route and could not therefore be ignored. It had its own private airstrip and was surrounded by a series of fortifiable hills. It was however overlooked by high mountains and, but for the airstrip, was completely cut off from Hanoi, some 275km away.

The 20km long by 13km wide perimeter was secured by six battalions of the French 1st and 2nd Airborne Battle Groups, including the 1st BEP, who immediately set about fortifying the perimeter by constructing a series of strong points, each reputedly named after one of the several mistresses of General de Castries, the base's commander. The Parachutists were then reinforced by four battalions of Legionnaires; the 1/13th DBLE, III/13th DBLE, 1/2nd REI and the III/3rd REI to create one of the most potent gatherings of elite forces since 1945.

Ho Chi Minh pondered on what action to take, and on Giap's advice eventually decided to accept the French challenge to battle, but under his own terms. Rather than rush his nearest available conventional troops into early combat to be destroyed piecemeal by the far superior French, he instead put into effect one of the finest logistical moves of modern history. True to the maxim, 'strike to win, strike only when success is certain, or do not strike at all', he ordered the mobilisation of two distinct armies. While he force-marched three regular infantry divisions (the 308th, 312th and 316th) and a division of artillery (the 351st) - about 50,000 men in all - towards Dien Bien Phu, a second army of 20,000 men, women and children began to hack new jungle routes for weapons and supplies.

Unarmed and untrained though this force was, it was yet an archetypal unit of special designation. It was brought together for the sole purpose of supporting the regular forces in the coming battle, and was disbanded immediately its purpose had been served. While untold thousands of procommunist peasants began to bring in enough rice to last the army for several months, brigades of bicycles - iron horses - were drafted in to move the rice forward. Avoiding the main roads because of the continuous French air patrols, and moving only at night, the two armies moved forward to encircle the unsuspecting Europeans.

During the months of preparation, and unseen by French aerial reconnaissance, the Viet Minh support army manhandled over 200 artillery pieces - many of them Soviet and Chinese 105mm howitzers - through the jungle. By superhuman effort involving nothing more sophisticated than muscle and flesh, relay teams roped to the guns pulled them inch by inch - 800m a day - through 80km of jungle. In the space of weeks Dien Bien Phu was turned from a fortress into a prison.

Although the French were expecting an attack they were overwhelmed by its ferocity. Unknown to them, Giap had amassed a fighting force over three times superior to theirs. His artillery, perfectly secreted in caves and trenches in the hills, overlooked the French making daylight movement above ground suicidal. The communist attack which followed, although fanatically brave, was militarily conventional. All 200 of Giap's artillery pieces were brought to bear in an hour-long barrage against the airfield and command centres. On the first day 'Beatrice', one of the closest outposts to the central section, was stormed by an entire division assaulting in 'human-wave' formations, and overwhelmed; 500 of the 700 officers and Legionnaires of the III/13th DBLE defending were killed or captured.

The days which followed were no better. 'Gabrielle' and 'Anne-Marie' fell on the two successive days, and by the third the airstrip was exposed and virtually unusable. Colonel Charles Piroth, the French artillery commander, his guns unable to counter the French ordnance in the hills, committed suicide. Despite parachute drops into the perimeter by five more airborne battalions, including the veterans of Lieutenant Colonel Bigeard's 2nd BEP, and by numerous untrained volunteers who came to fight alongside their comrades, the garrison of Dien Bien Phu was forced to surrender on 7 May 1954. The last unit fighting was the III/3rd REI at strongpoint 'Isabelle', which was overrun at dawn on 8 May. Over 9,500 French troops began a forced march into captivity from which few returned. They died in their thousands, not from brutality as is often suggested but from disease, exhaustion and malnutrition. They lived on two bowls of thin rice gruel a day, which they had somehow to cook themselves, both during the march into captivity and subsequently in the hastily improvised camps.

In a rare accord with the Geneva Convention, a batch of 885 prisoners taken at Dien Bien Phu were allowed to return to Hanoi some five months after the battle ended, including de Castries and his senior officers. In all, about 2,100 French prisoners eventually made it back to freedom.

A Hard Lesson Learned

Giap had won a famous victory, but at the cost of 7,900 men killed, the biggest number being 2,000 in the human-wave assault on Gabrielle by the 308th Division. A further 1,200 had died taking Elaine, and yet another 1,000 in the final morning. In addition, some 12,000 communists were wounded, of whom an unknown number succumbed. Administration within the Viet Minh was virtually non-existent with the notification of casualties regarded as a low priority. More often than not, families never heard of a death officially but had to assume it months or even years after not seeing a relative.

Giap had won the engagement before the first bullets had even been fired however, for Dien Bien Phu had been more than anything a battle of timing and logistics. The French command had expected to be attacked by two divisions of unsupported infantry which it felt confident it could annihilate. Instead it had been attacked by four fully equipped divisions, with Viet Minh artillery firing from areas that French Intelligence had regarded as impenetrable. Without his unique army of 20,000 men and women, true 'soldiers of special designation' yet all too often discounted as 'coolies' in many military histories, Giap could not have gathered together so overwhelming a conventional force, and would almost certainly not have succeeded.

The world gasped at the result of Dien Bien Phu. It taught peasant armies around the world that wars could be won by other than conventional means. If highly motivated irregular forces could be induced to take tremendous risks in support of conventional fighting troops, the latter would be granted such freedom of movement that they would eventually be able to overcome a more static, albeit more powerful, enemy. After Vietnam was partitioned Giap expanded and modernised the army, equipping it with second and third generation Soviet and Chinese weapon systems which to them were obsolete, but which to the Vietnamese were a big improvement on what they had. He created new divisions, new training centres, new doctrines. He established a commando training camp in which men were taught to use mines and explosives, the art of assassination and kidnapping, sabotage and demolitions. Concealment, camouflage, fieldcraft, unarmed combat and reconnaissance were honed to create a fighting force which twenty years later would humble the mightiest military machine in the history of the world.

The Algerian Crisis

Even before she began to withdraw from Indo-China, France became embroiled in yet another guerrilla war, this time across the Mediterranean in Algeria. Between 1 November 1954 and the declaration of Algerian independence on 3 July 1962, over 500,000 French troops were committed to a punitive and frequently bloody counter-terrorist campaign against the Front de Libération Nationale (FLN).

In general military terms the Algerian confrontation was a war of mobility, consisting of a series of brush encounters against small, mobile armed bands rather than set-piece battles. After the first few months of hostilities the French Parachutists and Legionnaires found themselves confronting groups of limited size, seldom larger than a 'katiba' - a strong company of between 150 and 180 'fellagha' or guerrillas.

All resources possible were made available to the troops. The French were quick to exploit the concept of airmobility, the use of air space in support of ground force operations. Elite units, many of them veterans of Indo-China, became skilled in heliborne operations. Approaching their objectives fast and low to avoid detection, heavily armed special purpose heliborne squads were trained to decamp within seconds of landing, thereafter to fan out into the countryside, seizing the key ground before the enemy had time to react. Support was provided by heliborne artillery (another new special purpose force concept) and by conventional infantry if necessary.

Despite the superior training and firepower of the French, their losses were considerable. Throughout the campaign the Legion alone lost 65 officers, 278 sous-officiers and 1,633 légionnaires dead. Eventually France was defeated, not on the battlefield but by domestic public opinion. Press accounts of women and children being herded into resettlement camps under the 'Challe Plan' (General Challe was appointed Commander in Chief in Algeria in December 1958), compounded with the growing number of seemingly indiscriminate civilian casualties turned French resolve against the war.

In April 1961, fearing that Algeria would be betrayed by the French Government, the military commanders in the colony staged a coup. The coup failed and, as a consequence of its involvement, 1st REP was disbanded for the third time in its short but bloody history. In 1962, the French Army left Algeria and returned to France. The Legion, with its roots in Sidi-bel-Abbès, found itself without a base and deeply distrusted by its government. That it survived is in itself testament to the Legion's resilience.

In the last thirty years the Legion has served in every area of the world in which France has influence. Between April and September 1969 three companies of the 2nd REP supported by a composite motorised company undertook a series of highly successful counter-insurgency search and destroy missions on behalf of the Government of Chad. In 1978 and again in 1983, when Chad found itself under threat from Libya's Colonel Gadaffi, the Legion returned to restore order.

On 3 April 1976 selected paratroopers from 2nd REP supported the successful GIGN rescue of French children from a terrorist-held bus on the Djibouti-Somalia border. Two years later, on 19 May 1978, the headquarters and three companies of 2nd REP jumped into Kolwezi in Zaire. In two days of heavy fighting, in one of the most audacious special forces operations of modern times, they secured the town against the violent excesses of the Katangan 'Tigers', saving the lives of hundreds of European residents for the loss of five légionnaires dead and 25 wounded.

In the spring of 1983 the 'Green Berets' of the 2nd REI, 1st RE and 1er Régiment Etranger de Cavalerie (1st REC) joined a Western peace-keeping force on the streets of Beirut. During its three month stay the Legion lost a further five dead and 25 wounded. However it impressed friend and foe alike with its discipline and unending good humour in the face of extreme provocation.

More recently, the Foreign Legion made an important contribution to Operation Desert Storm. As part of the French 6th Light 'Daguet' Division the 1st REC, 2nd REI and 6th REG held the Coalition left-flank, destroying the Iraqi 45th Division while advancing deep into Iraq. When the cease-fire was ordered Daguet was a mere 240km from Baghdad; in an excellent position, had the decision been taken, to strike at the Iraqi capital.

Rebirth of the SAS

In October 1945 a war-weary Britain disbanded the SAS. It almost immediately realised its mistake when an independent War Office study emphasised the absolute need for a special purpose force of highly skilled and motivated men, capable of operating singly or in small groups independent of the line infantry. The SAS was ideally suited to this role, yet the very concept of a 'private army' was anathema to a large number of influential politicians within the ranks of the then ruling Labour Party.

In 1947 a compromise was reached when a new Territorial Army unit, 21 SAS (Artists), was born. The original Artists Rifles had been raised in 1859 and affiliated to the Rifle Brigade. It had served with distinction throughout the First World War, earning eight Victoria Crosses in the process. The unit had served as an Officer Cadet Training Unit (OCTU) during the Second World War and had taken no part in the fighting. Nonetheless its reputation as an elite had remained, and it was considered ideally suited to take on the role of the SAS.

The Malayan Emergency

It took a bloody and protracted colonial war in the jungles of Malaya to resurrect the regular SAS. In June 1948 a cadre of experienced guerrillas under the leadership of Chen Ping, a veteran of the earlier war against the Japanese, returned to the jungle to launch a Marxist-style war of liberation against the British. His tactics were those of the typical Marxist 'liberator': the indiscriminate murder of estate owners, colonial officials and the police; the destruction and sabotage of estates, mines and factories; and the intimidation of the rural population into cooperation.

Between 1948 and 1950 the British responded with a series of conventional counter-insurgency holding operations designed to secure the lines of communications and key towns and villages. The introduction of compulsory registration and firearms controls, and the lifting of a number of obvious suspects contained the insurrection but did little to defeat it. The national servicemen who formed the vast majority of the garrison had little or no jungle training and were simply incapable of pursuing the enemy far from the comparative safety of their garrisons. When the communists changed tactics, broke up their regiments into platoons, abandoned the idea of establishing liberated bases and moved deeper into the jungle an uncomfortable stalemate ensued.

In April 1950 Lieutenant General Sir Harold Briggs was appointed Director of Operations and quickly brought a radically new perspective to the problem. Adopting the Maoist theories of guerrilla warfare he began to turn the communist terrorists (CTs) against themselves. He introduced some 410 'New Villages' capable of protecting the loyal population most at risk, and offered safe passage to the growing number of disillusioned guerrillas wishing to leave the jungle.

The New Villages, equipped with shops, medical centres, schools, electricity and water, were not only easier to defend and popular with their inhabitants, but were tangible proof of Malaya's potential as an independent country free of communist doctrine.

To spearhead his plan Briggs called for the deployment in the jungle of specially trained troops, capable of operating in this hostile environment for weeks on end, living with, cultivating and eventually winning over the local aborigines upon whom the terrorists had come to rely for food and intelligence. Responsibility for forming and leading these elite troops fell to Mike Calvert, the former commander of 1st SAS Brigade and a veteran of fighting the Japanese in the jungles of Burma.

Calvert's force, known as the Malayan Scouts, were drawn from three highly divergent sources: A Squadron comprised 100 volunteers selected from units then serving in the Far East; B Squadron was found from members of 21 SAS (Artists) and C

Squadron from Rhodesia. The Rhodesians were by and large highly disciplined and orthodox soldiers, marred only by the inability of the majority of their number to integrate with the aborigines whom by upbringing they had learned to despise. B Squadron, with its high standards of motivation, training and selection fitted in well. A Squadron however, which had been rapidly assembled without the proper selection processes crucial to weed out the unreliable, proved initially less satisfactory. It was from this somewhat unlikely beginning that 22 SAS Regiment was born in 1951.

When the High Commissioner, Sir Henry Gurney, was assassinated in October 1951 overall command in Malaya was vested in Sir Gerald Templer, with responsibility for the army, police and civil authorities. Templer arrived in Malaya in February 1952, with instructions that in due course the country was to become self-governing - a deadly long-term weapon against the aspirations of Chen Ping.

A dynamic personality in his own right, Templer wasted no time in fully implementing the Briggs plan. He turned all operational responsibility over to Major General Sir Robert Lockhart, who by the spring of 1952 commanded a total of 45,000 men, 25,000 of them British, in 24 battalions. The new energy and practicality which Templer brought to the war against Chen Ping was almost immediately effective. Stringent new food regulations, in which every crop harvested was recorded in detail and every tin of food sold had to be punctured by the seller to prevent hoarding, were introduced, and by the end of 1953 had reduced the communists to a position where they were forced to spend an estimated 90 per cent of their time organising food supplies.

Initially the role given to the SAS was as haphazard as was its early selection process. Patrols were tasked with food denial, with the furtherance of the hearts and minds campaign and only occasionally with the location and elimination of terrorist camps. However when John Sloane took over command from the gallant but by now sick Mike Calvert matters began to improve. The regiment was temporarily withdrawn from the jungle, regrouped and reappraised. Under the tutelage of the Second World War veterans John Woodhouse and Dare Newell a proper system of selection was reintroduced, and the element of indiscipline and adventurism which had threatened to mar the Regiment's return to active service was obliterated.

Over the nine years of the Malayan campaign the Regiment perfected its jungle operations. It honed to a peak the arts of navigation, camouflage and survival. It learned preventative medicine and how to deal with various tropical diseases; and learned tracking from the Iban and Dyak tribesmen, some of them former headhunters brought as trackers from Sarawak.

Above all the SAS mastered the art of tree-jumping, a tactically important yet critically dangerous method of deep-jungle infiltration. The first operation was carried out in January 1952, by 54 men of B Squadron who jumped into a small DZ in the Belum Valley. By a dropping error all but a few landed in the surrounding jungle with only a few casualties. From this it was anticipated that it was possible to jump into trees without sustaining unacceptably high numbers of casualties. Further experimental descents were made, first into rubber trees and then, in May 1952, into primary jungle.

Initially troopers jumping into deep jungle carried 30 metres of rope knotted every 45cm. Once the jumper crashed through the top jungle canopy his chute was caught, leaving him hanging below the canopy. He then climbed down the rope hand over hand until safely on the ground. Later a crude form of lowering device was evolved based on a mountaineer's abseiling gear. Although this considerably reduced fatigue a number of snags were experienced.

In January 1953, as part of Operation 'Eagle', B Squadron successfully jumped into primary jungle with an abseiling device with a 73m lowering line made of 4.45cm webbing with a 454kg breaking strain. However three fatalities occurred in January 1954 when the equipment malfunctioned when used again as part of Operation 'Sword'. Further developments were introduced and six months later a much improved system was used in Operation 'Termite' when 177 officers and troopers drawn from the three squadrons were dropped into the Perak jungle with only four minor casualties.

Tree-jumping, although dangerous, allowed for rapid deployment into areas inaccessible to helicopters and was thus continued, even when the Regiment's new commanding officer, Lieutenant Colonel Oliver Brooke, was injured during a descent. As the terrorists were forced to withdraw deeper and deeper into the jungle so they had to be located, attacked and eliminated. To have done so using conventional means of access would have been a criminal waste of highly specialist assets.

As Templer's campaign to win the hearts and minds of the local population intensified so the ability of the SAS to make friends became crucial. There were three culturally distinctive types of aborigine in the Malayan jungle, all of whom had to be won over by the Regiment's unique combination of earthy humour, medical assistance and sheer military competence.

It would be invidious to suggest that the SAS somehow single-handedly won the war against the communist terrorists in Malaya. They did not, but without their participation it might have become a more protracted and far more bloody affair. As Calvert made clear to his men in the early days, 'We in this unit are not going to win the war. All we can do is to play a particular part in what other Army units are not trained for or suited for'.

By the time the SAS left Malaya at the end of the emergency it had won its personal battle for the right to exist as a regiment. Whitehall finally agreed to its permanent establishment, and it became part of the British Order of Battle in 1958.

The Battle for Jebel Akhdar

As the emergency in Malaya drew to a successful conclusion the SAS found itself committed to a very different form of operation in northern Oman. Conventional troops would never have been asked to move from the jungle to the dry oppressiveness of the Gulf, and once there to engage a warlike enemy without a lengthy period of acclimatisation. That the SAS were able to do so successfully speaks volumes not only for its training and resolve but for the very principles of special forces warfare.

Between 1959 and 1967 the SAS fought three low intensity' campaigns of which the general public knew little. They were, nonetheless, important in the history of the Regiment, transforming it from a jungle force to the finest counter-insurgency force in the world.

The first of these mini-campaigns was fought for the control of Jebel Akhdar. Translated from Arabic Jebel Akhdar means 'Green Mountain'. It rises for over 2,000 metres straight out of the desert, although it has several peaks which are far higher. Its plateau can be approached only by a series of narrow, twisting and easily defensible tracks. It is the perfect setting for a tribal insurrection.

In 1954 Sulaiman Ibn Himyar, chief of the Bani Riyam, began to challenge the authority of the Sultan of Muscat and Oman with whom Britain had treaty obligations. Supported by the local Imam, Ghalib ibn Ali, and Galib's brother, the ambitious and powerful Talib, Sulaiman led two local tribes, the Bani Himya and Bani Riyam, into open revolt. In 1957 Britain dispatched an infantry brigade from Kenya to restore order. Nazwa, the regional capital and an important communications centre, was secured and Sulaiman's fort and power base in the village of Tanuf was destroyed by RAF bombing. Unwilling to surrender to an uncertain fate Sulaiman and Talib withdrew into the security of the Jebel from where they continued to attack isolated government posts. Britain dispatched reinforcements from the Royal Marines and the Trucial Oman Scouts to assist the Sultan's somewhat primitive armed forces, but neither unit had the training or resources to mount a full assault on the Jebel stronghold itself which it was clear would now be required to shift the insurgents from their lair.

Britain was in a dilemma. It desperately wanted to maintain its influence with the oil-rich states of Kuwait, Bahrain and Qatar, yet was conscious that its recent incursion into Suez had a catastrophic effect of Anglo-Arab relations. Whitehall had succeeded in withholding from the popular press the destruction of Tanuf, with its attendant civilian deaths, and now reasoned that were it to send a large force to the area the full extent of its earlier involvement would become known with disastrous results. After an appeal from the Foreign Office the Government decided publicly to do nothing, but secretly to send the SAS into the area.

The task of retaking the Jebel was delegated to 70 officers and men of D Squadron under the command of Major John Watts. The small team arrived amid the greatest secrecy straight from the jungle on 18 November 1958 and at once set about winning the hearts and minds of the indigenous population.

Working in small teams the SAS were deployed to the villages surrounding the Jebel. Adopting the policy of winning hearts and minds which had proved so successful in Malaya they gained the trust and respect of the locals. They watched, waited and above all listened for any scrap of useful intelligence however unwittingly given. Slowly and painstakingly they began to build up a pattern of the enemy's movements on and off the plateau. Watts appreciated that however much the policy of hearts and minds might weaken the enemy, it would not destroy him. That would take a more conventional form of military engagement preceded by a period of intensive and potentially dangerous deep reconnaissance. Against the strenuous advice of the Sultan's own experienced loan officers, night patrolling onto the Jebel was undertaken. Despite the obvious dangers of operating at night in an alien terrain against seasoned adversaries, the policy proved a success.

Two troops led by Captain Rory Walker and guided by a 'turned' local succeeded in scaling a twin peak on the northern side of the Jebel. Before their presence was detected they managed to construct a series of sangars on the plateau, some within 3,000 metres of the enemy's position, from which they were able to undertake a number of damaging nocturnal raids. Despite spirited counter-attacks from Talib's men,

5 The Post-War Years

Walker's team succeeded in maintaining their tenuous foothold on the mountain until the very end.

While the insurgents' attention was drawn by Walker's activities in the north a covert SAS deep-reconnaissance patrol in the south discovered the location of a well-protected arms cache hidden in a cave. Peter de la Billière, later to command the British forces in the Gulf but at that time an SAS troop commander, was ordered to attack the enemy position. Under cover of darkness his men made a long and tortuous approach through enemy held territory to within a few hundred metres of their objective. As dawn broke the defenders in the vicinity of the cave were greeted by a barrage of rockets and small arms fire. True to their martial traditions the insurgents did not break and run but rather went to ground returning the SAS fire. De la Billière was forced to execute a fighting withdrawal under the protective cover of Sergeant 'Tankie' Smith's Browning machine-gun. He did however manage to destroy the cave with much of its irreplaceable arms cache so driving yet another nail into the coffin of Talib's resistance.

In January 1959 Watts' hard-pressed men were reinforced by Major John Cooper's A Squadron which immediately deployed in support of Walker's two troops to the north of the Jebel. Now that the SAS considered itself strong enough to defeat the enemy in conventional battle a plan worthy of the regimental motto 'Who Dares Wins' was devised. Having advised a number of muleteers sympathetic to the rebels that the attack would be launched from Tanuf, top secret plans were implemented to assault the plateau along a series of previously untried routes from the friendly village of Kamah in the south-west.

Aerial reconnaissance was able to confirm that the subterfuge had worked to a degree and that Talib had moved the majority of his men to the area above Tanuf. Nonetheless the assault remained fraught with danger. The main force would have to navigate a 1,200-metre climb at night along unknown and ill-defined tracks with full packs and be in position before dawn if it were not to be cut to pieces by the remaining enemy marksmen.

The long climb began at 8.30pm on 26 January 1959. Masked by a diversionary attack to mask the inevitable noise both squadrons climbed steadily throughout the night. By 5.00am it became clear that progress had been slower than anticipated. Although A Squadron had reached its objective, three of the four troops of D Squadron were still bunched and vulnerable some way from the target. Fully aware of the consequences should his men be caught in the open, Watts ordered two of his troops to dump their heavy ammunition and equipment and push on. Unencumbered, they reached the comparative safety of their objective at 6.30am, just in time to receive an aerial resupply drop. By the time the enemy had become aware of his predicament the SAS was firmly in place. Supported by RAF Venoms the troopers began to send out fighting patrols to reconnoitre the largely uncharted plateau. The next morning the deserted village of Habib was occupied and on 30 January Sulaiman's cave, which he had been using as a headquarters, captured. Although a vast number of documents, and a substantial number of weapons were taken Talib, Galib and Sulaiman managed to escape to seek sanctuary in Saudi Arabia. Despite this obvious setback the insurrection had been crushed and the Jebel, together with the Walidom of Nazwa, returned to the Sultan.

After its successes in Malaya and the Oman the Regiment was brought home and reduced to two squadrons, A and D. B Squadron was incorporated into the other two while C Squadron, which had returned home in 1956 to be replaced by a New Zealand squadron, formed part of the Rhodesian Army.

Confrontation

The second and third of the SAS's low intensity campaigns in this period, the wars in Borneo and South Arabia, were potentially more serious. The first of these lasted from 1962 until 1966; the second from 1964 to 1967. For much of the time the SAS was involved in both campaigns simultaneously. Each squadron would serve in Borneo for five months, return to the United Kingdom for a brief period of leave and retraining and then deploy to South Arabia for up to four months. This was a stunning exhibition of the Regiment's endurance and skill and an absolute vindication of the Government's earlier commitment to the special forces ethos.

The Borneo Confrontation began as a local insurrection when a young sheikh, Azahari, led about 1,000 followers in a series of simultaneous attacks on a number of government buildings in Brunei. Troops from the Gurkhas, the Royal Marines Commandos and the Queen's Own Highlanders were rushed from Singapore, and within eight days had driven the insurgents deep into the jungle. Although the revolt was crushed, the general situation quickly worsened when neighbouring communist Indonesia began to mass troops along the 1,100km border.

Major General Walter Walker, the Director of Operations in Brunei, realised that the five battalions then under his command could not hope to secure the long, unmarked and mountainous frontier and called for special forces assistance. A Squadron, SAS was ordered to the area and at once set about the primary task of gathering intelligence of enemy movements. Its two- and four-man sabre patrols deployed were aided by the terrain, which allowed for only a limited number of infiltration points, and by the local tribes who were willing to provide the patrols with information.

The patrols brought the concept of hearts and minds, honed to perfection in Malaya, into devastating effect. Troopers moved into the border villages to make friendly contact with the Iban tribesmen. Relations were never forced, but quickly developed through mutual respect. The tribesmen provided food, accommodation, trackers and river transport when required and received in return payment and gifts, medical support and occasionally construction work.

The intelligence gathered by these patrols was crucial. The Indonesians tended to rely far too heavily on the rivers and known tracks for movement, and when they did venture into the jungle left easily defined trails marked by discarded cigarette packets and garbage (in sharp contrast to the SAS who were trained to remove every sign of their presence when patrolling; even their body waste was bagged and carried with them to safe dumping areas.)

When infiltration routes were identified, the SAS watched them covertly, giving early warning of approaching Indonesian patrols to the waiting conventional forces. As soon as the Indonesians entered Malaysian territory they were ambushed by Gurkhas and other fighting forces delivered to the scene by helicopter. D Squadron replaced A Squadron in April 1963, and spent much of its tour working with the

5 The Post-War Years

Gurkha Independent Parachute Company in training the cream of the indigenous tribesmen as scouts. These scouts proved an excellent asset, and were later to take part in a series of cross-border operations with the SAS.

As the war escalated Walker's initially small force was expanded until by the end of 1964 he had eighteen front-line British battalions, including eight Gurkha battalions, and three Malaysian Army battalions, a total of 14,000 troops, under command. The SAS itself was expanded when B Squadron, which in the eyes of many should never have been disbanded, was hastily reformed. At the same time it was mooted that Britain should form no less than nine special forces squadrons; the three regular SAS squadrons, two drawn from the Gurkhas and three from the Parachute Brigade and the Guards Independent Parachute Company. Although this far-sighted idea was never promulgated, the Guards Independent Parachute Company was later destined to form G Squadron, 22 SAS.

Towards the end of 1964 the SAS was given permission to take the offensive by mounting clandestine cross-border operations. Codenamed 'Claret', these incursions took the form of reconnaissance missions up to an attributable distance of 10km into Indonesian territory. Intelligence was gathered on a massive scale, but force was used only selectively, causing enough punishment to the front line Indonesian troops to demoralise them yet not enough to provoke their government into an escalation. Publicly neither belligerent admitted to this new and bloody phase in the Confrontation, as adverse reaction could have affected either.

To ensure anonymity, SAS troopers carried United States-manufactured Armalite rifles (not then on general British Army issue), wore non-regulation boots and carried no personal identification. To avoid compromise, movement on patrol was painfully slow. Patrols would pause for up to twenty minutes after often less than ten minutes of movement to pause and listen intently for anything unusual. Talking, unless essential, was banned and every step possible was taken to mask the very existence of the patrol. Normal social niceties such as cigarettes, and even soap and toothpaste, indeed anything which an alert enemy might have smelt, were discarded.

Although the SAS did not seek combat, unless leading Gurkha fighting patrols to their targets, there were a number of occasions when the two- and four-man patrols were forced to shoot their way out of trouble. On one such occasion, in February 1965, a small patrol probing an old Indonesian terrorist camp was itself ambushed. The leading scout, Trooper Thompson, and the second man in the patrol, the leader, Sergeant Lillico, were both hit. As the rest of the patrol went to ground Thompson managed to crawl back to Lillico's position to join him in returning the enemy fire. As he had seen Thompson on his feet, Sergeant Lillico was under the misapprehension that he could walk and therefore sent him back along the track to bring up reinforcements.

Thompson had in fact sustained a shattered bone in the left thigh and could only crawl. He nonetheless dragged himself along by the hands and, on arriving at the top of a ridge, fired several bursts in the direction of the enemy camp. Fearing that the bursts represented the arrival of reinforcements the Indonesians, who had suffered several casualties, he temporarily withdrew.

During the rest of the day Thompson continued to crawl to where he expected to find the remainder of the patrol. He applied a tourniquet to his thigh, remembering to release it regularly, took morphia and bandaged his wound as best he could. Thompson rested that night, and in the morning continued on his way. He had covered some 1,000m, about half the distance to safety, when he was located by a rescue party shortly before last light on the second day. An immediate attempt was made to winch him out by helicopter but this failed due to the height of the trees. Thompson was therefore forced to spend a second night in the jungle before being carried to a larger clearing from which he was successfully evacuated, some 48 hours after the contact.

For his part Lillico, who was in a worse physical state, succeeded in pulling himself into the cover of a clump of bamboo as soon as the enemy withdrew, took morphine, bandaged his wound, and collapsed. He awoke to the sound of a helicopter overhead but was unable to attract it due to the thickness of the bamboo. He rested that night and during the course of the next day dragged himself some 400m to a ridge from where he fired some signal shots to attract the attention of the search party which he knew would be looking for him. His shots were immediately answered by three bursts of automatic fire from the enemy then a few hundred metres away. He hid in the available scrub from where he was able to avoid the attentions of the enemy hunter force. That evening, with the enemy gone, he was able to signal to a rescue helicopter which winched him to safety. For their outstanding bravery Lillico was awarded the Military Medal and Thompson was mentioned in dispatches. Once more the SAS had shown that exceptional men could perform exceptional feats of gallantry and fortitude.

In the summer of 1965 the British battalions in Borneo were reinforced by the Australians and New Zealanders of the 28th Commonwealth Brigade. These included a New Zealand and Australian SAS squadron.

In August 1965 Singapore opted out of the Malaysia Federation. This was followed two months later by a coup in Indonesia which resulted in a power vacuum and the ultimate replacement of President Sukarno by the more moderate General Suharto. A peace agreement ending the conflict was signed in August 1966. The confrontation had cost 114 allied lives. Many of those killed were Gurkhas who had borne the brunt of the fighting. An estimated 590 Indonesians had been killed. The SAS lost three killed and two wounded.

South Arabia

On 29 November 1967 Britain ended 128 years of colonial rule in Aden. Although she had hoped for an orderly withdrawal she had made the mistake of publicising too early the proposed date of her leaving. In so doing she had played into the hands of a group of Marxist orientated dissident tribesmen, intent on making Britain's last years as uncomfortable as possible. On 10 December 1963 an attempt was made on the life of the High Commissioner, Sir Kennedy Trevaskis. Although the attempt failed, his assistant, George Henderson, and an Indian female worker were killed.

The British authorities, intent on nipping trouble in the bud, instigated Operation 'Nutcracker', a retaliatory raid into the mountains of the Radfan to the north. The operation was not an unqualified success. Although the three battalions of the Federal Regular Army (FRA) employed had succeeded in dislodging the dissidents from a few of their strongholds the army and RAF assets employed had failed totally to coordinate, leaving the forward infantry units dangerously exposed.

5 The Post-War Years

The Radfan Force, known as Radforce, was formed in 1964 to deal once and for all with the dissidents in the area. Overtly Radforce comprised 45 Commando, two battalions of the FRA, a company of the 3rd Battalion, the Parachute Regiment and a battery of 105mm pack howitzers of the Royal Horse Artillery. Covertly the force was joined by A Squadron, 22 SAS.

The SAS were sent in complete secrecy to the remote military air base at Thumier, near the rebels' mountain stronghold on the Yemeni border. The families had been told that the squadron was exercising on Salisbury Plain. They first learned the awful truth from a press report that Captain Robin Edwards and Trooper J N Warburton had been killed in action; and their bodies beheaded.

It later transpired that Edwards' patrol had been the vanguard in a punitive operation into the hills. They had set off on a night march to establish a safe DZ for incoming Parachute Regiment soldiers. Matters went tragically wrong when one man became sick early in the march. Instead of reaching its objective by dawn, the patrol was forced to take refuge in a totally inadequate, stone walled goat pen. It was quickly compromised and attacked. The ensuing gun battle lasted all day. Edwards and Warburton were killed as the patrol attempted to break out at dusk. The survivors, disorientated and weakened by lack of water, were harried by tribesmen throughout the night but nonetheless succeeded in effecting a successful withdrawal.

Thereafter the Regiment was regularly engaged in covert work in the Radfan mountains and the alleyways of urban Aden. In and around Aden city, SAS men dressed as Arabs and armed with 9mm Browning Highpower pistols, sought and intercepted terrorists, taking prisoners for interrogation wherever possible.

In the mountains, patrols provided covert artillery observation posts and sought DZs for the Royal Marines and paratroopers. During one particularly large operation an SAS troop, working in conjunction with 45 Commando Royal Marines, was helicoptered into the Radfan to reconnoitre for suitable DZs. The initial SAS heliborne insertion behind enemy lines was covered by the guns of the Royal Horse Artillery to keep the snipers at bay. The barrage was lifted as the Scout helicopters landed, was resumed for one minute and lifted again as the helicopters took off. Although three helicopter sorties were required to land the entire SAS party, the exercise was completed without loss in less than twenty minutes. Fittingly the last man out of the Radfan was an SAS officer, who remained, ostensibly as a civilian technician, to advise the South Yemenis on the administration of the Thumier military base.

The Battle for Murbat

In 1970 Britain was drawn with some trepidation into what was to be her last major colonial war. Since 1962 Sa'id bin Taimur, the aged and despotic Sultan of Oman, had been engaged in a losing battle with Marxist inspired guerrillas in the southern province of Dhofar. Using the now independent People's Democratic Republic of Yemen (PDRY) as a base they had mounted an increasingly successful campaign against the small government presence in the area and were now threatening to destabilise the entire region. In 1970 the unpopular and totally out of touch Sultan was deposed in a bloodless palace coup and replaced by his son, the Sandhurst-trained Anglophile Sultan Qaboos bin Said.

Qaboos requested and was immediately granted British military assistance to crush the insurrection. SAS teams were introduced within days (there is some suggestion that elements may already have been in position) and at once began to implement Operation 'Storm', the regaining of the initiative in the south.

The area of operations was alien to the SAS troopers, most of whom were fresh from the jungle. A narrow coastal plain some 60km long and 10km wide centred on the regional capital of Salalah. Inland the region was dominated by the mountainous Jebel Qarra, with its deep wadis and numerous caves running south and west to the Yemeni border. The Negd, a generally flat and treacherous area of desert between the mountains and the Empty Quarter completed the uninviting panorama.

The Dhofari people were largely unknown to the SAS. The town tribes of the coastal plain were basically of Kathiri origin; industrious, comparatively sophisticated and unsympathetic to the Marxist cause. By contrast the Qarra Jebalis of the mountains were hot tempered, highly intelligent and fiercely independent. Their loyalty was to self, livestock, family and tribe in that order. As the SAS discovered to their advantage the Jebalis made loyal friends if exploited sensibly, but bitter enemies if crossed. The Bedu of the Negd were nomadic herdsmen drawn from the Mahra and Bait Kathir tribes. They had their own languages and were equally as independent.

Lieutenant Colonel Johnny Watts commanding 22 SAS realised at once that his greatest battle would be for the hearts and minds of the much abused indigenous population. To this end he introduced an intelligence cell to monitor the activities and test the reaction of the Marxist insurgents. A psychological operations team (psyops) was formed to counter the Adoo, or Marxist rebel, propaganda. Doctors and SAS paramedics visited the villages to inoculate the tribesmen and their families against preventable but previously lethal diseases. Veterinary teams treated the camel and goat herds in the Negd, providing the nomadic Bedu with new-found economic security.

Crucially Watts gave the Dhofaris the opportunity to take up arms against the Adoo. Initially most Dhofaris had offered at least tacit support to the rebels, until the latter's Marxist-inspired hatred of family and religion had come to alienate the deeply conservative tribesmen. The newly formed groups of fighters were trained, armed and paid but not directly commanded by the SAS. Known as firqat they were allowed to elect their own leaders after which they were given almost total autonomy. The firqat were a true special purpose force; designed specifically for one campaign and wholly unable to carry the war beyond their own narrow geographical confines they were yet excellent soldiers. They soon began to trust the SAS, whom they greatly admired as soldiers, and by the spring of 1971 had gelled into a potent fighting force. In March of that year Watts elected to probe the enemy's dispositions in depth. He led a team of approximately 60 firqat and 40 SAS along a previously untried route into the mountains, and in twelve days of aggressive patrolling killed at least nine enemy before withdrawing.

Watts appreciated that he could not hope to control the area without first establishing a series of permanent mountain bases in the Jebel itself. In October 1971, immediately after the monsoon, he launched Operation 'Jaguar'. A joint SAS-firqat team under the command of Captain Branson made a feint into the Jebel from the east. Meanwhile Watts led the residue of the SAS squadron, two firqat guides and a squad of Baluchis into the mountains to seize the deserted airfield at Lympne. Having secured the airstrip he seized the village of Jibjat and began patrolling along the Wadi Darbat dislodging the unsuspecting Adoo in his path. On 9 October a secure base was established at White City from which Watts' 350 strong force was able to control the entire plateau above the coastal plain.

There followed one of the most spectacular events in the short but packed history of the SAS. On 27 November Watts organised what was later described as a 'Texas-style cattle drive supported by jet fighter cover and 5.5-inch artillery.' Over 1,400 head of goats and several hundred cattle were either airlifted or driven from the plateau to the coastal market of Taqa. Most of the animals belonged to firqat families. Those that had previously belonged to men serving with the Adoo were confiscated by loyal herdsmen during the drive.

Within a few months Watts' unique style of psychological operations and special forces warfare had all but destroyed the authority of the Adoo on the Jebel. Over 700 Dhofaris had joined the firqat and bases at least nominally loyal to the Sultan had been established throughout the Jebel.

The Marxists knew that they had to score a single, spectacular success against the authority of the Sultan if they were to regain the initiative, and chose as their target for annihilation a major military base near the coastal town of Murbat. The town was defended by a hotchpot of 30 Askiris from Northern Oman armed with ancient .303 inch Lee-Enfield rifles, a number of firqat, 25 Dhofar Gendarmerie armed with British 7.62mm SLR semi-automatic rifles and an SAS training team. The latter consisted of nine men under command of Captain Mike Kealy (later to die under tragic circumstances in the Brecon Beacons) based in the British Army Training Team (BATT) House. Their heavy weaponry consisted of a single 25-pounder artillery piece dug in close to the Gendarmerie fort on the northern defensive perimeter. This was supported by a .5-inch Browning machine-gun and a general purpose machine gun (GPMG), both on the roof of the BATT House near the perimeter centre.

The attack, executed by an estimated 250 well-armed Adoo supported by at least one mortar battery firing from the Jebel Ali to the north, was launched at 5.30am on 19 July 1972. The initial assault was launched by some 40 Adoo against the Gendarmerie Fort. Exploiting available dead ground to the full the attackers infiltrated between the BATT House and the Fort, turned towards the latter and broke into a run. As soon as they broke cover they were mown down by Corporal Chapman manning the .5 inch Browning on the roof of the BATT House. Now aware of the SAS dispositions the Adoo began to strafe the BATT House as well as the fort with machine-gun fire and mortar rounds.

Kealy took stock of the situation and reacted at once. Having radioed Salalah for assistance he decided to move to the 25-pounder gun pit adjacent to the fort to establish the exact position. Leaving Corporal Bradshaw in command at the BATT House he and Trooper Tommy Tobin, the SAS medical specialist, began a precarious 400m sprint to the comparative shelter of the gun pit.

Using the established principles of fire and movement to perfection the pair made it some 200m before the Adoo fully realised their intentions and brought concentrated fire to bear on them. Miraculously neither soldier was hit, and both reached the gun pit safely. The carnage which greeted them there was indescribable. Several gendarmes were dead, one was alive but quite mad. The Omani gunner was seriously injured, as were Troopers Savesaki and Labalaba, two Fijian friends serving with the SAS who had been near the gun at the time of the attack. The 25-pounder, although momentarily silenced, was still able to fire.

As the exultant Adoo moved in for the kill Labalaba, who had now received basic first aid from Tobin, brought the artillery piece into action. As he fell his place was taken by Tobin, covered as far as possible by Kealy, and by now supported by withering fire from the BATT House. The occasionally suicidal Adoo continued to launch their attacks, sometimes coming within feet of the SAS survivors, but were always beaten back by the courageous Kealy and his seriously injured team.

Just as it seemed that the exhausted SAS must be overrun, two Skymasters of the Sultan's Air Force appeared overhead. Disillusioned, their will to fight shattered, the Adoo broke and ran. As they did they were cut to pieces by the concentrated fire of ten GPMGs. Fortunately for the defenders elements of G Squadron due to take over responsibility for the sector had been in the area. They had at once boarded three available helicopters and made all speed to the assistance of their comrades. As the hapless Adoo fled they were met by 23 members of the squadron advancing unseen from the south-east.

The battle for Murbat, one of the shortest and most bloody in the history of the SAS, broke the Marxist will to fight and established once and for all the authority of the Sultan in the area. Kealy's personal bravery and leadership were recognised with the award of the Distinguished Service Order (DSO). Several of his companions had their names mentioned in dispatches but, in the tradition of the SAS, these were never published.

The Birth of the Green Berets

The US Army Special Forces were formed in 1952 specifically to counter the threat of communist military expansion. The North Korean Army had mounted a surprise offensive against South Korea in 1950, Marxist guerrillas were waging an intensive campaign against the British in Malaya and there were Communist-inspired civil wars in progress throughout the world. More worryingly Soviet forces were massing along the Western European border and a concerted attack was considered imminent.

During the Second World War the Office of Strategic Studies (OSS) had organised and supported resistance movements in many of the occupied countries of Europe and Asia, but it had been disbanded with the advent of peace leaving a dangerous political and military void.

It was decided to fill this void by creating a new special purpose force which would be skilled in guerrilla warfare, capable of harassing an invader and able to support the resistance groups which it was felt would spring up and pave the way for ultimate liberation. The task of creating this force fell to Colonel Wendell Fertig commanding the Special Operations Section, a group within the US Army Psychological Warfare Staff. Both Fertig and his Planning Officer, Colonel Russell W Volckman, had commanded guerrilla units in the Philippines while his Operations Officer, Colonel Aaron Bank, had served with the OSS in France and Indo-China. These three officers pooled together their experiences to produce a number of proposals, all of which met with hostility both from the more conventional elements of the US Army and the newly formed Central Intelligence Agency (CIA).

In 1952 proposals to create a new special purpose force specialising in unconventional warfare were accepted. Colonel Bank was ordered to find a site for the new Psychological Warfare School and chose as his base Fort Bragg, North Carolina. In June 1952 the new force, designated the 10th Special Forces Group (Airborne), was activated.

As befitted an elite, selection was rigorous. Many of the transferees had previous experience with the Rangers or Airborne, or had served with special operations during the war. Others were recruited from displaced personnel from Communist-occupied countries. All were skilled professionals, capable of operating either alone or as part of a small team. Apart from normal infantry training the recruits had to pass specialist courses including communications, demolitions, operational intelligence and field medicine.

Escape and evasion techniques, crucial for prone-to-capture troops destined to operate behind enemy lines, were honed. Supporters from the local civilian populations were used to provide exercise support in the form of intelligence gathering and shelter while the local police and National Guard acted as enemy. Mountain and winter warfare training was undertaken in Colorado and amphibious training in the swamps and coastal regions of Florida. By the end of 1952 the 10th SF Group had finished its training and was ready to deploy.

The years between 1953 and 1961 provided a period of quiet consolidation for the embryonic United States Special Forces. In early 1953 the 10th SF Group sent a detachment to Korea to act as advisors to Far East Command. Later that year a period of worker unrest in East Berlin made the US Army realise the importance of having special forces personnel permanently stationed in Europe. As a result half the Group was redeployed to Bad Tolz in Germany. The remainder stayed at Fort Bragg where they were redesignated the 77th Special Forces Group (Airborne).

In 1956 the Special Forces became increasingly interested in the worsening political situation in South-East Asia. Two training missions were deployed from Fort Bragg to Japan where they were used to form the nucleus of a new Group, the 1st SF Group (Airborne), activated on Okinawa. The 77th SF Group was redesignated the 7th in 1960, and together with the 1st SF (Airborne) deployed teams to Formosa, Thailand and Vietnam.

The year 1961 proved crucial for the Special Forces. President John F Kennedy, an active proponent of irregular warfare, visited Fort Bragg and was impressed with what he saw. He ordered the creation of four new Groups and authorised the wearing of the until then unofficial green beret by all SF personnel. The 5th SF Group was formed in 1961, to be reinforced in 1963 by the 3rd, 6th and 8th. Simultaneously the commitment to South East Asia was increased and training deployments intensified.

Rapid expansion is always a problem for an elite. Although a Special Forces Training Center was established, and additional funds were set aside for training and administration, standards inevitably fell. However expansion, coupled with the Green Beret's new-found notoriety, also brought its attendant benefits. Training was improved, both at individual and team level, and an exchange programme with other NATO special forces implemented.

During this period the role of the Green Berets broadened. They grew from a special purpose force concentrating on guerrilla warfare to a true special force skilled in the diverse disciplines of insurgency and counter-insurgency warfare, anti-terrorism and deep reconnaissance. They also became excellent teachers. Teams from the various Groups were deployed throughout the world, training the security forces of friendly governments in counter-insurgency operational techniques and assisting local populations in civic action programmes. The principles of hearts and minds, used so successfully by the British but until then alien to the US Army, were also implemented with considerable success.

Each SF Group was now allocated its own sphere of responsibility: the 1st and 5th SF Groups were deployed to South East Asia with teams operating in Laos, the Philippines, South Korea, South Vietnam, Taiwan and Thailand; the 3rd SF Group operated throughout Africa with particular responsibilities for the Congo, Ethiopia, Guinea and Kenya; the 6th SF Group with responsibility for the Middle East trained the special forces of Iran, Jordan, Pakistan, Saudi Arabia and Turkey. Finally the 7th and 8th SF Groups concentrated on Central and South America, areas of obvious strategic and political importance to Washington.

Irregular Warfare in Vietnam
The United States Military Assistance Advisory Group for Indo-China was active in Vietnam as early as 1950, four years prior to the French defeat at Dien Bien Phu. As the war escalated it was joined in 1957 by teams from the 1st and 77th Special Forces Groups. The 750 American military advisers in the country began to train the elite elements of the by now 243,000 strong Army of South Vietnam (ARVN) in unconventional warfare techniques and special operations. Based at the purpose built South Vietnamese Commando Training Center at Nha Trang, the 77th SF Group concentrated on training the first Vietnamese Rangers, whom it was hoped would ultimately be able to take over many of the special forces duties from the Green Berets.

By 1960 the rural infrastructure had begun to crumble. It was estimated that there were some 7,000 insurgents active in South Vietnam; an average of fifteen village chiefs were being assassinated or kidnapped each week, others were defecting and whole villages were slowly turning towards the communists. In December of that year the National Front for the Liberation of Vietnam was formed and quickly forged a new guerrilla force, soon to be known to the world as the Viet Cong. In essence a combination of the old Viet Minh and the new village converts, the Viet Cong grew in strength and potency until it was able to challenge the government for control of a number of the more vulnerable regional capitals.

A state of emergency was declared by the South's President, Ngo Dinh Diem, in October 1961. In the spring of 1962 Washington responded by increasing the number of armed forces personnel in the country to 4,000, many of them advisors and special forces personnel. By December of that year the number had grown to 11,300. In October 1963 President Kennedy raised the stakes considerably when he authorised the deployment to South Vietnam of the US Air Force's 7th Air Division, part of the 7th Air Force, with responsibility for all air operations throughout South East Asia.

Diem's position should now have been secure. But his government's lack of a democratic basis, maladministration, unbridled corruption and wholesale bias towards the small Roman Catholic minority left it vulnerable. While the Viet Cong were terrorising the countryside to eliminate anti-communist opposition the government secret police were purging the villages of anyone betraying even the slightest anti-Diem sentiments. An estimated 75,000 South Vietnamese were killed by their own government and a further 50,000 imprisoned during this period. The villagers, often in dread of the Viet Cong and constantly terrified of the government swayed with the wind.

Hearts and Minds in Vietnam

Diem attempted to counter the spread of Viet Cong activity and influence through the medium of the Strategic Hamlets Program, the forced migration of villagers into secure compounds free of communist intimidation. Superficially the policy was similar to that operated so successfully by the British in Malaya. In reality however the situation was wholly different. The Vietnamese were deeply tied to their ancestral roots and regarded enforced eviction as religious desecration. Diem realised that it would have taken his entire army to ensure the individual isolation of the 25,000 villages in the South from the estimated 45 active Viet Cong bands and compromised.

On 3 February 1962 Diem began to put the Strategic Hamlets Program into effect. Sir Robert Thompson, the head of the British Advisory Mission in Saigon and a veteran of the Malayan insurgency, helped the CIA implement the scheme. The South was divided into so-called prosperity zones: Yellow, under government control (about 32 per cent of the population), Red under Viet Cong control (43 per cent) and Blue for those still in dispute. Diem planned to establish fortified hamlets - yellow zones - within the red zones which would gradually be taken over by Government forces.

The United States Special Forces were used to establish the hamlets, many of which were large, in essence several villages joined by a defensive perimeter, and to identify pockets of Viet Cong influence surrounding them. The policy failed from the outset. The Green Berets helped the hamlets create elected councils which in theory controlled the daily lives of the inhabitants and created internal defense forces. In practice many councils granted the Viet Cong shelter at night and allowed them to escape in the mornings.

Millions of dollars in aid were poured into the project but little of it reached the hamlets. Consequently the peasants were often forced to live in virtual squalor while the officials sent to administer them grew rich. Nor did the hamlets offer any real protection. Government agents and hostile village headmen were rounded up by Viet Cong infiltrators and publicly beheaded or ritually disembowelled after summary nocturnal trials. Most of the hamlets were attacked, more than 2,000 of them more than once and one of them no less than 36 times! In one province 105 of 117 were attacked. In the Mekong area alone the Viet Cong destroyed more than 500 hamlets.

Diem's failure was largely self-inflicted. Neither Saigon nor Washington ever fully appreciated the subtleties of 'hearts and minds'. Unlike the British in Malaya; who had succeeded by clearing, dominating and holding the areas surrounding the friendly encampments, the Vietnamese and American forces ignored local intelligence, preferring to 'sweep' at random through selected target areas destroying any hint of what they perceived as resistance. Once the ARVN and Americans left, the Communists quickly reappeared to mete out their own form of bloody retribution to government collaborators. After Diem's assassination in a CIA-inspired coup in November 1963, the policy of collectivisation was abandoned.

The War for the Central Highlands

Late in 1963 the Viet Cong began the slow evolution from a guerrilla to a special purpose force. They started to create military formations ideally suited to the war of liberation ahead. Armed bands were expanded into battalions and battalions into regiments. In support of the Viet Cong, and under the direct command of the veteran Vo Nguyen Giap, the regular North Vietnamese Army (NVA) began to infiltrate the Central Highlands in the South.

In response the United States Special Forces became increasingly involved in the CIA-sponsored Civil Irregular Defence Group (CIDG) programme, and in late 1963 finally took it over.

The Central Highlands were of vital strategic importance and ideally suited to infiltration. A rugged, mountainous region the Central Highlands were peopled by 32 mountain tribes known to the French as Montagnards or mountaineers. These tribes were of two distinct ethnic backgrounds; Malayo-Polynesian and Mon-Khmer. Most lived in appalling conditions and only two, the Rhade and Jarai, had any form of written language. To the South Vietnamese the Montagnards were savages, worthy of the most vicious repression. To the Americans and Communists they were a source of potential mercenary manpower in a war of ideologies in which the tribesmen had little understanding.

In the early 1960s the Montagnards had seen the Communists as a form of protection against the excesses of the Diem regime. Tribes such as the Kor, Sedang and Bahnar had resorted to massacring South Vietnamese garrisons while the Hre had publicly gone over to the Viet Cong. However the Communists had overreached themselves when they had attempted to purge the tribal leadership. The kidnap and murder of thousands of Montagnards who had formerly fought for the French had resulted in many tribes abandoning the Viet Cong cause.

It was against this background that the CIA had begun working with the Rhade tribe in 1960. The aim of the Agency's Civilian Irregular Defence Group Programme had been to provide armed territorial units capable of protecting local settlements from Communist infiltration. Fortified camps had been built inside contested areas, and once established had been used to mount fighting patrols deep into Viet Cong territory. In the months that followed the CIA teams had been gradually supplemented by specialists from the 1st, 5th and 7th SF Groups. In mid-1963 the entire operation had been handed over to the military.

The Montagnards soon grew to accept the SF personnel, and as with the SAS and Ibans in Borneo quickly developed a bond of mutual respect. Food and accommodation were shared and the Green Berets' medicine and engineering skills used to improve the primitive lot of the tribesmen. The programme was successful from the outset. A total of 43,000 militia were trained in 1963 alone. Specialist training centres, such as the Mountain Commando training Center, were established and 18,000 of the better irregulars organised into strike forces for the execution of more offensive operations, such as the recapture of fortified Montagnard villages held by the Viet Cong.

In late 1964 the 5th SF Group was relocated to Vietnam and put in charge of the approximately 40 CIDG camps then operational. Whereas previously teams from the 1st, 5th and 7th SF Groups had spent six months in their allotted camps before handing over to a relieving team which had then had to gain the confidence of the locals afresh, personnel now began to spend a year in the camps before being rotated out as individuals.

The benefits gained by this new-found continuity were considerable, and allowed the Special Forces to expand their programme of offensive indigenous operations. Under the Border Surveillance Programme special purpose patrols comprising CIDG troops and Green Berets began to operate against the Communist supply lines along the Ho Chi Minh Trail.

In 1964, amid the greatest secrecy, a special purpose force of tribesmen led by Special Forces personnel was created for cross-border infiltration of supply routes. Named the Studies and Observation Group, the new force carried out clandestine operations deep into Laos (initially codenamed 'Shining Brass', later 'Prairie Fire'), Thailand and Cambodia ('Daniel Boone'). Using the special forces' armoury of psychological operations, sabotage and subversion so-called Spike Teams or Recon Teams of twelve Montagnard or Nung tribesmen led by SF personnel carried the war to the enemy in a way that would never have been possible using conventional troops.

Every effort was taken to mask the presence of the cross-border raiders whose very existence was deniable. Methods of infiltration and exfiltration varied but usually involved a low-level flight in a UH-1 (Huey) helicopter. Captured weapons were carried where possible and locally made camouflage uniforms worn. The political risks run in operating the Studies and Observation Group were high. However the intelligence gained, with particular regard to the enemy's strength and dispositions, was phenomenal.

Viet Cong reaction to the growing Montagnard involvement in the war was as predictable as it was savage. The isolated bases were attacked with suicidal bravery, but were mostly well defended. Occasionally the Viet Cong's nocturnal massed-wave assaults were successful and garrisons were overrun, but this was rare. The Green Berets countered by recruiting the most able of the indigenous personnel from the CIDG camps and forming them into battalions known as Multipurpose Reaction Forces or Mobile Strike Forces (Mike Forces). Capable of being deployed by parachute or helicopter the lightly armed Mike Force companies rapidly reinforced besieged bases, and by their timely intervention often turned a potential CIDG tragedy into a bloody Viet Cong defeat.

In 1966, Mike Force strength was increased to three battalions with an additional reconnaissance company and an ARVN Special Forces team in support. Two years later it was organised into the 5th Mobile Strike Force Command. By December 1968, 5th SF Group controlled 7,000 Mike Force personnel together with 27,000 'conventional' CIDG many of whom were also organised into other Mike Force-type units.

The special purpose forces Mike Force concept proved popular with the more far-sighted of the conventional military commanders who had already come to realise that United States firepower alone would prove insufficient to defeat an enemy as committed and elusive as the Viet Cong. During the summer of 1968 the 5th SF Group was joined by another four Mobile Strike Force Commands, attached to I, II, III and IV Corps Tactical Zones. Mike Force irregulars even undertook scouting and reconnaissance tasks ahead of the elite 1st Air Cavalry and 173rd Airborne Brigade, attempting to draw the enemy into battle until the heliborne United States forces could arrive.

A number of indigenous special purpose units were absorbed into the order of battle and given names reminiscent of the American Indian Wars. Kit Carson Scouts were composed of turned Viet Cong and NVA regulars and proved invaluable to green GIs desperately attempting to adjust to guerrilla warfare. Apache Force instructors drawn from Montagnard and Green Beret personnel attempted to teach new arrivals the action to be taken on contact with the enemy and doubtless saved hundreds of GIs from death in their first engagement.

Inevitably the success of the Montagnard irregulars was met with suspicion and antagonism in Saigon. In 1962 Montagnards from the Rhade and Jarai tribes were forcibly resettled deep within Communist controlled territory and were severely punished when they attempted to return to their old villages. The American Special Forces attempted to redress the balance, but were frustrated by the fact that they had to operate within the Montagnard camps in conjunction with the South Vietnamese Special Forces or 'Luc Luong Dac Biet' (LLDB). Contemptuous of the Montagnards and with little stomach for small-unit warfare, the Vietnamese LLDB were usually relegated to administrative roles within the camps, leaving the operational control firmly in the hands of the Green Berets.

Occasionally the Montagnard detestation of all things Vietnamese spilled over into open rebellion. In September 1964 tribesmen seized seven Special Forces camps, disarming the Green Berets before slaughtering their LLDB counter-parts. During the same month a force of 500 Rhade and M'nong overran a civil guard post and massacred the occupants.

Subsequently 3,000 hardcore rebels decamped for Cambodia, demanded regional autonomy and formed the 'Front Unifié de Libération des Races Oprimées (FULRO). In due course the Green Berets persuaded 600 of the rebels to return to the Highlands, but were never able fully to trust them again. Notwithstanding the FULRO episode many Montagnards remained loyal to Saigon, and during the Tet offensive of January 1968 gave an excellent account of themselves in the battles for Ban Me Thout and Nha Trang.

In 1971 the CIDG programme was officially ended and the indigenous troops absorbed into the South Vietnamese Army. Notwithstanding this, 37 of the former CIDG camps were retained as ARVN Ranger Camps, from which a number of Montagnards continued to operate against the Communist infiltration routes until overrun by the advancing North Vietnamese Army. Deserted by their former allies most ended their days in Communist extermination camps.

The United States Special Forces underwent a number of changes following the American defeat in Vietnam. In 1969 there were 2,300 SF personnel attached to the

CIDG programme alone, and when this was abandoned many found themselves redundant. At the end of 1969 the 3rd SF Group was deactivated. The 10th SF Group was recalled from Germany, leaving only a small element in Bad Tolz to face the threat from the Soviet Union. The 6th SF Group was deactivated in 1971, the 8th in 1972 and the 1st in 1974.

The Soviet Threat to Europe

For over four decades the West stood in awe of what it perceived to be the might of the Soviet military. NATO exercises presumed invasion followed by a deep penetration of Western soil, and many military commanders quietly accepted that it would be Allied rather than Soviet nuclear missiles which would be the first to be unleashed.

It was assumed that the Soviet special forces, or Spetsnaz, would attack key targets behind NATO lines and would almost certainly attempt the assassination of key military and political figures. Yet very little was known about Spetsnaz. In fact 'Voiska Spetsialnogo Naznacheniya' (VSN) had no equivalent in the West. In the eyes of the Soviet Union it was a force of special designation rather than a NATO-style special purpose force. A staggering 90 per cent of its members were conscripts among whom standards varied greatly.

Until 1989 references in the Soviet press to VSN were rare and usually couched in historical terms. Units were described in a 'special reconnaissance' (spetsialnaya razvedka) or 'diversionary reconnaissance' (diversiya razvedka) context, and never as units or subunits of special designation. The very existence of a multi-talented elite within the Soviet Army was discounted as Western propaganda. Troops specialising in reconnaissance were designated 'razvedchiki'. LRRP operators became 'iskatelia' (those who seek), HALO/HAHO specialists were known as 'vysotniki', and prisoner snatch groups as 'okhotniki' or capturers.

In 1989 the Kremlin partly lifted its veil of secrecy, and allowed a series of articles to appear in the Soviet military and civilian press referring in detail to the existence and performance of units of special designation. However much of the information leaked was of low grade intelligence value. It was already known to NATO analysts, and was almost certainly only released in an attempt to defuse the West's growing interest in Soviet special purpose forces. Moreover many of the units discussed, although doubtless elites, had little, if any, connection at all with Spetsnaz.

The Birth of the Soviet Elite

The evolution of the Soviet special purpose forces, or indeed the forces of special designation, was quite unlike that of their Western peers. The first recorded use of forces of special designation by the Soviets occurred soon after the Revolution. In the spring of 1918 the 'Chasti Osobogo Naznacheniya' (ChON), comprising detachments of pro-communist workers, moved into the major industrial complexes to ensure their total adherence to the new regime. A year later the force was expanded by the Cheka (the predecessor of the KGB) into a paramilitary territorial unit within the Red Army. As such it saw considerable action during the civil war and against the Moslem 'basmachi' (bandits) in the south, until it was itself disbanded in 1925.

The Demise of Empire

The Soviets pioneered the use of airborne special forces as early as 1927. Reconnaissance teams ('razvadchiki') were used to devastating effect against the basmachi in Central Asia until the latter's virtual suppression in 1931. By 1932 the embryonic regular airborne forces had become almost completely dedicated to deep reconnaissance ('spetsialnaya razvadka') and to the destruction of the enemy's command and control facilities.

By the early 1930s Soviet special operations units had successfully suppressed the majority of domestic dissent and felt ready to concentrate on the suppression of anti-Soviet activity abroad. In 1936 the Cheka created an Administration for Special Tasks to kill or kidnap enemies outside the USSR, and set about the ruthless elimination of its enemies. During the Spanish Civil War (1936-39) the newly formed NKVD and GRU (Military Intelligence) undertook terrorist, sabotage and guerrilla activities behind Nationalist and Republican lines on a scale never before envisaged.

The role of Soviet special purpose forces and forces of special designation during the Great Patriotic War has been fully documented in Chapter One. Immediately after the war the Soviets disbanded their forces of special designation, transferring responsibility for the execution of rear-area diversionary missions to the airborne units. During the late 1950s however they recreated their specialist units, structuring them within the existing KGB and GRU frameworks.

KGB Spetsnaz

By far the most secretive of these new organisations, KGB Spetsnaz, remained a mystery to all but a few in the West until its ultimate demise with the disintegration of the Soviet Union. Comprising a small cadre of professionals assisted by several hundred support personnel it focused on social, economic and political targets at the highest level. It was represented clandestinely in most major embassies from which it undertook relatively few, though painstakingly selected operations under conditions of extreme secrecy.

Its duties included strategic sabotage and 'mokrie dela' or 'wet affairs' such as the elimination in times of peace of key hostile personnel and regional political leaders. KGB Spetsnaz occasionally resorted to proxies, operating with the East German and Bulgarian intelligence agencies. They were present in Afghanistan, usually disguised in the uniforms of conventional airborne troops, and were responsible for the murder of President Amin and his entire family.

GRU Spetsnaz

The existence of the military wing of Spetsnaz, attached to the Second Directorate of the GRU, was formally admitted by the Soviets as part of their move towards Glasnost or openness, but was by then well documented by the West. In time of war Spetsnaz had several diverse roles. Of prime importance was the destruction of the enemy's political direction through the neutralisation of key personnel and the destruction of command, control and communications (C^3) centres. Airfields, naval bases and air-defence installations were reconnoitred and targeted. Although Spetsnaz did not have a tradition of close partisan liaison it established itself during the Afghan War as a most potent anti-guerrilla force.

5 The Post-War Years

Death in the Prague Spring

Spetsnaz forces were used to devastating effect during the suppression of the 'Prague Spring' of 1968. So as to mask their ultimate intentions from an unsuspecting world, immediately prior to the invasion the Soviets confined to barracks the majority of their conventional troops stationed throughout the northern confines of the Warsaw Pact. The Czechs were not unduly worried therefore when an unscheduled civilian Aeroflot aircraft landed at Prague's Ruzyne Airport late at night, taxied and parked at the end of the runway. An hour later a second Aeroflot aircraft landed. This time it disgorged its passengers, all of them fit and young, who having cleared customs, set out for the city centre. Two hours later the 'passengers', by now fully armed, returned to take over the main airport buildings.

Almost at once one, possibly two, further aircraft landed and immediately disembarked teams of uniformed Spetsnaz. A series of transports followed, each containing more Spetsnaz supported by conventional airborne troops from the 103rd Guards Airborne Division. Within two hours of the first uniformed Spetsnaz troops landing the airport and its environment were firmly in Soviet hands and troops were advancing on the capital. By daybreak the presidential palace, the radio and television studios, the transmitter, all of the main stations and the bridges over the Vltava were in Soviet hands.

Spetsnaz in Afghanistan

The role played by Spetsnaz in the invasion of Afghanistan was no less critical. Between 8 and 10 December 1979, some fourteen days prior to the invasion, Spetsnaz troops, in the company of an airborne regiment, deployed to Begram, a key town to the north of Kabul, to secure the Salang Highway with its critical tunnel. Between 10 and 24 December a battalion from the airborne regiment, supported by the Spetsnaz contingent, moved to Kabul International Airport less than 3kms from the city centre. Between 24 and 27 December troops from the 105th Guards Airborne Division, again supported by Spetsnaz, landed at and secured Kabul Airport and the air force bases at Bagram, Shindand and Kandahar. During the course of the following night the full offensive began. Paratroopers arrested the Afghan government whilst Spetsnaz teams demolished the central military communications centre, captured the still-functioning Ministry of the Interior, the Kabul radio station and several other key points.

Simultaneously two regular Spetsnaz companies, with KGB assistance and supported by an airborne regiment, attacked President Amin's palace at Darulaman. Amin, his family, security force and entourage were killed for the loss of 25 Soviet dead including the Soviet KGB Colonel Balashika, reportedly hit by 'friendly' crossfire.

The years of bloody turmoil which followed show the clear divisions between the potential of the small inner elite of Spetsnaz regular special forces and the far less well trained Spetsnaz conscript forces of special designation. Spetsnaz passed the first two years of the Afghan War quietly, defending their barracks and major installations. In 1983 however they went on the offensive. Working in conjunction with groups of between 500 and 1,500 heliborne troops they attacked isolated towns and villages which the Afghan Mujahideen had once considered safe. Guerrilla lines of communication were ambushed while villages suspected of offering the rebels aid or succour were razed to the ground in a scorched earth policy as vicious as any seen in Vietnam.

In the spring of 1985 Spetsnaz conscripts began to operate in close conjunction with conventional ground troops in an attempt to rid the valleys of large-scale enemy activity. During two well publicised sweeps along the Kunar Valley helicopter-inserted Spetsnaz troops moved along the high ground ahead of the advancing tanks and APCs in an attempt to catch the unsuspecting Mujahideen in the open. Casualties on both sides were heavy but, in the eyes of the Soviets, acceptable.

While the regimental Spetsnaz conscripts continued to operate as a conventional elite in close cooperation with the ground troops, the regular Spetsnaz detachments were given almost complete autonomy. Usually in their thirties, battle-hardened and totally acclimatised to mountain warfare, these special forces quickly began to register successes.

Some groups dressed as peasants to enable them to move comparatively freely about the mountain passes. Others were dropped many kilometres from their objective, travelling overnight to lay ambushes. Reconnaissance ('razvadka') units operated from hides high in the mountains reporting their findings direct through their own command structure to the Kremlin.

Spetsnaz activity in Afghanistan was necessarily curtailed when the Mujahideen began to receive shipments of Stinger surface-to-air missiles on a large scale. Regular units could no longer rely on the helicopter for safe transport to and from the mountains and were thus unable to take their specialist skills direct to the enemy.

The European Response

For over forty years the massed armies of the Warsaw Pact threatened the West along the entire length of the Iron Curtain. Spearheaded by the tanks and artillery of the Third Shock Army, the Soviets poised to strike across the Inner-German Border (IGB). NATO knew that it had neither the manpower nor resources to repel an attack in its early stages, and conceded privately that it would have to cede territory temporarily in order to draw the invaders into a series of kill-zones in which the West's greater technology could be brought to bear. NATO relied heavily on a number of elite units to slow the enemy armour as it attempted to deploy having breached the border defences. Most of these units evolved to fulfil their particular role. As such they were special purpose forces rather than true special forces. Nonetheless there can be no doubt that, had they been called upon to fight they would have severely slowed the enemy's advance.

Germany

Post-war West Germany never forgot the atrocities committed by the Soviet invaders in 1945 and made it clear to its NATO allies that in any future war it would fight an invader for every centimetre of its national soil. The execution of so uncompromising a policy of defence required the services of a number of elites. The role of disrupting the massed armour and mechanised artillery of the operational manoeuvre groups which would have spearheaded the Soviet advance westward fell to the three Luftländer brigades of the Fallschirmjäger, the successors of the German airborne forces who had fought so magnificently throughout the Second World War. Intended to act as a rapid response airmobile reserve within the three German corps areas, the brigades quickly gained an elite status as arguably the most potent tank-killers in NATO.

Germany appreciated that its corps commanders could only make a full assessment of the enemy's likely intentions and react accordingly, if they could receive timely intelligence on the size and activities of his reserves who would be called upon to spearhead any proposed breakout. In conjunction with the majority of her NATO allies West Germany introduced Long Range Reconnaissance Patrol Troops, or Fernspahetruppen, to obtain this information, if necessary from behind enemy lines.

The Bundeswehr operated three LRRP companies, one with each of its Corps. Administratively they were organised along conventional Federal German lines with a company headquarters providing logistics, supply, intelligence, transport and communications, but in other respects they were unique. Much of their selection and training was internal, although specialist aspects were catered for at the International Long Range Reconnaissance Patrol School at Weingarten, in southern Germany.

The LRRP were not conventional troops and were therefore not expected to engage the enemy in hostile activity. They were however highly trained in the arts of camouflage, escape and evasion and unarmed combat to enable them to extract themselves from a dangerous situation if necessary. Their methods of entry behind enemy lines remained secret, but were presumed to include parachuting, either static or free-fall, low level air transport, delivery by armoured personnel carrier driven by specially trained troops or by the utilisation of stay-behind parties.

The Gebirgsjäger, who operated in the high alpine regions of southern Bavaria, provided West Germany with her only special purpose mountain troops. Trained and recruited locally the Gebirgsjäger enjoyed a strong sense of tradition unusual in the Bundeswehr. They were well equipped and highly trained to carry out their assigned role, but would have been of little practical use away from their chosen environment.

Italy

Italian Navy special forces, or COMSUBIN (COmando SUBacquei INcursor), were reformed in 1952 to protect NATO interests in the Mediterranean. Comprising a mixture of operational and training companies, regular personnel and conscripts the unit became responsible for all offensive and defensive underwater activities off the Italian coast. The best of its regular personnel undertook an intensive ten months training programme at the Incursion School, during which they obtained both diving and parachuting qualifications before undertaking a further period of fourteen months special-to-arm training with the Operational Group. Conscripts, whose terms of service precluded such extensive training, undertook a one-month course designed to make them proficient in the less onerous yet equally crucial and highly specialised role of ground base defence.

While the bulk of the Italian Army was committed to the defense of the Gorizia Gap in the north-east of the country, the special purpose forces of the FIR ('Forza di Intervento Rapido') were tasked with guarding the long and vulnerable coastline to the south. Comprising the Folgore Brigade, which incorporated the 9th 'Colonel Moschin'

Above: Maintenance of physical fitness is a must for all elite forces - exemplified here by Russian airborne troops. (Guy Taylor)

Below: Soviet airborne forces were unique in having developed a family of AFVs for the support of parachute operations. (Guy Taylor)

Left: Training in eastern martial arts - such as karate seen here - is common to most of the world's military elite forces. (Guy Taylor)

Below: The former Soviet Naval Infantry maintained an armoured as well as amphibious capability enabling it to advance unsupported from a bridgehead once secured. (Leslie McDonnell)

Above: Soviet BMP-equipped battalions were trained to advance supported by armour, dismounting at the last minute to assault on foot. (Leslie McDonnell)

Below: A soldier of the former Yugoslav Army learns the importance of keeping his weapon - if not himself - dry at all times.

Above: A new generation of 7.62mm Russian pistols have been designed to fire 'silent' cartridges.

Below: The Makarov pistol, with its built-in silencer, was issued to Soviet Spetsnaz forces.

Above: Former East German Army engineers undertake a river recce before an assault crossing.

Left: During the Malayan Emergency helicopters such as the S55 Westland Whirlwind were deployed to give long-range recce patrols an added degree of mobility. (Westland)

Lower left: MH-53J helicopters of the 21st Special Operations Squadron USAF have been fitted with the latest Pave Low infra-red system for night operations. (USAF)

Right: Members of the 101st Airborne Division in Vietnam jump from a UH-1D Iroquois helicopter during a sweep close to the Demilitarized Zone. (US Army)

Below: Troops prepare to board a US Army Blackhawk helicopter during Operation Desert Shield. (DOD)

Above: A US Marine Corps Iroquois helicopter seen touching down during Operation Urgent Fury. (US Army)

Below: A soldier of the Spanish Foreign Legion takes aim with his CETME 5.56mm assault rifle.

Assault (Saboteur) Parachute Battalion, the true special forces of the Italian Army, and the Alpini Parachute Company, the Friuli Brigade and elements of the San Marco Marines, the RIP was fit, well trained and highly motivated.

The five Italian Alpini Brigades were true special purpose troops. Mainly conscripts who spent seven of their twelve months in specialist mountain warfare training they would have been of little use elsewhere. However the fact that most were expert skiers when they were conscripted, and by and large remained in the mountains and retained their fitness and skills once released, meant that they could have been mobilised with a minimum of delay in the case of an emergency.

The Northern Flank

For up to a century Sweden based her defence policy on non-alignment in time of peace and neutrality in time of war. During the Cold War however she became increasingly concerned by the number of incursions into her territorial water by Soviet Naval Spetsnaz teams reconnoitring her harbours and waterways, and came to accept that neutrality would be a luxury denied her in any future major conflict.

Finland, despite its policy of military non-cooperation with the Warsaw Pact would almost certainly have conceded the right of passage across its territory for Soviet troops in time of war. Consequently Swedish neutrality would have become untenable should the Soviets have wished to strike quickly against the relatively lightly defended NATO northern flank.

To counter this threat Sweden adopted a total defence concept in which virtually every able bodied man between 18 and 47 years received basic military training and might be expected to be called upon in an emergency. Both the Swedish army and navy operated special purpose companies to carry the war to the enemy. The army Parachute-Ranger Company, or 'Fallskarmsjägere', was LRPS and parachute trained and became expert at living off the land for sustained periods under all climatic conditions. The navy Coastal-Rangers Company, or 'Kustjargarskolan', formed part of the Naval Coast Artillery and specialised in combat, surveillance and targeting missions for the conventional troops in its parent brigade. Both units were highly mobile and trained to operate from landing craft or helicopters as necessary.

Although Norway did not allow the permanent stationing of foreign troops on her soil she willingly hosted a series of annual exercises involving a number of elite NATO units, notably the British 3 Commando Brigade. Her own army was small, but highly effective and motivated and could have been deployed quickly in the instance of a surprise attack. The standing army was small, comprising only 24,000 troops including 18,000 conscripts. However these were backed up by a staggering 146,000 trained reserves, many of whom were skilled skiers totally at home in arctic conditions.

Norway had a small company-sized special forces unit trained in long range reconnaissance, sabotage and demolitions. All members were parachute trained, LRRP experts and combat swimmers. The company comprised a small permanent cadre supported by regular soldiers on a two year attachment and trained regularly with the Royal Marines Commando Mountain and Arctic Warfare Cadre. It was considered one of the best special purpose units of its kind in the world.

5 The Post-War Years

Denmark formed a special operations company, or Jaeger Corps, in 1961 to supplement its small peacetime army of 17,000 officers and men including 6,800 conscripts. Although Denmark had no airborne capability all Jaegers were parachute trained and had to attain exacting standards before acceptance into the company. Training incorporated the usual special forces skills of demolitions, unarmed combat and communications, swimming, SCUBA diving and boat handling with special attention being given to fitness, endurance and the ability to live off the land. Unusually, Denmark relied heavily on its highly motivated volunteer Home Guard, or 'Hjemmevaernet', rather than its regular army, for protection.

6
Crême de la Crême
Selecting the Elite

During the Second World War elite forces and specialist units were invariably recruited and trained under conditions of absolute secrecy. Volunteers were sought but rarely told why, save perhaps that their services were required for 'special' operations. Once selected for training those who failed to make the grade, or who simply 'wanted out', became a security liability. Some were 'RTU'd,' returned to their old units. Others were forced to soldier on regardless. Airborne forces who completed parachute training, and accepted the financial rewards for doing so, were warned that they faced court-martial if they refused to jump in combat. The German 'Werewolves', some as young as 13, were summarily executed if they declined to join their suicide squads.

A Civilian Elite
SOE employed equally drastic, though rather more humane methods of preserving its anonymity. Initial screening was thorough, and gave the subject every opportunity to withdraw. As he or she progressed through the early selection stages the true nature of the Executive's clandestine work was gradually revealed, to allow the hesitant the opportunity to consider the full implications of irregular warfare. Those who wavered were rarely given a second chance.

Volunteers who were accepted for training by SOE were subjected to a long and gruelling assessment programme to ensure their suitability as agents. Those who failed were offered alternative employment within SOE or, if unsuitable, were sent on other courses for different work. Security risks were posted somewhere distant and insignificant, typically to a series of workshops in the remote Highland village of Inverlair (said to be the inspiration for the television series 'The Prisoner').

No records were kept of how many recruits were rejected, and at what stages, although it is known that Baker Street received detailed weekly progress reports on each student. Most reports were destroyed after the war, as were the majority of SOE records. However, from those which remain it is clear that many instructors clashed on their assessments, particularly of women candidates.

The entire training programme took place in a series of schools, many of them located in country homes requisitioned for the purpose. All were staffed by FANYs and, despite the rigidity of the training, were relatively palatial. Preliminary training was in physical fitness, with considerable time dedicated to cross country runs, elementary map reading and rudimentary weapons handling. Where practical theoretical lessons were conducted in the student's 'field' language.

6 Crème de la Crème

Security was unrelenting. Trainees were known by codenames and were told not to discuss their personal lives with each other, although inevitably human nature prevailed at times and it seems that many did. Supervision was constant. Each house was provided with a well-stocked bar which the recruits were encouraged to use to test their security under drink. On a few occasions discreet overnight 'companions' were even provided to ensure the agents did not talk in their sleep and, if they did, in what language!

Wanborough Manor, a secluded manor house situated off the Hog's Back near Guildford, was the best known of the schools. Run by Roger de Wesselow for F Section, responsible for agent infiltration into France, it quickly attained a reputation for excellence. Locals were advised that the house had been commandeered for Commando training but nothing else, and were left to decide for themselves why so many of the students appeared to be middle aged men or attractive women.

Those who failed the first stage of training, or felt that they lacked the aptitude, were returned to normal life, perhaps after a short period in Inverlair. The rest were sent to the west coast of Scotland, to a site close to Gubbins' home (see chapter four), where they mastered the physical aspects of resistance. Intensive physical training, endurance exercises and rock-climbing were interspersed with lessons in advanced weapon handling. Candidates learned to strip and reassemble not only the British Sten and Bren guns but all types of French and German medium machine-guns under pressure and at night. Unarmed combat, silent killing (always a contentious issue), demolitions and sabotage were also taught as the course progressed as was basic Morse Code, which was required for identification purposes on the drop zone.

Survivors were sent to Beaulieu to learn the defensive aspects of espionage; how to recognise the enemy by uniform and rank, how to avoid the attention of collaborators and how to behave when stopped at a routine road block. As their time at Beaulieu progressed students were tested in their ability to resist interrogation. Shaken awake in the middle of the night they were taken to cells and questioned (though never tortured) for hours, perhaps days, to test the strength of their cover story under duress. Failures were retested after further training or, if necessary, transferred to other duties.

Technical training followed on from Beaulieu. Parachuting was taught by Department STS 33 from a large house at Altrincham near Manchester, with drops into the grounds of Tatton Park. Wireless operators were sent to Thame Park, near Oxford, where they received a thorough grounding in Morse Code, the theory and practice of transmission and reception, and coding and cyphering techniques.

No amount of training could prepare the agent for the numbing shock of seeing so many enemy uniforms on the streets. Nor could it quell the feeling of sheer terror experienced when first presenting a set of forged identity papers for inspection. It has become the vogue in certain quarters to question the effectiveness of SOE to the war effort and to deride its methods of selection and training. Certainly it made a number of mistakes, some of which proved fatal to its operators in the field. However no one can doubt the dedication of the men and women who, after months of selection and training willingly dropped (in a number of cases more than once) into enemy territory.

The Basis of Special Forces Selection

The training and selection of military elites has always depended upon the role envisaged for the particular unit. Whereas applicants for all special purpose forces must share a number of essential attributes such as fitness, tenacity and strength of character, other requirements may vary drastically. Excessive aggression, lauded in a paratrooper, is regarded as dangerous in a marine who may have to spend months closely confined on board ship. Equally, introversion, common within the ranks of the SAS and Green Berets, is despised by larger elites with more 'formal' military traditions.

Not surprisingly therefore, every major elite has developed its own selection process, the length and complexity of which reflects the number and diversity of that unit's operational tasks.

SAS Selection

The SAS has become renowned for its willingness to embrace every type of unconventional warfare and demands of its candidates for selection a high degree of mental dexterity as well as physical fitness.

Today it comprises three regiments, coordinated by SAS Group Headquarters. 22 Special Air Service Regiment (22 SAS) is a regular army unit, made up of approximately 650 men, and is barracked at Stirling Lines, on the outskirts of Hereford. Soldiers selected for 'the Regiment' (as it is universally known within its own ranks) will be invited to stay as long as their services are of value. Officers serve for a two-year tour on attachment, after which they return to their parent units. The best are invited to volunteer for second and subsequent tours as their army careers progress.

21 and 23 SAS are Territorial Army (reserve) units with headquarters in the Duke of York's Barracks, Chelsea and Birmingham respectively. The two TA regiments are of roughly the same size as 22 SAS and have a number of satellite squadrons located throughout the country. They are staffed by Permanent Staff Instructors (PSIs) from the regular regiment with whom they maintain close links.

The selection and training of the Special Air Service is the most arduous in the British armed forces. There is no direct recruitment to 22 SAS. Every member of the Regiment has volunteered for service from another regiment or corps, a fact which often gives rise to the charge that the SAS 'poach' some of the best officers and soldiers. Attendance on one of the Regiment's twice-yearly selections is not always a good career move. Those who RTU, by far the majority, are often seen by their parent units as misfits while those who succeed may have to take a voluntary drop in rank and will sometimes miss the opportunity for accelerated promotion.

Selection begins in the Brecon Beacon mountains in Wales, with a series of fitness and map-reading tests over ten days which are designed to bring every candidate up to the same basic level of fitness. These exercises are carried out in groups of twenty men; the distances to be covered and the complexity of the routes to be followed are increased over this period.

On successful completion of the first phase, the emphasis is switched to solitary marches and map reading exercises, designed to test the individual's self-reliance. Many soldiers, accustomed to working in section-sized units fail at this stage. At the end of the ten days of tests, a forced march of 65km awaits the candidates; this must be completed in twenty hours, while carrying 25kg of equipment, water and rifle (without sling). Known by the candidates as 'Sickener Two', the march takes place in the Beacons or on the Black Mountains of Wales. It is as much a hill-walking exercise as a run, with scheduled checkpoints which must first be located from the map. Standards are uncompromising and injuries and illness are not regarded as reasonable excuses for failure to reach a rendezvous on time.

The candidates who pass basic selection, on average less than twenty per cent, proceed after a week's leave to Continuation Training. This lasts for around six months and tutors the potential recruit in all the SAS patrol skills: weapons handling, combat and survival, reconnaissance, medicine, demolitions, camouflage and concealment, resistance to interrogation and other skills. Continuation includes a five-day escape and evasion exercise which concludes in an interrogation phase, and culminates in the soldier being tested, along with three other hopefuls, in a four-man patrol jungle exercise in the Far East. The failure of any one man in the patrol will result in the failure of the entire team.

During the entire period of the assessment, candidates are screened for any qualities which might make them unsuitable for service in the SAS. A good deal of mental stress is added to the physical pressure of the selection; it is customary for recruits to be asked to make a logistic plan, or perform some intricate task requiring patience and concentration when already exhausted by exercise. Any tendency to irritation under stress, immaturity or lack of judgement will ensure the failure of a candidate who might perform the physical tests admirably.

At the end of the Continuation Training, and on completion of a basic static-line parachute qualifying course, the candidate is at last 'badged' SAS and awarded the coveted sand coloured beret. However, training will continue for a further eighteen months, until the recruit has completed specialist courses in the various disciplines which are required within the SAS.

Such courses may include: signalling, proficiency in languages, demolition, field medicine, free-fall parachuting, close protection driving, combat and close quarter shooting, underwater swimming, boat handling, unarmed combat and mountaineering. At the end of the specialist training the recruit will become a fully-fledged member of the Regiment, though training for certain types of SAS operations (notably the anti-terrorist role) will require yet further intensive periods of study and practice.

Training and selection for 21 and 23 SAS follows the same pattern, although selection is spread over a far longer period and is inevitably less severe. It begins with a 9km run - twice the distance of the British Army basic fitness test - to test stamina and incorporates fortnightly exercises of increasing difficulty culminating in a two-week camp. Successful attendance at every weekend is mandatory, and absence for any reason will result in the recruit having to withdraw to the next assessment course.

The gruelling training programme and 'sickener' exercises, designed to deter recruits attracted by the mysterious ethos of the Regiment which shrouds itself in secrecy, result in an exceptionally high calibre of SAS officer and trooper. 22 SAS has been described as a 'bunch of misfits who happen to fit together,' an apt description for a unique unit in which many of the tenets of conventional military discipline have been dispensed with in favour of the self-discipline of the individual soldier.

Australian Variations

The Australian Special Air Service Regiment (SASR) works in close conjunction with its British equivalent. Cross-postings are common and information is regularly shared. Yet its selection process is fundamentally different. The SASR is based at Campbell Barracks, Swarbourne near Perth, Western Australia, far from the majority of the country's population and the rest of the Army. This poses problems in recruiting as success may well result in the soldier (and his family) being posted to a social backwater.

During their military careers many of the best infanteers elect for a tour with one of the crack Regional Force Surveillance Units (RFSUs), such as NORFORCE based in Darwin, and as such are not available for SASR selection. The Regiment has therefore had to look increasingly to recruits from the support arms, and has had to concede that many may not be up to the required level of fitness when presenting themselves for candidature. Before joining the three-week selection course, aspiring candidates are advised to start exercising heart and lungs and to develop stamina. As in all facets of training this is most efficiently achieved by running. However clerks and technicians, however well motivated, may well not be given the time to prepare themselves fully; unless, of course, they are blessed by that most unusual of beings, a sympathetic commanding officer!

SASR selection is in essence a test of character which, on average, just under 50 per cent of the recruits pass. The majority of the failures either leave voluntarily or are retired due to injury or an inability to cope with the punishing schedule. The SASR Reinforcement Wing, responsible for selection and training, uses the first few days of the course to weed out those not fully committed to the special forces ethos. The numerous runs and assault courses are timed and every candidate, whatever his standard of preliminary fitness, is expected to show a constant improvement. Conventional military discipline, which is largely discounted in Hereford, is rigidly adhered to in Swarbourne with regular room inspections and severe punishment for those who fail to keep their rifles clean or within arms length at all times.

The first selection test, the timed run, is carried out carrying a rifle, two magazines, two full water bottles and a day's rations, weighing in total 10kg. The course is over 14.5km and must be completed in 90 minutes. In marked contrast to Hereford, failure to attain the required time will not automatically result in a candidate being returned to unit. A soldier forced to join the course less than fully fit, and who just fails the run while obviously giving 100 per cent, may not be rejected if the staff instructors regard him as 'trainable'.

During this phase the aspirant is also tested on his willingness to walk alone at night in the bush and cope with confined spaces and heights. In training he will be expected to swim with his rucksack across rivers and may be required to undertake combat-swimmer missions. All recruits must therefore pass a swimming test, although the poor swimmer will find the staff eager to provide additional coaching.

Self-discipline, initiative and strength of character are tested in the final stage of selection, the endurance march. The course moves to the arid Sterling Ranges of South-West Australia, which boast several peaks in excess of 800m. After an introductory twelve-hour navigation walk over a single peak, the candidate is expected to negotiate five peaks in as many days while carrying a 50kg rucksack. Heavy and awkward, the unwanted load not only alters completely the soldier's centre of balance thus impeding him during the climbs, but constantly snags in the dense undergrowth.

Selection is followed by an SAS Patrol Course which teaches the individual patrol skills; then by an obligatory static-line parachute course. At this point the soldier is posted to the Regiment and enters the Reinforcement Training Cycle to learn basic demolitions, weapon handling and survival skills. A Regimental Signaller's Course follows, conducted by 152 Signals Squadron, at the conclusion of which each soldier must demonstrate the ability to send and receive Morse Code at a speed of ten words per minute. Finally students complete a combat medical course with emphasis placed on the treatment of injuries, particularly gunshot wounds.

Following these courses 'reinforcements' are posted to their squadrons, but before joining them they receive continuation training in their new specialisations. These may include small boat handling and underwater swimming for the Water Operations Troops (Australia has no equivalent of the Special Boat Service), free-fall parachuting or an SAS-orientated drivers' course for those who have chosen a Vehicle Mounted Troop.

The complete selection and training cycle takes approximately ten months after which the new Ranger is posted to his squadron to continue 'Advanced Training' in shooting, fieldcraft, land and astro-navigation, small unit tactics and a myriad ultra-specialisations peculiar to his particular troop.

New Zealand Rangers

The New Zealand Special Air Service Squadron, known as the 1st Ranger Squadron New Zealand Special Air Service, was originally formed in 1955 under the command of Major Frank Rennie. From its earliest days the squadron has been closely associated with both the British 22 SAS and the Australian SASR. Indeed the New Zealand Minister of Defence, the Honourable Tom Macdonald, made the following announcement about the decision to form the New Zealand SAS:

'The New Zealand squadron will be in all respects similar to the squadrons of the 22nd Special Air Service (British) Regiment at present in Malaya...Every member of this regiment is a volunteer and in the British Army it is considered a high honour indeed to be selected for the Special Air Service'.

The initial recruitment policy in 1955 was unusual in that 138 of the initial volunteers were drawn from civilian life and only the 40 officers and NCOs from the regular army. Of these less than 100 were ultimately selected for service seven months later. The period from raw recruitment to operational status was so short that the troop was forced to complete its parachute training and in-theatre jungle warfare courses in Malaya. On return from Malaya the unit was temporarily disbanded, however following observation of the value of special forces in Malaya, it was reactivated in 1959.

In 1963 New Zealand commemorated the centenary of two units which had operated during the Maori Wars, the Forest and Bush Rangers, by renaming the squadron the 1st Ranger Squadron New Zealand SAS. The unit has not seen active service since its withdrawal from Vietnam in 1971. Today it recruits solely from the regular and Territorial Armies. The selection process is rigorous and similar to that of the British and Australian SAS units; testing fitness, intelligence, endurance and commitment. Training involves the usual special forces skills such as parachuting, survival, navigation and amphibious operations, with particular regard to tracking, a skill for which the large number of Maoris in the unit have made it world renowned. The *Rainbow Warrior* incident, in which French special intelligence forces blew up a Greenpeace ship in New Zealand waters killing one of the crew, and the hijacking of a New Zealand Boeing 747 in Fiji in 1987 has almost certainly caused the Government to reappraise the role of the SAS; increasing its capability in counter-terrorism and as a hostage rescue unit (HRU).

US Army Special Forces

The US Army Special Forces, known as the Green Berets, were introduced specifically to develop, organise, equip, train, and direct indigenous military and paramilitary forces in unconventional warfare. They are far more integrated into the conventional armed forces than their European equivalents, and as such most candidates for membership will already have proved their physical worth during airborne training or when undertaking a Rangers course before applying for selection.

The acceptance criteria for personnel volunteering for the Special Forces are very high. Applicants must pass a preliminary security vetting before the commencement of training - (SAS personnel also require 'PVTS' status - positive vetting top secret - before being accepted into the Regiment), must be airborne-qualified, or be willing to become so, and must be good swimmers, capable of swimming over 50m in boots and clothing. All must be High School graduates, must have passed their Advanced Physical Readiness test, advanced individual military training and Junior NCOs' cadre (E4-E7).

On arrival at Fort Bragg candidates face a gruelling three week preselection course, known as Special Forces Assessment and Selection (SFAS), designed as a cost cutting procedure to weed out the potential failures before too much valuable time and money are expended on them. Approximately half of an average class of 300 survive SFAS to win a place on the Special Forces Qualification Course ('Q Course').

The common-skills phase of the Q Course lasts five weeks and covers patrolling, close combat, airborne insertion, survival, and land navigation. Survival, camouflage and concealment, abseiling and navigation are taught by the Land Navigation and General Subjects Committees; the art of patrolling within the four-man 'A' Team by the appropriately named Patrolling Committee. The students are tested over twelve consecutive nights during which they are required to complete a complex navigation exercise, alone, in heavy woodland; a factor which in itself causes many to fail.

Survival, Evasion, Resistance to Interrogation and Escape (SERE) are taught as an independent package by Green Berets who were themselves captured in Vietnam. In marked contrast to other NATO 'prone to capture' troops, who are ordered to give only 'The Big Four' (name, rank, number and date of birth) to an enemy, United States forces operate a policy of controlled release allowing them to divulge non-military or redundant information should they be subjected to unbearable levels of physical or psychological abuse. Recent experience in the Gulf suggests that the United States policy is far superior; it was in fact successfully adopted by SAS Sergeant Andy McNab when tortured by the Iraqi security forces. The SERE course concludes with a three-day man-hunt in the Unwharrie National Forest during which the students, armed only with a knife, are expected to live off the land while evading a capture force drawn from elements of the 82nd Airborne.

At the end of week six, the surviving students are expected to specialise in one of the 'A' Team basic skills or 'military occupation specialities': weapons, communications, combat medicine or engineering. The basic signals course lasts 25 weeks and aims to make the students proficient in the operation of all radios in use by the Special Forces while giving them a grounding in the sending and receiving of Morse at up to eight words per minute - dangerously slow in covert operations. An advanced course will teach them basic radio repairs while increasing their Morse speed to a more acceptable rate of fifteen words per minute.

The Engineering course covers both demolition and construction techniques, bridge building and demolition and the manufacture and use of explosives. Weapons specialists learn to fire, strip, clean and reassemble a variety of heavy and light calibre weapons from around the world. Special Force medics undertake what is generally considered to be the most intensive field medical course in the world. The first eighteen weeks of their three phase course is spent at Fort Sam Houston in Texas, where they are instructed in basic medicine. They return to Fort Bragg for the advanced phase where they are taught preventative medicine as well as the treatment of disease, gunshot and shrapnel wounds. Students spend 21 weeks at Fort Bragg before putting their newly acquired skills into practice during the final four-week phase of the course spent in the casualty department of a military hospital. Those with the aptitude may then volunteer for a longer, and even more intensive advanced course in which they will learn major field surgery techniques such as amputation.

All commissioned and warrant officers undergo a nineteen week Detachment Officer Course in which they study the structure and operational techniques of the Special Forces, with particular regard to the command attributes required to handle the skilled personnel with whom they will be operating.

Although they will also be expected to qualify as weapons, engineer, signals or medical specialists, sergeants applying to transfer to the Special Forces may also undertake a sixteen week Operations and Intelligence Course to hone their skills in intelligence gathering, collation and evaluation.

All students are tested on their newly acquired physical and academic skills during the final phase of selection, a gruelling period of five weeks during which they are parachuted into the Unwharrie National Forest as part of Exercise 'Robin Sage'. In a simulated hostile environment the students have to locate 'friendly natives' drawn from the local population, demonstrate their skills to teach them weapon handling and organise them into an effective guerrilla force. During the final stages of the exercise the Green Berets lead their guerrilla forces in ambushes and raids against the 'aggressor force' again drawn from the 82nd Airborne.

In response to suggestions that Green Beret selection is too geared to the past lessons of Vietnam, the American Army Special Forces are currently experimenting with a new officer-selection scheme based on the Australian SASR course. Should this prove successful it may be extended to the selection process for all candidates.

After acceptance into the Special Forces the new members may volunteer to undertake any number of additional courses. A five-week military freefall parachuting course will teach them high-altitude/low-opening (HALO) or high-altitude/high-opening (HAHO) techniques essential for covert airborne infiltration. Should they prefer they may elect for one of three five-week underwater operations courses; Combat Diver, Combat Supervisor and Diving Medical Technician, in which they will learn to use both open and closed circuit breathing apparatus to depths of up to 41m.

Ranger Selection

Unlike their compatriots in the Green Berets, the Rangers are exclusively fighters with no interest in indigenous personnel training. They are inherently light shock-action troops, geared to the specialist arts of ambush and interdiction behind enemy lines. To apply for Ranger training soldiers must be medically fit and be able to pass the Army Physical Readiness Test. Those not airborne-qualified must attend a three-week jump course with the 4th Airborne Training Battalion at Fort Benning, Georgia to raise them to the required level of proficiency.

The parachute course is divided into three phases: Ground Week, Tower Week and Jump Week. Training is aggressive to instil the airborne spirit in the candidates from the outset, and undertaken at the double with morning runs and physical training the norm. Successful candidates then undertake the four-week Ranger Indoctrination Programme (RIP) designed to weed out the bulk of those considered unsuitable for Ranger training.

The course begins with two days of static-line parachute descents after which the students are tested on their basic infantry skills, on their performance in helicopter insertion (including a 65m abseil descent), their climbing, raiding and ambush skills. Throughout the third week the students' reserves of mental as well as physical stamina are tested during an operation from a simulated patrol base in which they are continually kept active, avoiding and setting ambushes and patrolling in a 'hostile' environment. The students are constantly assessed, with command regularly changing to allow the candidate to be examined both as leader and led. Inevitably many of the course fail to attain the high standards demanded by the Rangers, indeed it is not unusual for up to two-thirds of their number to be returned to their units at this stage.

Even those who pass the RIP are expected to spend from nine months to a year with a Ranger battalion, and may even then have to undertake a pre-Ranger School course before being considered ready for the Ranger School at Fort Benning. Unusually for special forces selection and training, most of the students they will meet on the Ranger course itself will be drawn from other units, particularly the Marine Corps and Airborne Divisions which use the School to advance the leadership potential of their best officers and NCOs.

Candidates must expect to work for up to eighteen hours a day, seven days a week throughout the course, which was recently extended from 58 to 65 days to accommodate additional training on the mountain phase. The first nineteen-day phase, which teaches basic skills such as map reading, patrol techniques and communications, is held at Fort Benning. Thereafter the students move to Camp Frank Merrill in Georgia where they are introduced to mountaineering skills. The third phase is orchestrated by the 2nd Ranger Company in Utah, and involves desert training to equip the soldiers with the techniques required for survival in extremely hot climates. Finally the 'swamp phase', held at Eglin Air Force Base in Florida, involves the perfecting of skills such as reconnaissance and boat operations in jungle and swamp conditions.

When qualified Rangers reach their units they serve a 22-month tour on an unrelenting 48-week annual training cycle in a variety of climates. They may train in advanced skills, such as parachuting techniques, sabotage or reconnaissance to build up their specialised skills, and will be kept in the peak of fitness to ensure that they remain constantly ready for any operation demanded of them as part of the United States Rapid Reaction Force.

Delta Force

Operational Detachment-Delta, usually known as 'Delta Force' or simply Delta, was created on 19 December 1977 to increase United States capability in counter-terrorism and hostage rescue. The motivating force behind the unit's creation was a colonel in the Special Forces, Charles Beckwith. He had been seconded to the SAS in 1963 and had become convinced of the need for the creation of an anti-terrorist unit modelled on the British lines.

Under Beckwith's command, selection and training processes were virtually identical to those of the SAS. However it is possible that since he relinquished command these have been refined to take into account Delta's more specialist role.

Delta personnel are recruited from qualified members of the United States Special Forces who undergo a period of further intensive physical and specialist training before acceptance. All potential transferees must attend a lengthy and very searching preliminary interview with a number of serving officers and NCOs of the group. Crucially they must also undergo psychological assessment to ensure that they are sufficiently self-possessed and mature to endure the hours, perhaps days, of sheer frustration and monotony which invariably precede an operation. Any signs of the 'Gung-ho' attitude so prevalent in certain of the United States special purpose forces would almost certainly lead to a candidate's rejection.

Fitness is of the essence. As well as completing timed speed and endurance marches, candidates have to perform an inverted crawl over 40 yards in 25 seconds, swim 110 yards fully clothed and in boots, and complete 37 sit-ups and 33 press-ups each in less than one minute. Deadly accurate, yet safe, speed-shooting is demanded, with candidates obtaining 100 per cent accuracy with a variety of weapons at 600 yards and 90 per cent accuracy at 1,000 yards. Close quarter battle skills are tested, and later honed, in a 'killing house' to enable accurate, snap combat-shooting at moving targets within the confines of a building. Siege-breaking exercises involving assaults on aircraft and buildings also figure prominently in the selection and refresher training.

Intelligence gathering skills receive considerable attention, as does training on state-of-the-art communications equipment and tuition in a variety of languages. A variety of more esoteric skills are also practised; including vehicle theft, aircraft refuelling, negotiation and hostage reassurance.

United States Navy SEALs

The United States Naval Sea-Air-Land (SEAL) units have their origin in the naval frogmen of the Second World War and are probably the most highly trained of all American Special Forces. Created on 1 January 1962 under the direct patronage of President John F Kennedy, their very title epitomises the sheer breadth of their ability.

The role of United States SEALs encompasses all the functions expected of modern day Special Forces, including tactical/strategic assault on specific targets of value, intelligence gathering, reconnaissance, counter-insurgency and anti-terrorist operations. They are the Naval equivalent of the Green Berets, but would not concede a jot of superiority to their Army counterparts; sharing all of the Army Special Forces skills, in addition to a number of maritime specialities of their own choosing.

Until their disbandment in 1983 SEAL Team personnel were drawn from the ranks of the Underwater Demolition Teams, themselves expert in underwater operations including conventional SCUBA and closed-circuit diving, demolitions and mine-laying. Officers and men undergo identical basic training, save that officers are expected to bear the added responsibility of team leadership.

Trainees undergo a vigorous 23-week course at the Basic SEAL Training Department of the Naval Amphibious School, Coronado, from which approximately 45 per cent emerge successful. The initial four week period is spent on runs, water sports and physical training, after which the recruits are tested to ensure that they have amassed sufficient strength and stamina to operate alone or in small teams in the midst of the enemy, while carrying enough equipment to operate for several days.

The residue of the course is conducted under simulated combat conditions with sleep, regarded as a luxury, kept to a minimum. During the final stages of the course, students transfer to San Clemente Island where they practise heavy underwater demolitions and complete a series of long swims, culminating in a five-mile marathon.

Once accepted into the unit, SEALs undertake continuation training in counter-insurgency oriented low intensity operations, study foreign languages and complete a HALO parachute course. Further specialised training takes place in techniques of infiltration and the freeing of ship-board hostages.

A SEAL team will be cross-trained in a number of specialisations which may include hand-to-hand combat, sniping, espionage, medicine, escape and evasion, camouflage, survival and close-quarter battle. The extremely high standard expected of SEAL personnel, together with the requirement to master more than one discipline, accounts for the long period of specialist training - up to one year, twice the duration of that of the Green Berets.

Swiss Paratroop-Grenadiers

Occasionally political and geographical conditions dictate the mode of training and even the structure of a country's Special Forces. Nowhere is this more true than in Switzerland. Since 1945 Switzerland has sat uneasily on the crossroads of East and West. Patently capitalist in her economic and social outlook, she has nonetheless remained, as far as her economic links with the West will allow, politically neutral. She is a member of neither NATO nor the European Union, and has never sought election to the United Nations.

6 Crême de la Crême

Since the recognition of her permanent neutrality in 1815, Switzerland has been determined to rely upon her internal resources rather than the fickle whims of her neighbours for protection. Control and training of the army was centralised in 1848 and has altered little since.

All fit males are liable for service in the militia. After a period of seventeen weeks continuous basic training undertaken at the age of eighteen, they become liable for up to 21 days service for the next eight years, and for ten days service for a further four. After thirteen years 'Auszug', or call out, they are deemed to have fulfilled their obligations to the 'active' list, and are transferred to the 'Landwehr' or Home Guard with which they serve for up to fourteen days per annum until the age of 42. Thereafter they transfer to the 'Landstrum' or Last Reserve with which they remain until the age of 50. Recently military involvement has begun to prove both commercially disruptive and politically unpopular. Equally importantly it has failed to produce an elite realistically capable of engaging in the rigours of modern warfare. However dedicated the reserves they are only able to operate within their own parameters, a problem which the Swiss Government came to realise would be compounded as a series of planned manpower reductions were to be implemented. To solve this problem the Parachute-Grenadiers, a regular army force capable of operating with minimum support in the most inhospitable of terrains, was formed in 1968.

All Parachute-Grenadiers are parachute trained and jump regularly under all conditions. Initial selection and aptitude tests take place at an early age whilst the potential recruit is still at school. Successful candidates are enlisted at the age of eighteen after which they undergo a two week civilian parachute course under non-tactical conditions. Those who make the grade receive a civilian qualification before passing on to the recruit school for a further five months training during which they make a further 80 descents by day and night, under all conditions, with and without weapons and heavy equipment. Parachuting technique is increasingly honed throughout training, with particular regard paid to the maintenance of tight formation during high and low altitude drops. More conventional training is introduced to ensure that at the end of the course successful Parachute-Grenadiers are proficient in night combat and navigation, close-quarter combat, recognition, navigation, survival and the use of enemy weapons.

The very best are encouraged to apply for membership of 17 Company, Parachute-Grenadiers, an elite within an elite formed in 1980 to undertake long-range reconnaissance and intelligence gathering missions. Uniquely the Company has no formally defined war role, and as such its members are expected to excel in every facet of operational military life. So exacting are the standards of entry for the Company, that of the 300 potential entrants annually short-listed fewer than 30 are ever selected for training, of whom no more than fifteen are ultimately selected.

Training within 17 Company, Parachute-Grenadiers is tough and exacting, emphasising totally the unremitting nature and terrain in which its members would be expected to operate. All normal special forces techniques are taught, with particular regard given to physical and psychological training, survival, escape and evasion and parachuting.

As ever parachuting skills are regarded as paramount. All Company members are taught the use of high performance military ram air parachutes (including tandem systems), and have experimented in the use of helmet-mounted secondary radar transponders. All have to master the calculation of glide paths, drop release points and opening altitudes for use in HAHO insertions, the preferred method of ingress during hostile operations. Unique among all airborne forces, the members of 17 Company frequently practise emergency procedures by actually uncoupling their main canopy and deploying their reserve.

Despite the unremitting hostility of the terrain, and their willingness to jump under all conditions including snow and even fog, Swiss Paratroop-Grenadiers have not sustained a single fatality in over 45,000 descents, a unique record of which they are justifiably proud.

Prior to acceptance into 17 Company, potential entrants spend a week training among the steep cliffs and gorges of Centovalli, a remote and inhospitable area close to the Italian border. Night navigation, tactical movement and fieldcraft, the sine qua non of the deep reconnaissance operative, are tested exhaustively. No quarter is offered or expected, and no comforts given. To survive, the students are expected to dig snow holes for protection and to live off the land. Injuries, occasionally serious, are common but at the end of the course the successful applicants know that they can regard themselves as members of one of the true parachuting elites of the world.

South African Recce Commandos

Despite the huge social and political changes overtaking the country, the Republic of South Africa remains the unrivalled military and economic powerhouse in the region. Traditionally it maintained security for its white minority rulers through the expenditure of massive sums on its armed forces, particularly its special and elite regiments. Many of the personnel in these units were drawn from the body of white national servicemen undertaking their two year period of conscription. Others were found by the reserve Citizen Force to which the national servicemen transfer at the end of this period to undertake a further 720 days of military service over six two-year cycles.

The Reconnaissance Commandos, otherwise known as the Recces or SpesOps, were the South African equivalent of the British SAS or the United States Green Berets. Established out of a need for a group with specialist reconnaissance and sabotage skills, the first unit - 1 Reconnaissance (Recce) Commando - was created in Durban on 1 October 1972. Since that time a number of additional units have been established; 2 Recce Commando in Pretoria, 3 and 5 Recce at Phalaborwa in the northeastern Transvaal close to the Kruger National Park, and 4 Recce at Langebaan in the Cape.

The Recce Commando remains one of the most secretive of all special forces units and much of what is written about it must remain speculative. In the past many volunteers had seen previous service with the ex-Rhodesian Selous Scouts, the SAS or the Rhodesian Light Infantry. Some had seen service with the Portuguese in Angola, a few were even reputed to have been mercenaries from Britain, Australia and the United States. However it may be assumed that, in the new political climate, such individuals are less welcome.

Unusually the unit accepts national servicemen, citizen force and regular soldiers. Prior to call-up for national service all prospective conscripts are supplied with a questionnaire in which they are asked to state whether or not they are interested in serving with the special forces. On the basis of these questionnaires applicants are called forward for preliminary selection.

During their first two weeks of training, national servicemen who have shown an interest in special forces training are subjected to the most rigorous physical, medical and psychological examination. Whilst every effort is made to stress the need for above average intellect as well as physical prowess, the pre-physical selection test is considerable. Every recruit must be able to complete: a 15km route-march with 30kg of equipment in two hours; a 5km cross country run in 20 minutes; 50 press-ups and eight pull-ups non-stop; 80 sit-ups in two minutes; 200m carrying a fellow soldier in the fireman's lift in one minute; 85 shuttle kicks in two minutes, and physiological tests to determine muscle and heart-lung functions.

Successful candidates undergo basic Recce training for three months. Following this they undertake an individual acclimatisation course of roughly four weeks duration. This is followed by a week-long selection course in the wilds of Zululand and the borders, to test candidates in simulated operational situations. Roughly 40 per cent of the initial course have normally dropped out by this stage. However, those successful now commence their initial special forces training proper at the Recce training school in Durban.

As with the selection course, the standards required in the eight month Recce course are extremely tough and are designed to push all candidates to their limits. Training includes instruction in the handling of explosives, demolitions and minewarfare, boating and sailing, parachuting, bushcraft, tracking and survival techniques, domestically produced and foreign weapons, unarmed combat, battle tactics, signals, medicine and land-air logistical and strike coordination techniques. Parachute training is identical to that undertaken by the Parabats (see below) and includes instruction in HAHO and HALO techniques. Throughout the course the soldiers are subjected to further exhausting physical endurance tests, during one of which they are expected to spend several nights alone in lion country with only a rifle, ammunition and box of matches.

Of those who initially volunteer for the Recce Commandos fewer than ten per cent ultimately graduate through the selection and training procedures. In a typical year, of 700 applicants, no more than 45 make the grade. At the end of their service national servicemen are transferred to 2 Recce for the duration of their Citizen Force liability. Some, however, apply during their second year of national service to join the special forces as regular soldiers or in a short-service capacity.

The Makings of a Special Purpose Force
The Parachute Regiment
The selection process for membership of the British Airborne forces is among the most arduous of its kind in the world. Traditionally the Parachute Regiment selects directly from the streets rather than from other regiments or corps. Selection begins after a period of basic infantry training which includes weapon handling, field craft and elementary first aid, although the principal aim is to get the recruits sufficiently fit to tackle the rest of the course. The Aldershot area in which the bulk of selection tradi-

Selecting the Elite

tionally took place is relatively flat. Steep and muddy artificial hills were therefore built into the Army's driver training area in nearby Longmoor to enable the Depot instructors to test the young aspirants' physical resources to the limit. However, basic training has since been transferred to Catterick where both the climate and the terrain are far harsher. An assessment exercise, known within the Regiment as 'Basic Wales' and held in the Black Mountains around Sennybridge, keeps the recruits under continuous physical and mental pressure and completes the first stage of their selection.

For the first few weeks of selection recruits who feel that they lack the aptitude for the Parachute Regiment, or who simply cannot stand its iron discipline and thirteen-hour training day, may leave on payment of a nominal discharge fee. Others, who in the opinion of the instructors fail to come up to the mark, or who fail the series of endurance runs, confidence courses and assault courses which span the basic selection phase, are weeded out.

The next stage involves more physically demanding exercises and support weapons familiarisation. The pressure is still not relaxed and the recruits are constantly assessed on their fitness, weapon handling and marksmanship skills. At the end of this phase the instructors review the individual recruits' progress to decide whether they are suitable for further training. If found wanting in certain qualities they may be transferred to a line infantry regiment, or if their physical abilities and military skills are letting them down, back-squadded to repeat all or part of the basic training cycle.

Those who pass the assessment face pre-parachute selection, or 'P Company', one of the most demanding physical tests in the British Army. Now in the peak of physical condition, the recruits undergo a variety of tests designed to assess their determination and self-confidence. These involve mastering the Trainasium, a terrifying structure of scaffolding poles and narrow cat-walks, 7-15m high and cunningly constructed to test the recruits' nerve and reaction to orders. After leaping gaps, leopard crawling across wires and standing unaided on the 15m 'shuffle-bars', the recruits are faced with a standing jump across a 2.5m gap. On each obstacle the recruits are given just three opportunities to overcome their natural fear, a mental process which they will have to overcome every time they stand by the open door of an aircraft. Failure is rare, but for those who refuse to jump it means the end of selection training.

Recruits must also prove their ability to negotiate two circuits of a 1,425 yard obstacle course twice in an average time of 17.5 minutes, complete a ten-mile squadded battle march carrying 50lbs of weapons and equipment in less than 105 minutes, and perform satisfactorily in a 'log race'. Teams of eight men carry a log the size of a telegraph pole over a 1.75-mile course of sand hills in twelve to fourteen minutes. Team members who drop out, or who in the opinion of the instructors fail to carry their due weight, are rejected.

Controlled aggression has always been the hallmark of the airborne soldier, and the old 'milling' tradition lives on in P Company. Recruits take part in a 60-second boxing match during which their courage and self-discipline are assessed. The instructors are not looking for boxing finesse, but for the ability to 'get stuck in' to the opponent regardless of personal feelings and pain.

Recruits who succeed in passing P Company are awarded the coveted red beret, and are then sent for four weeks fieldcraft and section tactics training in Sennybridge in Wales. Recruits are assessed on all their infantry skills, such as camouflage, concealment and movement, and on the more advanced techniques of patrolling and raiding. They learn to cease being individuals, and to function as a four-man team (known as a 'brick') within their section and platoon. At the end of this phase trainees carry out a live firing exercise in which they assault an 'enemy' position on one of the open ranges.

On completion of fieldcraft training the recruits are sent for parachute training at RAF Brize Norton. Starting initially with practice exits from a mock-up of a Hercules aircraft, the troops progress to controlled drops from towers, then from a captive balloon and finally seven qualifying jumps from a Hercules C-130 transport. At the end of the course, parachutists' wings are awarded to the successful recruits.

After two or three years experience in a rifle company, there is the possibility of further specialised training with the numerous support platoons and sections, or advanced parachute training with the 'Pathfinders' of 5 Airborne Brigade.

There is no permanent establishment within the Pathfinders and officers serve for two years with the unit and soldiers for three before returning to battalion duties. The Pathfinder platoon numbers only 30 men and the competition to join is intense. The total selection course is compressed into three weeks of sheer activity and comprises a series of navigation and endurance walks covering approximately 100km in three days, and culminates in a 50km tab across the Welsh Mountains or Dartmoor's North Moor carrying an equipment load of 25kg. The survivors are organised into four-man patrols for a tactical phase involving live firing and close quarter battle drills before undertaking a four-day long-range reconnaissance patrol exercise. Successful applicants are HALO trained before being awarded the coveted Pathfinder flash.

82nd Airborne Division

During Operation 'Urgent Fury', the invasion of Grenada in October 1983, the 82nd Airborne Division deployed into action from its base at Fort Bragg in less than eighteen hours. It is the US Army's primary reaction force and the mainstay of the United States Central Command Rapid Deployment Force.

Prior to joining the Division all personnel, regardless of their military occupation speciality (MOS), must complete the US Army's jump school at Fort Benning, Georgia. The training is carried out by the 4th Airborne Training Battalion and is designed to inculcate in the candidate, among other qualities, the correct attitude of mind in the airborne soldier. Training is hard and aggressive, and students are expected to perform their tasks quickly and without question.

Unusually there are a number of women in the United States Airborne forces and, although they are not expected to fight in combat they are airborne-qualified and serve in the support areas, releasing the men for combat duties.

The three-week Basic Airborne Course (BAC) is divided into three segments: Ground Week, Tower Week and Jump Week, and is designed to train both officers and soldiers in the art of military static-line parachuting. Before being accepted for the course students must prove themselves medically and physically fit and, regardless of age, must pass the Army Physical Readiness Test in the grade established for 17- to 25-year olds.

Ground Week is dedicated to the development of the students' confidence while improving their fitness. Each day begins with an hour of strenuous physical training, which includes a number of stretching exercises and callisthenics, and finishes with a 5km run. During the intervening hours the trainees learn the basics of static-line parachuting including aircraft drills, exit procedure, parachute control and the parachute landing fall.

Students are constantly monitored, and those considered satisfactory are allowed to proceed to Tower Week. While progressing from the 10m tower to the 76m free tower they master the skills of mass exit drops, crucial to the success of an opposed landing, learn to control the angle of their landing approach and how to steer their parachutes. Not only must they demonstrate the ability to perform all the skills that they have been taught in the first two weeks, but must prove they are completely familiar with the emergency drills in the case of a canopy malfunction before being allowed to progress to Jump Week.

Jump Week, the final phase, is the culmination of the previous two weeks' training. Students make five static-line jumps of increasing difficulty from both C-130 Hercules and C-141 Starlifter aircraft. The first jump is made from 1,250 feet using a basic T-10 parachute. The second jump is from 1,500 feet and executed carrying combat equipment which is suspended under the reserve parachute and lowered on a strap once the main has deployed. The third jump, also made from 1,500 feet, utilises a more complicated MC1-1B chute, the fourth returns to 1,250 feet but is made with a full pack at night and the fifth, generally regarded as the easiest, is a day jump from 2,000 feet.

Over 21,000 personnel a year successfully complete their fifth jump, are badged 'airborne' and become eligible to wear the coveted wings on their left breast. Of these a select few move to Fort Bragg and the 82nd Airborne Division.

The Fallschirmjäger

Historically the Fallschirmjäger, the West German paratroops, were regarded as among the finest of NATO's airborne elite forces. They have lost little of their motivation since German unification, and remain one of the most potent special purpose forces in the world. Essentially lightly equipped shock troops but with considerable anti-armoured potential, the Fallschirmjäger were until recently entrusted with the task of plugging gaps in the NATO front line until more conventional reserves could be brought into play. Although they had only a limited airborne role, they were nonetheless, and indeed remain, expert paratroopers.

Basic training is carried out at brigade level. Recruits undergo a series of physical and psychological tests prior to acceptance for training, and as a prerequisite must prove their ability to: run 5,000m in under 23 minutes, throw a shot put at least 8m, be able to long jump over 4m, sprint 100m in under 13.4 seconds and swim 200m.

Having been accepted for parachute training, the recruits first undertake a three-month basic infantry training course to learn the rudiments of weapons handling, fieldcraft, tactics to company level, and marksmanship. Thereafter they report to the German Army Parachute Training Centre at Altenstadt in Bavaria where they spend up to four weeks under the command of non-commissioned officers drawn from the 1st German Airborne Division.

6 Crême de la Crême

Training is intensive, and with one instructor for every eight students, highly personal. Having spent the first two weeks mastering canopy control and landing techniques the recruits progress to the 'Tower' where they are tested on what they have learnt. By the time that they are ready to parachute for real the recruits will have completed at least fifteen Tower jumps, and a number of 'dry runs' in a C-160 Transvall. During the fourth and final week of the course the students make five jumps: the first two without equipment from a height of 400m, the third with an equipment container, the fourth in darkness without a container and the fifth conventionally during daylight.

The course is hard, with a failure rate of up to 20 per cent. Those who succeed are awarded their coveted wings, which they wear on the right breast, and are assigned to a Luftländesbrigade as fully fledged Fallschirmjäger.

The new paratroopers spend the first ten to twelve months of their service with the battalion receiving further training in the use of their equipment and on tactical exercises from platoon to corps level. The best may apply for further training at the Airborne Training Centre - 'Luftlande und Lufttransport Schule' - situated in Schoengau, Bavaria. The centre offers 32 different courses including freefall, junior leadership, aircrew survival and a four-week Ranger course.

The Ranger course is considered one of the toughest of its kind in the world with over half the students failing on their first attempt - a particularly high figure considering the fitness and experience of the applicants. Infiltration, survival, ambush drills, prisoner taking and field interrogation are among the topics taught in this course, which finishes with a four-day escape and evasion exercise itself preceded by a 40km cross country speed march.

Fallschirmjäger passing the Ranger course are eligible to command a platoon in either an airborne infantry or air-mobile anti-tank company. Those who wish may apply for long-range patrol (LRPS) duties or seek membership of the Fernspähe companies, the German equivalent of the SAS specialising in HALO parachute-insertions behind enemy lines.

French Commandos de l'Air

France, with its independent strategic and tactical nuclear capability and its numerous overseas commitments, relies on a unique paratroop formation, the Groupement Fusilier Commandos de l'Air (GFCA), to provide its domestic and foreign air bases with the necessary level of security. The Air Commandos have a total strength of around 9,000, 75 per cent of whom are conscripts and nearly all of whom are airborne trained.

The GFCA contains its own elite squadron, the Escadron de Protection et d'Intervention (EPI). Almost unknown outside the French Air Force, the EPI is composed of professional servicemen or short-service volunteers, and contains some of the most experienced NCOs in the Air Commandos. Prior to joining the squadron volunteers must pass rigorous selection which concentrates on assessing their mental and physical abilities while under stress. Various tests at individual and group level must be passed throughout the selection course, which has a high failure rate. A high level of fitness is necessary for acceptance; the forced marches and cross country battle runs account for many of the drop-outs.

Aspirants with sufficient ability and self-motivation are allowed to proceed to continuation training, during which they concentrate on advanced military skills and small unit tactics. Like the Army's Compagnies de Reconnaissance et d'Action Profondeur (CRAP), EPI units operate in small groups, occasionally behind enemy lines. Unlike normal LRRPs however, the Air Commandos must be capable of operating in an urban environment necessitating a high degree of FIBUA proficiency.

Unarmed combat and close quarter battle (CQB) techniques are an essential part of the EPI's training programme, and the highest standard of martial arts must be attained by all personnel. Additionally the squadron's NCOs must achieve black belt standard in one or more of the martial arts. Further training includes the basic signals course, held at the GFCA headquarters at Nîmes, and advanced training at the Air Force's communications school.

Due to their special role, EPI paratroops receive additional training at both Air Force and Army establishments. They regard themselves as paratroopers first, yet enjoy the significant advantage of Air Force membership; unlike the Armée de Terre's 11th Parachute Division whose members make an average of fifteen jumps per year, the availability of aircraft to the GFCA enables its troops to average 70 to 80 parachute descents annually.

Parachute training in France is undertaken by the Army at its airborne school at Pau in southern France. All Air Commandos undergo their basic static-line courses at the school, and may go onto the more advanced courses such as HALO and heavy-drop.

11e Division Parachutistes

French paratroops constitute one of the world's largest airborne arms. Since their formation 'Les Paras' have conducted more operational drops than any other force and over the last quarter century have earned themselves a reputation as particularly tough troops. Before the Second World War, France's paratroops were part of 'L'Armée de l'Air', or Air Force, and the Army's first airborne units were not formed until 1956. Since then they have seen service in Egypt, Indo-China, Suez and Algeria. In more recent times France's paratroops have also served in Central Africa, particularly in Chad.

The present French airborne division, 11e Division Parachutistes (11th DP), was formed in 1971 by the merger of 11e Division d'Intervention and the 20e and 25e Brigades Parachutistes. The new division is completely self-contained, its 14,000 officers and men (over 75 per cent of whom are, again, conscripts) forming an important part of the Force d'Action Rapide (FAR), the French equivalent of the United States Rapid Deployment Force.

The airborne infantry elements of 11th DP comprise the 1e Régiment de Chasseurs Parachutistes based at Souge; 9e Régiment de Chasseurs Parachutistes based at Toulouse; 1e Régiment Parachutistes d'Infanterie de Marine (RPIMa) based at Bayonne; 3rd RPIMa based at Carcassonne; 6th RPIMa based at Mont de Marsan; 8th RPIMa based at Castres and 2e Régiment Etranger de Parachutistes (REP) based at Calvi, Corsica. 1st RPIMa has a para-commando/special forces role and operates under the direct command of the Divisional Headquarters. 3rd RPIMa, 8th RPIMa and 2nd REP comprise the Groupement Aeroporte, and as fully professional units may be deployed overseas without the prior consent of the French Government. Two other fully professional airborne units function outside the control of 11th DP: 2nd RPIMa and 13e Régiment de Dragoons Parachutistes, the latter a special forces reconnaissance unit paralleling the British SAS.

To qualify for the coveted 'brevets parachutistes,' the French parachutists' wings worn by all qualified members of 11th DP, volunteers must first pass through an intense training course at Ecole des Troupes Aeroportées (ETAP), near Pau, in southern France. Courses at ETAP are run throughout the year in all aspects of military parachuting, from basic static-line descents to advanced freefall and heavy drop (cargo resupply). The training is tough and the standards high, particularly as 'Les Paras' have a reputation within the airborne fraternity for getting the maximum number of men out of the aircraft door in the shortest space of time. In addition the French have a surprisingly good safety record.

Légion Etrangère/French Foreign Legion

One of the most legendary military formations in the world, the 'Légion Etrangère', the French Foreign Legion, came into being on 9 March 1831. Composed of foreign nationals rather than French citizens, the Legion soon proved itself to be one of the most capable and effective fighting forces in the world.

Today the Foreign Legion comprises a highly trained, well-equipped modern armed force of some 8,000 officers and men with its own infantry, armour, engineers and support units. All are totally professional and none more so than the Legion's dedicated Parachute Regiment - 2e Régiment Etranger de Parachutistes (2nd REP).

2nd REP was originally raised as the 2e Bataillon Etranger de Parachutistes (2nd BEP) at Satif, North Africa in 1948, where it spent three months undergoing airborne training before deploying to Indo-China. It was parachuted into Dien Bien Phu, by then surrounded by General Giap's Vietnamese forces, on 9/10 April 1954. By the time the French garrison fell on 7 May the 'paras' of 2nd BEP had fought constantly for 27 days and nights. The battalion was almost totally destroyed by the end of the battle, with the few survivors herded into captivity by the Viet Minh victors. The battalion however refused to die, and by using volunteers from other units was reformed prior to leaving Indo-China in November 1955.

Now established as a regiment and designated 2nd REP, the unit was deployed to Algeria between 1954 and 1962. During that time it accounted for over 4,000 of the enemy for the loss of some 741 of its own men. In seven years of sustained fighting its members were awarded a total of 38 Croix de la Légion d'Honneur, France's highest military decoration for bravery.

In June 1963 the Regiment came under command of Lieutenant Colonel Caillaud and slowly began to change its role from that of conventional paratroopers to paracommandos. It began to train in sabotage, mountain and ski warfare, amphibious operations and long range reconnaissance. Selection became tougher, and training more diverse. The Legion paras adopted their new role enthusiastically spending the next two years acquiring the requisite skills and techniques.

The entire 2nd REP is parachute trained and capable of conducting both airborne and airmobile operations. Legion paratroopers receive their basic infantry training on the French mainland with 4e Régiment Etranger, at Castelnaudary. All légion-naires enlist for a minimum for a minimum of five years, and those who volunteer and are selected to serve with 2nd REP are among the top recruits who pass out at Castel-naudary.

27e Division Alpine

The Force d'Action Rapide has its own specialist mountain warfare unit, the 27e Divi-sion Alpine formed in 1976 from the merger of the 17th and 27th Alpine Brigades. Over 2,500 of the 9,000 men who constitute the division are alpine trained and attached to one of the six Chasseur Alpins battalions. All Chasseurs must prove themselves physically fit and mentally alert before being accepted into the alpine elite, after which training remains on-going and rigorous. Each battalion has its own mountain training centre capable of holding a full company and it is not unusual for up to 20 per cent of the entire division to be involved in exercises or training at any one time.

The Italian Folgore Brigade

Italy was among the pioneers of military parachuting, having established a fully trained parachute company as early as 1938. By 1939 this had been expanded into two battal-ions each of 250 men, both of which were deployed to Libya. A third battalion of 300 was raised at Castel Benito in 1940, and in 1942 all three battalions, together with their logistic support, were reformed into the Folgore Airborne Division.

After the war the Italians retained a nucleus of airborne troops, using them to re-establish the Parachute Training School at Tarquinia in 1946. A Parachute Brigade was created in 1952 and it was from this that the present Folgore Brigade evolved. Today the Brigade forms part of the FIR (Forza di Intervento Rapido) with responsi-bility for the defence of southern Italy.

All members of the Folgore Brigade are volunteers. Training, which lasts for sixteen months, is very intense with great emphasis being placed upon physical fitness and personal reliability. An initial 18 weeks is spent in fitness training, after which the recruit spends ten weeks studying communications, fifteen weeks mastering underwa-ter operations including demolition, six weeks in parachute training, twelve weeks with the artillery and eight weeks in alpine familiarisation and skiing.

The 9th 'Colonel Moschin' Assault Parachute Battalion, the special forces of the Italian Army, is formally part of the Folgore Brigade. With an approximate strength of 225 men, the Battalion comprises a headquarters, a training company and an opera-tions company, with an additional company authorised in wartime. The Battalion, which is trained to operate in groups of between two and twenty men, keeps itself at the peak of readiness. Although not as proficient as some of its rivals in general spe-cial forces skills, the Battalion is nonetheless regarded as one of the most able of spe-cialist units in NATO.

South African Parachute Brigade

Prior to the formation of the Recce Commandos in 1972 the South African Parachute Brigade (Parabats) constituted the country's elite reaction force. the Parabats were trained as a quick reaction force using helicopters and aircraft. In a conventional scenario their role ranged from raiding in the enemy's rear to reinforcing hard-pressed ground troops. In the counter-insurgency (COIN) role they were trained either to operate as stopper groups in support of the mechanised divisions or in the airmobile assault role. They were used extensively in cross-border incursions, particularly against SWAPO insurgents, but are now developing a less contentious profile.

The selection and training standards of the Parabats are extremely tough, and some 60 per cent of prospective entrants fall out along the 22-week training course. This takes place at parachute school attached to 1st Parachute Battalion (1 PARA) in Bloemfontein. Volunteers are recruited and selected from the national service battalions and then transferred to 1 PARA with whom they complete the standard three-month basic training course. Parabat basic training places great stress on physical fitness, so much so that some twenty per cent of the recruits accepted for basic training fail to finish the course.

Basic training is followed by six weeks of advanced individual training, which includes instruction in driving and vehicle maintenance, weapon handling, signals and unarmed combat. Physical training is intensified, and includes fourteen days of dedicated fitness enhancement during which the recruits complete a series of 16km runs carrying tar-covered poles or dragging motor car tyres tied to the ends of chains. Physical training is carried out in groups of twelve to create feelings of camaraderie among the trainees. Those who report sick for any reason are returned to their units. Over 50 per cent of the original survivors drop out or are returned to unit during this tortuous phase.

Before a student is allowed to progress to the jump phase he must fulfil yet more physical requirements including: scaling a two-metre wall with full kit; climbing a five-metre rope; running 200m in 75 seconds in full battle kit while carrying a fellow student, also in full battle kit with rifle; completing 67 sit-ups in two minutes; completing 49 seven-metre shuttle-runs in 90 seconds; and completing 125 squat kicks and 32 push-ups in two minutes each.

The sole aim of the physical training phase is to ensure that the recruit has the aggression, determination and above all perseverance to make a good Parabat. Those whom the Regiment feels pass this test begin formal parachute instruction with two weeks of hangar training, including simulated jumps from a training tower or 'Aapkas' (literally 'Ape-cage'). The first actual jump takes place after ten days of dry training, and is usually from an altitude of approximately 600m. Wings are awarded after the successful completion of seven jumps, including two at night and four with equipment.

A number of the best graduates are invited to volunteer for the elite Pathfinder group. This six-week course grants them skills comparable to those of the Recce Commandos, and in the past would possibly have found them operating with 'turned' guerrillas in pseudo-terrorist operations.

The Israeli Paratrooper

No soldier in the world has seen so much concentrated action or played so crucial a part in the survival of his country as the Israeli paratrooper. 'Hatzanhanihm' - the Paratroops - were formed on 26 May 1948 during the War of Independence and at the time consisted of a loose collection of British-trained soldiers, resistance fighters, Holocaust survivors and the occasional mercenary. Today the 'Zahal' - Israeli Defence Forces - maintain three regular paratroop brigades, the 202nd, the 890th and the 50th Na'ha'l (Pioneer Fighting Youth), as well as three reserve brigades.

All fit Israeli men are liable to undertake three years national service (four years for officers) followed by regular periods in the reserve until the age of 54. Many volunteer for the parachute brigades and ancillary units but only a few are accepted. Initial selection ('Gibushon') lasts for just over a day during which the applicant must prove his physical, mental and spiritual worth. Those selected undertake six-months basic training with one of the airborne brigades during which they may volunteer for one of the specialist parachute reconnaissance units, for which they must undergo a longer and more complex 'Gibush.'

The first phase of basic training lasts for fourteen weeks and is geared to physical fitness during which the recruit is taken to the limits of his physical and mental endurance. During weapon training he familiarises himself not only with domestic and Western firearms but with a whole series of weapons which he is likely to capture from an Arab enemy. Most of the training is under field conditions and much of it consists of long, harsh forced marches('Masa'ot'). Although there are indications that these are being reduced in intensity due to the high incidence of stress fractures among new recruits, two marches remain of particular importance. During the first, held at the end of the first phase of basic training, the recruit receives his unit tag; at the end of the second he is awarded the coveted red beret, and is registered as a 'rifleman 3rd class'.

Before the commencement of the second phase of basic training those considered inadequate for the 'Hatzanhanihm' are posted out. The survivors join a training platoon with which they spend two months mastering helicopter operations, FIBUA and their assigned weapon-role: machine-gunner, radio operator or mortarman. The final phase of training is spent at the Tel Nof Jump School where, having undertaken five successful static line jumps, they are awarded their coveted wings. With basic training over they are posted to an operational unit where advanced training continues. All paratroopers are expected to complete 'Kours Ma'kim' (squad leader course) upon the successful completion of which they may either return to their unit or elect to become instructors for the next wave of new recruits.

During any period of training the recruit may ask to be considered for transfer to a 'Sayaret' or Reconnaissance unit, all of which are parachute trained but independent of the brigades. Of these the finest are considered to be the highly secretive 'Sayaret Matkal' under the direct control of the Defence Minister, the 'Sayaret Haduzin' consisting entirely of Druze Muslims, and the 'Sayaret Golani', made up entirely of regular soldiers.

Naval Special Purpose Forces
Royal Marine Commandos

Today the Royal Marine Commandos are organised into a brigade strength unit, 3 Commando Brigade, which has its headquarters based at Mount Wise, Plymouth. Three commandos comprise the strength of the Brigade; 40, 42 and 45 Commandos, Royal Marines, each roughly equivalent to an Army battalion of 650 men. The Brigade possesses its own air squadron, signal squadron, air defence troop, logistical support regiment and raiding squadron. Heavy-weapon support is provided by 29 Commando Regiment, Royal Artillery, while engineer support is provided by 59 Independent Commando Squadron, Royal Engineers and the Territorial Army unit, 131 Independent Commando Squadron, Royal Engineers.

Commando training, which is generally considered to be one of the most physically exhausting courses in the British armed forces, is administered from the Royal Marine base at Eastney, near Portsmouth, though most actual training is conducted from Lympstone in Devon and Poole in Dorset. Initially all recruits must pass a potential recruits course during which they are not just assessed by the instructors but assess their own suitability for life as a Royal Marine. Those who are accepted spend a total of 26 weeks, extended to one year for officers, undergoing basic training.

Part One of the training course lasts fourteen weeks and concentrates on establishing a high standard of physical fitness, with regular forced marches and runs incorporated to build stamina. Conventional training in weapon handling, tactics and communications is given, interspersed with an introduction to the more specialist arts of emplaning and deplaning from helicopters and landing craft, abseiling, mountaineering and rock climbing techniques.

Part Two training, or group training as it is known lasts a further twelve weeks and includes lectures on the remaining infantry support weapons, basic seamanship and amphibious operations. Recruits are also taught the basics of internal security tactics and rapid deployment from vehicles. The course culminates in a final four day regime of assault courses, the 'Tarzan' course, weapons proficiency and swimming tests, a nine-mile speed march and a 30-mile endurance march across Dartmoor with full equipment and weapons.

On successful completion of the Commando 'Pass Out' tests the recruits become Commando qualified Royal Marines and are awarded their coveted green berets and shoulder flashes. They then receive further instruction in arctic and jungle warfare, skiing, underwater swimming (using SCUBA and closed-circuit oxygen rebreather), and canoeing. Having successfully completed all aspects of their training they become eligible to volunteer for one of the specialist units within the Corps; Comacchio Squadron, the Mountain and Arctic Warfare Cadre and the Special Boat Service.

The men of the Mountain and Arctic Warfare Cadre are based in Plymouth and are tasked with teaching mountain and arctic warfare skills to their fellow Royal Marines. They are trained to operate alone or in small groups behind enemy lines on long-range reconnaissance, intelligence-gathering or sabotage operations anywhere in the mountains but particularly in the frozen wastes of northern Norway.

Selection is through continual assessment and is based on both classroom and field work. The course is arguably the hardest of its kind in the world with a pass rate as low as 20 per cent. It begins with a cliff-climbing phase on the coastal pinnacles of Lands End in Cornwall before moving to the mountains of Wales, and thence to survival and resistance-to-interrogation training in the Scottish Hebrides. A large section of the instruction phase (radio transmission, reconnaissance and sniping) is then conducted at the Cadre's headquarters at Stonehouse Barracks, Plymouth, during which the recruits must plan and execute a raid on a coastal signals installation.

The winter warfare and survival phase of the course is preceded by the military ski instructors course at Rjuken and comprises three months of intense arctic training. It culminates in an eleven-day exercise mirroring the Cadre's wartime role of providing 3 Commando Brigade with tactical reconnaissance. This takes the form of a 200-mile long-range reconnaissance patrol in simulated wartime conditions during which the four-man teams lie up in snow holes and carry out detailed reconnaissance missions against specified targets. They establish liaison with and brief 'partisan' groups from the Norwegian special forces who in return supply them with food and act as a tenuous safety line by replacing any faulty items of equipment such as radio transmitters.

After spending the winter in Norway the students complete a Pathfinder course in the Ben Nevis area of Scotland, followed by a static-line parachute course at Brize Norton. Finally they spend the final few months of the course in the Lake District, Cumbria, learning and teaching alpine technique which is tested on Exercise 'Ice Flip' in Switzerland.

Members of the Special Boat Service comprise the special forces element of the Royal Marines and thus justifiably regard themselves as an elite within an elite. Trained for long stays behind the lines the unit specialises in insertion by two-man Klepper canoes and small inflatables. The two-week preselection period for the acceptance course, which is designed primarily to dissuade the uncommitted and curious, is arduous in the extreme.

Preselection starts with a 20-mile endurance march, after which the candidate spends the night alone and without benefit of survival equipment before making a 30-mile march home. During the two days the men are diverted over numerous water crossings requiring them to swim a number of rivers carrying their bergens. Later the survivors are required to swim with their equipment to a landing craft 400m off the beach. The trainee's suitability for diving is established in the cramped and claustrophobic conditions of the 'lock-out' chamber used to leave and enter submerged submarines. Many students find that, however fit and self-assured they may be, they are simply incapable of adapting to the near zero visibility of North Sea diving.

The selection/training course is divided into aptitude testing and trade training, and encompasses the usual special forces techniques enhanced by the additional skills required of a water-borne specialist. These include beach survey and photography, endurance canoeing and swimming exercises, small boat training, parachute descents into the sea and coastal, astro and underwater navigation.

US Marine Corps

Although not regarded officially by the United States Government as part of its special forces, the Marines nonetheless undergo rigorous selection and training. The cream of the United States Marines volunteer for the Force Reconnaissance Units responsible for intelligence gathering prior to an amphibious landing. Known as 'Recons', the unit receives training similar to , but independent of, the US Army Special Forces and US Navy SEALs. Recon units are divided into Force Recon Company groups, operationally and structurally similar to the British SBS, and less specialist Battalion Recon Company groups.

6 Crème de la Crème

Force Recon training is long and intensive. Applicants must first have passed through the Marine Corps eleven-week 'boot camp' at either San Diego or Parris Island, and have served for a period with a Marine battalion. They must be proficient in all the usual basic infantry skills and many will have seen service with the Battalion Recon. They must be airborne qualified, or be willing to become so, and must be good swimmers and divers capable of using both open and closed-circuit breathing apparatus. Finally they must prove their ability to master one or more of the specialist skills of small boat handling, forward air controlling, artillery spotting and long-range reconnaissance.

COMSUBIN

As has already been seen no country in the world has a prouder history of mini-submarine warfare than Italy. The Italian Navy Special Forces, known as COMSUBIN ('Comando Subacquei Incursori') were formed in 1952 and now carry on this tradition.

COMSUBIN is based at Varigano, a small centre near La Spezia on the northwest coast, and is organised into five units, two in support and three operational. Support comprises the 'Gruppo Scuole' (Special School) and the 'Centro Studi' (Research Centre.) The 'Gruppo Scuole' trains not only COMSUBIN personnel but also other allied underwater specialists and the police. It is itself divided into the Underwater School, the Incursion School and the Installation Defence School.

The Underwater School is responsible for the selection and training of frogmen and deep sea divers and, unusually, is the only organisation in Italy capable of issuing a military diving licence. Frogmen, who attend an eighteen-week course at the School, are all conscripts. Deep sea divers, who are all professional servicemen, undergo a far more comprehensive six months instruction whilst the assault paratroopers of the 9th 'Colonel Moschin' Battalion undergo an intensive and diverse ten week training course.

Nowhere within the COMSUBIN are the traditions of the Italian 'human torpedoes' of the Second World War more revered than in the Incursion School. It is here that future 'Incursore' are selected from among volunteer officers and NCOs of the regular navy. The ten months training which follows initial selection, incorporating as it does lessons in tactics and equipment, ordnance and weapons, climbing, diving and unarmed combat, together with a period at the Military Paratroop School, Pisa (where HAHO and HALO techniques are taught) is so intensive that only five per cent of those originally accepted for the course can hope to pass out successfully. Even then the fledgling 'Incursore' must spend a further fourteen months undergoing in-house training before being considered fully qualified.

The elite 'Demolitori Ostacoli Antisbarco' (Shore Demolition Unit) of the 1,000 strong 'San Marco' Marine Battalion must pass a gruelling ten week course at the School. The 'Servizio Difesa Installazioni' (Installation Defence School) selects and trains conscripts in the role of shore base defence in a one month course covering matters as divergent as the physical security of buildings to countering attacks by enemy frogmen.

The COMSUBIN operational group comprises the 'Gruppo Operativo Subacquei' (Underwater Operational Group), the 'Gruppo Navale Speciale' (Special Naval Group) and the 'Gruppo Operativo Incursori' (Incursion Operational Group). Underwater divers are trained not only in the defence of domestic bases but in submarine rescue, and thus have to prove their ability to master diving bells, deep diving systems and even mini-submersibles as well as using air lines and conventional respirators. The Incursori, the offensive arm of COMSUBIN, is small comprising fewer than 200 men of all ranks, and is necessarily extremely secretive. It operates in teams of between two and twelve and spends much of its time in 'live' simulations of mine and sabotage attacks against the hulls of unsuspecting naval and merchant ships in the area.

The Russian Experiences

When the Soviet Union split up into its constituent states attempts were made to keep the armed forces centralised under the control of the Commonwealth of Independent States (CIS), formed in December 1991. However when it became clear that several states, led by the Ukraine, would accept nothing less than total military independence the scheme was abandoned. President Yeltsin issued a decree in May 1992 establishing the Russian Armed Forces and creating a Ministry of Defence. Russia then took control of all armed forces then based in Germany, Poland and the Baltic republics, the 14th Army based in Moldova and most of the units still in the Trans-Caucasus republics.

As the majority of elite units within the former Soviet Union were of Russian or Ukrainian extraction it seems highly likely that most former special forces troops are now serving in their newly independent armies. However, although a new formula has yet to evolve it is clear that selection, which in the past was based heavily on ideological competence, will have to undergo a radical change.

Spetsnaz, the former Soviet Union's coveted special forces, were the most feared troops within the Warsaw Pact. They were attached to the 2nd Directorate of the GRU ('Glavnoe Razvadyvatelnoe Upravlenie') and were thus responsible to Soviet Military Intelligence and not, as was often mistakenly thought, the KGB. As such their role was vastly different to that of the smaller, more highly trained NATO special forces.

Selection for Spetsnaz was by continuous assessment and began well before the potential recruit began his national service. Most men and women selected for the Soviet special forces had parents in the Communist Party, with impeccable political backgrounds. As young children most would have joined the Octoberists, transferring at the age of ten years to the Pioneers. Their impressionable minds would have been exposed to highly idealised stories of Red Army valour often told by highly decorated veterans of the Great Patriotic War. Xenophobia was encouraged, with the Soviet Union depicted as an island surrounded by its capitalist enemies.

Recruits were introduced to basic military training at the 'zarnitsa' (summer camps) under the watchful eye of retired officers. They were introduced to drill, guard duty, civil defence and first aid with basic soldiering and tactics introduced as a game. At the age of fifteen the politically aware transferred to the 'Komsomol' (Young Communist League) with whom they attended 'orlyonok' (Little Eagle) camps to develop skills in map reading and weapon handling. Throughout their time in Komsomol the progress of the recruits was monitored by the KGB, GRU and the Party itself, each of which competed with the others for potential recruits.

6 Crème de la Crème

While a member of Komsomol potential recruits joined DOSAFF (The Voluntary Society for Co-operation with the Army, Air Force and Navy) with which they undertook further orlyonok camps in addition to a minimum of 140 hours of training spread over two years. The best were taught parachuting, diving, radio skills, vehicle maintenance and other skills required of special purpose troops.

Conscripts drafted into the Soviet Army joined in one of two massive inductions undertaken each year. Those already earmarked by 'Komsomol' and DOSAFF as above average were sent to the rocket troops, the KGB (which maintained its own armed forces wholly independent of the Ministry of Defence,) the airborne or Spetsnaz. Training was harder for the airborne and Spetsnaz recruits. During an initial one-month training period they were taught basic fieldcraft, navigation, camouflage and weapons training. Those who failed to maintain the standards expected of them were transferred to the infantry. The best were sent to training battalions to undertake a six-month course to become sergeants. Although only the best young men were sent on these courses, standards were so high that many were returned to their units. Unlike successful sergeant-trainees in the conventional Soviet Army, Spetsnaz sergeants returned to their units as privates to provide a reserve for existing NCOs who became casualties in training or who failed to maintain the high standards demanded of them.

After initial selection potential officers were trained at the Reconnaissance Faculty of Kiev Higher Command Arms School and the Special Faculty of the Ryazan Higher Airborne School. They were integrated as far as was possible with the conventional officer cadets against whom they were constantly assessed. Failure to attain or maintain standards resulted in immediate transfer.

7
Weapons and Equipment of the Special Forces

Elites have always demanded the best in arms and equipment. They have expected to fight the bloodiest of battles for their commanders and to sustain great losses; in return they have regarded it as their right to bear the best available weapons.

Occasionally radically new weapons have evolved which have revolutionised the battlefield, necessitating the creation of a new elite to service them. The Sumerians were the first to appreciate the advantages of speed and mobility in battle when, as long ago as the third millennium BC, they introduced the primitive four-wheeled battle-wagon. This was drawn by teams of four donkeys or asses and was totally lacking in manoeuvrability. This lumbering platform offered no protection to its crew which immediately became a target for the enemy's archers, and were of necessity relegated to the rear echelons.

The War Chariot
However 500 years later three independent innovations, bent-wood construction technology, the horse and the composite bow evolved simultaneously to bring about a renaissance in the art of charioteering. The first horses to be domesticated were not ridden, but were harnessed to chariots in teams of four. The development of bent-wood techniques allowed the chariots to be constructed for the first time with lightweight bodies and spoked wheels with rims made of curved felloes. The new composite bow introduced a rapid-fire delivery system which in the hands of trained archers was capable of exploiting the battle platform offered by the new, highly manoeuvrable chariots.

The combination of chariot, and teams of four highly trained horses was extremely expensive to establish and maintain, requiring an entire support echelon including drivers and warriors, horse breeders and trainers, wheelwrights and chariot builders, composite bow-makers, metal smiths and armourers. Not unnaturally the employment of chariots in battle became the exclusive prerogative of the rich and powerful, allowing corps of elite mercenary charioteers to hire out their services dearly to the highest bidder.

Chariots were built with little protection for their two-man crews. The driver controlled the team of horses, and at the same time managed a light shield on his left arm. His partner likewise needed both hands for the task of archery. The chariots were equipped with a large stock of arrows which were shot from a small but powerful composite bow. The specially bred horses, which by 1600BC had been reduced to teams of two for easier control, were harnessed to a yoke attached to a single, long, curving shaft.

7 Weapons and Equipment of the Special Forces

The chariot was not only highly prestigious and expensive, but vulnerable. It was kept in reserve until a weakness in the enemy line became apparent. It was then introduced to create a breach in the enemy ranks which could be exploited by the supporting infantry. Thereafter the chariot might be used to harry and hunt down the dispersed enemy, preventing an orderly retreat, maximising losses in men and equipment.

The first to form an elite corps of charioteers, capable of undertaking independent action at great distances, were the Hittites of what is present-day Turkey. They had discovered the technology of bronze processing and were far ahead of their neighbours in the manufacture of weapons. They introduced sturdy, single-axle combat chariots capable of accommodating a driver and two warriors which they used to great advantage in their subjugation of the Semitic Amorites and Canaanites of the eastern Mediterranean.

The combination of chariots and bronze weapons in battle proved so convincing that both were quickly adopted by the Semitic tribes themselves and used in the vanguard of their expansion into Egypt.

Early Horsemanship

In 1530BC the Kassites came out of the mountains north-east of the Tigris and began to expand south-west, conquering Babylon and destroying the Amorite state in the process. Little is known of the Kassites save that they were among the first to employ horsemen in support of their charioteers, although it seems highly unlikely that these played more than a peripheral role in the ensuing battles.

Cavalrymen had become an integral part of the more advanced armies by 1000BC, but for about 1500 years thereafter remained an adjunct to the infantry. The more far sighted of the commanders, men such as Philip II of Macedon and Hannibal, realised the potential of an elite independent mounted force, but even they failed to formulate general rules for the organisation and role of the horse in battle.

Early cavalry rode bareback without the benefit of stirrups and saddle, and of necessity had to spend much of their time in the simple but essential task of remaining mounted. Inevitably this affected their mobility and steadiness, and it was not until the introduction of body armour that massed cavalry felt secure enough to engage enemy heavy infantry in close-quarter combat.

As the cavalry became more important, and gained the upper hand over the combat chariots, social attitudes towards the horse began to change and the social elite, who had once been driven into battle, now began to ride. This enhanced the status of the horse as an instrument of war, and many established armies began to create both heavy and light cavalries. The finest horsemen of this time were however irregular. The Scythian horse archers of the fourth century BC were masters of the curved composite bow. When the arrow was released it was driven forward with tremendous force by the combined effect of the released tendon and the straightening sides of the stave. Archers could fire forwards or backwards at the trot, discharging up to ten arrows a minute to a range of 400 paces.

One of the greatest advances in cavalry warfare came in the seventh century AD with the introduction of the saddle and stirrups. Riders could now control their horses more easily, giving them more freedom to use their hands, perhaps to carry a larger and heavier shield. The rider could lift himself in the saddle and deliver stronger blows at greater distances than his opponents, thus allowing controlled close-quarter battle.

Feudal Cavalry

After the fall of the Western Roman Empire in 476AD, parts of its former territory were settled by Germanic tribes who quickly established new social patterns and military elites. Horsemen belonged to the richer classes and were thus better equipped. As such they became more effective in combat and soon became the mainstay of military power. The Visigoths, inhabiting the area between Gibraltar and the Loire, were among the first to adopt mail or scale armour, helmets and rounded shields. The Langobards, from Tuscany and the Po Valley carried long spears (kontos) and broad swords (spathions) and occasionally maces, bows and javelins.

In western Europe feudal organisation gave birth to a tiered nobility with the large landowners; the dukes and barons in the higher echelons and the lesser nobility, the knights, below. Knights could afford better weaponry, horses and servants and quickly became an effective elite in combat. Prior to the twelfth century most knights carried double-edged swords and a short lance which could double as a missile if required. Throwing battle-axes were also favoured, although in Britain and northern France these were often replaced by heavier two-handed Norman axes.

From the end of the twelfth century, lances became longer (5m) and were steel-tipped. The double-edged sword remained, but with a longer hilt to enable double-handed use. Daggers were employed in close battle, as were short-handled maces with spiked iron balls. The axe remained in use, and was joined by the battle hammer. Knights equipped themselves with a growing weight of protective armour which, by the fifteenth century, covered not just the rider but his horse as well.

Between the tenth and fourteenth centuries the knights' armour made them unstoppable. Light cavalry and infantry could not withstand their weapons in combat, while the archers and crossbowmen could only afford to unleash a few missiles before being forced to flee before the hooves of the knights' charging horses. However the late fourteenth century witnessed the renaissance of the infantry, which again appeared on the battlefield in highly trained elite formations. In 1315, at the battle of Mogarten, Swiss pikemen successfully used their halberds to unhorse the opposing knights who then fell easy prey to the marauding infantrymen. A century later, at Agincourt (1415), the Welsh bowmen, unleashing their arrows from 100lb-tension longbows, heralded the demise of the armoured cavalry elite by slaughtering the cream of the French nobility.

Early Firearms

During the late fifteenth and early sixteenth centuries changes in the structure of feudal society, coupled with the introduction of primitive firearms, brought significant changes in the character and composition of the European cavalry. Mercenary elites formed to sell their services to the highest bidder and brought with them new weapons and styles of warfare. Only heavy cavalry on armoured horses remained a match for the pikemen and arquebusiers of the Swiss mercenary infantry; the more opportunist light cavalry was relegated to occasional attacks against infantry or artillery on the march.

7 Weapons and Equipment of the Special Forces

By 1550 even the feudal heavy cavalry had been usurped by the mercenary elites. During the wars among the German Protestant dukes (1546-55), the mercenary 'schwarze reitern' (black riders) abandoned their spears in favour of pistols and swords, separate helmets and light body armour. They were thus able to throw themselves in tight masses against the conventional heavy cavalry. Their pistols proved triumphant, successfully penetrating the cumbersome armour of their opponents at close range.

Gradually the heavily armoured cavalry abandoned their horse-armour and much of their body armour in favour of greater mobility, until by the early seventeenth century they had become 'cuirassiers'.

Improved weaponry and training led to a reduction in the depth of cavalry battle formations from ten or more lines to six. Shallower formations using the same number of men created wider fronts with more exposed flanks and required greater control and discipline. The cavalry of the day was thus forced to abandon its individualism to became a highly trained elite, acting as an organised troop.

By 1600 heavy cavalry consisted of the cuirassiers, most of whom wore three-quarter armour and were armed with two pistols and a straight thrusting sword. Light cavalry - carabiniers and dragoons - wore a helmet and corselet (shot-proof breastplate and pistol-proof backplate) and were also armed with pistols and a straight sword.

New Infantry Elites

At the beginning of the sixteenth century the infantry element of most armies comprised pikemen, halberdiers and archers. This medieval array was forced to adapt quickly to the introduction of the arquebus, early versions of which were tucked under the right arm and fired from an inclined rest spiked into the ground. The arquebus had a very limited range, was inaccurate and slow to load. Nonetheless in 1503 an elite force of Spanish arquebusiers under Gonzalo de Cordoba inflicted a convincing defeat on a conventional Franco/Swiss army at the battle of Cerignola. In open country the arquebusiers were clearly vulnerable. This problem necessitated the creation of specialist units, or 'tercios', in which the arquebusiers were stationed in front of or on either flank of specially trained pikemen; supporting the advance of the latter with their fire and retiring under the protection of their long pikes if assaulted.

The firearm heralded the demise of the halberdier and the archer, whose arrows were by now of limited use against the latest generation of armour; by 1595 even the English trained bands were equipping themselves with firearms rather than bows. Gradually the arquebus was replaced by the matchlock musket, which was in turn replaced by the flintlock towards the end of the seventeenth century.

A tactical breakthrough occurred when Gustavus Adolphus reduced the weight of the musket to 11lb enabling it to be fired from the shoulder without a rest, and introduced the paper cartridge incorporating both charge and ball. These measures increased the musketeers' efficiency to the point where their dependence on the pikeman was reduced, and the proportion of musketeers to pikemen was therefore increased. Simultaneously it became possible to reduce the musketeers' ranks from ten to a maximum of six, allowing units to hold a wider area.

The introduction of the bayonet in the late seventeenth century spelled the end of the pikeman. Initially bayonets were plugged into the barrel but this prevented the weapon from firing. However, ring bayonets began to enter service in 1678, to be replaced by socket bayonets by the end of the century. These eliminated the need for supporting pikemen. With the pikemen went the last vestige of infantry armour. In its place infantrymen began to wear a uniform coat of national colour with distinctive facings and buttons, allowing the introduction for the first time of a uniformed elite.

Even as the pikemen began to leave the battlefield their place was already being taken by the grenadier. Trained as assault infantry, the duties of the grenadier were best performed by the tallest and strongest men available. Inevitably it was not long before grenadiers, distinctive in their high, stiffened mitre caps, came to be regarded as an elite.

Although certain improvements were introduced into the weaponry of the 1714-1815 period, with few exceptions the capabilities of armaments remained to a large extent unchanged. The musket remained slow to load, and inaccurate at ranges of much more than 100 yards. Artillery was smooth-bored and muzzle loading. With the exception of the limited number of howitzers available the trajectory of cannon was so low that it could not fire over the heads of friendly troops, and thus had to be positioned among or in advance of an army's front line.

Cavalry utilised the impetus of the charge. From the late eighteenth century the lance was reintroduced in a number of armies. Generally it was of little use against a mounted enemy with sabres, but against infantry it was a lethal weapon in the hands of elite troops sufficiently disciplined and confident to press home a coordinated, mass frontal assault. The infantry continued to manoeuvre in slow moving lines and columns, treating the battlefield as if it were a parade ground. Against cavalry the universal defence was the square, a formation with all sides facing out to present an impenetrable hedge of bayonets on every side. The bayonet was carried by all troops armed with muskets but rarely used aggressively, its merit in battle being almost entirely psychological. Bayonet charges were normally only made when the enemy was already wavering as a result of artillery or musket fire.

Particular circumstances did occasionally require unusual tactics. When the Duke of Cumberland's regiments met Charles Stewart's Highlanders at Culloden in 1746, he ordered them to remain in line to accept the clansmen's assault. The Highland warriors carried a limited number of firearms, traditionally favouring the broadsword and dirk. Their only item of protection was a small round shield worn on the left forearm. Cumberland appreciated that when they raised their sword arm to strike, the Highlanders left their entire right side vulnerable. He therefore ordered his infantry to fix bayonets, but instead of attacking the opponent to their front, as they would normally, they were to strike at the exposed side of the clansman to the right. This unique tactic did not, in itself, lead to victory as the Highlanders' assault, when it eventually came, was ragged and their numbers had already been decimated by the guns of the Royal Artillery. It did however indicate that, if properly trained and led, quite conventional troops could use their limited repertoire of tactical moves to great advantage in defeating an unconventional enemy.

Napoleonic Advances

Skirmishers - light troops covering the front of an army's advance - had long been present in battle, but until the later eighteenth century they had usually been expendable irregulars. However, the overwhelming defeat of General Braddock in 1756, at the hands of a small French force supported by American skirmishers, taught the British the need for change. Consequently each infantry regiment formed a 'light' company of its best troops, usually detached from the parent unit for covering the advance, or for some other special mission.

By the time of the American Revolution it was common British practice to separate the light companies from their regiments for action, organising them into provisional units. In addition the grenadier companies - also one to each regiment - were separated and merged into special units in combat. Inevitably both the light and grenadier companies became elites, which led to the eventual establishment of 'light' and 'rifle' regiments in the British service.

Nowhere was the concept of a light infantry elite more vigorously pursued than in revolutionary France. During the War of the First Coalition (1792-1798), the habit of skirmishing spread throughout the French infantry to the extent that by 1793 all battalions were acting as light infantry, dissolving into skirmisher swarms as soon as action was joined. These fighting methods, sometimes called 'horde tactics', were in turn superseded after 1795 by a tendency to return to conventionally controlled, deeper assault formations, themselves preceded by skirmishers to scout the ground and disrupt the enemy by individual aimed fire.

French skirmishing during this period was undertaken not by specially trained elites but by the bulk of the infantry masses. Nonetheless special light troops were retained in the French order of battle for the next 50 years.

The character of light infantry and of warfare were greatly changed by the introduction of the rifle. For fighting individually, in dispersed order, an accurate weapon was crucial to the development of the light infantry concept. The introduction of Ezekiel Baker's rifle did much to enhance the potency of the British light and rifle units of the Napoleonic era. Capable of rapid fire by the use of sub-calibre bullets, or individual aimed fire when loaded with conventional bullets, the Baker rifle had a range of more than twice that of the Brown Bess musket which then equipped the British infantry of the line. Rifles were, however, expensive and, more seriously, relatively slow to load. They were therefore confined to elite units and select individuals in line companies until well into the nineteenth century.

The American Civil War

In 1861 the election of Abraham Lincoln to the Presidency of the United States precipitated a vicious war between the North and South. The conflict introduced the world to the awful realities of total war. In four years of bitter fighting more than 160,000 soldiers died in action - an estimated 90,000 of their wounds, 60,000 in prison camps and perhaps 10,000 in accidents. In many instances, details of Confederate casualties simply do not exist. In the early stages of the war the superior capabilities of many of the weapons carried into battle by the badly trained volunteers, who swelled the regiments of both sides, were beyond the ability of their users to exploit them. The war produced few true elites. It did however play a large role in the evolution of the infantryman.

At the outset of hostilities neither side was in any way prepared for the rigours ahead. The North had made no real attempt to mobilise, while the South, despite its military tradition, had no standing army. Of the 1,098 officers serving in the army at the outset of the war, 785 remained loyal to the Union while 313 resigned their commissions in order to offer their services to the Confederacy.

The North eventually raised 1,666 infantry regiments, plus a total of 306 independent infantry companies. In 1861 volunteer regiments of both sides consisted of ten companies, each comprising 100 men commanded by a captain with two lieutenants, thirteen NCOs, two buglers, a wagoner and a maximum of 82 private soldiers. In addition, each regiment had a headquarters consisting of six officers, a chaplain, two NCOs, a hospital orderly and 26 bandsmen, giving a total regimental strength of 1,046 officers and men.

A regular regiment was larger, comprising two battalions each with eight companies, a total close to 1,700 all ranks. These figures were however purely theoretical; units did not receive battle replacements and were often fought down to 40 per cent of operational strength before they were disbanded. The North raised a total of 1.5 million men throughout the war, the South about one million - a remarkable feat from a male population of only 1.14 million! Both sides fielded a maximum of 500,000 men at any one time, and purchased approximately 1,500,000 infantry rifles and muskets of over thirty different types.

Many regiments in the North consisted of ethnic minorities who had been forced by poverty to live in overcrowded, insanitary ghettos and who now chose to serve together. From these unlikely beginnings were born a number of elites. The Irish Brigade was formed by Thomas Francis Meagher, a leading Irish-American, exclusively from New York, Philadelphia and Boston immigrants. The 79th New York (Highlanders) were formed from Scottish immigrants, many of whom had seen service with the British army in the Crimean War. Even when they were expanded to ten companies, by the introduction of Irish and English expatriates, they refused to compromise their traditions, continuing to parade in the full dress uniform of the 79th (Cameron Highlanders) from whom they took their traditions.

The standard infantry weapon on both sides was the rifle musket, so called because when rifled longarms were first introduced into Britain in the 1840s the Duke of Wellington balked at calling them rifles 'lest the whole army clamour to be dressed in green', the colour then reserved for the elite Rifle regiments. Volunteers were drilled for many hours in the dozen commands and twenty specific motions required to fire the rifle musket. Even so, the marksmanship of the average Civil War soldier remained lamentable. The nominal standard rifle in Union service at the outbreak of war was the Model 1855 Percussion Rifle, manufactured at Harper's Ferry Arsenal between 1857 and 1861. A number of these rifles fell into Confederate hands when Harper's Ferry fell to the South and were copied to excellent effect by the Fayetteville Armoury, North Carolina and the Richmond Armoury, Virginia. The finest rifles to enter general service on either side were purchased from the Royal Small Arms factory, Enfield. A total of 428,292 Enfield .577 rifle muskets were purchased by the North, as well as 8,000 short Enfield rifles.

Other foreign rifles to enter service included the Austrian .54 calibre Lorenz M1854, of which 226,000 were purchased, Belgian (57,400), French (44,250), Prussian (60,000), Prussian Jäger (29,850), Prussian commercial (30,000) and Italian (6,000) rifles. Added to this were over 100,000 smooth-bore muskets purchased from foreign sources, principally Prussia and the various states of the German Confederation.

European countries had no qualms at unloading all their obsolete and obsolescent weapons at highly inflated prices; enabling them to re-equip their own armies with the new generation of rifles entering the market. This was particularly true of Prussia which was keen to equip its forces with the new, revolutionary bolt-action Dreyse needle-gun.

Sniping rifles were used by both sides with considerable success. The marksmen of Hiram Berdan's Sharpshooters were perhaps the best exponents of this skill, although there were other specialist companies, and almost every regiment had its snipers who were provided with the best rifles that could be procured.

Berdan's Sharpshooters, who were formed on 30 November 1861, were a true elite. Before being accepted into the ranks every man had to be able to place ten consecutive rounds within the ten-inch diameter of a bull's eye at 200 yards as well as provide excellent references as to his character, yet service proved so popular that a second battalion was soon raised.

Initially the volunteers brought their own hunting rifles, but when this created acute problems of ammunition resupply they were issued with revolutionary revolving five-shot .56 calibre Colt Military Model rifles. However when the Colt proved unreliable, due to overheating and the propensity for all cylinders to discharge at once as a result of flash-over, the Sharpshooters received the coincidentally named, and far superior, single-shot breech-loading Sharps rifle.

As tactics progressed and the volunteers, now seasoned by combat, began to improve their musketry skills, the infantry's marksmanship became more lethal. As a consequence their commanders began to find it less necessary to rely on skirmishers to disrupt the enemy's front line. More fundamentally, experience was proving that skirmishing lines were simply too flimsy to withstand the sustained attack of massed rows of bayonet-wielding infantry. By 1864, therefore, the status of the Sharpshooter as a military elite was considered largely redundant. In the autumn of that year the 1st and 2nd Regiments merged, and in February 1865 the entire unit was disbanded.

The role of the cavalry as an elite was reinforced during the Civil War. At the outset of hostilities the Union had no more than six cavalry regiments: the 1st and 2nd Dragoons, the Mounted Rifles, and the 1st, 2nd and 3rd Cavalry. By 1865, however, these had been expanded to 258 regiments, with a further 170 independent cavalry companies. The Confederate Army of North Virginia mustered four cavalry divisions made up of six brigades each holding an average of four regiments.

The European-style massed cavalry charge did not lend itself well to the American situation. Although both sides introduced the lance in small numbers both quickly relegated it to the rear areas, favouring instead the sabre, carbine and pistol. For the first half of the war the Southern cavalry rode supreme, and were regarded by many as the finest mounted infantry in the world. Many Confederate troopers were experienced hunters, used to firing from the saddle. Most were accomplished riders, and all were expected to provide their own horses, tackle and weapons. This was an excellent short term method of building an elite cavalry arm from nothing, but in the long term it proved to be disadvantageous. As the war progressed, volunteers were still expected to supply their own mounts and to transfer to the infantry should these be killed. In theory compensation was offered for killed or injured horses, but in practice payment was invariably late and inadequate, making it difficult for the trooper to purchase a new horse and resume his place in his old unit. Regiments were decimated for the want of men able to provide their own mounts, while experienced cavalrymen fumed and fretted in the unwelcoming ranks of the infantry.

By mid-1863, the Union cavalry, which in the early days of the war had lacked both experience and élan, felt confident enough in its training and organisation to face the Confederacy in open battle. On 9 June it received an opportunity to prove that it was now at least as good as its much-vaunted adversary. In the Battle of Brandy Station, General Stoneman's cavalry corps held Stuart's Confederate cavalry for the first time, routing the 2nd South Carolina and 4th Virginia regiments in the process. The supremacy of disciplined, massed cavalry over Confederate mounted infantry, too keen and eager to fight as individuals was established, and was reinforced in a series of subsequent engagements.

In 1865 the majority of volunteer regiments were disbanded. A year later the cavalry was returned to a peacetime footing. Four new regiments were formed, two of them, the 9th and 10th Cavalry, were manned by black enlisted men (the famous 'Buffalo Soldiers') with white officers.

Towards the end of the nineteenth century cavalry armament was partially modified after the introduction of firearms with greater rates of fire. Lances remained in use with the Russian Cossacks, the British light cavalry and the German and Austro-Hungarian Uhlans. The breastplate was abandoned by Austro-Hungary in 1881, and relegated to ceremonial use by the Germans in 1883.

The Boer Commando

The appearance of the machine-gun and rapid-fire artillery piece further limited the use of the cavalry and diminished its role as a fighting elite. Britain used eighteen cavalry regiments, supported by about 10,000 yeomanry mounted infantrymen, in the Boer War (1899-1902), but was forced to deploy them on foot for most of the time. In contrast the Boers used fast horses to mount a series of highly successful guerrilla operations which proved severely embarrassing to the British professionals for the first year of hostilities.

The Boers grouped themselves into commandos varying in strength from 100 to 3,000 men, depending on the local population. Every individual was a marksman, armed with a modern (usually Mauser) repeating rifle, and every man was mounted. The riders of the veldt were hunters, trained from childhood to take advantage of cover and terrain. They were capable of producing irregular fire sufficiently devastating to pulverise the ranks of any close-order formation before it could get close enough to respond. The Boers abhorred the bayonet and were wholly incapable of withstanding the close assault of a British infantry battalion. They were however masters at extricating themselves from danger and were rarely forced to meet the enemy at close quarters.

It took the British two years and eight months to subdue an enemy with a total manpower potential of 83,000 males of fighting age, and which never fielded more than 40,000 of its men at once. British Imperial forces engaged in the beginning totalled no more than 25,000, but by 1901 this number had been increased to 500,000.

For the first time in 80 years the British Army had met a hostile elite of mounted marksmen, and had proved itself all but incapable of countering them.

Great War Advances

Military planners noted with concern the increasing lethality of weapons during the latter half of the nineteenth century. However they did little to counter them. The leading military thinkers paid inadequate attention to the lessons of the American Civil War, and in four years of carnage paid the penalty with the lives of an entire generation. During the late 1880s Britain drifted almost accidentally into camouflage, and later learned the necessity for expert marksmanship when confronting the Boers. However even she, with her uniquely all-professional army, declined to differentiate between a social and a military elite among her regiments.

Unlike Britain, Continental Europe entered the Great War with conscript armies. During the years prior to hostilities 50 per cent of German youth reaching military age was conscripted for two years' service with a spell in the reserves thereafter. France, with a smaller population, called 80 per cent of her available youth for three years' service. Both attempted to weld their units into fighting cohesion with the aid of a hard core of career officers and NCOs.

France regarded her entire army as an elite. Its tactics concentrated entirely on the traditional offensive, discounting completely the potential of barbed wire to disrupt, and defensive machine-gun fire to annihilate, an unsupported massed assault. When General Marshal had the audacity to suggest that the French 'poilus' (as the infantry were affectionately known) should be dressed in something less gaudy than their much-loved but highly impractical blue greatcoats and red pantaloons, he was hounded from office for daring to undermine the very 'élan vitale' of the French Army. Within a year of hostilities the vast majority of the French army had abandoned its traditional uniform in favour of camouflage.

In comparison the all-regular British Army was an elite. Composed of volunteers enlisted for a seven year period, and led by well-qualified officers, its morale, discipline and steadiness were second to none. The 150,000 men of the British Expeditionary Force (BEF) were armed with the legendary .303-inch Short Magazine Lee Enfield rifle and were trained to fire fifteen aimed rounds per minute, a factor destined to have a devastating effect during the early battles of Mons and Le Cateau.

The Tunnellers

By late 1914, as trench warfare began to overtake the war of movement, both sides began to look for ways of breaking the deadlock. When the war began in August 1914 none of the combatants had been equipped with operational directives for tunnelling or mining. The Germans, however, possessed special purpose Engineer Companies skilled in the art of tunnelling and were quick to exploit their advantage. On 20 December 1914 they exploded ten mines along a half-mile stretch of the British front line near Festubert, causing the hapless Indian Sirhind Brigade, which had been holding the sector, to break and run.

Fortunately for the Allies, the Germans had no full-blown assault force poised to flood through the breach which had been created. The mining operation therefore became little more than a live-firing experiment. Even so, it introduced to the Western Front a new and highly specialist dimension of special purpose warfare. The initiative remained with the Germans for much of 1915, forcing the British and French into the defensive ploy of counter-mining: listening for sounds of underground activity and then tunnelling forward to neutralise the enemy mine before it could reach under the Allied line. As mining intensified each side attempted to entomb the other's miners by placing small explosive charges, or camouflets, against their saps; there were also frequent vicious underground combats when rival tunnellers met.

To reduce the possibility of surprise tunnellers worked as nearly as possible in silence, muffling their picks and shovels and stopping every few seconds to listen for the tell-tale sounds of enemy activity. Many carried revolvers, knives and even home-made cudgels and knuckle-dusters to deal with the unexpected arrival of the enemy.

The speed of the British response to the threat of German mining owed much to Major John Norton Griffiths MP, a politician and tunnelling contractor who persuaded Lord Kitchener to approve the formation of a special mining unit to be recruited from civilian tunnel workers. The nucleus of this unit consisted of men employed by Griffith's peacetime company to dig sewer tunnels under the city of Manchester. The teams, who were recruited into the Royal Engineers, used the 'clay-kicking' technique. Lying at an angle of 45 degrees on wooden frames, they used both feet to drive a spade into the clay at the tunnel face. As the loosened clay was removed the clay-kicker moved forward on his frame to extend the tunnel. It was appalling, exhausting work, usually carried out in foul air which the crude ventilation bellows could do little to freshen. The tunnellers received enhanced pay, but this did little to compensate for the ever-present risk of being killed by cave-ins or counter-miners.

Griffith only began recruiting his tunnelling specialists in January 1915, yet the first British success in tunnel warfare came comparatively early in the form of the storming of Hill 60, on the southern face of the Ypres Salient, in April of that year. Work on three tunnels began on 8 March in appalling tunnelling conditions of almost liquid mud. By 16 March the tunnellers had detected the sound of counter-mining, and one British tunnel subsequently pierced a German gallery which was successfully demolished with a camouflet. After a month of exhausting labour the tunnels had been driven under the German positions and the explosive charges, the largest of them 2,700 lbs had been tamped in place. The three mines were detonated on 17 April with shattering effect, blasting deep craters in the German line which infantry of the 13th Brigade had no difficulty in seizing.

The devastation caused by mining was unquestionably better at cutting the enemy's barbed wire defences than the heaviest artillery bombardment, and tunnelling continued unabated throughout 1915, 1916 and 1917. The climax of the tunnellers' war occurred on 7 June 1917, when nineteen mines containing a staggering 950,000 lbs of ammonal were detonated under the German lines at Messines. The bang was not only clearly heard in London, it was reported in Dublin, about 500 miles away. According to one observer it made the clay boil like porridge as it vaporised countless numbers of German troops. As the men of General Plumer's Second Army advanced into the carnage to secure the new front line they found thousands of German troops dazed and in many cases driven quite mad by the sheer force of the explosion.

7 Weapons and Equipment of the Special Forces

Messines was effectively the postscript to the tunnel war. The massive artillery bombardments of late 1917 had effectively turned the terrain east of the Ypres Salient to primeval swamp, making further mining operations in the area impossible. That year the German armies withdrew behind the prepared defences of the Hindenburg Line. In the final great German offensive which followed, mining was destined to play no part at all.

Operation 'Michael'

It was the Imperial German Army in the latter stages of the war which created the first truly elite infantry units. Operation Michael, the last-ditch attempt to cut through the Allied lines around Amiens, saw the large scale use of special purpose storm troopers for the first time. These units, filled with hardened veterans, enjoyed the luxuries of better food, pay, training and equipment. Troopers went into battle in small, tight-knit units, carrying plentiful supplies of grenades and, where available, the first truly effective sub-machine-gun, the MP 18.

Unlike conventional units, which still relied on the frontal assault to capture entire trench systems, the storm troopers made use of dead ground to probe for enemy weaknesses. On 27 May 1918, during the Second Battle of the Aisne, Ludendorff ordered an assault against a lightly defended sector held by General Duchêne's Sixth French Army. General Duchêne was taken completely by surprise, despite an ominous increase in German line-crossers (which invariably preceded an assault), strong indications that the Germans were massing in the area, and the misgivings of the three veteran British divisions 'resting' in the French line and temporarily under his command.

The German success was made the more complete by storm troopers who infiltrated deep into the British 50th Division's position during the hours of darkness immediately preceding the assault. Using the swampy dead ground of the River Miette for cover, they crawled completely unseen between the 2nd Northants and the 2nd Royal Berkshire Regiments to create chaos and confusion in the British rear.

Ultimately Operation Michael failed, as did all German assaults in the area, and before long their armies were rolled back along the entire front. This was not, however, the fault of their shock troops, nor of the artillery units, which had been specially trained to offer them close support by putting down a creeping barrage in front of their advance. The German military analysts did not forget the lessons of 1918; they incorporated them into the policy of 'blitzkrieg' (lightning war) which was destined to prove so successful in the opening stages of the Second World War.

Blitzkrieg Unleashed

Blitzkrieg did not require the introduction of a plethora of new weapons, but rather the concentrated use of existing weapons by special purpose elites on a massive scale. The strategy, which required the use of fast moving armoured formations capable of slicing through the enemy's front line to disrupt his command and control systems, was based on the ideas of the British military experts Broad, Fuller and Liddell Hart, but was refined by the German tank expert Heinz Guderian. Under Guderian's tutelage, and against the wishes of the more conservative general staff, the first German panzer division was formed in 1935. Two years later Guderian published his influential textbook *Achtung! Panzer!*, in which he advocated his ideas about high-speed warfare. When war came he was able to put his theories into devastating effect at the head of an armoured corps in the Polish campaign in September 1939, and nine months later spearheaded the German breakout from the Ardennes. Guderian regarded initiative as the key to success, and trained his officers to exercise a previously unheard of degree of personal responsibility in the highly volatile battlefield situations which he created.

The German Army which spearheaded the invasion of France and the Low Countries in June 1940 was numerically inferior to the Allies both in men and ground equipment. Its ten Panzer divisions mustered a total of 2,439 tanks, over half of which were Mark Is and Mark IIs useful for little more than reconnaissance. By comparison the French had around 3,000 tanks and the British Expeditionary Force had 210 light tanks and 100 Matilda infantry tanks. Only in aircraft were the Germans numerically superior. The Luftwaffe boasted 2,738 aircraft against the Allies' 1,375. To compound the latter's problem the Royal Air Force refused to release its few available Spitfire's to the defence of France, while many of the French fighters were completely out of date and no match for the German Messerschmidts.

The German superiority in aircraft allowed Guderian the crucial advantage of mobility. It also allowed him to use his Stuka dive bombers in the role of aerial artillery. The Ju87 Stuka was slow, with a top speed of only some 250 mph and was no match against conventional fighters, however its pinpoint accuracy made it an ideal weapon in support of the advancing panzers. The nature of its attack, falling on targets in a near-vertical dive, siren wailing, and pulling up at the very last moment struck terror into the already demoralised Allied troops.

The Spirit of Resistance

On 15 June 1940 General Joseph Georges, commanding France's north-west front, announced to his army commanders that the government had started negotiating for an armistice. Many Frenchmen and women, refusing to accept defeat, vowed to fight on and began to form themselves into primitive resistance cells. Groups from other occupied countries quickly followed suit. In July the newly appointed British Prime Minister, Winston Churchill, created the Special Operations Executive (SOE) to 'set Europe ablaze' through the medium of economic sabotage. The term 'economic sabotage' was deliberately left open to a variety of interpretations which broadened as the war progressed. Irregular, but often highly effective, special purpose clandestine units were created from the embryonic resistance cells. With the assistance of the SOE, and later of the United States OSS, these cells refused to accept defeat, and instead chose to perpetuate the spirit of resistance during the dark years of occupation.

Each independent resistance group, or 'réseau', required a small number of highly trained specialist agents at its heart; an organiser in overall command, a courier to maintain liaison between the organiser and the different groups within the réseau and a radio operator to keep communications with headquarters in England, or possibly later in North Africa. Once in the field, responsibilities tended to merge. Couriers in particular tended to work closely with their radio operators, finding them safe houses, providing them with lookouts and arranging for transportation of their sets from place to place. The more resilient also helped to deputise for the organiser in his dealings with local groups, helped organise the reception of arms drops and even took an active part in sabotage operations.

Many couriers were women, and as such were able to move about the towns and countryside without attracting undue attention. They were encouraged to memorise messages whenever possible. When these were simply too long or complex they were taught to transcribe them in minute handwriting on to tiny sheets of rice paper which could be easily hidden and even swallowed in an emergency. Couriers learned to manufacture 'sympathetic', or invisible, inks usually from non-prescription drugs easily obtainable on the Continent. Typically one part of alum, used widely for tanning rabbit skins, might be mixed with 100 parts of water to make an invisible ink developed by passing a hot iron over the sheet of paper.

In the early days agents were inserted into enemy territory by parachute or boat. Two obsolescent Whitley bombers were formed into 419 Flight, RAF, and made available to SOE in September 1940. They were joined by a third Whitley on 9 October and by a fourth in February 1941. On 25 August 1941, the Flight was expanded to form 138 Squadron, RAF, and was re-equipped with ten Whitleys and four larger and newer Halifax bombers. In March 1942, the squadron redeployed to Tempsford, Bedfordshire, where it formed a close liaison with 161 Squadron, its sister special operations squadron which specialised in pick-ups. No 138 Squadron grew steadily throughout the war until, by May 1943, it boasted twenty Halifaxes. These were replaced by 22 Stirlings in July-September 1944. For its part, No 161 Squadron was formed with seven Lysanders. It later used Whitleys, Halifaxes and Hudsons, and added Stirlings from September 1944.

Communications between home base and the resistance groups in Europe was by radio. The radios the agents used were modified as the war progressed, but basically comprised a receiver, transmitter and about 65 feet of aerial. They were tuned with slices of quartz, known as crystals. Cut to a precise dimension, which determined the wavelength, the crystals were about the size of a postage stamp. Each was mounted in a small rectangular Bakelite box, with a pair of prongs to plug it into the set. Crystals were notoriously fragile, and prone to loss, yet without them the set was useless. Sets had to be capable of operating by day or night over ranges from as little as 100 miles for a clandestine station located in northern France, up to as much as 1,000 miles for stations in Czechoslovakia and the Balkans.

Special Weapons Development

Many of the weapons dropped via the SOE and OSS agents to the Resistance groups were conventional. Others however were highly specialised, tailored to the job in hand, mobile and relatively easy to conceal. The OSS in particular was able to call upon the considerable resources of the United States war economy to develop systems which were so advanced that they were to destined to remain in the United States special forces' arsenals for decades to come.

Whereas the SOE had been formed hurriedly, with little direction and with a very general mandate, the OSS was created with more specific objectives and had the benefit of the resources of an already established body of scientists. The National Defense Research Committee (NDRC) was formed by Presidential Executive Order in the summer of 1940 to advise the armed forces in 'the development of the instrumentalities of war'. In contravention of the then prevailing United States laws of neutrality the NDRC established an office in London in February 1941 to draw on Britain's extensive knowledge of new German weaponry and to learn of her early attempts at counter-measures. In exchange the NDRC acted as a willing conduit for the British acquisition of much-needed technical equipment and electronic components. Later in 1941 the NDRC was absorbed into the Office of Scientific Research and Development (OSRD). When the OSS was established on 13 June 1942, the OSRD was itself subordinated to the Research and Development Branch of the new organisation. The NDRC itself was expanded and reorganised into 23 administrative divisions, panels or committees, each headed by a specialist in that particular field.

From the point of view of clandestine warfare, by far the most interesting of these sub organisations was Division 19 responsible for 'Miscellaneous Weapons'. With its own research and development laboratory in Maryland, it was able to call upon the expertise of the other 22 divisions in the research and development of special weapons for the OSS and its British allies. Although the scientists of Division 19 were given virtual autonomy they were closely monitored by representatives of the Technical Division of the OSS to ensure that their research did not exceed the limits of operational practicability. The final testing of devices was undertaken by a User Trial Committee drawn from the NDRC, the OSS Procurement Branch and the British Liaison Mission.

By July 1944 the list of unorthodox weaponry and equipment had grown to such proportions that the OSS was actually forced to publish a catalogue describing each piece of specialised equipment available to its agents. Copies of this amazing catalogue remain, and form the basis for H. Keith Melton's excellent book entitled *OSS Special Weapons and Equipment*.

Clandestine Weapons

Between 1940 and 1944 sub-machine-guns represented 47 per cent of all firearms dropped into occupied Europe. A further 30 per cent were rifles, fifteen per cent pistols, five per cent automatic rifles, two per cent carbines and one per cent anti-tank weapons. Early attempts by the SOE to equip its teams with Thompson sub-machine-guns met with failure due to the sheer cost of manufacture. However the ubiquitous Sten gun proved far easier to obtain. Designed by R. V. Shepherd and H. J. Turpin and manufactured by the Royal Ordnance Factory at Enfield (and later under licence at a number of factories), the Sten proved as resilient as it was easy to manufacture.

Although wartime stories that the Sten cost less to manufacture than its magazine of ammunition are untrue, at £1 10s per weapon it was indeed cheap to manufacture. About three and a half million Stens were produced throughout the war, of which over a million were distributed by SOE to its various guerrilla groups. Each gun was normally dropped with up to eight magazines pre-loaded with their conventional complement of 28 rounds. The Sten was designed specifically to accept the 9mm Parabellum ammunition used by the German MP 40 sub-machine gun to make replenishment easy, using stolen or captured stores.

The commonest Sten to be deployed with SOE was the Mark II, usually fitted with a distinctive skeleton-frame butt, but sometimes fitted with a cruder tubular butt.

7 Weapons and Equipment of the Special Forces

It arrived in three pieces - barrel, body and butt - with simple multilingual instructions for its assembly. It could be easily disassembled for concealed carrying in a basket, rucksack or suitcase. Less easily hidden was the less common Mark III, which could only be disassembled into two parts.

Notwithstanding its popularity with the réseaux, the Sten had a number of dis-advantages. Its ultra-short barrel - only 7.5ins long - made it inaccurate at ranges in excess of 50 metres. It was prone to blockage and jamming, particular if its magazine was filled to its maximum, and it had a tendency to misfire if knocked or dropped whilst cocked.

When United States parachute drops began in July 1944, M3s and Thompsons were substituted for Stens whenever possible. The M3 was heavier and more expensive to produce than the Sten. It was completely manufactured out of stamped sheet steel and could accept 9mm or .45-calibre ammunition with the aid of an interchangeable barrel and bolt; it could however only fire fully automatic.

According to figures provided by Colonel Maurice Buckmaster, head of F Section SOE, of the 418,083 weapons delivered to France during the war, 57,849 were automatic pistols or revolvers. Automatics were far more popular with the resistants, who accepted less sophisticated (though far more reliable) revolvers only grudgingly. Where possible Remington-manufactured Colt .45 automatic pistols were distributed. In general use with the French and American armies, Colts were sturdy and thoroughly reliable. Yet their small magazines and large-calibre rounds made them heavy and outmoded.

The 9mm Browning High Power pistol was far more practical, but so scarce that its distribution was limited almost exclusively to conventional SAS, Commando and Airborne elite units. A few were delivered as a status symbol to Resistance network organisers. However, the jealousy which often ensued within the group when such a weapon was produced tended to make its presence counter-productive. Capable of holding thirteen rounds of 9mm ammunition the Browning had a comparatively short range, limited stopping power and was liable to jam unless properly maintained. Yet it was light, relatively easy to strip, hide and reassemble and thus well suited to clandestine warfare.

The Smith & Wesson 0.38in/200 typified the revolvers issued to the Resistance groups. Produced in the United States to a British specification, it was conventional in its design yet robust in the extreme. The weapon was opened by pushing the six-round cylinder to the left, after which the spent cartridge cases could be cleared quickly with the aid of a sprung ejector rod. Single or double action could be used, for accuracy or for speed respectively, although a constant shortage of 0.38-calibre rounds forced Resistance groups to husband their ammunition.

Although of limited use in the cut-and-run warfare usually associated with the Resistance, rifles were delivered in large numbers, particularly in the final stages of the war. Of these the most popular were the Short Magazine Lee Enfield (SMLE), the standard weapon of the British infantry during most of the war, and the United States Springfield.

More specialist weapons included the silenced .22 calibre automatic pistol and the Welrod, a specially constructed 0.32in single shot silent pistol accurate up to 50 yards but most effective when used with the muzzle against the target. The famous 0.45in Liberator, or Woolworth Gun, was produced in large numbers but was considered so impractical that its use was almost exclusively limited to the Far East. Despite the advances of modern technology some British Commando and special forces units utilised medieval weapons such as the crossbow for certain operations.

Post-War Advances

The year 1945 heralded peace, marred by the almost immediate threat of another war. In Europe the Iron Curtain came down across the face of Europe as the Soviet Union refused to demobilise, and slowly but surely began to create an Empire of its own. In the Far East communist nationalists refused to disarm, and made it clear that they would no longer accept government from the discredited colonial powers which had proved so impotent against the Japanese.

In order to combat this new threat the West realised that it would have to create a small group of special forces from the large number of special purpose units, both regular and irregular, which were then being forced, not always willingly, into retirement. Many special forces units, the SAS in particular, were created (or re-created) for action in a particular theatre, but quickly proved themselves so invaluable that they were incorporated into their country's permanent order of battle.

Where possible these units remained independent, away from the chain of command of begrudging senior officers, and thus found themselves with unusual freedom in the choice of their own weapon systems. Special forces also became adept in using the weapon systems of the enemy, both as a means of resupply behind the lines and, occasionally, to enforce 'deniability' in particularly covert operations.

In the last three decades, two factors have led to a massive increase in the numbers and types of weapon systems available to a potential enemy. When the United States forces left Vietnam in 1975, they abandoned a staggering 1,100 aircraft, 400 naval vessels, 50,000 motor vehicles, 800,000 M16 rifles, untold millions of rounds of ammunition, hundreds of tons of bombs and several thousand tons of explosives. Most of this fell into the hands of the North Vietnamese authorities and was either sold for barter or hard cash to friendly powers, or more ominously donated to various communist resistance movements around the world.

The more recent disintegration of the Soviet Union has led to similar problems. Undisclosed quantities of weaponry and armaments technology have been sold to the highest bidder by the newly independent states of the former Soviet Union, adding considerably to the arsenals of some of the most politically unstable countries in the world. Equally ominously, Russian conscripts, their morale shattered as they await confined to barracks for repatriation, have been openly selling their arms and equipment on the black market, adding to the pool of guns available to an ever more violent underworld.

The Choice of Modern Weaponry

A considerable amount of ordnance used by today's special forces, particularly in the fields of ballistics, explosives and surveillance, remains secret. Certain units, such as the French counter-terrorist GIGN, have always been willing to allow a controlled demonstration of their firepower potential as a deterrent. Other units, for equally sound operational reasons, have not. The use by the SAS of a flash-resistant all-black fighting rig, and its employment of stun grenades and the Heckler & Koch MP5 sub-machine-gun were only made public when its dramatic lifting of the Iranian Embassy siege in London received worldwide publicity.

Despite current financial constraints the SAS has fought hard to retain its Operational Research Wing which gives it special access to state-of-the-art weapons, surveillance systems, communications devices, protective clothing, transportation and survival equipment. It is no coincidence that when Lieutenant General Rose required immediate intelligence from the frontline town of Gorazde, in the former Yugoslavia, in April 1994 he chose to deploy an SAS forward observation team rather than rely on conventional communications.

Weapons and support systems selected by special forces troops for any given mission must always satisfy certain criteria. Above all they must be absolutely reliable. As most special forces actions involve short, violent contacts with the enemy the weapon must work not just on the first, but on every occasion that the trigger is pulled. The Soviet AK-47, and to a lesser extent the AK-74, are crude by Western standards but a Russian special purpose force team using them knows that they can always be relied upon, even when caked in mud or covered in snow. Similarly British SAS and German GSG-9 hostage-rescue units (HRUs) know that they can rely utterly on the MP5 series of sub-machine-guns in the invariably close confines of a siege-busting operation.

Special forces weapons often have to meet different requirements from conventional service equipment. The weapon should be as small as possible, easy to operate and quick to bring into the aim. Special forces teams have to operate in all climates, and of necessity occasionally have to fire while wearing gloves. It is not sufficient merely to remove the trigger guard from a weapon, all controls such as the cocking handle and safety catch must be capable of being operated by a gloved hand.

Elite personnel are trained to react immediately to the unforeseen, and to fire from a range of positions - sitting, prone, from the shoulder or hip, static and moving. In a world in which delays or misses can prove fatal and the expression 'the quick and the dead' has a terrible reality, personnel have to be able to react and bring the weapon to bear on an enemy in a split second, disabling him with the first round. Most conventional military weapons fail to satisfy this criterion. The United States M16A2 and the British SA-80 (at 37 inches and 30.9 inches respectively), although excellent weapons, are considered too long for close-quarter combat. On the other hand the German H&K MP5, the Israeli Uzi and the Czech Skorpion are all regarded as suitable.

Minimum weight and maximum firepower are also critical factors. Many special forces missions are conducted on foot and over difficult terrain, or require HALO/HAHO parachute insertion for which weight reduction is vital. The 1980s witnessed the introduction into general military service of a number of important weapons with smaller calibres than their predecessors. In particular the 5.56mm SA-80 replaced the 'long' round 7.62mm SLR in British service, while the 5.45mm AK-74 replaced the 'short' 7.62mm round AK-47 with the Soviets.

The smaller rounds resulted in an overall reduction in weapon size and recoil while losing nothing in lethality. Both weapons are relatively light and on the face of it are suitable for special warfare exploitation. However the comparative unreliability of the SA-80 has made it unpopular with the British special forces, who were invariably seen carrying the American M16A2 during the Gulf War.

Elite Combat Rifle Development

The US Army's Advanced Combat Rifle (ACR) Program is currently carrying out trials on a combat weapon for the twenty-first century. It is considering four potential replacements for the M16A2. In the hands of a trained infantryman firing under controlled conditions, each weapon under trial claims to offer a 100 per cent hit potential at 300m reducing to 80 per cent at 600m with little diminution under battlefield conditions. Although this is clearly contingent on the training and experience of the individual marksman, it may be hoped that special forces personnel, who will eventually be equipped with the chosen weapon, will be of a standard of excellence to exploit it fully. However current indications suggest that it will be difficult to improve on the M16A2 to any great extent.

The Heckler & Koch G11 is without doubt the most innovative weapon under trial. Quite unlike any other weapon in appearance, the entire rifle, including the barrel, is enclosed in a smooth outer casing with a combination optical sight/carrying handle above and a pistol grip and trigger below. There are no projections or holes through which dirt and debris can enter (save for the muzzle) and the only control is a rotary disc set into the butt. A simple switch by the trigger can be used to select single, automatic or three-round bursts. The G11's automatic cyclic rate of 600 rounds per minute (rpm) is similar to that of a conventional support weapon. However, its three-shot burst mode has a cyclic rate of 2,000 rpm, ensuring that all three rounds are chambered and fired before the recoiling parts have reached the buffer at the end of the recoil stroke. Consequently the three rounds are en route to the target before the firer's shoulder registers the recoil and begins to react. This produces a significantly tighter grouping at 100-300 yards/metres than three rounds fired by a conventional weapon.

Heckler & Koch have produced a unique form of caseless ammunition specifically for the G11. Each rectangular block of propellant has a 4.7mm calibre bullet projecting from one end. When fired, all the propellant is consumed within the chamber leaving no case to eject, thereby avoiding the traditional jamming problems associated with cartridge ejection.

The number of heavier weapons available to the special forces is more limited. Sniper rifles have tended to retain the 7.62mm round, which provides stability and good ballistic qualities for long-range shooting. The role of the sniper remains highly specialist, and not confined to conventional special forces warfare. Modern snipers rarely operate alone, and are chosen at least as much for their fieldcraft and reconnaissance skills as for their marksmanship. They rarely seek targets of opportunity but instead operate under strict control after careful planning and preparation. Many do not wear conventional uniforms, relying on their 'war diaries' to confirm their right to protection under the Geneva Convention.

One of the finest of the established sniper rifles is the Russian SVD or Dragunov. A semi-automatic weapon, it uses the same basic operating principles as the AK-47 assault rifle allied to a revised gas-operated system. A joy to handle, it is long but perfectly balanced with a quoted accuracy to well over 800m. The SVD was used extensively by Spetsnaz in Afghanistan (where several fell into Mujahideen hands) and remains an important part of the Russian armoury.

Hostage Rescue Units sometimes favour 0.22in or 0.250 'soft kill' rifles for their low penetration qualities. Whereas a 7.62mm round may exit the criminal and then strike a bystander or hostage, a smaller round will not, presenting the marksman with a far greater safety margin when deciding whether or not to engage a target.

Rifles such as the Accuracy International L96A1 - favoured by the SAS - are known as hard kill weapons. The L96A1 has an effective range of 1,000m, is equipped with a 6x42 telescopic sight as standard, and may be fitted with a selection of large light-gathering scopes.

GSG-9, with its far narrower role, selected the Heckler & Koch 7.62mm G3 SG/1 rifle. Designed for semi-and fully-automatic fire at targets up to 600m, the weapon employs a roller delayed blow-back action to enhance accuracy.

Close Assault Weapon Systems

Close Assault Weapon Systems - or shotguns - have long been a favourite weapon of the special forces. Highly reliable and with a good spread of shot they have proved invaluable in both jungle and close-quarter battle conditions. At present Heckler & Koch and the AAI Corporation of Baltimore are attempting to develop a new form of flechette ammunition for a future generation of specialist shotguns. A flechette is one of a cluster of small arrow-like finned projectiles fired from a single cartridge at high velocity. It is no newcomer to war having seen service in Vietnam, yet its large-scale application by elite forces is still awaited.

Special Forces Ammunition

Combat ammunition can be divided into three types; military, police and special forces. Military ammunition has to be reliable in all climatic conditions. It has to be operational in a variety of weapons for which it was not necessarily specifically designed, and adhere to the Geneva and Hague Conventions. It need not kill; indeed a round which simply incapacitates may ultimately prove more effective in that it removes from the battle not only its victim but an estimated seven rear-echelon soldiers needed to transport him to safety and restore him to health.

Police rounds should ideally not kill, but incapacitate the target, enabling him to recover and be brought to justice. They should not expand unduly inside the target, should effect minimum penetration and should not ricochet. On the other hand special forces ammunition should kill, or at the very least incapacitate the target, upon impact. Statistically 87 per cent of people shot with conventional ammunition survive. This is a luxury which special forces units cannot afford to concede to an enemy who invariably outnumbers them and whom they have to attack cold.

Unfortunately for Western special forces most of their preferred HRU and close-quarter battle (CQB) weapons are 9mm, and as such have excellent penetration and killing power, though poor stopping power. Ammunition manufacturers have attempted to overcome this problem in a number of ways; by enlarging the projectile, by enhancing the wound channel capabilities, by adding a hollow- or soft-point design to the bullet, by introducing frangibility (bullet break-up) and by increasing the velocity to produce a higher kinetic energy.

A number of so-called fourth generation rounds have been produced as a result, and are now in general special forces use.

Shotgun ammunition is more readily interchangeable and thus more versatile. The standard 12 bore/gauge manually operated, small-magazine-capacity shotgun so popular with the special forces can shoot a vast number of different cartridges ranging from birdshot to grenades. Fired at close range birdshot will not penetrate internal walls. Small buckshot fired at medium range will not kill non-combatants outside its operational area, while large buckshot will penetrate hard cover at close range and stop a soft target at a range of 30m.

Support Equipment

In addition to personal weapons and ammunition, elite troops also need a diverse range of specialist equipment to enable them to operate to their full potential. Adequate transport to and from an operation is essential. The lethal consequences of the United States Government's inability to provide its special forces with suitable air transportation during Operation 'Eagle Claw', the Iranian hostage rescue fiasco, offers terrible testament to this obvious fact.

Special purpose forces such as the United States Marine Amphibious Units (MAUs) rely on a complex armada of amphibious support ships, amphibious transport docks, dock landing ships and tank landing ships to enable them to function independently in any part of the world. For its part the Royal Navy is in the process of replacing its assault ships *Fearless* and *Intrepid* to enable the Royal Marines to retain their out-of-area capability.

The insertion of small teams onto an enemy coastline has long been practised by special forces. Recent improvements in radar and sonar systems, however, have virtually ruled out the use of large vessels such as fishing boats, and canoes or submersibles are now preferred. The latest generation of canoes can be parachuted into the sea with their team. Once ashore, they can be dismantled or filled with water, and left submerged to await the team's return.

A number of small dedicated submarines have been developed to carry special forces insertion teams close to their targets. One such craft, the Vickers 'Piranha', has an overall length of only 87ft yet is capable of delivering a seven man crew, ten combat swimmers and two swimmer-delivery vehicles close inshore. This excellent craft has a range of 1,800 nautical miles surface, 70 nautical miles at 4 knots submerged, can negotiate shallow waters and on the surface offers the minutest of radar signatures.

The final approach to the beach is usually made in one of a variety of small, dedicated submersibles. One such remarkable boat, the Submarine Products Limited 'Subskimmer', is powered on the surface by an 80hp outboard motor. Close to the shore the outboard's exhaust is sealed and a powerful suction pump is activated to suck the air out of the hull. The craft may then run with only the swimmers' heads above the surface or fully submerged for a range of 4.75 nautical miles at a speed of 2.5 knots. Subskimmer can be left on the bottom of a river while the team infiltrates inland and later recovered to return them to the mother submarine. Helicopters have traditionally played a crucial part in the special forces dimension. The US 20th, and later 21st, Special Operations Squadrons played an important role in support of the special forces in Vietnam. A decade later, Soviet Spetsnaz and airborne units relied heavily on Mi-8 Hip transports and Mi-24 gunships to take the war against the Mujahideen into the mountains of Afghanistan. In January 1991, the US 20th Special Operations Squadron used its Sikorsky MH-53J Pave Lows to devastating effect in the Gulf War.

The United States in particular is so impressed with the potential of the helicopter in special forces warfare that it is currently re-equipping the 160th Special Operations Aviation Regiment with 51 Boeing MH-47E Chinooks, with a covert mission range of 345 miles and 23 Sikorsky MH-60K Blackhawk special-operations helicopters.

8
The Specialist
A Modern Raison d'Etre

By their very nature special purpose forces have been introduced in response to specific threats or to overcome a particular difficulty. Usually they have been disbanded once that threat has been neutralised or the difficulty surmounted. Special forces on the other hand have invariably remained, a potent reserve against the unexpected.

The Threat
Traditionally the threat to special, or special purpose forces has been military. It has come from a numerically larger, or better equipped conventional enemy or from rival elites. However the second half of the twentieth century has seen terrorism grow as an increasingly potent weapon in the hands of the political extremists. Marxist-Leninism has always regarded terror as a bona-fide means of political influence, which its disciples have never been afraid to export. Until her own internal collapse, the Soviet Union, either directly or through her satellite proxies in East Germany and Bulgaria, hosted and trained - and where necessary even pay-rolled - countless terror groups. Established organisations such as PIRA and ETA were encouraged to maintain a close liaison with closely with, and even to call upon the dubious assistance of the more volatile Red Brigades where necessary. This created a level of instability which the established security services found difficult to counter.

Today Eastern Europe no longer plays host to terror groups, indeed Russia has sought the advice of MI5 in its fight against internal disorder and has recently taken the unprecedented step of inviting the United States to open an FBI office in Moscow in an attempt to counter the growing threat from organised crime. State sponsored terrorists have long ago been expelled from Egypt, and more recently from Syria. However they remain a potent force in Iran and Iraq, and in the guise of Muslim fundamentalism are presently threatening the stability of the secular regimes of the southern Mediterranean. Terrorism remains rife in the more remote areas of South America, in the Philippines and in large tracts of central Africa.

The Mailed Fist
It is virtually impossible for a country to fight terrorism with terrorism without losing at least the outward respect and support of its allies. Occasionally governments have decided the price is worth paying. When terrorists of the 'Black September' movement murdered eleven Israeli athletes during the 1972 Munich Olympics, the Israeli defence and intelligence apparatus swore revenge. Vengeance, when it came, was spectacular.

8 The Specialist

On the morning of 9 April 1973 a team of 30 Israeli reconnaissance paratroopers from the elite 'Sayaret Maktal' landed from a flotilla of six Zodiac rubber craft on Dove beach, Beirut. They were met by a team of Israeli Naval Commandos who had earlier secured the beach head, and by a group of MOSSAD agents. Dressed in civilian clothes the agents and paratroopers were driven to their various targets in cars rented by fellow MOSSAD agents. One group headed towards a luxury apartment complex known to house three Black September officials responsible for the organisation of the earlier massacre. The PLO sentries were quickly disposed of and the Black September targets eliminated without compassion.

At the same time a second team of paratroopers attacked the headquarters of the Democratic Front for the Liberation of Palestine (DFLP) and, in a bloody close-quarter fire-fight, eliminated most of the gunmen present. A third team succeeded in destroying the Black September bomb factory, killing scores of terrorists guarding the facility.

As the attacks went in, Israeli Air Force helicopters hovered overhead ready to remove the wounded to safety and to carry off masses of captured PLO files. As the paratroopers and their MOSSAD aides made their escape to the beach head and the waiting Zodiacs, the helicopters dropped spikes on the major routes to frustrate pursuit. On the face of it the raid was an unequivocal success. The PLO suffered a severe setback while Black September virtually ceased to function as a major terrorist organisation. However the eighteen months of planning which the raid had required severely drained the resources of Israeli Intelligence, distracting it from its other, more mundane responsibilities. Routine assessments of Arab conventional military strength were allowed to become clouded and complacent. In October 1973 Israel paid dearly for its omissions when its armed force were taken almost completely by surprise on the holiest day of the Jewish year - Yom Kippur.

To compound Israel's problems Sayaret Matkal suffered a political disaster on 15 May 1974, when the Popular Democratic Front for the Liberation of Palestine (PDFLP) killed five civilians and seized a school in Ma'alot. In the resulting rescue, which was rushed and badly planned, 22 children were killed and another 60 were injured. A subsequent inquiry revealed that Sayaret Matkal had lost the element of surprise, had assaulted the wrong floor of the building and had used phosphorus grenades so strong that they had blinded both terrorist and rescuer alike. Sayaret Matkal was retained for hostage rescue duties abroad, but internal responsibility passed to a new HRU ('Yaman'). This was deployed by the border police and supported by an army battalion of technical specialists known as 'Shal-dag'.

Hostage Rescue Units

The death of the Israeli athletes at Munich impressed on all the major powers the need for highly-trained personnel to respond to terrorist incidents. The German attempts at a rescue had been brave but disastrous, and had done much to add to the carnage. It was accepted that hostage rescue units, or HRUs, would usually have to operate at a complete disadvantage. They would rarely be able to choose their combat ground and would not always be able to plan their assault.

Candidates for an HRU would need to be excellent combat marksmen in a variety of weapons and would need to be highly competent in the skills of fighting in a built-up area (FIBUA). They would need to be fit and resourceful, capable of operating on their own or in small groups. They would need to be trained in hostage management, close personal protection and insertion techniques. They would need nerves of steel and be able to demonstrate total coolness under fire. In short they would be too precious to waste on the daily mundanities of conventional soldiering or ordinary police duties.

Many countries turned to their special forces to supply these units. Other countries, notably West Germany and France, created special purpose forces from within the police. Drawing on its unique politico-military structure, the Soviet Union created units from within the KGB and MVD.

The Police Solution

West Germany's Grenzschutzgruppe-9 (GSG-9) was formed by government order on 26 September 1972. Originally led by Colonel (later General) Ulrich Wegener, it has since evolved into one of the finest units of its kind. GSG-9 draws the majority of its recruits from the Bundesgrenzschutz (BGS), the paramilitary Federal Border Protection Service created in 1951 to guard the internal border between West and East Germany. Following the reintroduction of the German Federal Armed Forces (Bundeswehr) in 1955 the role of the BGS was redefined and extended to cover the protection of all West German borders and ports of entry, the security of government buildings and embassies.

The BGS includes an Air Unit, equipped with helicopters and based at Bonn-Hangelar. Operational standards for both flying and ground crews are high, and compare well with those of the Army.

The GSG-9 is ordered into action by the Ministry of the Interior when local or state police units are unable to cope with a problem. It is divided into Special Tactical Troops (Specialeinsatztruppen -SET) five of which - plus a Command Troop - form a company, or Strike Team, under a Hauptkommissar. Strike Team Two is comprised of combat-swimmers and specialises in maritime operations and North Sea oil rig protection. Strike Team Three is trained in High Altitude Low Opening (HALO) parachuting techniques, which it employs as a means of silent infiltration into a terrorist-held area. The other teams are trained in surveillance and close personal protection duties, and operate in support of federal police SWAT teams attached to each of the German states.

Not surprisingly, the entry qualifications for GSG-9 are exacting. An initial interview selects candidates with a high proficiency in conventional police work; this must be coupled with high academic qualifications and the basic social graces and self-confidence required of a future VIP close-protection officer. Thereafter practical training lasts for four months and is followed by an operational posting. Proficiency is maintained by practising a series of simulated hostage rescues from cars, trains, aircraft, boats and buildings. Marksmanship skills are honed during three half-days and one additional evening per week spent on the range, during which each combat team expends in excess of one million rounds of ammunition per year.

GSG-9 achieved an outstanding success in October 1977, when hostages in a Lufthansa Boeing 737 at Mogadishu Airport, Somalia, were rescued and their Palestinian captors were neutralised.

8 The Specialist

The French hostage rescue unit, the 'Groupement d'Intervention de la Gendarmerie Nationale' (GIGN), was formed from the 'Gendarmerie Nationale' in November 1973. The Gendarmerie Nationale' is itself the model for most of the world's paramilitary police forces. It is organised on military lines, its officer candidates are invariable recruited from the regular or reserve army officer corps, and it is quartered in barracks ('Casernes'). It comprises three main forces: the Headquarters ('Commandement'), responsible for planning and administration and answerable directly to the Ministry of the Armed Forces; the Departmental Gendarmerie and the Mobile Gendarmerie.

The smallest unit within the Gendarmerie comprises the brigade, with up to fourteen agents. There are two types of brigade, the 'Brigade Territoriale' for general duties and the 'Brigade de Recherches' which has an investigative role. The brigades themselves are formed into companies, the companies into a 'groupement', and the 'groupements' into regional areas ('circonscriptions régionale'). Each regional area corresponds to one of the seven military regions into which mainland France is divided.

The Departmental Gendarmerie is deployed throughout mainland France, policing rural areas and towns with less than 10,000 inhabitants as well as acting as a military police force. The Mobile Gendarmerie may be called to the assistance of any Department, or political region, in the case of an emergency or civil unrest, and in the case of serious disturbances may be supplemented by Ministerial Reserve units temporarily seconded from the Departmental Gendarmerie.

The Gendarmerie Nationale has a modern and well-equipped helicopter section responsible for the provision of communications services, support for the brigades on the ground and assistance in search and rescue duties. Selection for Gendarmerie enlistment is tough. Candidates must have completed military service and meet the uncompromisingly high academic and physical standards demanded.

After training and a successful period in an operational unit, candidates may apply for transfer to GIGN. Aspirants have to complete basic parachute and diving courses before selection for the training course which emphasises mental and physical fitness, strength and marksmanship. On average, GIGN agents fire 9,000 rounds of revolver and 3,000 rounds of rifle ammunition on the range annually. They are expected to hit a moving target at 25 metres or more in two seconds; faced with multiple targets they must hit a vital spot on six targets at 25 metres within five seconds.

GIGN enjoyed its greatest success at Djibouti in February 1976 when, in conjunction with the paratroopers of 2nd REP, it rescued French school children from a terrorist-held bus. In January 1978 in intervened when two inmates at Clairvaux prison seized a deputy warden and two prison officers. The incident ended successfully with precision sniper fire which did much to enhance the GIGN reputation for uncompromising action in the face of terror. When French diplomats were taken hostage at the French Embassy in Salvador, the 'leaked' news that a GIGN team had arrived in the country convinced the terrorists that it was time to surrender.

Responsibility for domestic hostage rescue within the United States lies with the FBI which maintains its own HRU. Known as the Hostage Response Team, the 50-strong force is reputed to be among the best in the world. The Bureau also maintains small counter-terrorist teams in each State, although localised hostage rescues, resulting from purely criminal activity, are likely to be dealt with by state, county or city police SWAT teams.

Other counter-terrorist intervention teams are maintained by the Secret Service Executive Protection Division, the National Park Police and the United States Marshal's Service. The security of nuclear weapons and weapons-grade fuel is the responsibility of the Energy Department Nuclear Energy Search Team (NEST). United States overseas army and air force bases are protected by the Military Police and Security Police respectively; the latter are reputed to have been trained by GSG-9. Hostage rescue abroad is the responsibility of Delta Force and is described in more detail below.

Paramilitary HRUs

South Africa, with its history of political unrest, relied until recently on a heavily armed special purpose HRU unit drawn from the ranks of the police. The Special Task Force was organised after the 1975 Israeli consulate siege in Johannesburg. Comprised entirely of South African Police volunteers over the age of 21, it was formed in 1976 by the then SAP riot control supremo, Lieutenant General 'Bert' Wandrag.

Recruits accepted after the gruelling selection course were schooled in marksmanship, parachuting, diving, mountain rescue and specialist hostage rescue assault tactics. Basic training lasted for ten weeks and was followed by a trial period of two months. This, in turn, was followed by a further year of specialised training which included the handling of a wide variety of hostage rescue scenarios.

Weapons employed included: 9mm Super Star pistols; S-1 and BXP 9mm submachine-guns; R-1 and R-4 assault rifles; 37mm stopper grenade-launchers capable of firing baton, stun, irritant or illuminating rounds; and a locally-developed stun grenade. Weapon familiarisation and accuracy were honed at a 'Killing House' situated at the unit's headquarters in Pretoria. To add realism to the training, the facility reputedly included target video-footage taken of actual hostage rescue incidents.

The Special Task Force saw extensive service during the Soweto unrest of 1976/77. However, its real baptism of fire came during the 1980 Silverton bank siege when a group of ANC cadres was wiped out after holding 27 civilians hostage. After that the unit was deployed on several occasions to free hostages taken in prison escapes or revolts. One of its most notable achievements was the suppression of the Bophuthatswana homeland coup in 1988, which resulted in the reinstatement of the puppet President, Lucas Mangope.

In September 1988 the unit came to the attention of the international media during a Papal visit to Lesotho. When 71 Catholic pilgrims were held hostage by four members of the Lesotho Liberation Army, the ruling Military Council sought the assistance of the Special Task Force in freeing them. The unit stormed the bus in the grounds of the British High Commission having first blinded the gunmen with a dazzling arc-light. Three of the novice guerrillas were killed in the ensuing shootout, and the hostages rescued without loss.

The Railways Police Special Task Force, a highly specialist HRU, was formed in October 1975. Despite its name, within ten years of its inception it became responsible for resolving all smaller-scale internal hostage rescue situations involving buildings, aeroplanes, trains, boats and buses. Training placed considerable emphasis on physical fitness, and there was extensive schooling in house-clearing techniques and in the use of helicopter assault methods. Members were equipped with helmets, respirators, bullet proof vests and an array of pistols, sub-machine-guns, shotguns and stun grenades.

The unit was used extensively for VIP protection during the 1976/77 Soweto unrest. In 1981 it was involved in the negotiations with the hijackers of an Air India Boeing 707 airliner, following the abortive Seychelles coup led by the mercenary, Colonel 'Mad' Mike Hoare. Suggestions that the unit maintained a close liaison with special purpose HRUs in Singapore and Israel were never proved.

The Military and Hostage Rescue

The British military were among the first to become actively involved in countering international terrorism. In 1969, 22 SAS Regiment was tasked with forming training teams to protect friendly overseas heads of state, and with the protection of British embassies in potential trouble spots. In 1973 a Counter Revolutionary Warfare (CRW) Wing was established at Hereford with a permanent staff of twenty, and it now trains all members of the Regiment's sabre squadrons in every aspect of counter-terrorist skills.

A major part of the training involves the perfecting of close quarter battle (CQB) techniques, which includes a six-week course in marksmanship. Training begins in a conventional electronic CQB range, consisting of remotely-controlled targets, some depicting gunmen and others hostages; these spring up at various heights and angles in front of the advancing soldier. Although CQB ranges are excellent in preparing individuals for fighting in a built up area (FIBUA), they lack the sophistication required to train experts in hostage rescue.

To perfect the specialised HRU disciplines of rapid entry and target identification a Killing House has therefore been built at the SAS headquarters at Stirling Lines in Hereford. Techniques practised in the Killing House include rapid magazine changing, malfunction clearance drills, shooting on the move and from unconventional positions. Rapid target acquisition, exact shot placement and double tapping are also taught to the highest level to ensure that they all become second nature to the student. Personnel discharge a minimum of 5,000 rounds per week during the course, though the Special Projects Team will fire far more.

Until 1986 the Killing House comprised one basic room adjusted to represent a series of hostage-rescue scenarios. The room contained a potentially lethal combination of SAS men acting as victims and dummies depicting terrorists. To add to the realism live ammunition was used and the room was often in darkness. The students were required to burst into the room, identify the hostages within four seconds and neutralise the terrorists before they had time to react. The system worked well until a highly respected SAS senior NCO, acting as a 'victim', was incorrectly identified and shot dead.

Sophisticated technology now ensures a far greater degree of safety. The Killing House now has two rooms; one containing the 'terrorists' and 'hostages', the other the assault team. Cameras are fitted, and a real-time image of each room is simultaneously displayed on a life-size wrap-around screen in the other. The students and 'terrorists' can thus see and fire at the images of each other in relative safety. In addition, the entire sequence is recorded on video to allow comprehensive debriefings. At any one time an SAS squadron is on 24-hour standby for anti-terrorist and hostage-rescue operations. The duty squadron is divided into four operational troops, called Special Projects Teams, each comprising an officer, usually a captain, and 15 other ranks. The Special Projects Teams are again divided into four four-man assault teams; one is permanently based in London and the others in Hereford.

Logistics support for the CRW Wing has improved beyond all measure in the last decade. The Regiment now holds a computerised data-base of all public buildings and likely terrorist targets and can down-load this information onto a portable computer to allow a field commander instant access to such crucial tactical information as dead ground, blind spots and arcs of fire. Respirators and the now-famous black flame-proof suits have become closely associated with the SAS in its CRW role, as have stun grenades, which detonate with a deafening bang and a blinding flash. Frame charges - capable of blowing precision holes through doors, brickwork, windows and even steel - were openly employed during the Princes Gate siege as was a range of dedicated light aluminium climbing equipment. Less obviously, CRW personnel are issued with a variety of body armour, specifically designed to be light while offering maximum stopping power through the use of such materials as Kevlar. Typically the GPV 25 vest, which is worn for hostage-rescue work, offers protection at close range from the impact of any high velocity 9mm automatic or sub-machine gun, .357 Magnum pistol and 7.62mm rifle rounds.

A dedicated SAS signals support squadron maintains a satellite-communications system capable of providing world-wide links with Stirling Lines, and thence, by more conventional though equally secure means, with the Director Special Forces (DSF) in Duke of York's Headquarters, Chelsea. A range of compact communications kit is available to every individual in a hostage rescue team to ensure that information can be passed, and orders relayed, unambiguously and at once.

Operation 'Nimrod'

Of all the operations carried out by the SAS since its re-establishment after the Second World War, none has captured the imagination of the world, nor been carried out on so public a stage, as the operation to end the siege at the Iranian Embassy. On 30 April 1980 six Arab revolutionaries - Makki, Ali, Shai, Faisal, Hassan and their leader, Oan - burst into the foyer of the Iranian Embassy in Princes Gate, London, and seized 26 hostages, including PC Trevor Lock from the Metropolitan Police Diplomatic Protection Group. The six terrorists, who were members of the Mohieddin al Nasser Martyr Group, were fighting for the autonomy of Arabistan, an oil-rich province of south-west Iran, which had been annexed by that country in 1926. Despite being well armed; having at least two 9mm machine pistols, three Browning Highpower automatic pistols loaded with hollow-point ammunition, a .38 revolver and several Russian hand grenades; crucially they showed little initial desire to use their weapons.

Within minutes the five-storey, 50-room building was surrounded by the local police. Gradually they were joined by elements from D11 (the police 'Blue Beret' marksmen), by C13 anti-terrorist officers, Special Patrol Group teams, Scotland Yard's C7 Technical Support Branch and - more covertly - by a team from the CTW who came in plain clothes to assess the situation. The terrorists' initial demands - the immediate release of 91 Arabs being held in Iranian jails and their transfer to Britain, and the provision of Arab ambassadors to mediate on their behalf - were quickly tempered after discussion with Police negotiators. The threat to execute the hostages should the embassy be attacked remained, nevertheless.

While negotiations were going on, Prime Minister Margaret Thatcher sought the advice of COBRA - the Cabinet Office Briefing Team of MI5, MI6, MOD and SAS experts constituted for just such a contingency - and ordered the deployment of an SAS Special Projects Team to the area. In complete secrecy the CRW experts moved to an old Royal Corps of Transport barracks in Albany Street, near Regents Park, and at once began to study a model of the Embassy. Thermal imagers were used to determine which rooms were in occupation, and by how many individuals. Further intelligence was steadily added by C7 using microphones and surveillance devices in the chimneys and walls of adjoining buildings until the SAS had sufficient information to determine a basic assault plan.

It was agreed that one four-man team would abseil down the rear of the building to the ground and first floors while a second team, crossing from the balconies of neighbouring buildings, would enter the building from the front. The teams would use frame charges to effect their entry and would then lob in stun grenades to disorientate the terrorists. All team members were to be dressed in black anti-flash suits, bullet proof jackets and respirators and would be armed with Browning automatic pistols and Heckler & Koch MP5 sub-machine-guns.

On the morning of 5 May the situation within the Embassy suddenly deteriorated when the terrorists lost confidence in the police negotiators. That evening they murdered a hostage and dumped his body on the pavement. Control of the incident was passed from the police to the MOD, and 'Pagoda' Troop, the code-name for the Special Projects Team, was ordered to bring the siege to a satisfactory conclusion.

At a given signal two troopers abseiled down to the first-floor rear balcony while a second pair abseiled to the ground. The men on the balcony were unable to detonate their frame charges as a colleague had become entangled in a rope above them. Instead they used sledge hammers to make an entrance to the rear of the building, lobbed in stun grenades and entered. Seconds later the team at the front of the building blew in the window with frame charges, threw in stun and CS grenades and entered. The terrorists were taken by complete surprise. The building, which had had its power cut, was in darkness and soon filled with smoke and tear gas. Carefully and deliberately, Pagoda troop moved through the building in search of the terrorists. Oan was killed on the first-floor landing. Two terrorists guarding the hostages in the second-floor telex room were killed and a third wounded, but not before they had themselves murdered one of their hostages and wounded two others. A fifth terrorist was killed in the hallway near the front door of the Embassy, and the sixth in an office at the back of the building.

The entire operation took no more than seventeen minutes. The hostages and remaining terrorist were evacuated from the by now burning building, allowing the

SAS to depart as they had come, in almost complete secrecy. Other than a few burns, Pagoda Troop suffered no casualties.

In 1987 the SAS extended the scope of support of the civil powers when they successfully rescued a prison warder held at knife point in HM Prison, Peterhead. In the process they demonstrated a powerful array of previously unseen specialist anti-riot/HRU equipment available to them. This included a high-powered cannon capable of breaching walls with water-filled shells, a thermal lance designed to cut through prison bars in seconds and a range of new disabling gases. There can be no doubt that the SAS has continued to develop new tactics, and has taken delivery of much new equipment, since 1987.

Delta Force

The United States 1st Special Forces Operational Detachment (Delta Force) was activated on November 1977, following GSG-9's successful hostage rescue mission at Mogadishu, and is now responsible for United States hostage rescue missions abroad. It was the creation of the legendary United States special forces pioneer, Colonel Charlie Beckwith, who served with the SAS in 1963. Under Beckwith's command the Delta Force structure, selection and philosophy closely mirrored those of the SAS; it is possible however that since he relinquished command these have been refined to take into account Delta's more specialist role.

All potential transferees to Delta must attend a lengthy and very searching interview with a number of serving officers and NCOs of the Group and must undergo psychological assessment before they are even accepted for selection. This is to ensure that they are self-possessed and mature enough to endure the hours, possibly days, of extensive monotony which invariably precede the few minutes of sheer naked aggression which mark the final stages of most hostage rescues.

Training covers all aspects of conventional soldiering, with particular regard being paid to the handling of foreign weapons and deep reconnaissance, together with the more esoteric skills of vehicle theft, aircraft refuelling and hostage reassurance. Like the SAS, Delta has its own CQB House used to sharpen its hostage rescue and room-clearance drills. Larger than the SAS Killing House, the aptly named Delta 'House of Horrors' has four rooms: the first a warm up room containing pop-up friend-or-foe targets; a second with entry and immediate engagement scenarios; a third dedicated to night-shooting and assaults; and a fourth in the form of an aircraft cabin.

The size and organisation of Delta is secret, although it is considered to have an establishment of about 400 personnel, of whom about half are combat operators organised into two squadrons. In line with traditional SAS thought the standard operational group is the four-man squad, each member of which has a primary and secondary specialisation which may include communications, demolition or advanced field medicine. Four squads form a troop, and two or more troops, together with their support, a squadron.

Delta's most famous and tragic action was Operation 'Eagle Claw', the ill-fated attempt in 1980 to rescue the United States hostages from Iranian hands. As a direct result, a top-level re-evaluation was made of all counter-terrorist resources. A new Joint Special Operations Control (JSOC) was established at Fort Bragg, North Carolina, and now comprises SEAL Team Six, Delta (which was retained virtually intact), Helicopter Task Force 160 and USAF special operations assets.

The US Army has recently decided to involve all combat units up to battalion level in basic counter-terrorism/counter-insurgency training. Home-based units now rotate through the Joint Readiness Training Center at Little Rock, Arkansas, which is staffed by 500 SOF personnel under Delta Force supervision.

A number of smaller nations have excellent dedicated HSUs. A typically example is 7 (NL) SBS, the Special Boat Section of the Royal Netherlands Marine Corps. It is responsible for the security of Dutch oil rigs in the North Sea, and is trained in counter-terrorist techniques, operating in that role with the Close Combat Unit based at Doorn.

On 23 May 1977 the Close Combat Unit demonstrated its expertise to the world when South Moluccan terrorists hijacked a Dutch train travelling between Assen and Groningen, taking 49 people hostage. After a three week siege the train was successfully stormed by the CCU. SAS advisers, who had been invited to the scene, had offered stun grenades to the Marines for their assault, but in the event the terrorists were distracted by fighter aircraft flying low over the train.

The Soviet Response

The socio-political problems facing the Soviet Union immediately prior to its disintegration were immense. The 285 million Soviet citizens belonged to 104 different nationalities, of which only 22 boasted more than one million people. Fifteen of those nationalities enjoyed the protection of their own republics, another twenty were autonomous republics and a further eighteen lived in national districts. In addition the Soviet Union hosted at least ten ethnic groups ranging from East Slav to German.

Many of the problems in the south were rooted in religious intolerence and mistrust. The Azerbaijanis had converted to Islam in the seventh century, the Turkestanis had converted in the eighth century, and the Bulgars some 200 years later. Many Azerbaijanis, were Shi'ites, and as such had become deeply influenced by the fundamentalist revolution in Iran. The Christian republics of Armenia and Georgia, ever scornful of their Muslim neighbours, had come to fear their intentions. Nothing they had seen in Iran or Afghanistan had led them to change their minds. Pent-up nationalist emotions had led to public disorder which had manifested itself in ethnic unrest, rioting, and even - at its worst - localised pogroms.

Not surprisingly the Soviet national airline, Aeroflot, became the target for a number of vicious, usually ethnic, hijacks. On 8 March 1988, eleven members of the family jazz band Ovechkin hijacked a Tu-154 airliner en route from Irkutsk to Leningrad. Concealing shotguns among their instruments they seized the plane and demanded to be flown to London. Feigning compliance with their demands the pilot landed in Leningrad, pretending that it was a refuelling stop in Finland.

This simple ruse was exposed when the hijackers saw Soviet police and troops milling about on the runway. After a period of fruitless negotiation a hastily convened MVD assault team attempted a rescue. The team was completely untrained for such an operation, which it attempted to execute devoid of specialist equipment and without direction. In the ensuing fire-fight, nine people were killed and a further nineteen wounded. The assault ended in gruesome fiasco when the hijackers detonated an explosive device, turning the rear of the aircraft into an inferno.

The ensuing adverse publicity enabled the KGB to assume control of aircraft-related hostage-rescue operations. A special group was formed under the command of Colonel R. Ishmiyarov and divided into two main departments, dealing with analysis and operations respectively, with support from communications specialists and trained negotiators. The group, which most closely resembled GSG-9, drew its recruits from the KGB Border Guards. It came under the jurisdiction of a Deputy Chairman of the KGB, with operational control subordinated to the 'Urgent Action Crisis Headquarters' in Moscow, staffed by officials of the KGB, MVD, Foreign Ministry and Ministry of Civil Aviation.

The new unit first came to the public attention in December 1988, when four hijackers seized a school bus in Ordzhonikidze. Quietly and calmly the hijackers were allowed to ransom the children for weapons, money and an Il-76T airliner which they then forced to fly to Israel. With tacit Israeli support the KGB followed behind; their orders to recover the plane, its crew and the hijackers with as little incident as possible. Two days later, under considerable pressure from both the Israelis and Soviets, the hijackers were persuaded to surrender, and were last seen by the western press being hustled aboard the Tu-154 pursuit aircraft.

Although control of aircraft-related hostage rescue passed to the KGB, control on the ground remained largely with the MVD. During the spring of 1989 a new MVD cadre emerged. Photographs appeared in *Novosti* showing fit young MVD personnel wearing the latest 6ZBT- M-01 flak jackets and carrying AKS-74 assault rifles with an extra magazine taped to the loaded one. These men were issued with conventional camouflage trousers and jackets, but wore bright scarlet berets in the floppy style of the Soviet paratrooper. In action they wore equally distinctive white helmets.

The new 'MVD unit of special designation' was variously referred to as Oznaz or Omon in the Soviet press and formed the Interior Ministry's latest anti-terrorism, hostage-rescue team. Suggestions that the unit comprised 'ordinary looking soldiers recruited from all corners of the country' were spurious. The group was in fact lead by Captain Viktor Spiridonov, a former army paratroop instructor. Its closely-knit members referred to themselves as 'the brotherhood', all were army veterans, many were ex-parachutists or Spetsnaz, and nearly all had seen action in Afghanistan.

An article in the journal *Krasnaya Zvezda* which appeared in the summer of 1989 suggested that the unit formed part of the elite Dzerzhinsky Internal Troops Division. Its members were said to undertake a six months training programme (which was possibly increased to ten months soon thereafter) at its own training centre in the Moscow area. The curriculum included specialist gymnastics, shooting, long-distance endurance running, unarmed combat and simulated assaults. Training aids in the form of an SAS-style Killing House and dummy aircraft were utilised to refine hostage rescue techniques.

Although the unit was small, possibly no more than a company in size, its very existence added credence to the theory that at that time the Soviet Union looked to the Ministry of Internal Affairs, rather than the army, to counter the growing threat of domestic terrorism.

8 The Specialist

The Military In Aid of the Civil Powers

All military forces are trained to act in support of the civil powers in an emergency. In a democracy however it is rare for a government to call upon the assistance of its conventional armed forces to control civil unrest. Instead most will maintain a quasi-military organization, or series of organizations, to assist in the maintenance of order during periods of localised unrest. The United States has its 50 National Guards which may be mobilised by the state governors without recourse to Washington. They are all volunteers, mostly drawn from the local community which generally supports them in their activities. Continental Europe has its paramilitaries, who although being on the face of it policemen, are armed, trained and disciplined in the manner of a military force. Even Britain, with its traditional abhorrence of an armed police force, has come to accept the necessity for an increasing number of its officers to carry side arms in the normal course of their duties.

Totalitarian regimes, however, have rarely shown the same restraint, and it is far from uncommon for localised civil unrest in Asia and South America to be countered by front line troops. The years immediately preceding the disintegration of the Soviet Union saw massive unrest, as long-frustrated aspirations to nationalism began to manifest themselves in the birth of often violent, political pressure groups. The role of the army and of the Interior Ministry in attempting to suppress these groups is as complex as it is diverse. Afghan veterans, who were not trained in riot control, yet who were ordered to clear dissenters from the streets, often acted violently. An incident in Tbilisi, in April 1989, was a typical example of such over-reaction.

The Tbilisi Incident

Throughout 1989 civil unrest within the Soviet Union grew. On the night of 8-9 April, disturbances in the Georgian capital of Tbilisi erupted into bloody near-civil war when Interior Ministry troops, supported by paratroopers from the 104th Guards Airborne Division, attacked an estimated 10,000 demonstrators then occupying Lenin Square in the city centre. After less than two hours of vicious fighting sixteen demonstrators, fourteen of them women, lay dead. Although 75 soldiers were reported hurt, none was seriously injured.

During the days and weeks that followed, the Soviet authorities attempted to justify the actions of its elite troops but with little success. It soon became apparent that the unrest had been anticipated, indeed engineered, by the local Communist Party supported by Politburo hard-liner Yigor Jigachev and Defence Minister Dmitiri Yazov. They had decided to take advantage of the fact that Mikhail Gorbachev had only just returned from a trip to the United Kingdom. Aware that he had yet fully to regain the reins of power, they were determined to destroy once and for all the seeds of Georgian nationalism, by force if necessary.

For a number of weeks the unofficial Georgian National Front movement had been fomenting unrest. It had organised demonstrations at the university and strikes among the public sector and transport workers. When 400 National Front members had marched to the Communist Party headquarters and organised a much publicised hunger strike, the local Party had threatened to call the Militia to clear the square. 10,000 demonstrators had spontaneously surrounded the hunger strikers' encampment forming a human barrier between it and the authorities. The stage had been set for confrontation.

On the morning of Saturday 8 April heavily armed elements of the 104th Guards Airborne Division, based at Korovabad, began to parade in the streets of the Georgian capital in a deliberate show of force. The sight of elite paratroopers did not alarm the demonstrators unduly as they had long been associated with the control of civil disorder. The 7th Guards Airborne Division had been used to regain order after large scale rioting in Kaunas, Lithuania as far back as 1972. More recently the 104th Airborne Division itself had deployed to neighbouring Nagorny Karabakh in an attempt to stop the prevailing sectarian slaughter. Their inherent toughness, better training and higher motivation had been thought to lend itself ideally to urban confrontation.

Unknown to the general population however, the local Communist leadership in conjunction with the MVD had drawn up plans to clear the square. At approximately 4.00am a line of BTR 60PB armoured personnel carriers, followed by men of the MVD and paratroopers, moved in. Fighting broke out in which sixteen demonstrators died and many hundreds were injured. The exact sequence of events during the short-lived confrontation remains confused. What is known is that spades were used openly as weapons against the unarmed crowd. In the words of one eye witness, 'Militiamen and Special Interior Ministry Troops' wielding shovels and metal clubs seemingly lost control, turning the area immediately in front of the Communist headquarters into a slaughterhouse.

In the post mortem which followed, the MVD and army blamed each other for the carnage while the Party blamed both. Rodinov, in overall charge of the task force, was removed from his command, but was later appointed as head of the General Staff Academy.

A hastily convened commission accused the military authorities and local Communist leadership of five offences: using the Soviet Army against civilians without declaring a state of emergency; using weapons proscribed by law; using illegal chemical agents; attacking civilians; and finally (and perhaps most alarmingly) attacking members of the local MVD who went to the assistance of such civilians.

The status of the 'illegal chemical agents' used at Tbilisi is of particular interest. Rodinov admitted that his paratroopers and not the MVD had fired 27 canisters of 'Cheremukha' (Cherry) into the crowd. Identified as chloracetophene - a weapon of First World War vintage designed to debilitate the nervous system and internal organs whilst impairing sight and breathing - the gas is far more potent than anything used by security forces in the West. However it was the use of the gas by the Army, not the substance itself, which was criticised. Ironically, the use of the same gas would have been lawful had it been discharged by the MVD.

In a little-publicised decree of 28/29 July 1988, the Supreme Soviet had extended the powers of the Internal Troops to incorporate the use of 'special means' to counter threats of mass violations of public order. Although the precise extent of these 'special powers' had deliberately been left vague, it was generally accepted that they included the controlled use of tear gas. However, not only were the MVD Internal Troops at Tbilisi not equipped with chemical agents, they were not even carrying respirators. It is highly unlikely, therefore, that they even knew that gas was to be used, a theory strengthened by the fact that a number fell victim to the effects themselves.

8 The Specialist

It was subsequently conceded by the authorities that the Decree of July 1988 did not in itself legalise the use of firearms against civilians, save in self defence. The point was of no more than academic interest in the case of Tbilisi as firearms were used neither by the Army nor the MVD. However subsequent assertions made by the Army in its newspaper *Krasnaya Zvezda*, that its use of shovels as offensive weapons was in strict accord with the no-use-of-arms order, and therefore lawful, was incorrect. The very presence of the Army without a prior declaration of a State of Emergency had been in contravention of Article 119, point 14, of the Soviet Constitution, and was therefore unlawful.

The Tbilisi incident drove a near irreparable wedge between the MVD and the Army. The MVD felt, with some degree of justification that it had been unfairly pilloried for the excesses of the paratroopers. Its Internal Security forces, which unlike the Army did not require a declaration of a state of emergency to deploy, had acted lawfully, and in most instances with considerable restraint. Indeed a number of its personnel had been injured by the airborne forces when they had attempted to restrain the latters' excessive zeal. They had not employed chemical agents, although entitled to do so, yet had found themselves criticised by association when the paratroopers had. For its part the Army made it abundantly clear that it would no longer tolerate being used as a political pawn. In its opinion it had received explicit, albeit flawed, orders to clear Lenin Square, and had carried them out to the letter. The Soviet authorities heeded the warning, and never again attempted to use the Army in the suppression of peaceful political dissent.

The PLA in Tiananmen Square

The violent end to the democracy movement's peaceful rally in Tiananmen Square in June 1989, when unarmed demonstrators were crushed by seasoned troops of the Chinese People's Liberation Army (PLA), shocked the world. But it should not have. The PLA merely remained loyal to its political roots.

The 38th Group Army, which was based in the area surrounding Beijing and which was the first take up position on the city's outskirts, was the most modern and well equipped of China's armies, but it was not a true elite. Unlike the MVD and paratroopers in Tbilisi its officers and men had not recently seen action, nor had they been specially trained in the role of counter-insurgency. When the 38th first appeared in the suburbs of the capital it was immediately apparent that its armoured personnel carriers had been in storage for some years. As if to emphasise the unit's unpreparedness for war, in several cases the tarpaulin covering its armoured vehicles' machine-guns had actually stuck to the barrels.

The units of the 38th were subjected to at least four hours of political indoctrination and an hour's political study per day for up to two weeks prior to entering Beijing. Commissars were appointed to every company-sized formation (approximately 130 men). They marched with the men, ate with them and shared their recreation, yet they could do nothing to overcome the latent ideological conflicts in the minds of the young soldiers, many of whom had friends among the demonstrators.

When a state of martial law was declared and the troops began to move towards Tiananmen Square many were unarmed. A few, reputedly, were not even in uniform. Soldiers allowed their vehicles to be halted and surrounded by the students and their worker allies, with whom many of the young soldiers sympathised. A large number of vehicles turned round, refusing to go further, others actually surrendered to the demonstrators.

After the failure of the 38th Group Army, the Government made detailed plans for Group Armies from distant parts of China to be deployed around Beijing. Passenger trains were cancelled, as were domestic air flights, as the 27th Group Army made its way from Shijiazhuang. It was followed by major units from the 39th Group Army in Shenyang, the 15th Airborne from Wuhan, the 14th Group Army from Sichuan, the 24th from Chengde, Inner Mongolia and the 1st and 12th Group Armies from Nanjing. The 6th Tank division, already in Beijing and considered loyal, was reinforced by the 1st Tank division from Tiajin. In all, over 150,000 troops were moved to the capital.

The assault against the demonstrators, now publicly labelled 'criminals' by the authorities, was led by the 27th Group Army. To minimise possible sympathy for the protesters, its soldiers were denied access to newspapers and radios for a number of days prior to the confrontation. Jonathan Mirsky, in his excellent contribution to Jane's *China in Crisis*, suggests that, as the 27th Group Army crashed its way into Tiananmen Square it truly believed that the figures it saw moving about in the smoke and flame were not students and workers but 'liu-mang' or hoodlums, who had combined with bad elements, reactionaries, class-enemies and counter-revolutionaries to overthrow the Government, the Party, the State, and indeed Communism itself.

Whatever the truth, the men of the 27th Group Army continued to use their weapons indiscriminately long after any perceived danger to themselves, and to the State, had passed. The next day, on more than one occasion they continued to shoot into crowds of frantic parents and friends who had come to search for the bodies of those gunned down and bayoneted the night before. Doctors and nurses, who true to their vocation risked their lives to help the wounded, risked summary execution at the hands of these soldiers, many of whom seemed unable to restrain their blood lust.

The death toll in Tiananmen Square will never be known for certain. Bodies were piled into funeral pyres and burned without record. Nor can the wholesale difference in reaction between the 38th and the 27th Group Armies be easily explained. It is not enough to say that they came from different parts of China, or that they enjoyed conflicting political aspirations. Elements of the PLA were purged after Tiananmen Square, but by and large it was left intact. It had been ordered to clear the streets of Beijing and had done so. After that it had dutifully left the streets without question.

It is perhaps significant that the PLA did not introduce its elite and totally loyal paratroopers onto the streets of Beijing, keeping them in reserve instead. Nor has it taken steps to introduce a force such as the Soviet Omon. Clearly the Chinese Government feels that it can rely on the Army as a whole to provide it with support and protection in the face of future political or social disquiet.

Drugs and the Elite

The increase in the trafficking of illegal drugs on an international scale has long been seen as the greatest risk to the stability of the modern world. Drugs manufacture and distribution is now on such a scale that it threatens the very stability of a number of third world countries.

8 The Specialist

Traditionally the West controlled drug manufacture at source by providing the indigenous harvesters with alternative sources of wealth, either in the form of civil aid projects or direct subsidy. It then organised the growers into local militias strong enough to combat pressure from domestic purchasers. The modern drug industry however is on too large a scale to be countered by so simple a solution. It is supported by organised crime and terrorism, and has massive firepower at its disposal.

Until recently more than 80 per cent of the Lebanon's Bekaa Valley was used to grow opium and hashish under Hezbollah control, providing that unfortunate country with an estimated 30 per cent of its gross national product. Recent pressure from Syria, and to a lesser extent Israel, has reduced the size of this harvest, but it remains formidable.

The coca plant represents one of the main cash crops in Colombia, Peru and Bolivia. In Colombia, the largest of the narcotics producers, the traffic is controlled by two main syndicates; the 'Medellin' and 'Carli' cartels. Each has its own army dedicated to the manufacture and distribution of narcotics and each has proved itself capable of murder, kidnap and corruption on a vast scale. Internal terrorist groups such as the Marxist 'Fuerzas Armadas Revolucionarias Colombianes' (FARC), the Maoist People's Liberation Army (EPL) and the Cuban-inspired M-19 levy a ten per cent tax on the peasants who grow the coca leaves, in exchange for protection, having an excellent understanding with the traffickers. In 1987 rural Colombian guerrillas acted as proxies for the traffickers when they crossed the Venezuelan border to attack National Guard units who were destroying drug plantations. M-19, with its more sophisticated urban roots, has been held responsible for a number of drug-related murders of judges, government officials and army officers, who were regarded by the traffickers as a threat.

In November 1985, in one of the worst outbreaks of violence, members of M-19 seized the Palace of Justice in the capital city of Bogotá. Over 80 people were killed, including half of the members of the Supreme Court. The Palace was retaken by unspecified 'anti-terrorist' forces with the loss of many hostages. No terrorists survived the assault which the Government therefore claimed as a success. Nonetheless it understandably left the judiciary extremely shaken.

On 10 February 1988 José Blandon, a former aide to the then Panamanian dictator, General Noriega, testified before a United States Senate subcommittee that Fidel Castro and Noriega had been working in conjunction to promote 'drug-financed guerrilla movements throughout Latin America'. He stated that Medellin cartel chief, Pablo Escobar Gaviria, was supported by Castro who provided his cartel with a naval base on the islet of Piedra, off the northern coast of Cuba. From the protection of Cuba speed boats took the cocaine, hashish and methaqualone to distribution networks in Florida. From there large numbers of Cuban agents distributed the drugs with the aim of increasing addiction, violent crime and corruption throughout the United States.

Simultaneously drug barons in Peru, who were responsible for virtually half of the world's cocaine, were being protected by the Maoist Sendero Luminosco (Shining Path) movement, in exchange for fifteen per cent of the proceeds plus aircraft landing fees of $15,000. The drugs were being concentrated in the inaccessible, and highly fortified Huallaga Valley and transported from there by light aircraft to distribution centres in Mexico and the Caribbean.

Alarmed by the comparative ease with which drugs were crossing the Caribbean into Florida, the United States Coastguard introduced a new air-elite into the equation. In 1985 the then Vice-President George Bush set up the National Narcotics Border Interdiction System. It was equipped with a varied collection of aircraft, including several confiscated from the smugglers themselves. The Interdiction System contains the South Florida Task Force, and within that the Miami Air Branch, based at Homestead AFB. Most of the Air Branch pilots are ex-service, and have developed a close liaison between the various civil and military agencies involved in the narcotics war.

The Miami Air Branch was originally established in 1972 with a single Bell Jet-Ranger helicopter, supported by an Aerostar aircraft. These were later reinforced by former US Navy S-2 Tracker aircraft and by Cessna Citation IIs, acting as 'mini-AWACS' aircraft. The highly sophisticated range of instrumentation fitted to the Cessnas greatly facilitated the United States Customs' ability to track suspect aircraft and boats. Nonetheless, the advantage remained with the traffickers. Equipped with boats and planes faster than those issued to the United States Coastguard, and able to monitor the Customs radio frequencies, they became adept at the use of decoys, even resorting to false 'Maydays' in the macabre knowledge that pursuing Customs craft would be duty bound to respond.

The addition in the mid-1980s of two modified Black Hawk helicopters, on extended loan from the US Army, has markedly enhanced the Miami Air Branch's ability to counter the traffickers. Modifications to the helicopters, including additional internal fuel tanks, have given the aircraft an endurance of over five hours. Special radios ensure secure communications between the helicopters and narcotics agencies while a 30 million candle-power Spectrolab Nitesun searchlight affords a supremely useful night-interception capability. The Black Hawks have proved to be excellent pursuit helicopters, usually getting airborne within four minutes and often surprising the smugglers with their sheer speed (184 mph). At present, the Black Hawks fly about one in ten of the total hours undertaken by the Miami unit, but have a far higher percentage success rate.

Under the umbrella of Operation 'Snowcap' the United States Drug Enforcement Agency (DEA), the Pentagon and the CIA have been spearheading efforts to overcome the traffickers on the South American mainland. Spy satellites using infrared imagery are being used to identify plantations, air strips and processing factories while specialist heliborne police units have been carrying out fast search and destroy missions.

United States Special Forces have recently been seen training the Peruvian police in a range of SF-patrol tactics, culminating in heliborne assaults by the elite Military Anti-Guerrilla Command on the drug factories in the Huallaga Valley. Britain has sent specialist jungle-trained instructors from 22 SAS in support of the Colombian authorities. Unlike the United States Special Forces in Peru, who favour more direct means, the SAS and their police commando students, drawn from the elite ten-man Special Operations Groups (GOES), are employing the LRRP tactics which proved so successful in Borneo.

Helicopters are used, but only to drop off long range insertion patrols and strike forces close to the areas of known drug activity. From these remote LZs the patrols enter the contested areas on foot, employing lead scouts and flankers and using their reconnaissance skills to avoid detection. The Colombians carry Israeli made personal weapons, and have learned from the SAS to cover long distances in the most inhospitable of terrains, pausing only for the occasional sip of water.

The introduction of special purpose forces into the South American drugs wars has led inevitably to an increase in hostilities and has occasionally brought strains into the relationship between the militaries and their governments. In 1989 the Shining Path alone lost 1,026 members killed in action against the security forces at a cost of 293 police and military and 1,016 civilians killed, including 123 mayors assassinated as part of the terror campaign.

Northern Ireland and the Fight Against Political Terrorism
The Background
The fight for control of Northern Ireland is now more than 25 years old. It began as a comparatively bloodless confrontation between the rival Loyalist and Nationalist communities but quickly developed into something far more sinister. The Army was first involved in August 1969 after the Royal Ulster Constabulary (RUC), supported by the highly sectarian B Specials, had proved unable to control local rioting.

Responsibility for the maintenance of public order passed to the Army whose numbers gradually swelled until, by 1972, they had peaked at around 22,000. However the shooting of thirteen demonstrators by 1st Battalion The Parachute Regiment in Londonderry in the January of that year led to an inquiry into the Army's behaviour. It was understood by politicians and senior officers alike that it would soon become necessary to reduce the Army's profile on the streets.

By 1977 the Army's presence had been reduced to fourteen battalions of about 650 men each, together with a small number of support elements. The majority of units were serving on a four-month unescorted tour of duty and were deployed in fixed areas, known as Tactical Areas of Responsibility (TAORs). A few battalions were serving for two years and were generally held in reserve to come to the assistance of any unit within its own area of responsibility which found itself particularly heavily committed.

Parachute Regiment battalions and Royal Marines Commandos were deployed in Northern Ireland as conventional troops, taking their turn on the four-monthly roulement tours with the line infantry. Even the SAS, when it first deployed in 1969, openly wore uniform, complete with beige berets and winged dagger badges. However, the war in Oman meant that the Regiment had insufficient resources to maintain a sizeable presence in the Province, and although a few officers and NCOs remained, the majority of its members were withdrawn after D Squadron had finished its tour.

As the Army presence grew in size and complexity, so the command structure has been expanded to incorporate three brigade headquarters; 39 Brigade in the Belfast area, 8 Brigade in Londonderry and 3 Brigade in Portadown covering the border. Each of the brigade commanders reports to the Commander Land Forces (CLF) at Headquarters Northern Ireland (HQNI) in Lisburn, a major general who is the top Army commander in Ulster. Above him is the General Officer Commanding (GOC), a lieutenant general in overall command of all the armed forces in the Province, and is responsible for top level liaison with the police and government.

The RUC are also organised on a hierarchical system, with their police stations grouped into sixteen divisions corresponding roughly to the Army TAORs. Several divisions are grouped into one of three regions - Belfast, South and North - each with its own assistant chief constable who keeps close liaison with the Army brigadiers. The three Assistant chief constables answer to the Chief Constable at RUC headquarters at Knock, East Belfast.

Despite attempts to integrate Army and RUC activities closely, there has long been an antipathy between certain police and Army officers on the ground. Although the primary effort of the security forces, both police and Army, has traditionally been directed against the republican movements, the Provisional IRA and the smaller Irish National Liberation Army (INLA), it has recently swung towards Protestant extremism in the form of the Ulster Defence Association (UDA) and the Ulster Freedom Fighters (UFF).

Many military intelligence operators find it difficult (usually quite erroneously) to accept that the Loyalist majority in the rank-and-file of the police can be wholly trusted in the fight against Loyalist extremism. Conversely elements of the RUC (with perhaps more justification) regard the Army as outsiders, who come for short tours and then return to the comparative safety of the British mainland without ever really appreciating the true parameters of the Irish problem.

Between 1977 and 1979 rivalry between the police and Army became acute, so much so that it threatened to challenge the all-important processes of intelligence gathering, crucial to the combatting of any terrorist organisation. At the time the majority of RUC intelligence was gathered by E Department, the Special Branch. However the Special Branch had lost responsibility for interrogations to C Branch, the Criminal Investigation Department (CID). The Army relied upon Field Intelligence NCOs (FIN-COs), and relatively untrained officers from the roulement battalions, to run its own agents.

Routine intelligence was collated by 12 Intelligence & Security Company, an element of the Intelligence Corps formed specifically for service in Northern Ireland in 1972. Although the Company dealt with low-level agent-handling at the time, it was far more involved in routine administration. The Army rarely talked to the police; the police rarely talked to the Army; and subunits within both guarded their information jealously, relying on the principles of 'need to know' to pass on as little intelligence as possible to anyone.

Overdue Improvements and New Elites
In 1972 the Army introduced the Special Military Intelligence Unit (Northern Ireland) - (SMIU - NI), an organisation of approximately 50 officers and men tasked with acting as go-betweens between the Army and RUC Special Branch. Initially many of the operators appear to have been chosen more for their gregariousness than ability as intelligence gatherers and sifters and mistakes were certainly made.

In addition both of Britain's security services, MI5 and MI6, were active in the Province and, as ever, often working in near open conflict. Both ran agent networks (occasionally employing the same agents!) and both maintained liaison officers with Lisburn and Knock. To compound its problems the influence of MI6 was heavily reduced in 1972 when it was unable to refute totally suggestions that it had encouraged two of its agents, Kenneth and Keith Littlejohn, to rob banks in the Republic of Ireland.

In an attempt to build bridges between the various intelligence agencies, the Army set up a new elite surveillance unit, which later became known as 14 Intelligence Company. Initially, however, it had the reverse effect, and matters worsened at grassroots level.

Determined to rationalise the control and administration of its special forces the Ministry of Defence introduced a new Directorate Special Forces under the command of a brigadier (DSF). At the same time it introduced a third, highly secret, elite which quickly gained the same status and prestige as the SAS and SBS. The unit, formed specifically for Northern Ireland, operated under a number of cover names to preserve its anonymity for as long as possible.

The new unit took over the role of the Mobile Reconnaissance Force (MRF), when the latter was disbanded in 1973. The MRF had been formed by the counter-insurgency expert, Brigadier Frank Kitson, on his appointment as Commander 39 Brigade in 1970. The role of the MRF was pre-emptive. Soldiers, many of them Irish and able to pass as locals, would stake out areas of known terrorist activity and await events. Often they would operate in conjunction with 'Freds', turned terrorists who had thrown in their lot with the security forces.

As the MRF became more experienced, its activities expanded and became more unconventional. In one instance it set up its own massage parlour; in another female soldiers posed as door-to-door cosmetics saleswomen. One particularly daring, and ultimately tragic, operation involved the setting up of the Four Square Laundry. Laundry vans were used to carry out surveillance in Republican areas, while dirty washing actually deposited for laundering was submitted to forensic testing before return. The operation was compromised when a Fred was 're-turned' by the IRA. A laundry van containing two MRF soldiers, one of them a woman, was ambushed in West Belfast. The male soldier was killed but the woman escaped. The Fred was subsequently executed by the IRA.

14 Company

It gradually became clear that the MRF laboured under a number of weaknesses. Its almost total reliance on intelligence provided by the far from reliable Freds left it vulnerable; as did its inability to call upon the assistance of dedicated conventional quick-reaction troops in case of emergency.

The surveillance group which replaced it - and which later became known as 14 Company - set itself higher standards. Its members are drawn from volunteers trawled from throughout the Army, all of whom have passed a selection process as gruelling as (if somewhat different from) that of the SAS. Selection takes place twice yearly and is centred on an SAS training centre. It emphasises the need for self-reliance, psychological strength and resourcefulness. Most applicants are bright and in their late twenties. They are neither unusually tall nor short, nor do they have distinctive facial or other features. Quite simply they are men and women who can blend into a hostile background, to watch and listen without themselves becoming the objects of suspicion.

By 1975 the unit had formulated its present structure with one detachment, or 'det', of a captain and approximately twenty soldiers per brigade. The unit has learned not to compromise its standards and is frequently understaffed. Nonetheless, when available further junior officers are accepted to act as liaison or operations officers.

Early attempts were made to disguise the name of the unit to afford it greater cover. Originally soldiers posted to it were said to be joining one of the NITAT teams in either Germany or southern England. NITAT, the Northern Ireland Training Advisory Team, was made up of high calibre soldiers with recent Northern Ireland experience and was used to train battalions due for roulement. It was not however in any sense a special purpose force, and when it was felt that it was becoming too closely associated with covert activity in the Province the implied connections between it and the unit were severed.

Subsequent attempts to disguise the unit as part of the Intelligence and Security Group based at Ashford, Kent were abandoned when the very real division between the covert role of the unit and the more overt role of 12 Intelligence and Security Company, actually serving in Northern Ireland, began to blur. In the early 1980s the present title of 14 Intelligence and Security Company, usually shortened to 14 Company or even 14 Int, was introduced.

Although membership remains secret Mark Urban, in his excellent analysis of the Company in his book *Big Boys' Rules*, has managed to identify some of the major incidents attributable to it. Most missions carried out by 14 Int involve either the setting up of covert observation posts (as opposed to conventional overt vehicle check points (VCPs)) or watching people from unmarked 'Q' cars.

The use of covert OPs and Q cars in localised areas of almost total paranoia such as exist in Northern Ireland is fraught with danger. In 1974 Captain Anthony Pollen of the Coldstream Guards, attached to 14 Int, was cornered and shot dead while trying to take photographs on the edge of the Bogside, a Catholic estate in Londonderry. Three years later three soldiers manning an OP in South Armagh were compromised. They were targeted from across the Irish border by an ASU armed with an M60 machine gun, stolen from the United States National Guard, and again were shot dead.

Occasionally 14 Int operations lead to suggestions of military overreaction. However it must be remembered that the volunteers are often working alone or in pairs, and that although support in the form of a Quick Reaction Force is always relatively close an individual soldier may occasionally have to take drastic action in support of his own safety, or that of others. On 12 December 1977 a lance-corporal attached to 14 Int became the victim of a potential hijack when two members of INLA attempted to steal his car. In the process one of the terrorists, Colin McNutt, was shot dead. A day later, in an unrelated incident, Corporal Paul Harman was stopped by an unknown number of assailants in West Belfast. It seems that he tried to talk himself out of the situation rather than use force. He was shot dead, his car was set on fire, and a considerable amount of delicate communications intelligence was captured by the Provisionals.

Despite the obvious dangers of covert work, new surveillance units were introduced in the late 1970s. In 1978 Major General Dick Trant, Commander Land Forces, introduced 30-man Close Observation Platoons, special purpose units drawn from the cream of the two-year resident battalions and of the South Armagh roulement battalion. The seven COPs became important in establishing regular patterns among both known and suspected terrorists, and became adept at providing both 14 Int and the SAS with specific targets.

Bronze Section

In 1976 the RUC's mobile anti-terrorist unit set up a specialist firearms and observation unit known as Bronze Section. Many of the Section's activities, which were largely based in the Belfast area, relied on old or faulty intelligence and were thus prone to failure. A year later, in an attempt to emulate the successes of 14 Int, Special Branch formed its own surveillance squad, E4A, within its Operations Division. Later, the RUC set up its own special firearms units to act on the intelligence gleaned not only from E4A but also from the myriad of technical surveillance experts employed within the larger E4.

In 1979 Chief Constable Newman set up the Bessbrook Support Unit (BSU), an undercover outfit of 28 policemen commanded by an inspector with three squads of nine each headed by a sergeant. The members wore camouflage clothing, and were well trained in the field of surveillance, but rarely exercised in close liaison with the Army.

By the end of 1979 the security forces were operating a plethora of special purpose units in Northern Ireland; three detachments of 14 Int, seven Army Close Observation Platoons, the Special Patrol Group's Bronze Section and three squads from E4A.

The SAS in Northern Ireland

The SAS was redeployed to Northern Ireland in 1977 when it was sent to South Armagh to counter the increase in PIRA activity in the area. The Regiment's presence was temporarily increased to two squadrons in an attempt to saturate the area, and for a while terrorist activity subsided. The role of the SAS in Northern Ireland is extremely dangerous yet it does not include, and indeed never has included, a policy of shoot-to-kill. It runs its own agents, conducts its own surveillance and intelligence gathering missions and, when required, executes its own ambushes.

Between 1976 and 1989 the SAS accounted for 37 terrorists dead, including the three in Gibraltar (in an operation described in the next chapter) for the loss of four men killed. Until recently it conducted covert cross-border raids to arrest wanted terrorists; such as Sean McKenna, Kevin Byrne and Patrick Mooney apprehended in 1976. However the adverse publicity, and highly embarrassing trial, which resulted when eight members of the Regiment were themselves arrested in the Republic of Ireland forced the curtailment of such operations.

Regrettably, despite careful planning, several SAS ambushes have resulted in the deaths of innocent people. In 1978, in one of the worst instances, John Boyle, a 16-year-old schoolboy was shot dead by a four-man SAS ambush team. His family had discovered an arms cache in the local graveyard and had reported the matter to the authorities. The Army had called in the SAS without informing the family to stay away from the area. James had returned to the cache, and in all innocence had begun to remove a weapon when two members of the ambush party had mistaken him for a gunman and fired, killing him instantly.

Despite these setbacks the SAS have scored a number of notable successes. In May 1987 eight members from two East Tyrone Brigade PIRA ASUs were killed in a failed attempt to blow up the police station at Loughall. In 1986 a mechanical digger with a large bomb in its bucket had been used in a successful attack on an RUC station at The Birches, County Armagh. When a second digger was stolen a few months later, and was discovered at a derelict farm ten miles from Loughall, the vehicle was put under surveillance by E4A who subsequently noticed explosives being taken to the farm. When E4 intercepted a telephone call from one of the potential terrorists, supplying the date and target of the intended attack, SAS soldiers and RUC snipers moved into the deserted police station at Loughall while other SAS troopers deployed into the surrounding countryside to prevent the escape of any of the terrorists once the ambush had been sprung.

At 7.20pm on 8 May the digger, accompanied by a stolen Toyota van, crashed into the perimeter of the police station. As the terrorists began to shoot indiscriminately into the police station the SAS and RUC returned fire. The bomb was detonated, destroying a large part of the station, but all eight terrorists were killed, four in the van and four in the open. Tragically two motorists who inadvertently drove into the area of the ambush were mistaken for terrorists and one was killed. The IRA swore vengeance for the massacre and began to plan an attack on a soft target. The story of this, the Gibraltar incident, is told in the next chapter.

9
Overt or Covert
The Lifting of the Veil of Special Forces Secrecy

The concept of open government is an ideal to which few countries genuinely aspire. Despite protestations to the contrary Britain has effectively strengthened several key aspects of her Official Secrets legislation, and has only recently released many First World War records to the public domain. The United States has its much vaunted Freedom of Information Act, yet even now neither the CIA nor the military have shown the slightest inclination to disclose many covert aspects of the Vietnam War.

Generalisations are dangerous, however it would not be unfair to say that when the major security services are given the opportunity to circumvent open government, they take it. Knowledge is power, and the release of too much information on the internal structure of a security force can easily undermine its ability to operate. Worse, it can lead to the compromise of its operators and to the possible death of its agents.

It is the duty of special purpose forces involved in the maintenance of security to protect their parent society against disorder, intimidation and terrorism. Many agencies prefer to operate in uniform, or at the very least their staff work overtly with full peer group support. Occasionally, however, victimisation or intimidation will force agents to operate with police protection, often with disastrous results. By way of example in South Vietnam in the late 1960s there were many villages in which the local officials operated freely by day, issuing licences and permits and collecting taxes, but they and their policemen and soldiers all moved out to spend the night in a defended compound outside the village. This suited the Communists absolutely. While visiting politicians, news teams and others reported the villages as 'under government control' the reality was very different. Control rested with the Viet Cong who emerged after dark to summarily try and to execute any who had collaborated with the government.

Agent Handling and the Need for Secrecy
It follows that the public, if they are to dare to give information to the police or the security services, must feel confident that they can do so without recrimination. Despite recent technological advances HUMINT, the exploitation of human resources, still provides the bulk of intelligence input at all but strategic levels. Information, to be of real use, must not only be accurate but timely. To operate effectively anti-terrorist units require a profound insight into the political aspirations and military intentions of their adversaries. This can often only be obtained by the painstaking joining together of a thousand jigsaw pieces of sometimes trivial information into a single intelligence plan.

The Lifting of the Veil of Special Forces Secrecy

The creation of an intelligence system capable of piecing together such a jigsaw requires the trust of its sources. Whether they are ordinary members of the public who walk into a police station to give information on a crime, or are paid informants working for an organisation as covert as 14 Int, they must know that they are safe. If necessary their identities must be hidden and their families protected.

First rate HUMINT can often only be obtained from within an organisation, either by infiltrating an agent into one of its cells or by turning an existing member. Turning is best achieved by targeting a participant whose heart is not in it or who is suffering from obvious family pressures. Initial meetings with the target may only be conducted by highly trained operators, and for obvious reasons must take place in the utmost secrecy. The 'need to know' principle, whereby only those within the intelligence network who actively require details of the agent are given them, must be imposed rigidly; even if, as occasionally happens in Northern Ireland, this creates a rift between two departments.

There is nothing more demoralising to hard-core terrorists than the fear of internal betrayal. They will try to stifle this by ruthless exemplary punishments. Occasionally this increases the desire of the waverers to escape from their nightmare. As sympathisers are detected and terrorists arrested, they become increasingly susceptible to turning in the hope of withdrawing themselves and their families from further violence. This leads to further arrests, and ultimately to the disintegration of terrorist support among the local populace, as it becomes clear that their cause is lost.

This policy worked with excellent results against the Mau Mau in Kenya and against the communist terrorists in Malaya, and to a lesser extent against various other guerrilla organisations in South America. However it met with far less success with the Freds in Northern Ireland, and has since led to a series of highly embarrassing 'supergrass' trials in which the evidence of turned (and well paid) informers has been brought into disrepute.

If allowed to, terrorists are quite capable of using basic psychological operations techniques to frustrate the special purpose forces sent to combat them. Recent disturbing reports from Northern Ireland suggest that Loyalist paramilitaries are being supplied with the names and addresses of the relatives of Protestants whom they wish to coerce into support. It is rumoured within the community that the more intimate aspects of this information are being supplied from within the security services. Whatever the truth or otherwise of this wholly unsubstantiated suggestion, the mere intimation of internal compromise is frustrating the ability of the bona fide intelligence gatherers in their attempts to win the trust and support of the population as a whole.

Lifting the Veil

Occasionally unforeseen circumstances, such as the tragic crash of the RAF Chinook helicopter on the Mull of Kintyre in June 1994, inadvertently shed some not always welcome light on the complex world of covert intelligence. At 6.04pm on 2 June no less than 25 intelligence operatives, travelling from Belfast to a top secret security meeting on the outskirts of Inverness, died when their aircraft crashed in thick fog. Although the precise cause of the crash remains a mystery sabotage was almost immediately ruled out.

9 Overt or Covert

After a short delay the Government announced that it would release the identities of all the deceased, although at the same time it issued a D-notice asking the media not to publish the photographs or addresses of six Northern Ireland Office security specialists, thought to be MI5 officers.

The list gave a rare insight into the depth and complexity of security in Northern Ireland. As well as the six members of the NIO the list included the head of the RUC Special Branch, Assistant Chief Constable Brian Fitzsimons, two of his detective chief superintendents and four superintendents, including the head of the Belfast region Special Branch and his deputy and the head of the RUC's E4 covert surveillance unit. The Army lost a full colonel, the first to die since the commencement of the present troubles in 1969, three lieutenant colonels and a major from the Intelligence Corps, as well as a number of other staff officers detached from their regiments and undertaking routine security duties in the Province.

The list of the dead is in itself testimony to way that the elite of the police, the Army and the security services have come together covertly in an attempt to offer one coherent response to terrorism. In the words of Blair Wallace, Deputy Chief Constable of the RUC and a friend of many who died, 'The duties they [the dead] performed were of the highest order of courage and dedication. It is no exaggeration to say that they and their colleagues over the years saved innumerable lives and saved the province and the mainland from the worst ravages of terrorism.

'That was the scale and magnitude of their work and their worth. By the nature of their work, their achievements could never be explained or publicised. But it was of the very greatest significance, and I feel it deeply incumbent on me to tell the people of Northern Ireland what a loss we and they have suffered'.

Death in Gibraltar

On occasions it is necessary for elite counter-terrorist troops, normally more at home in uniform, to operate in plain clothes. It may even be necessary for the full extent of their activities to remain secret, even after their activities have been brought to the attention of the international press. On 6 March 1988 a team of SAS soldiers confronted and shot dead on the streets of Gibraltar three members of a known Provisional IRA Active Service Unit (ASU), Daniel McCann, Sean Savage and Mairead Farrell.

Following the SAS killing of eight IRA terrorists at Loughall in May 1987 the British security and intelligence services went on full alert in anticipation of a retaliatory attack, probably against a soft target. In November 1987 the terrorist experts in Spain's 'Servicios de Informacion' informed the British authorities that Savage and McCann had been sighted in the Malaga region using false identities. It immediately became apparent that they were intending either to kill a prominent British citizen living in Spain or to attack a military installation in Gibraltar.

The next few months witnessed an intense amount of surveillance and cooperation between the British and Spanish police, security, and counter-terrorist agencies. When it became clear that the target was almost certainly the changing of the guard and band parade ceremony performed by the 1st Battalion, the Royal Anglian Regiment outside the Governor's residence, an advisory group was set up in Gibraltar. Surveillance was increased and the parade, due to take place in December, was postponed to buy the anti-terrorist agencies some more time.

In late February 1988, MI5 recorded several journeys made to the Rock by Mairead Farrell, travelling under the false name of Mary Parkin. She was observed paying particular attention to the guard changing ceremony, and on 1 March was seen to follow the route taken by the bandsmen. The next day the Joint Intelligence Committee in London notified the Joint Operations Centre, with its SAS liaison officer, as a result a sixteen-man SAS Special Projects Team was promptly dispatched to Gibraltar.

The precise terms of the briefing given to the Special Projects Team on its arrival remain secret, although certain aspects were released to subsequent enquiries. What is certain is that an MI5 officer briefed the group that the three targets were dangerous terrorists, that they would almost certainly be armed, and that they would be likely to use their weapons if confronted. Equally, it seems certain that the MI5 officer told the briefing that the use of a timer to set off the bomb was considered highly unlikely in the light of the IRA's experience in Enniskillen in Northern Ireland the previous November, when the use of a timer had resulted in a high number of civilian casualties. The use of a remote-control device was thus considered to be far more likely.

This is a key point in justifying the actions of the SAS in killing the three IRA members, any one of whom, they later argued, might have 'gone for the [remote control] button' to detonate the bomb at any time. Although the SAS were given specific orders to arrest the terrorists they were told that they could use their 9mm Browning Highpower pistols if (in the words used at the inquest in September 1988) 'those using them had reasonable grounds for believing that an act was being committed or about to be committed which would endanger life or lives and if there was no other way of preventing that other than with firearms'.

On 4 March Savage and McCann flew into Malaga airport where they were met by Farrell. Their subsequent movements are unknown as, at that critical moment, the Spanish police temporarily lost them. It was later discovered that they had hired two cars, one to transport the bomb (this was subsequently found in Marbella with 60kg of Semtex and other explosives), the other to act as a 'blocker' (an empty vehicle used to occupy a space which would subsequently be filled by the car containing the bomb).

On the morning of 6 March Savage drove the blocker across the border, left it in the assembly area and walked off to join Farrell and McCann, who had crossed into Gibraltar on foot. At this point Joseph Canepa, the Gibraltar police Commissioner, formally handed over control of the operation to the SAS.

The events which followed are confused, although a general picture of the events can be gained from the evidence given by the SAS at the inquest. Shortly after 4.00pm two SAS men walked up behind Farrell and McCann, who had by then split from Savage, and opened fire on them. The soldiers testified that they were, at most, 33 feet, and possibly only 3 feet, from the two when McCann glanced back and saw them, and the smile left his face. According to Soldier A, McCann's hand moved 'suddenly and aggressively across the front of the body'. Soldier B testified that Farrell almost instantaneously half turned and grabbed for her shoulder bag. In so doing 'she made all the actions to carry out the detonation of a radio-controlled device'. The soldiers shot them twelve times, but denied suggestions they had fired while the two were lying on the ground.

Savage meanwhile was tailed by Soldiers C and D. They testified that when he heard the shots which killed Farrell and McCann, he spun round. Despite an order from Soldier C to stop, Savage continued to move his arm towards his jacket pocket, adopting 'a threatening and aggressive stance'. The two SAS men then shot him fifteen times until he was 'no longer a threat to initiate that [radio controlled] device'.

The death of the three terrorists, who were subsequently found to be unarmed and not to be carrying triggering devices, resulted in questions being asked about the amount of control being exercised by the SAS, whether they had a licence to kill, and whether the British Government had ever intended to take the three alive.

In June 1994 a report by the European Commission on Human Rights, subsequently accepted by a majority of eleven to six, declared that there had been no 'conspiracy theory' to kill the terrorists, and that the fact that they had deliberately been allowed to enter Gibraltar did not in itself constitute evidence of a premeditated plan to kill them. Notwithstanding the exoneration of its personnel, and the fact that the operation had successfully eliminated an IRA ASU, the publicity surrounding the affair was deemed negative from the perspective of pro-SAS propaganda. Although there can be no doubt that the Regiment, if so ordered, would undertake such an operation again, it would clearly prefer to keep its clandestine activities wholly deniable.

Deniable Operations

According to the purest tenets of international law it is an act of war for one country unilaterally to order its armed troops across the borders of another. Given the large number of clear instances in which one nation has felt the need to meddle in the affairs of another, short of an actual declaration of hostilities, governments have become adept at fighting wars by proxy.

In time of notional peace, United States deniable operations are planned and executed solely by the CIA. They must be approved by the President, they usually enlist the aid of foreign resources (such as tribesmen in Vietnam and Laos) and are invariably led by civilians trained to operate covertly with military special purpose forces.

Air America

The United States was quick to realise the necessity for dedicated air support for its non-attributable activities. After the Second World War the CIA formed its own clandestine air force - Air America, which it subsequently used for the insertion of field agents, mercenaries and supplies into a series of minor wars, many of them of its own making.

Many CIA activities involving Air America were so secret that they have still not been admitted to, several decades after the event. Shortly after the Communist takeover in China the CIA supported the defeated Chinese Nationalists in no less than three unsuccessful invasion attempts from bases in the Shan States. When Communist China invaded Tibet in 1950 Air America ran supplies and CIA-trained Khamba tribesmen to support the Tibetan resistance.

In 1959, when the United States Military Assistance Advisory Group (MAAG) to Vietnam was increased from 342 officers and men to 685, sixteen US Marine Corps

Sikorsky H-34 helicopters were secretly transferred to Air America. The H-34s were made as anonymous as possible (all military markings were removed) and shipped to Laos to be flown by Agency pilots in support of the Meo tribesmen who were then at war with the Communist Pathet Lao. CIA support in the area of immediate Chinese influence was finally phased out as a prerequisite of President Nixon's visit China in 1972. Air America however continued to support CIA operations in Indonesia, the Congo, Laos and Vietnam.

In Laos the Air America pilots were joined by 'Ravens', forward air controllers (FACs) drawn from the cream of US Air Force pilots serving in Vietnam. The Ravens, who flew slow single-engined propeller aircraft such as the Cessna 0-1 Bird Dog from airstrips scattered around the Plain of Jars, flew in civilian clothes. Although nominally under the command of 56th Special Operations Wing, the Ravens in fact operated closely with the Royal Laotian Army, the Special Guerrilla Units of General Vang Pao's Hmong tribesmen, and other CIA-led indigenous units which were then attempting to prevent the flow of men and equipment down the Ho Chi Minh Trail.

Occasionally Air America has found itself involved in covert humanitarian missions. Operation 'Frequent Wind', the final United States evacuation from Vietnam, owes its success in no small part to Air America. Throughout 29 April 1975, a full day before the armed forces were given the order to intervene, Air America Huey helicopters began flying from roof top to roof top in Saigon, transporting survivors to the temporary safety of the CIA compound in the airfield. When further use of the airfield became untenable, the pilots shifted their efforts to the Embassy and ultimately to the ships of the Seventh Fleet anchored offshore. Inexplicably, when the Air America helicopters landed on the United States aircraft carriers their CIA pilots were disarmed and confined below decks, and were allowed to play no further part in the evacuation.

A somewhat modified clandestine air-transport company still exists in support of special operations. Known as Seaspray, it was formed in March 1981 to circumvent President Carter's Executive Order 12036, which banned the armed forces from conducting clandestine operations. Seaspray is based at Fort Eustis, Virginia, although it is reputed to operate a number of small fixed-wing aircraft and helicopters from Tampa International Airport, Florida. Functioning under the umbrella of Aviation Tech Services, or for Army administrative purposes, the 1st Rotary Wing Test Activity, it is reportedly tasked with the transportation of US Army Special Operations Forces, particularly Delta counter-terrorist teams.

In 1982 Seaspray became involved in Operation 'Queen Hunter', a highly sensitive surveillance mission on behalf of the National Security Agency. A number of aircraft were purchased through a front company, 'Shenandoah Aerolease'. These seemingly innocent aircraft were then modified to carry advanced radio direction-finding equipment and reputedly were subsequently used to pin-point Salvadorian rebel bases and arms traffic routes between Honduras and Nicaragua.

'Deniable' Espionage

The United States, and to a lesser extent the United Kingdom, has a long tradition of overflying other countries' airspace without permission. During the height of the Cold War, CIA pilots regularly violated Soviet airspace on espionage missions. The Soviets were well aware of the intrusions, but at the time were powerless to halt them. They therefore chose not to protest internationally for fear of publicising the comparative impotency of their air defences.

The Lockheed U-2, the most famous and enduring of spy planes, first flew operationally in 1955. It was designed to have a limited lifespan, yet it so effectively bridged the gap between tactical and strategic intelligence that it remained in service for over 35 years. The earliest batch of U-2s were delivered direct to the CIA, who in turn hired pilots from the elite of the US Air Force to provide them with at least a notional civilian status. Every effort was made to disguise the true purpose of the U2. The first aircraft to arrive at the US Air Force base at Lakenheath in England flew under cover of the National Advisory Committee for Aeronautics (NACA) as part of the 1st Weather Reconnaissance Squadron (Provisional). NACA insisted that the U-2 was nothing more than an ultra-high-altitude specific meteorological test bed, a fiction happily supported by the United States and British Governments. The reality could not have been more different.

The first U-2 mission over Soviet territory was flown on 4 July 1956. The aircraft flew into friendly West German air space, ascending to over 70,000 feet before turning east. The pilot entered Warsaw Pact airspace over Czechoslovakia, continued east to Moscow, plotted a course north to Leningrad and thence west across the Baltic to Lakenheath. The flight, which had been personally authorised by President Eisenhower, was a great success, producing thousands of needle-sharp photographs of Soviet military installations and production centres.

Between 1956 and 1960 the CIA conducted Operation 'Overflight', the collective name given to the hundreds of U-2 border incursions into Warsaw Pact airspace, and the estimated 30 long-range flights over the Soviet Union itself. By no means all U-2 flights were confined to anti-Warsaw Pact espionage. Frequent missions were flown over the Mediterranean, the Gulf and the Middle East. The Arab-Israeli War and the Franco-British build up to the Suez invasion in 1956 were both closely monitored by a far from sympathetic CIA.

Francis Gary Powers

It is crucial that covert missions should remain so, but on 1 May 1960 a U-2 aircraft flown by CIA pilot Francis Gary Powers was shot down by a Soviet SA-2 surface-to-air missile near Sverdlovsk. Powers had taken off from Peshawar in Pakistan for a flight of 3,700 miles. His route was to take him via the missile centre at Tyuratam, the industrial complexes at Sverdlovsk and Kirov and the naval and defensive installations at Archangel, Severodvinsk, Kandalaska and Murmansk. The flight was due to terminate at Bodö in Norway.

The repercussions were as drastic as they were immediate. Not knowing that Powers had survived, Washington embarked upon a desperate damage-limitation exercise. They claimed that an unarmed and wholly innocent U-2 reconnaissance aircraft working for NASA had inadvertently strayed across the Turkish border into Soviet air space.

However, when it was announced that Powers had survived and had admitted his espionage mission, and when photographs of the downed aircraft were released, clearly demonstrating the remains of a Hycon camera with its 900mm lens, Washington was forced to concede at least part of the truth. Krushchev walked out of the Paris International Summit and Eisenhower was forced to give a public undertaking not to fly further espionage missions over the Soviet Union. Powers was tried for espionage and imprisoned by the Soviets, but was quietly released only two years later.

The U-2s were almost immediately withdrawn to the United States, however within two months they were flying again. Two aircraft were secretly transferred to Taiwan and six Nationalist Chinese pilots were trained in their use. The operation was jeopardised in September 1962 when one of the U-2s disappeared under mysterious circumstances and Washington was forced to concede her part in their initial provision. However further U-2s, possibly as many as nine, were subsequently transferred to Taiwan and continued to provide the CIA with invaluable photographic imagery of mainland China.

The Cuban Missile Crisis

Fortunately for the United States her undertaking not to overfly Soviet air space did not extend to the latter's Cuban surrogate. In August 1962 a routine U-2 overflight of the island brought back photographs of two previously unknown SA-2 missile sites. Considerably alarmed, President Kennedy called for increased aerial surveillance, only to be frustrated by a wholly unrelated Congressional demand for a moratorium.

When the flights recommenced in early October they produced evidence of frantic construction work throughout the island. US Air Force U-2s from the 4028th Strategic Reconnaissance Squadron were ordered to augment the CIA U-2s, to provide what was by now completely overt round-the-clock surveillance. On 14 October 1962, a U-2 flown by Major Steve Heyser USAF photographed an SS-4 Sandal surface-to-surface missile site near San Cristobal, west of Havana. Within a few days a total of nine SS-4 missile sites, and about 40 Il-28 bombers, old but nonetheless capable of nuclear delivery, were discovered on the island.

On 22 October, Kennedy admitted his espionage activities to the world when he announced a maritime blockade of Cuba which would last until all Soviet offensive missiles and bombers were removed from the island. On 29 October, Khrushchev relented and ordered the dismantling of the missile sites.

Lost Lives and Human Errors

Deniable activities are always dangerous, even when they go undetected. When compromised they will occasionally provoke the target into acts of violent retaliation. During the 1980s US Air Force RC-135 electronic reconnaissance aircraft regularly carried out covert Telemetry Intelligence (TELINT) missions along the borders of the then Soviet Union, China, North Korea and Vietnam. Each aircraft carries a crew of between 20 and 30 Communications Intelligence (COMINT) and Signals Intelligence (SIGINT) specialists as well as the flight crew. The RC-135 is superficially similar to the Boeing 707 airliner, although numerous variations, such as its thimble-shaped radome, clearly identify it as a military aircraft. The RC-135 has neither the speed nor the altitude to violate the air space of a sophisticated adversary. It tends therefore to fly along established flight paths, although it will occasionally deviate to establish its target's electronic response.

9 Overt or Covert

Had it not been for the highly regrettable destruction of a Korean Air Lines Boeing 747 airliner over the Kamchatka Peninsula, with the resultant loss of 269 lives, it is highly unlikely that many non-experts would ever have discovered the existence of the RC-135. After the incident the Soviets argued that the pilot of the Sukhoi Su-15 which had shot down the civilian aircraft had mistaken it for a military RC-135 known to have been in the area earlier. A large radar trace was produced demonstrating the course of both aircraft and showing that at one point their radar images had merged. No attempt was made to show why the highly experienced Sukhoi pilot had failed to differentiate between a Boeing 747 and the significantly smaller RC-135 on a clear night at relatively close range, nor why he had not attempted to order the intruder to land.

The United States conceded that an RC-135 had carried out a reconnaissance mission east of Kamchatka earlier, and that it had indeed crossed the KAL 747's flight-path at a distance of 75 miles The RC-135 had, however, returned to its base in Alaska and had been on the ground for an hour at the time of the incident. Even with the advent of Glasnost and the demise of the Soviet Union the full truth behind the tragedy is unlikely ever to be made public. It is probable, however, that the death of so many innocent people was caused by a fundamental miscalculation on the part of an unusually edgy pilot and by a ground control overly keen to teach the United States a lesson.

Hidden Conflict in Korea

No country in the world pursues or abuses the concept of covert action more aggressively than North Korea. Despite the cessation of open hostilities with the Republic of Korea in 1953, the North's special forces (an estimated 12-15 per cent of her total Army strength of 700,000) have continued the conflict by every covert means available.

In January 1968, a 31-man team from the 124th Army Unit was ordered to begin training for a top secret and near-suicidal mission. They were given a provincial headquarters building as a base and ordered to practise assaulting it under all conditions. During their final practice assault they were pitted against 500 members of the Workers' Peasant Red Guard acting as enemy. Such was the reality of the exercise that during the successful storming of the building some 30 of the peasants were hospitalised with injuries. When not honing their assault techniques the special forces improved their fitness until finally they were able to carry 60lbs of sand over a 40-mile course in no more than six and a half hours.

After eight days of relentless training the special squad was given its orders by Lieutenant General Kim Chung Tae; to go to Seoul and cut off the head of President Chung Hee Park. The team were to wear South Korean Army uniforms covered by dark overalls and, to ensure deniability, were to kill themselves to avoid capture.

On the night of 17 January the team was led across the minefields and security fences of the Demilitarised Zone, and were possibly escorted through one of the many tunnels dug under the border. Once safely established in the South the team split into small groups, and during the course of three nights made its way to a rendezvous on the outskirts of Seoul. Removing their overalls the men began to move slowly towards the President's official residence, the Blue House. Their tenacity might well have borne fruit had not a group of keen-eyed woodcutters grown suspicious and, at the very last minute, alerted the security forces to the incursion. The team, posing as a South Korean counter-intelligence unit, was ambushed by security police. In the ensuing fire-fight 28 North Koreans were killed or killed themselves, 68 South Korean soldiers and civilians were killed and another 66 were wounded.

Unabashed by the ensuing international outrage, the North Korean special forces have tried on several subsequent occasions to kill the President. In 1974 an unsuccessful attempt resulted in the death of the President's wife. Not all attempts have been confined to the Korean peninsula. In 1982 the Royal Canadian Mounted Police uncovered a third plot on President Park's life.

In 1983 a three-man North Korean special purpose forces team, comprising a commander and two demolitions experts, made an attempt on the life of President Park's successor, General Chun Doo-Hwan. On 17 September the team entered Rangoon, Burma, aboard the freighter *Tong Gon Ae Guk Ho*. On 22 September the team left the ship in the company of other crew members and were met at a safe house by a woman agent of the North Korean Intelligence Service. Two days later the team received orders to assassinate the President as he laid a wreath at the Martyrs' Mausoleum. On 7 October the team gained access to the mausoleum, and laid its charges in readiness for Doo-Hwan's visit two days later.

On the day of the visit the assassins made a fatal error. Mistaking the South Korean Ambassador's motorcade for that of the President they detonated their charges early, killing the wrong man. The Burmese security forces instigated an immediate man-hunt. Shortly afterwards the team leader, Major Zin Mo, was seen swimming a river and captured. Two days later the other saboteurs were located hiding on a river bank. Captain Kim Chi-o was killed in the ensuing fire-fight, and Captain Kang Min-Chul was captured as he attempted to kill himself.

Not all of North Korea's covert incursions have been against the person of the President. In October 1968 a special purpose propaganda force landed along an isolated stretch of the South's eastern coast and immediately began to preach revolution to the locals. Incredulous and unimpressed the loyal peasants informed the security forces, and most of the 100-man force were captured or killed.

In 1978, in an act of particular daring, North Korean long-range reconnaissance personnel kidnapped two southern film stars, Shin San Ok and his wife Choi Un Hui, and spirited them north to train North Korean special purpose forces in the ways of the south. During the 1980s North Korean combat swimmers again landed along the coast, this time to establish guerrilla groups and collect intelligence on the local military installations.

In 1987, North Korea embarked upon a covert direct-action operation so delicate that it was entrusted to the Intelligence Service rather than to the military's special forces. On 29 November a man and a woman, both carrying forged passports, believed to have been issued by the North Korean residents' association in Japan, placed a bomb concealed in their luggage on board Korean Airlines flight KAL 858. The aircraft was destroyed en route from Abu Dhabi to Seoul and a massive manhunt ensued. When it was realised that neither the man nor the woman had in fact boarded the aircraft they became immediate suspects. Both were intercepted on their way back to North Korea, at which time the woman attempted suicide. Subsequent interrogation revealed that both were members of the North Korean Research Department for External Intelligence, were multilingual, and had been extensively briefed for the operation.

In July 1994, Kim Il Sung, North Korea's despotic 82-year-old leader, died. Only China mourned; the rest of the world either remained mute or made no attempt to hide their rejoicing at his passing. Whether North Korea will now attempt, at least in part, to return to the international fold or whether she will continue her covert special forces raids against the hated regime in the south remains to be seen.

Censorship, Elite Combat and the Press

'The essence of successful warfare is secrecy; the essence of successful journalism is publicity'. These words were first uttered during the Suez crisis in 1956 and were later repeated during the Falklands War. They remain the hub of a perennial conflict.

The issue of media access to combat information is as complex as it is vexatious. Many countries exercise ongoing censorship, or so control their national newspapers that censorship in unnecessary. Others traditionally rely upon the inherent patriotism of their media proprietors to ensure that nothing detrimental to the government or to its war effort is printed.

In Great Britain, while elements of the press persist in publishing the most lurid of scandals concerning politicians and the Royal Family, none would dream of deliberately compromising national security, nor of putting the lives of servicemen at risk. In the Falklands War of 1982, the government controlled the means of communication and were thus able to exert considerable influence on the timing and method of casualty releases. On at least one occasion, however, this policy proved disastrous.

When the LSL *Sir Galahad* was bombed at Fitzroy the Ministry of Defence released the fact almost immediately. It admitted that at the time of the incident the ship had been heavily laden with troops, but declined to give details of their regiment. Friends and relatives of all those serving in the theatre were kept on tenterhooks until it was at last announced that the majority of the losses had been sustained by the 1st Battalion The Welsh Guards. Even then a further delay ensued while the Army gathered together sufficient trained personnel to break the news to those who had suffered a bereavement.

Immediately before the historic assault by the 2nd Battalion The Parachute Regiment on the Argentine position at Goose Green, a representative of the BBC inadvertently disclosed the unit's position and intentions. The Commanding Officer, Lieutenant Colonel 'H' Jones, who was subsequently awarded a posthumous Victoria Cross in the battle, was beside himself with rage and threatened to sue the BBC. It has never been suggested that the actions of the BBC were either malicious or particularly negligent, and fortunately they did not, in the end, add to the carnage of the battle. Such events are however indicative of what can happen when something as seemingly innocuous as a unit's situation report (SITREP) is transmitted without considering the omnipresent demands of long-term security.

The special forces played a significant part in the Falklands campaign, and were largely responsible for the initial recapture of the island of South Georgia. However, as they tended to operate either from the air or from submarines, it was easy to keep their activities secret from the press. When the Ministry of Defence did feel the need to publicise a particularly successful special forces' operation the information was released at well informed press conferences to the reasonable satisfaction of both the military and the media.

The Gulf Experience

From the Iraqi invasion of Kuwait in August 1990 to the cease-fire over six months later, there was no aspect of the Gulf War which was not directly affected by the mass communications media. Israel, Jordan, Saudi Arabia and Iraq all imposed severe controls without provoking significant outcries from their journalists. Iraq, Jordan and Israel in particular attempted to manipulate the media. Jordan reported consistently that Iraqi forces were winning, and only when the Coalition proved victorious finally revealed the devastating degree of the Iraqi defeat.

Israeli manipulation was most evident in the reporting of Scud missile attacks. The sites of impacted Scuds were quickly cordoned off, and the press only granted access once the government had decided its response. Press reports therefore stressed the concern of the public and depicted a government having difficulty coping with public demands for a military response. This complemented precisely Israel's demand for defensive missiles, and led to a marked increase in the Coalition's special forces Scud-busting activities in western Iraq.

The state-controlled Iraqi media, through false news reports, led the Iraqi public to believe that they were winning, and never publicly informed them that they had lost the war. Although foreign reporting was encouraged it was totally manipulated, and all reporters' movements were controlled to ensure that they saw only what the government wished.

CNN in the United States and ITN in Britain attempted to bring their watching public near constant coverage of the war. After lengthy negotiation with the Iraqi Ministry of Information CNN was allowed to install a portable satellite station in Baghdad, but at a price. They were pressured into allowing two officials of the Ministry of Information to use their phones. The precise reason for this activity has never been made clear, but it is said that the Iraqis were deeply grateful. Later the French private station Le Cinq was promised visas, but only if they provided their Iraqi minders with the code for a phone abandoned when a Le Cinq crew left Baghdad hours after the bombing started. The minders got their code, and according to witnesses, used the satellite phone practically day and night.

Most reporters in Baghdad were working with communications systems far more advanced than they were used to. When a Tomahawk missile lumbered into sight en route to its target or a Coalition bombing raid took place the foundation of journalistic professionalism -accuracy rather than immediacy - was inevitably compromised in the insatiable demand for saturation news coverage. During air raids, reporters who were largely ignorant of the technology of modern combat talked extensively about the 'lit skies' over Baghdad. They were seemingly unaware that most of the flashes that they could see were caused by tracer rounds - fired blind from antiquated anti-aircraft batteries - which were falling well short of the high-altitude bombers overhead.

Iraq used the language barrier and the lack of fuel to ensure that its guest journalists saw only what the government wished them to see. This affected even the experienced CNN's reporting, and reached a climax when the highly respected Peter Arnett reported on the precision bombing of Amiraya bunker. The Coalition had struck Amiraya because it believed it to be a military installation, not knowing that its upper levels were being used as a shelter for the families of local government officials. Clearly distressed by the loss of life, the CNN crew emphasised the civilian dead rather than the building's military importance. In so doing they gave Baghdad a major propaganda victory and forced a reconsideration of the Coalition bombing policy; thenceforth the Pentagon controlled the bombing.

In a subsequent interview with David Frost, General Schwarzkopf described the reporting of this incident as 'aiding and abetting the enemy', claiming that it implied that he was 'deliberately lying to the American people that [he was] targeting civilians'.

The United States and the Press

The situation between the United States military and the press became soured at the time of Vietnam War. In the view of the media assigned to South-East Asia the military actively restricted information in order to influence reporting and, through this, public opinion. To the military, reporters were the enemy and were considered so biased against the United States' cause as to be virtually traitors. Relations between the two simmered throughout the war, but erupted once it became clear that the United States had lost. The conservative establishment began to accuse the 'liberal' press of bias and anti-American reporting. Unwilling to accept the fallibility of their own military machine, they lay the blame for their defeat squarely, and unfairly, at the feet of the media.

This problem continued with the Grenada operation, where reporters were not allowed to accompany the combat forces and were given no assistance in getting to the island. United States special purpose forces undertook a number of totally covert and highly successful operations on the island, yet the public at home, used to immediate coverage, had to rely on highly selective newsreel footage disseminated sometime later to appreciate their expertise. It soon became clear that the answer lay in the formation of a press pool, comprising reporters acceptable to the government, who would be conveyed to a combat zone under military protection (and presumably control.)

The first use of the press pool, in the Panamanian intervention in December 1989, proved a failure. Inadequate planning, inadequate support, too large a pool and frequent long delays in disseminating pool reports were blamed. To prevent press leaks, the pool was not mobilised until the invasion was underway; it was therefore unable to report the activities of the special forces spearheading the five pronged attack. Once again a fine opportunity for the United States press to report favourably on the activities of the elite formations of the US Army and Marine Corps was squandered. Operation 'Just Cause' was anticipated days ahead of the event, and had the press wished it could have compromised the entire mission by announcing the public departure of the 82nd Airborne Division from its bases. That it chose not to suggests that the Pentagon was unreasonable in its distrust of the media. Yet these lessons were not learned and nothing had changed by the start of the Gulf War.

The United States press pool was activated and arrived in Saudi Arabia on 13 August 1990, only eleven days after Iraqi forces invaded Kuwait. Initially matters went well, with adequate press accommodation provided at Dhahran. Morning CENTCOM briefings were given normally at 10.00am EST (6.00pm Saudi Arabia time) by Brigadier General 'Butch' Neal USMC. These were followed at 3.00pm EST by almost daily Pentagon briefings usually conducted jointly by Lieutenant General Thomas Kelly and Rear Admiral Michael McConnell, the joint Chiefs of Staff. Where possible further information was elicited from the field. However the almost jingoistic military tenor of the reporting was disrupted, for security reasons, when the ground offensive began on 24 February 1991 and the daily briefings were suspended. The Pentagon subsequently defended this action, arguing that the US Marine Corps feint along the east coast was crucial to the Coalition plan, and if revealed inadvertently by the press could have resulted in disaster. The press countered by arguing that the British and French were far more open about the war, yet the bulk of their combat troops were equally exposed on the Coalition left flank.

Throughout Operation 'Desert Storm' the United States Defense Department imposed a number of ground rules on the press which the latter subsequently described as oppressive. Pool spaces were reserved for television crews, wire services, a number of radio groups and a few fortunate newspapers and magazines. Pool reports were cleared by the censors who, on more than one occasion laid themselves open to accusations of blatant political bias. Reports which proved unpopular with the censors were simply delayed, often until they became so stale as to be unusable. Reporters who asked hard or probing questions were warned by their military liaison officers that their actions were 'anti-military'; should they continue not only might that reporter's future visits to the field be prejudiced but subsequent requests for interviews with senior military commanders might also be denied.

Occasionally the media tried to circumvent the rules by advancing into 'no-go' areas or hiding out with combat units, occasionally with drastic results. On 7 February 1991 the Bob Simons CBS crew went to the Kuwaiti border without clearance. They were captured, taken first to Basra and then to Baghdad, kept in isolation, beaten and interrogated. Pressure on Iraq, including the personal intercession of President Mikhail Gorbachev, eventually prompted their release, but not until Saddam had succeeded in milking the situation of every possible propaganda advantage.

On 5 March, during a second incident, an international band of over thirty journalists was reported missing near Basra. The United States authorities expressed their concern, but declined to become actively involved in an incident which they regarded as irrelevant to the prosecution of the war.

Questions Posed and Lessons Learned

The Gulf War did little to reduce the military's paranoid attitude towards the media. Given that the protection of those in combat is one of the highest responsibilities of government, it is surely correct that the release of information potentially useful to the enemy should be controlled. However this must not be allowed to lead to abuse. In the Gulf, unnecessary censorship was largely controlled by General Schwarzkopf's high ideals and determination to 'tell it like it was'. During the final hours of the war, photographs of the carnage on the Basra-Baghdad highway were released to a shocked world which had not fully appreciated the potential of modern military technology.

This did much to bring about what many later came to regard as a premature cease fire. The press however should not be blamed for public opinion.

There were no instances of special forces or special purpose forces operations being compromised by media leaks. When the Coalition wanted its Scud-busting activities publicised to placate Israeli fears the press obliged, but only in such generalisations that it did nothing to compromise the men on the ground. Again, the press readily reported the activities of the Marine Amphibious Unit (MAU) located off the Saudi coast, yet did nothing to suggest to the Iraqis that ultimately it would not be used in an amphibious landing.

Television is an expanding force which is likely to play an important role in any future global conflict. Since the end of the Gulf War coverage has spread virtually everywhere. The BBC has introduced World Service Television in competition with CNN, while the European Broadcasting Union is planning yet another 'instant dissemination' channel - Euronews.

Realistically the military will no longer be able to control these giants within its existing structured pools. There are strong suggestions that it should revert to the Second World War policy of attaching uniformed newsmen to individual units and allow them to take their chances at the front. They would be subject to military discipline, would have the protection of the Geneva Conventions if captured and would be constrained in their immediate reporting abilities by accompanying press information officers. Crucially however they would be confined to conventional communications links with the rear area, and would be denied the use of the increasingly sophisticated satellite links with which outside broadcasting has become associated. Any forward link which emitted an electronic signal would quickly be detected by the enemy's Electronic Warfare units and, apart from compounding their position, would run the risk of attracting artillery or air attack.

Reporters deemed mentally and physically capable might even be allowed to accompany special purpose forces on their raids. It would however be unwise to allow any with a high degree of accumulated knowledge on 'prone to capture' operations. Interrogation of captured members of the press is given a high priority, and it is unlikely that military accreditation would provide a reporter-POW with more than theoretical protection if taken by an enemy who fails to subscribe to the Geneva accords.

Occasionally the military finds itself working closely with members of the press over whom it has little or no control. This is not always a recipe for disaster; indeed such circumstances can lead to the press exercising a high degree of restraint. In Bosnia not only has the media been accompanying the belligerents, but it has also been closely observing the activities of the United Nations monitoring forces. When General Rose called upon the services of the SAS to act as forward air controllers the media in the area duly reported the fact. Yet they were scrupulous in ensuring that the soldiers' identities remained secret and that any photographs that appeared had their faces fully blacked-out.

Freedom of Information
During the two World Wars the majority of journalists accepted that their national existence might be threatened by irresponsible reporting, and took great care to ensure that

they did nothing to compromise the national interest. In the words of one war correspondent, John Steinbeck, 'Gradually it became part of us all that the truth about anything was automatically secret, and that to trifle with it was to interfere with the War effort'.

Significantly it was at the specific request of the press itself that the United States introduced during the Second World War, and later during the Korean War, direct military censorship in the field in order to avoid the problems and uncertainties of self-censorship. The military, however, disliked the responsibility, and despite representations from the media, refused to instigate formal censorship in Vietnam. The field censorship units were downgraded to reserve status and, in 1977, were finally disbanded.

From Vietnam onwards the United States government placed the onus of journalist accreditation firmly on the shoulders of the media itself. In Saudi Arabia it provided facilities for the journalists in theatre, but took no responsibility for them, nor for their stories.

Legislation on the subject of United States media freedom is, to say the least, sparse in relation to most European countries. Indeed, before the passage of the Freedom of Information Act in 1966 the only edict on the subject was contained in the First Amendment. There is no United States legal authority for restriction, control or censorship of the press in peace or war. However, while the Constitution forbids censorship, it does not specifically guarantee the media a right of access to information. In 1983 the American press considered suing the United States government over its media handling of the invasion of Grenada, but eventually decided to defer lest the ruling set a precedent for even tighter restrictions.

Ultimately, in conventional warfare, the government controls the media through access to the battlefield. However the position is less clear when dealing with 'mavericks' who neglect to apply for accreditation, or in unconventional or counter-terrorist situations. The ability of the SAS and other special purpose agencies in Northern Ireland to mount successful operations against known terrorist targets has been severely compromised by a number of unsubstantiated reports implying the existence of a shoot-to-kill policy.

10
The Civilian Spin-Off

The Mercenary Tradition

There have been accounts of mercenaries since the earliest days of recorded military history; indeed there are some who would suggest that mercenary soldiering is the oldest, and most enduring, (male!) profession in the world. As early as 401BC, Cyrus employed 10,000 Greek mercenaries in his endeavour to win the throne of the Persian empire. The attempt failed, but the mercenaries survived defeat and the death of Cyrus. They ultimately succeeded in retreating in good order back through Asia Minor, in a march of epic proportions which was recorded for posterity by the writer Xenophon.

Nearly two millennia later the political plot of medieval Europe was heavily influenced by mercenary bands. Some five centuries later mercenaries fought on both sides in the American War of Independence, and fifty years later died for the freedom of Texas. Mercenaries fought in relatively equal numbers for the rival Nationalist and Republican causes in the Spanish Civil War, and have since featured in the majority of third-world 'brush-fire' wars. Recently a substantial number of volunteers from around the world, with varying amounts of military experience, have made their way to enlist in one or other of the warring factions in the Balkans. Most recently, in early 1994, Azerbaijan was reportedly seeking British and American ex-military personnel to act as trainers for the Eyesore forces fighting against Armenia.

Britain has employed mercenaries at various times during its history, particularly Swiss and German regiments. In more recent times Britain has, for more than a century, maintained a brigade of Gurkhas, and until recently has also had a number of Fijians serving in the Army, many of them in the special forces. Unlike its older and better known French equivalent, the Spanish Foreign Legion was always constituted almost entirely of Spanish nationals, and indeed since 1987 has completely ceased recruiting foreigners. France, in contrast, has no such qualms, and the 'Légion Etrangère' continues to recruit internationally. However the Legion no longer harbours the scum of the earth; Interpol computers screen out hardened criminals, and only petty offenders who are thought to be capable of reform are admitted. Many applicants are rejected during the course of the first interview, while others cannot take the mental and physical pressures and quit during the first few weeks of training. And even after six months' service, when a man has qualified as a fully trained recruit, the Legion still reserves the right to reject anyone it considers to be unsuitable.

Service by Proxy

Increasingly today, highly-motivated ex-special forces personnel are being employed as government-sponsored mercenaries to further obscure the roots of deniable activities.

In September 1962 the government of the Yemen was toppled by an Egyptian-backed, Marxist-inspired coup, bringing a heightened level of instability to an already volatile area. Conscious of the threat to the Oman in the north and to the Aden Protectorate to the south- west, Britain attempted to counter the coup by proxy. As thousands of Egyptian servicemen entered the country, a mercenary force, which comprised former French, Belgian and British special forces personnel, supported by SOE and SAS veterans, was formed to assist the Royalist forces who were then fighting a guerrilla war. Operating from safe-houses in Aden and resupplied from the air by Rhodesian Air Services and the Shah's Iranian Air Force, the mercenaries worked in the tried and tested format of teams of three (commander, radio operator and medic). They were, however, hampered by the Royalists' insistence on using conventional tactics against an enemy prepared to use every weapon system available - including chemical warfare.

In June 1967 the British withdrew from Aden, and within three months the Soviets and Chinese had moved into the resulting power vacuum, allowing Marxism a firm base from which to spread its influence. Aden became the People's Democratic Republic of Yemen; an official Marxist state which soon attracted revolutionaries from around the Arab world. Dhofar, the most southerly province of the Sultanate of Oman, was considered ripe for revolution.

Due in no small part to the ageing Sultan's reactionary rule, the Omani people were oppressed and poverty stricken. The Army consisted of less than 1,000 men, half of whom were Baluchi mercenaries, with a handful of British volunteers in command. The Marxists feared no outside intervention, since the Sultan had no friends but the British, and rightly gauged that the British, still smarting from memories of Suez, would not wish any major involvement in Dhofar. The British government would, if pushed, rather withdraw than face a major furore in Parliament and the press.

Britain responded by allowing any Army officer who wished, to volunteer for two years' detached service with the Sultan's Army. Britain continued to pay its officer-volunteers, and in return gained the use of a vital Middle East transit base on the Omani-owned island of Masirah and transit camp facilities on a small airfield on the Salalah Plain. The relationship between the seconded British Army officers and the 'contract' officers, mercenaries from Britain, India, Pakistan, South Africa and (the then) Southern Rhodesia, who provided the Army with the balance of its leadership, was often fraught. All wore the same uniform, but divisions of class and income remained strong (contract officers, whom the British regulars regarded as socially inferior, were in fact better paid).

When Sultan Qaboos replaced his father in a bloodless coup, the worst repressions were immediately swept away. The British government felt confident enough to admit its participation in the region, regular units including the SAS were posted in, and the role of the seconded officer waned.

Due in no small part to earlier British military intervention, modern Oman is no longer seriously threatened from the south. However a number of British Army officers and NCOs are still seconded to its forces, and even now coexist somewhat uncomfortably with the diminishing number of contract officers in the Sultan's direct employ.

Occasionally countries allow 'volunteers' from their own armed forces to fight for the cause of a political ally. During the American Civil War it was strongly rumoured, though never proven, that the Confederate privateer *Shenandoah* was officered largely by British Royal Navy personnel who were on extended leave. Over a century later, the Nigerian government had the assistance of East German Mig-19 pilots and Egyptian crewed Ilyushin bombers in its bloody war against secessionist Biafra. In its turn Biafra was supplied with mercenaries from the former French colony of Gabon, which was itself then under the protection of a French mercenary force.

With Our Blessing... But!

As already discussed, when the involvement of conventional troops would prove politically unacceptable, governments will occasionally employ civilians to further their military aims. These civilians may be contracted directly by an attributable agency such as the CIA, or by wholly private companies working with the complicity of the authorities.

Many of these companies are completely open in their activities. Airwork for example, operating from offices in Hampshire, advertises publicly for skilled ex-military advisers for short-term contracts with friendly powers, often in the Gulf and Far East. It has the complete support of the British Ministry of Defence, who will occasionally put it in touch with servicemen on the verge of leaving the armed forces.

Other organisations, although completely independent of government control, will nonetheless do nothing to embarrass the domestic authorities. Watchguard, an organisation run in the early 1970s by Colonel David Stirling, operated from the offices of a front company in London's fashionable Sloane Street. It provided prone-to-assassination heads-of-state of friendly African and Middle Eastern countries with teams of well-trained, experienced (often ex-SAS) bodyguards, and as such it met with the quiet approval of the British government.

When, however, the company became involved in a plot to release 150 political prisoners from a prison in the Libyan city of Tripoli - the so-called Hilton Assignment - MI6 intervened. Stirling was reputedly offered a contract, by Umaral al-Shalhi, a millionaire supporter of the deposed King Idris of Libya, to engineer the overthrow of Colonel Gadaffi who had recently seized power in a military coup.

Stirling accepted the contract, but because he was loath to involve himself in anything which might embarrass the British government diplomatically, recruited the majority of his mercenaries from France. Unknown to either the mercenaries or their recruiters the plot against Gadaffi had been penetrated by British Intelligence who informed the CIA. At the time the CIA was still favourably disposed to the young Libyan dictator who, being a devout Moslem, was considered to be passionately anti-Marxist.

United States agents traced four of the mercenaries to the *Conquistador*, a coastal patrol vessel which had been purchased for the occasion and which was then berthed in the Italian port of Trieste. Afraid that any power-shifting in the region might favour the Soviets, the CIA appealed to the Italian secret service, the Servizio Informazione Difesa (SID), for assistance. The Italians moved quickly, raided the *Conquis-*

tador and arrested the mercenaries. With its cover blown, the Hilton Assignment rapidly fell apart.

Although it had no way of stopping it, the British secret service tried hard to frustrate the hiring of mercenaries after Southern Rhodesia's unilateral declaration of independence, and it intervened again when ex-SAS soldiers were recruited to topple the government in the African state of Togo.

The Seychelles Fiasco

On the morning of 25 November 1981 a Fokker F-28 of the Royal Swazi Airlines took off for the Seychelles, and by the afternoon had precipitated an international incident. According to its manifest the flight was carrying 46 rugby players from the fancifully named 'Ye Ancient Order of Frothblowers'. In reality it contained Colonel 'Mad Mike' Hoare and 45 co-mercenaries contracted to wrest control of the islands from the left wing government of France-Albert René.

The operation went badly wrong when one of the mercenaries, Kevin Beck, inexplicably went through the red channel at customs control, had his bag searched, and was discovered to be carrying a firearm. The alarm was raised, and in the ensuing mêlée a local policeman was injured and a mercenary, Johan Fritz, was killed - accidentally by one of his fellow mercenaries!

Unabashed, the mercenaries continued the task of securing the airfield. When an Air India jet en route from Salisbury to Bombay requested permission to make a routine landing it was granted, but the authorisation came from Charles Goatley, one of the mercenaries holding out in the air traffic control tower. Unaware of the drama unfolding below, Captain Umesh Saxena brought his aircraft in to an unexpectedly eventful landing, clipping the aircraft wing against an abandoned vehicle in the process.

Realising that the situation was hopeless, and seeing the aircraft as their only salvation, those mercenaries who were able to extract themselves during the temporary cease-fire occasioned by the aircraft's arrival trooped quietly on board and demanded to be taken to South Africa. Captain Saxena was allowed to take off, and at 5.00am landed at Louis Botha Airport, Durban. After prolonged negotiations with several South African authorities those mercenaries on board were handcuffed and removed to Zonderwater Prison near Cullinan.

South Africa vehemently denied any part in the attempted coup, but on 2 December, despite international demands for their punishment, released 39 of the hijackers. The other five, including Mike Hoare, were formally charged with kidnapping and were then released on bail.

On 7 December the full involvement of the South African Government in the attempted coup became obvious. That day the Seychelles authorities displayed to the international press Martin Dolinchek, one of the seven captured mercenaries and an officer in the South African National Intelligence Service, to the international press. After months of prevarication the South Africans bowed to world pressure and placed all the mercenaries on trial. After a lengthy hearing, part of which was held in camera, all were found guilty of endangering the Air India jet and its passengers, and seven were also found guilty of the more serious offence of hijacking. The majority were imprisoned for six months, the ring leaders for periods of between one and five years. Hoare himself was sentenced to ten years in prison with a further ten years suspended, but was released after less than four. In the eyes of many his punishment was not for leading a mercenary coup, but for failing in the attempt, and for embarrassing the South African government in the process.

The Rhodesian Experience

It is perhaps the counter-insurgency war in Zimbabwe (formerly Southern Rhodesia), fought between 1965 and 1980, that offered the elite mercenary soldier the most inter-esting recent opportunity to practise his military skills. There were probably around 1,500 non-Rhodesian mercenaries in the Rhodesian security forces; including British, Australians, Canadians, Dutch, French, Germans, Greeks and Scandinavians. Little official recruiting went on outside the country; such recruitment as there was taking place by word of mouth and written invitation. The Rhodesian Information Office advised applicants on the enlistment processes, after which aspirants had to make their own way to the training centres. Successful mercenaries did however have their fares refunded.

Mercenaries who joined the Rhodesian armed forces did so for a minimum term of two years and were treated identically to local volunteers. Their basic salary, although a little higher than that then paid in the British Army, was far from generous, and was certainly not in itself sufficient reason for enlistment. Most men joined because they liked the life, the comradeship and the excitement; few for reasons of overt racism.

Mercenaries served in every element of the Rhodesian armed forces, including the SAS (which was reputed to have a tougher selection process than its sister-unit in Hereford), the Selous Scouts and the Rhodesian Light Infantry (RLI). Others served in the counter-insurgency wing of the rather confusingly-named British South Africa Police (BSAP) Special Branch.

With the coming of independence and the formation of Zimbabwe in 1980, a number of elite units - including the SAS, the Selous Scouts and the RLI - were dis-banded. Those mercenaries who remained left quickly, many joining the now unem-ployed Rhodesians from these former units in the move south to seek employment with the South African Defence Forces. It is believed that at least one unit crossed the bor-der with its armoury and entire fleet of vehicles.

Laws of Convenience

Most countries do not prohibit their citizens from serving as mercenaries, provided that treason is not involved. However under existing legislation it is an offence for a United States citizen to fight for a foreign power. The Neutrality Act forbids the recruiting of mercenaries, or even the planning of a mercenary operation on United States soil. However this particular piece of legislation has always enjoyed a flexible interpreta-tion; Americans have a tradition of honourable service in the French Foreign Legion, and a large number of United States pilots served with distinction in the 'Flying Tigers' in China and in the Eagle Squadron of the RAF during the darkest days of the Battle of Britain and the Blitz. More recently, American mercenaries have often interfered violently in the affairs of Central America, and in a few instances have even fought for the Mujahideen against the Soviets in Afghanistan, however none has been prosecuted for it.

Tom Posey, a former member of the National Guard and head of Civilian Military Assistance, an organisation which sends men to fight against Communists in Central and South America, is typical of those who recruit openly in the United States. Many American would-be mercenaries subscribe to *Soldier of Fortune*, a magazine founded by the American anti-communist mercenary, Robert K. Brown. Formerly in the United States Special Forces, he has fought and trained others to fight in Guatemala, El Salvador and Nicaragua, as well as further afield in Afghanistan and Southern Rhodesia. As a self-styled 'Journal of Professional Adventurers', *Soldier of Fortune* draws the attention of potential mercenaries to areas of anti-communist unrest. It does not actively recruit, for to do so would be illegal, but instead it offers ex-soldiers with the relevant training and experience active 'support' in obtaining suitable work fighting communism abroad.

Light Work and Good Money
It is an unfortunate fact of life that elite soldiers often make bad civilians. Many are unable to adjust to retirement from active service at a relatively young age and simply cannot settle into the nine-to-five routine of a second career. Inevitably some band together to form security and personal protection companies in the forlorn hope of carrying their military experience into the civilian environment. A few succeed, and are able to exploit the volatility of the current international situation to earn comfortable livings. Most fail however, falling victim to their own naivety and commercial inexperience.

Many who fail as independents do succeed in finding conventional work or gain employment with one of the established security companies. Others however drift into the murky world of the freelance mercenary, from which few escape unscathed. In late 1967 some 50 mercenaries enlisted for service with the breakaway Biafran government of Colonel Ojukwu. In their first battle, an unauthorised assault on a Nigerian position at Calabar, the force was badly mauled. Most of the survivors left Biafra for good, not only older and wiser but - as they had received six months' pay in advance - substantially better off!

In May 1975 a group of some 90 assorted mercenaries met amid considerable publicity in the Devonshire Room of the Regent Centre Hotel in London. They had responded to advertisements placed in two national newspapers by John Banks; a convicted blackmailer, thief, self-confessed would-be assassin, mercenary and a former member of the 2nd Battalion The Parachute Regiment until dishonourably discharged in 1969. The advertisements read:

'Ex-Commandos, paratroopers, SAS troopers wanted for interesting work. Ring Camberley 33456.' The terms of service were good -£150.00 per week with life insurance of £25,000 - but the contract on offer was unusual in that it involved fighting for Joshua Nkomo's Zimbabwe African People's Union (ZAPU) against Ian Smith's secessionist white government of Southern Rhodesia. A number of the would-be mercenaries, mostly ex-servicemen from South Africa and Rhodesia, objected and left. Those who remained were told that they would be sent to a training camp in Zambia where they would be split into four-man penetration teams to carry out sabotage missions against key roads, railways and military installations. In the end, however, the mission came to nothing; an advance party of seventeen mercenaries were ordered to congregate at the Sky Line Hotel, near Heathrow Airport, to await their flight out. The next day, when their promised advance payments had not arrived, the men went berserk and, in two days of drunken violence, drew so much attention to themselves that the operation was aborted.

The Angola Tragedy

Unabashed by the total failure of his Rhodesian enterprise, and the glare of bad publicity which followed, Banks decided to make use of the military expertise which he had tapped, and in August 1975 he set up SAS - Security Advisory Services. Banks claimed that SAS could provide clients with a complete anti-terrorist security service, although in reality it was little more than a recruiting agency for mercenaries.

In January 1976 Banks was approached by Nicholas Hall, a former member of the 1st Battalion The Parachute Regiment. Hall had been discharged from the Army and imprisoned for robbing a number of post offices during a tour of Northern Ireland, and was now recruiting for the FNLA in Angola. Banks was asked to assemble a small group of veterans for mercenary work in Angola and quickly produced a team of nineteen under the command of Peter McAleese, an ex-SAS sergeant.

The military credentials of the party were impressive; all but two had military experience and most were former paratroopers or SAS. Of the 'civilians' one, Dave Tomkins, was an accomplished safe breaker! On 18 January the party flew out of Heathrow leaving Banks to continue his recruiting drive. He was greatly assisted by the enormous publicity which the first departure had engendered, indeed in at least one instance a newspaper had happily provided details of Banks' telephone number to a potential applicant.

Nearly 100 mercenaries were recruited during the following week, and those who flew out to Angola on 28 January were a singularly mixed bunch. The oldest, 'Jock' McCartney, was in his fifties, a former sergeant-major and fluent in Russian. The youngest, David Smith, was just seventeen with no military experience. A number of the military 'veterans' had been dishonourably discharged from the armed forces, at least one was on the run from the police. Two had served short spells in the Royal Navy as submariners, and had assumed that they were being recruited as trainers rather than combatants. A few had even left well paid, but to them, boring jobs and had elected for the life of the mercenary in the hope of gaining a fulfilment which until then had been missing from their lives.

Perhaps inevitably the entire sorry episode ended in tragedy. Fourteen of Banks' 'Dogs of War' were murdered on the orders of Costas Georgiou - better known as 'Colonel' Callan - a mercenary fighting on the same side. After returning to England Banks, who had accompanied the main party to Angola, was convicted on charges of blackmail and making threats to kill, and was jailed for two years. He has since been hired by Winnie Mandela, and other top African National Congress (ANC) members, as their personal bodyguard.

11
Special Forces 2050
A Look into the Future

Unconventional forces have become an essential ingredient in the successful prosecution of modern warfare, yet they frequently remain unpopular and mistrusted by politicians and the senior military hierarchies alike. In a world in which media presence has become paramount, their covert ways have often made them easy targets for the sensationalism of the modern press and have left their political masters vulnerable to the vagaries of an ill-informed mass media. In a world in which the end no longer automatically justifies the means, they have seen their operational successes analysed and criticised to the point of obsession.

In Britain, the SAS has been shielded, somewhat, from internal intrigue by its tradition of limiting its successful officer entrants to two-year tours. Although the best may be invited to return for second and subsequent tours (and often then go on to reach senior command positions) the majority of officers will serve only once, electing to spend the rest of their careers with their parent units. A large number of field and general officers have therefore served, albeit briefly, with the special forces, and as such are aware of their potential without fearing their autocracy.

The peace dividend has brought with it an understandable and near universal desire for a reduction in defence spending, yet crucially it has not brought about stability. Indeed the world is plagued with more brush wars and potential flash points than ever before. Consequently the major powers are finding themselves increasingly committed as peacekeepers to situations which demand either the deployment of large numbers of often no longer available troops, or the intervention of a small number of highly trained specialists.

Crucially, international public opinion will no longer tolerate the spilling of what it often naively regards as innocent civilian blood, nor will it countenance the outright humiliation of one sovereign state by another. The Coalition forces in the Gulf War could easily have taken Basra, and thereafter could have swept northwards into Baghdad. However they were constrained from so doing by a combination of media-led Western revulsion at the (much exaggerated) slaughter along on Baghdad-Basra road, and by Arab distaste at having a fellow-Moslem state humiliated by the West.

Conscious of the need to placate public opinion, special forces are trained to operate where possible in a surgical manner, minimising damage to non-combatants and non-military targets, while causing significant damage to enemy military forces. Occasionally special forces will even resort to psychological operations in an attempt to coerce an enemy into bloodless submission. This is often particularly valuable after a crisis when former enemy troops, who have been defeated but not humiliated, can be used to help rebuild an economy.

Thus, despite the reservations of many politicians and the more conservative of the military hierarchy, special forces and special purpose forces are enjoying, and are likely to continue to enjoy, an unexpected renaissance.

Future Trends in Special Operations

Several recent low-key special purpose humanitarian operations have provided an insight into the vast, but as yet still largely untapped, potential for small groups of highly mobile elite forces to render both economic and military assistance to friendly governments.

After the successful conclusion of Operation Desert Storm, a number of United States Naval Special Warfare Task Units (NSWTUs) were ordered to remain in the Gulf as part of an Amphibious Ready Group (ARG). When Bangladesh was devastated by floods, with massive damage and loss of life, special purpose naval forces from the ARG were able to alleviate much suffering almost immediately by deploying their rigid inflatable boats in support of the relief effort.

Recently the role of the United States military in Somalia has come in for a fair degree of justifiable criticism. However most errors emanated from poor intelligence and staff work, rather than from the abilities of the special purpose forces on the ground. In 1991, in an exercise ideally suited to their training and panache, a combined force of United States Marines and SEALs were helicoptered into Mogadishu to protect the embassy staff from bands of increasingly violent local militia. Landing in the Embassy compound, the troops secured the area until ships from their parent ARG were able to close the coast and dispatch more helicopters to evacuate the embassy staff. Despite the numerical superiority of the militias, and the constant if ineffective sniper fire, the evacuation was completed without casualties to either side.

In 1992 the United States conducted Operation 'Restore Hope' in an effort to alleviate the mass starvation brought on by the civil war in Somalia. Prior to the United States Marine amphibious landing, SEALs conducted a number of clandestine beach surveys. A degree of initial embarrassment was caused immediately prior to the Marines' dawn assault when a number of uniformed and heavily camouflaged personnel were identified as SEALs when they were caught in the media's photographic lights which had been set up on the beach in anticipation. Whoever these men were, they were not SEALs. Their uniform and the timing and method of their arrival were completely wrong. It may be safely assumed that SEALs did land, but hours earlier and in complete secrecy, to ensure safe passage for the Marines following.

In August 1993 the United States government learned a salutary lesson when it dispatched 400 Rangers in an attempt to apprehend the local warlord, Mohammed Aideed. Denied adequate field intelligence and forced to operate relatively overtly, the Rangers were able to employ little of the innovation and initiative for which they are renowned. Although they made several night heliborne assaults on Aideed's presumed positions they inevitably found that their information was wrong or that he had moved. Eventually, frustrated by their lack of success, the Rangers were withdrawn.

Brain Not Brawn

Increasingly it is the academic contribution as much as the military versatility of the special forces which leads to an operational success. The SAS in Malaya and Borneo pioneered the policy of hearts and minds. Living with the indigenous peoples of the jungle, they learned their languages and adopted their ways in an effort to win their confidence and respect. Over twenty years later the United States continued the tradition admirably by exploiting the linguistic abilities of a Russian speaking female, a Sergeant First Class from the 18th Airborne Corps, attached to the United States Special Operations Command (USSOCOM).

In early 1992, when Mongolia requested United States expertise to develop an internal defensive infrastructure, the Pentagon found its efforts to assist frustrated by a total lack of suitable Mongolian speakers. Appreciating that most Mongolian officers could speak Russian (Soviet troops had occupied the country until the disintegration of the Soviet empire only a few months earlier) they seconded the NCO-linguist to Ulan Bator to teach English to the Mongolian General Staff. Enthralled by the fact that their tutor was both a woman and a paratrooper the Mongolians invited the NCO to participate in an airborne jump with their own paratroopers. She did so successfully, and thus became the first American soldier in history authorised to wear the Mongolian airborne qualification badge.

In the winter of 1991-92, when many of the Asian states of the former Soviet Union were beginning to starve due to the sheer inadequacy of their transportation system, United States special forces linguists again intervened to enable food and supplies to be airlifted to the most stricken areas. When it was discovered that the C-141 Star-lifter crews could not communicate with the Russian-speaking air traffic controllers and ground liaison staff, Russian-speaking special forces personnel flew in each cockpit to translate. True to the universal military maxim 'soldier first, technician second', when it was discovered that ethnic fighting on the ground was endangering the operation, the United States special forces established a liaison with their former-Soviet Spetsnaz counterparts, the very men whom traditionally they had been trained to fight, to maintain the security of their aircraft.

Special purpose forces are rapidly developing a tradition of supplying medical, as well as linguistic, aid to the needy; particularly, it must be said, when those needy inhabit non-aligned or friendly countries. In March 1992 members of the US 3rd Special Forces Group (Airborne) were deployed to no fewer than eight African countries. In Cameroon alone, reservist medical specialists from the US Army Civil Affairs and Psychological Operations Command (USACAPOC) inoculated more than 58,000 people against meningitis and treated another 1,700 for a variety of other ailments. Less dramatic, although equally vital, special purpose forces medical personnel provided discreet medical and educational support in an attempt to stem the spread of AIDS, now close to epidemic proportions in some parts of the African continent. Humanitarian aid and national assistance to friendly powers will continue to represent major arenas for future special forces, and more particularly for special purpose forces. Equally, special forces liaison teams will remain ideally suited to the formation and training of friendly governments' special purpose forces facing insurgents or unconventional enemies. British SAS personnel performed excellently in the anti-narcotics war in Colombia, and although their efforts were on too small a scale to more than inconvenience the powerful drugs cartels, they amply proved the potential for future, larger operations. Military exchange tours, which are both cheap and easy to effect, will continue to provide a close liaison between the special forces of the major powers and the elite forces of their smaller allies.

The United States, with its huge amphibious capability, has no need to rely on the availability of a friendly staging post from which to launch its counter-insurgency activities. However it seems increasingly likely that less advantaged powers such as Britain and France, which no longer maintain massive blue water fleets yet which continue to enjoy considerable out of area interests, will begin to negotiate mutual support packages with friendly third-world governments.

In January 1994 it was conceded that Britain was negotiating the construction of a secret special forces base at Mersing, near the southern tip of Malaysia, as part of the much-criticised Pergau dam project. It is anticipated that Britain will wish to exercise her rights under the long-standing Five Power Defence Arrangement - with Malaysia, Australia, New Zealand and Singapore - to station troops and equipment there during joint exercises. Mersing will be available as a covert base for Special Air Service and Special Boat Service troops in the area and will play a key strategic role in the region when Britain hands Hong Kong back to China in 1997.

Low Intensity Operations

Low intensity conflict has been defined as 'armed conflict for political purposes not involving combat between conventional forces'. It follows few defined patterns and as such is exceedingly difficult to counter.

Modern technology is steadily improving the low-intensity insurgent's chances of success. Shoulder-launched anti-aircraft systems have already proved their worth with the Mujahideen in Afghanistan and with PIRA ASUs in Northern Ireland and are now becoming more accessible. A plethora of hand-held anti-tank weapons are available, easily capable of penetrating lightly armoured personnel carriers to create carnage among the passengers within. At the same time technological trends are creating more opportunities for the insurgent and terrorist; communications centres are growing in size and complexity, power generating plants - particularly nuclear power stations - are increasing in number; even aircraft, a tempting terrorist target, are getting bigger.

It is unlikely that special forces will be used to export state-sponsored terrorism on a large scale. However, they will almost certainly continue to be used to counter it. Reprisal air raids and missile strikes against known areas of terrorist activity are often counter-productive as they invariably result in the loss of innocent lives. A government suspected of supporting terrorism has only to produce evidence of heavy civilian casualties sustained during a retaliatory raid to divert attention from the initial purpose of that raid. Much of the evidence produced may be fabricated (as it was after the United States bombing raid on Libya), but experience has shown that such evidence is often enough to convince a shocked and militarily unsophisticated media that, however great the provocation which occasioned it, the attack was little more than an outrageous atrocity.

In contrast a well-planned and professionally executed commando action can retain its surgical integrity. Its target can be identified and eliminated with relative certainty while minimising collateral damage occasioned to innocent civilians. Crucially the knowledge that there are special forces trained and available to carry out such retaliatory commando raids has had a marked psychological affect on terrorist groups in the past, and has in itself been enough to temper their worst excesses.

Despite her status as the only remaining world superpower, the United States does not have an enviable reputation for commando-style intervention. Her attempts at hostage rescue in Iran proved a humiliating failure, while her performance in Grenada was marred by an awkward and confusing mix of units and inter-service headquarters. On one occasion US Marine Corps Cobra helicopters sent to support an Army unit in the Salines area were unable to locate either friendly or enemy positions as their pilots had not been informed of the Army's radio frequencies. When this fundamental error was overcome it was found that they were still unable to render substantial help as the Army and Marines had been issued with different maps!

It seems probable that the United States will attempt to address this problem by enhancing the size and potency of its Ranger Regiment. The Rangers were universally acclaimed for their performance in Grenada, and are probably the finest light infantry force in the world today. Trained to operate independently, or in support of special forces teams such as the SEALs, they can be transported as a single unit in the existing US Air Force transportation fleet and would represent a potent challenge to any but the largest and best organised of insurgents.

Quick-Reaction Warfare

For four decades both NATO and the Warsaw Pact trained for conventional mechanised warfare. It was envisaged that Soviet armoured units, spearheaded by the Third Shock Army, would attempt to smash a series of routes through the NATO defences deep into the West German heartland. It was anticipated that NATO would attempt to channel the advancing Soviets into a series of killing zones in which their concentrated divisions would be annihilated by the technologically superior Western armies.

It was accepted NATO doctrine that the air-land battle, as envisaged, would have a crucial role for special purpose forces. There would be an offensive role for the SAS and others, and also a compelling need for elite troops trained in covert target acquisition. There would however be little need for airborne or maritime special purpose forces. Mechanised forces depend on the existence of long supply lines which are vulnerable to special forces attack. The SAS and Green Berets were therefore trained to operate in small bands, using their experience and initiative to probe for targets of opportunity in the enemy rear. Primarily they were expected to employ the infiltration means, clandestine communications systems and target designators available to them to locate targets of particular value for NATO air interdiction. When an air attack was not feasible they were trained to attack directly, using the various stand-off weapon systems available to them. Targets were prioritised thus: nuclear delivery means, army and corps headquarters, command control and communications centres, choke points and heavy artillery.

The demise of the Warsaw Pact brought about a complete re-evaluation of the role of special forces in mechanised warfare. It became clear to the Western allies that they would no longer be able to plan for a defensive battle but would in future have to consider the possibility of fighting a variety of potential engagements far from their home bases. The role of airborne and heliborne troops was re-evaluated and enhanced, and a new force, the ACE (Allied Command Europe) Rapid Reaction Corps, formed. Command of the new Allied Rapid Reaction Corps (ARRC) passed to Britain, considered to be the historical experts in the field.

The Rapid Reaction Corps

The ACE Rapid Reaction Corps, as it is usually described, established its headquarters in Rheindahlen and undertook its first exercises in early 1994. It contains a number of constituent parts, and is able - in theory - to deploy worldwide at battalion, brigade, divisional or even corps level. Apart from a dedicated headquarters its troops are 'double-hatted', having national responsibilities elsewhere when not required by ARRC.

The Corps comprises up to five divisions. With the exception of the British 3rd (Armoured) Division, which is permanently based in the United Kingdom, it is highly mobile and relatively lightly armed, relying heavily on its elite airborne and marine special purpose forces to give it the edge in battle. Britain provides a second, United Kingdom-based division comprising two mechanised infantry brigades and 5 (Airborne) Brigade. Recent defence cuts have reduced the lift potential of 5 (Airborne) Brigade to one battalion. Nonetheless the potential of this most versatile of units, part of which was deployed to Rwanda in July 1994 to spearhead Britain's aid assistance programme, is such that it is still regarded as one of the finest special purpose forces in Europe.

The multinational Central Division is made up of two German parachute brigades, a Dutch airmobile brigade and the British 24th (Airmobile) Brigade. Current plans exist to equip this brigade with a fleet of attack helicopters. Given that the plans, which are in an advanced state, survive the on-going defence cuts they will give the British a heliborne offensive potential which has been sadly lacking hitherto.

A second multinational division in the south comprises an Italian parachute brigade, a Greek mechanised infantry brigade and a Turkish commando brigade. Finally, an Italian mechanised division contains two Italian mechanised brigades and a Portuguese airborne brigade.

The ACE Rapid Reaction Corps may be expected to provide a blueprint for the future. Not only does it offer NATO a counter to any envisaged threat short of high-intensity mechanised warfare (in which instance its troops would be deployed elsewhere) but it makes excellent use of a number of special purpose units, particularly airborne, which would otherwise have been without a role.

Amphibious Warfare

Nowhere is the change in military focus more apparent than in amphibious warfare. European nations in particular are carefully reviewing their strategic needs and in many cases are actually increasing their marine capability. The United Kingdom is revitalising the assault landing capability of the Royal Navy while Portugal and Italy are expanding their amphibious potential; as part of its restructuring NATO is fielding a new on-call amphibious task force for the Mediterranean.

Marine special purpose forces are not only robust but versatile; because they are sea-based they can be positioned without basing arrangements, overflight requests or landing rights, and can be maintained for extended periods at a high state of readiness close to all but a few potential flashpoints. On the NATO flanks and in the volatile regions of sub-Saharan Africa their ability to provide their own mobility and command and control will continue to make them an attractive option. They do not require airfields or ports and thus can operate to their full potential without over stretching their host nation's possibly delicate infrastructure.

As rapid reaction becomes the mainstay of the NATO platform, amphibious units will inevitably grow in importance. NATO's Combined Amphibious Force, Mediterranean (CAFMED) will soon be able to call upon the amphibious elites of the United States, United Kingdom, Holland, Spain, Italy, Greece, Turkey and Portugal. It will provide the NATO southern region with a quick reaction force, as potent as the ACE Rapid Reaction Force, able to deploy quickly and at any level of engagement.

Despite universal defence cuts European amphibious forces remain well-armed, well-equipped and, above all, well-trained. The Royal Marines have been reduced by only four per cent against an overall military cutback of fifteen per cent and will soon receive a new helicopter assault ship. The Royal Netherlands Marine Corps is actually expanding while, in Italy, the San Marco Battalion is actually growing by 50 per cent, while long term plans exist to create a joint-service amphibious light brigade. Portugal is equipping its Fuzeleiros with improved small boats and personal weapons while the Spanish marines are upgrading their air defence, communications and electronic warfare capabilities.

Given the unsettled nature of the world's current security environment it seems certain that the role of amphibious special purpose forces will continue to grow. Given that it is now accepted that forward presence, deterrence, crisis management and humanitarian support are best accomplished by naval-based forces, it seems likely that amphibious forces will continue to receive increasingly larger shares of their respective nation's defence programming.

Military Home Defence

Faced with defending large land masses and long borders, Canada and Australia are learning successfully to apply the rapid-deployment force concept to their domestic defensive strategy.

Although Canadian participation in NATO is diminishing her relatively small Army plays an increasingly important part in United Nations peacekeeping operations. As such it is retaining a positive profile at home and continues to attract recruits of the highest calibre. Canada maintains a 3,000-strong highly mobile 'immediate reaction' Special Service Force (SSF) based at Petawawa, Ontario.

The Canadian Airborne Regiment and the 1st Battalion Royal Canadian Regiment provide the unit's mechanised infantry; the light armour of the Royal Canadian Dragoons provides the reconnaissance and direct fire support, and the 2nd Regiment Royal Canadian Horse Artillery the indirect fire support. A combat engineer regiment, a tactical helicopter squadron, a service battalion, a field ambulance and a military police platoon provide the balance of the force.

While continuing to train for conventional conflicts and United Nations intervention operations the soldiers of the SSF are increasingly called upon to perform a wide range of internal duties which will almost certainly guarantee the unit's survival into the twenty-first century. A number of the Canadian paratroopers have qualified as para-medics and would spearhead a rescue attempt should an airliner crash in the Arctic. Others specialise in mounting long-range reconnaissance patrols, or in providing security and counter-terrorist support to the Royal Canadian Mounted Police (RCMP).

The role of the Australian Operational Deployment Force (ODF) is in many respects similar to that of the SSF, although the climate and terrain in which the two units operate could not be more different. The ODF is responsible for the defence of northern Australia, with millions of acres of scrubland, desert and near-tropical rain forest. Based at Townsville, Queensland, on the southern tip of the Great Barrier Reef, the ODF is kept at constant short notice to deploy. Despite having a substantial reserve element it is able to mount a full company deployment without prior notice within seven days and can be fully mobilised within a month.

The ODF is considered to be primarily a reconnaissance unit and would not usually be expected to fight for information, nor does it operate closely with the SASR. It relies heavily on the Regional Force Surveillance units (RFSUs), as well as more conventional government and military sources, to act as its eyes and ears. The RFSUs are manned by army reservists, with small regular components to deal with daily administration and training, and as such are similar in many respects to a British Territorial Army battalion.

RFSUs are true special purpose forces. Their members are chosen for their expertise in the field and for their intimate knowledge of local areas rather than for their potential as conventional soldiers. Most are born and bred in the country, learning the principles of survival at their father's knee. Many are bushmen or Aboriginals and as such share a mutual respect rarely found in an urban environment. Long-range reconnaissance patrols, which are generally undertaken by six-man teams, can last for five to six weeks under the most exacting of conditions. Easy to manage and cheap to operate the RFSUs are proving highly successful and will almost certainly be expanded in the years to come.

The Gulf War - Lessons for the Future

Approximately 5,000 special forces, most of them British and American, were deployed in the Gulf War. They comprised a mere fraction of the total Allied force, yet their contribution in the latter stages of the operation was crucial. They included components of the SAS and SBS, including a small number of reservists, the 5th US Army Special Forces Group, United States Delta Force and three US Navy SEAL teams. The men on the ground were supported by RAF special duties flights and elements of the US Air Force 8th, 16th, 20th and 21st Special Operations Squadrons. General Schwarzkopf reportedly requested two Ranger battalions, but these were held in reserve and only one company of Rangers was actually sent to the Gulf.

A large number of special purpose forces were also sent to the theatre. Saudi Arabia fielded an airborne brigade, Syria a special forces brigade and Morocco two commando battalions. More importantly, the US Marine Corps sent to the Gulf the 1st and elements of the 2nd Marine Expeditionary Force (MEF), well over half its active strength.

It was clear from the outset that political factors rather than purely military considerations would govern the prosecution of the war. Saddam Hussein made no secret of the fact that he regarded Israel as a legitimate target. In a newspaper article published in the government-controlled *Al-Jumhuriyah* (and later broadcast on Republic of Iraq Radio) he described Israel as 'the unjust force of aggression planted on Arab land', threatening to make the Jewish state the first target of his 'devastating and ruinous blows'. Well aware that Israeli retaliation to Iraqi missile strikes might lead to a premature disintegration of the Coalition, Schwarzkopf determined to use the special forces available to him to neutralise as many Scuds as possible before they could be fired.

In some instances warning of Scud launches came from EW units monitoring transmissions between the transporter-erector-launchers (TELs) and their command centres. At other times warnings came from the infra-red cameras mounted on United States surveillance satellites. The data was passed to Alice Springs, Australia and then to the United States Command Centre in Colorado. From there it was passed to Washington and onward to Saudi Arabia and Israel; all this taking only a few minutes and well within the missile's time of flight.

Special forces teams were helicoptered into south-west Iraq in an attempt to locate the launchers before they were activated. During the final stages of the war, United States and British special forces ground teams were credited with the discovery of some 40 Iraqi mobile Scud TELs, an estimated 29 of which were 'locked and loaded' and targeted on Israel. The last Scud to be fired was launched on the 41st day of hostilities, about 48 hours before the cease-fire. Had the 29 missiles poised against Israel not been destroyed, the penultimate day of the war might have been the first day of a far bigger one.

The ground teams were inserted by RAF Chinooks and MH-53J Pave Lows of the 20th Special Operations Squadron. Although, as ever, the squadron's activities in this area remain secret it has been authoritatively suggested that its Pave Lows flew some 60 missions in support of the special forces, actually locating a number of Scud sites on their own radars.

Towards the end of the Gulf War, a number of special forces ground teams switched from reconnaissance and intelligence-gathering to direct-action sabotage missions. SEAL teams stormed nine Iraqi-held oil platforms off Kuwait, while a combined SBS-SEAL assault on Faylakah Island contributed to the deception plan to suggest that Allied forces would launch a seaborne invasion around Kuwait City; offshore a small SEAL team provided acoustic deception to support this illusion. In a number of instances special forces teams infiltrated with large tripod-mounted laser designators to within 1,500 metres of high-grade targets to enable the Allied air forces to bomb their targets with pinpoint accuracy.

RAF and US Air Force specialist squadrons played an important role in supporting conventional air and ground operations in the Gulf. On the morning of 17 January 1991 four MH-53J Pave Low helicopters from the 20th Special Operations Squadron, part of the 1st Special Operations Wing, opened the way for US Army Apache attack helicopters to blast a route through the Iraqi air defence network. As a direct result, US Air Force F-117 stealth bombers were able to lead the first undetected raid on Baghdad, signalling the start of the air war. While en route back to base the

Pave Lows were fired upon by two SA-7 missiles launched by Iraqi Bedouins inside Saudi airspace. The Pave Lows' warning receivers alerted them to the presence of the infra red guided missiles and they were able to drop decoy flares. However the very existence of the armed Bedouin so far south ably demonstrated that Iraq had mobilised special purpose irregular forces of her own.

MC-130E Combat Talons of the 8th Special Operations Squadron helped open the ground war on the night of 6 February, when they dropped two giant BLU-82 Daisy Cutter bombs to blast a corridor through the Iraqi minefields and defences for the United States Marines. The effect was devastating; the 15,000lb bombs were so powerful that they killed every Iraqi soldier within a 3-mile radius, allowing the Marines to advance unscathed through the first two defensive lines. The shock waves were so great that an SAS patrol 110 miles away reported that Kuwait City had been hit by a nuclear weapon.

Combat search and rescue in the Gulf was undertaken jointly by helicopters from 20th Special Operations Squadron, operating from Saudi Arabia (and subsequently from Kuwait and Southern Iraq) and by 21st SOS based at 'Batman' in Turkey. When any Coalition aircraft was downed, its approximate position was recorded by other pilots on the sortie and by the crew of the E-3A Airborne Warning and Control aircraft (AWACS) tasked with tracking every mission. Where possible special operations ground teams were then inserted, by vehicle or helicopter, to search for the wreckage. If survivors were located their precise position was transmitted to the search and rescue flight via secure means, an SAR helicopter was then dispatched to recover the crew and, if they had been helicoptered in, the special forces personnel guarding them.

There can be no doubt that United States and British special forces made a significant contribution to the Coalition victory in the Gulf. In recognition of this, it was announced on 28 June 1991 that the British special forces had been awarded 52 medals and other honours for their actions during the Gulf War.

Certainly the special forces had been provided with the very latest equipment available, much of it hitherto unproven. However, had the men of the special forces not conducted themselves so magnificently their equipment would have given them little advantage. The conditions under which they operated were, at times, appalling. On 23 January 1993 an eight-man SAS patrol led by Sergeant Andy McNab was compromised while operating north-west of Baghdad. The Iraqis attacked with armour, and after a fierce fire-fight the patrol was forced to disengage and attempt an escape and evasion towards the Syrian border, 120km to the north-west. In the first night, in pitch darkness and conditions cold enough to freeze diesel fuel, the patrol covered over 85km During the days that followed, though stricken by hypothermia and other injuries, the patrol fought on. Four men were captured, destined to suffer appalling torture before their repatriation. Three were killed; only one escaped. Yet the patrol left in its wake 250 Iraqi soldiers dead or wounded. There can be few instances of greater valour in the history of special forces warfare.

Grounds for Optimism

It has been said of the special forces that they do not win wars, that they are expensive to maintain and that they are dangerously unaccountable. While each criticism is true in detail, none gives grounds for supposing that the concept of elitism in war will other than prosper in the years to come. Special forces are a catalyst not a solution, and as such they are rarely if ever responsible for bringing conflicts to a conclusion. They cannot take the place of the ordinary combat soldier, of economic and mental attack, exhaustion or of political action. They can, however, act as force-multipliers, reducing considerably the size and complexity of the conventional force required to achieve victory. In a world in which warfare is being conducted more than ever under the gaze of the media, and in which casualty figures are now a sensitive issue, this is crucial. So long as special forces continue to have a disproportionate effect on the enemy relative to their numbers they will be tolerated, if not loved, by the politicians who ultimately commit them. British losses in the SAS-led Borneo and Dhofar Campaigns were minimal. In six years of campaigning in the inhospitable Dhofar region, the SAS lost only twelve dead. In the three year Borneo campaign, casualties were also remarkably light - fewer than twenty British dead against one hundred times that number of enemy dead.

As the major armed forces retrench for the out-of-area operations and brush wars ahead they must surely appreciate the value of small if admittedly, for their size, expensive force-multipliers. An enemy which knows it is facing an elite is invariably wary, often to the detriment of its morale and fighting efficiency. Argentinian conscripts in the Falklands fled into the hands of an advancing Guards battalion rather than face the Gurkhas whom they had been told (quite erroneously) would take no prisoners. The role of the SAS in Northern Ireland has been magnified beyond all reason by the paramilitaries of both persuasions. Suffice it to say, had every alleged SAS sighting in the Province over the past twenty years been true it would have been necessary for the entire SAS Regiment, regular and territorial, to have been committed throughout.

The likelihood that future military operations will require smaller, more flexible, rapidly deployable forces has been made abundantly clear since the Gulf War. Former adversaries of NATO and the Warsaw Pact increasingly find themselves serving side by side under United Nations direction. As former Warsaw Pact nations seek closer links with NATO, their organisations are moving towards the maintenance of a rapidly deployable spearhead. The Russian armed forces, with fewer conscripts, are looking at a force structure which reflects to a degree the thinking behind NATO's ARRC. Its highly motivated Airborne Forces and Naval Infantry divisions provide core elements. The Czech Army has established the parachute trained 71st Rapid Reaction Battalion. This unit has already exercised with elements of the Dutch Marines and is scheduled to be expanded to brigade strength.

Finally, there is the matter of excellence. Armies comprise a number of regiments, keen rivals in time of peace but inseparable allies in time of war. Special forces provide a home for the true elite, men of idealism whose self-motivation is enough to spur them to acts of superhuman endeavour yet who would have no place in the conventional armed forces. Their intervention, real or supposed, in a campaign can have immeasurable advantages to the morale, and ultimate fighting ability, of line troops. This fact alone is reason enough to secure the survival of the special forces into the twenty-first century.

Bibliography

Published Sources

Adams, James; Morgan, Robin; Bambridge, Anthony: *Ambush: the War Between the SAS and the IRA*, Pan

Andrade, John: *World Police and Paramilitary Forces*, Macmillan

Asher, Michael: *Shoot to Kill: A Soldier's Journey Through Violence*, Viking

Barrie, Alexander: *War Underground: The Tunnellers of the Great War*, Tom Donovan Publishing

Beckwith, Charlie; Weeks, John: *Delta Force*, Arms & Armour

Bishop, Chris; Drury, Ian: *Combat Guns*, Temple Press

Braddon, Russell: *Nancy Wake*, Pan

Brent, Peter: *The Viking Saga*, Weidenfeld and Nicolson

Burgess, Major William Jnr: *Inside Spetsnaz*, Presidio

Caesar, Julius: *The Conquest of Gaul*, Penguin

Cassin-Scott, Jack: *The Greek and Persian Wars 500-323BC*, Osprey

Cernenko, Dr E. V.: *The Scythians 700-300BC*, Osprey

Clutterbuck, Richard: *Terrorism and Guerrilla Warfare*, Routledge/New York

Collins, John M.: *Green Berets, SEALs and Spetsnaz*, Pergamon-Brasseys

Commager, Henry Steele: *Illustrated History of the American Civil War*, Orbis

Cross, Henry: *The Guinness Encyclopaedia of Warfare*, Guinness Publishing

Darman, Peter: *A-Z of the SAS*, Sidgwick & Jackson

Davis, William: *Fighting Men of the Civil War*, Salamander

Dempster, Chris; Tomkins, Dave: *Firepower*, Corgi

Derry, Archie: *Emergency in Malaya: The Psychological Dimension*, National Defence College

Dickens, Peter: *SAS: The Jungle Frontier*, Arms & Armour Press

Dupuy, R. Ernest; Dupuy, Trevor N.: *The Encyclopaedia of Military History*, Collins

Eaton, Captain H. B.: *APIS; Soldiers with Stereo*, Intelligence Corps Association

Elton, G. R.: *England Under the Tudors*, Methuen

Escott, Bickham Sweet: *The Baker Street Irregulars*, Methuen

Eshel, David: *Daring to Win: Special Forces at War*, Cassell

Fiennes, Ranulph: *Where Soldiers Fear to Tread*, Hodder & Stoughton

Foot, M. R. D.: *SOE, The Special Operations Executive*, Mandarin

Garrett, Richard: *The Raiders; The World's Elite Strike Forces*, David & Charles

Geraghty, Tony: *This is the SAS*, Arms and Armour Press

Grabsky, Phil: *The Great Commanders*, Boxtree

Hackett, General Sir John: *Warfare in the Ancient World*, Sidgwick & Jackson

Harclerode, Peter: *The Elite and Their Support*, Strategic Publishing Company
— *Para*, Arms & Armour Press

Healey, Tim: *Secret Armies*, Purnell

Hinsley, F. H.: *British Intelligence in the*

Second World War, HMSO

Hitchcock, Raymond: *The Tunnellers*, Constable

Hogg, Ian: *Weapons of the American Civil War*, Bison Books

Hogg, Ian; Weeks, John: *Military Small Arms of the Twentieth Century*, Arms & Armour Press

Horner D. M.: *SAS Phantoms of the Jungle*, Allen & Unwin

Jane's Information Group: *China In Crisis*, Jane's

Jones, Liane: *A Quiet Courage*, Corgi

Jones, R. V.: *Most Secret War*, Hamish Hamilton

Judd, Denis: *The Boer War*, Granada Publishing Ltd

Katcher, Philip: *US Cavalry on the Plains 1850-90*, Osprey

Katz, Sam: *Israeli Defence Forces Since 1973*, Osprey

Keegan, John: *Who Was Who in World War II*, Bison Books Ltd

Kennedy, Michael Paul: *Soldier 'I' - SAS*, Bloomsbury

Laffin, John: *The World In Conflict*, Brasseys

Lang, Walter N.: *The World's Elite Forces*, Salamander

Ladd, James D: *Royal Marine Commando: The History of Britain's Elite Fighting Force*, Hamlyn

Lloyd, Mark: *Combat Uniforms of the Civil War*, Brian Trodd Publishing

— *The Guinness Book of Espionage*, Guinness

— *The Guinness Book of Helicopters Facts and Feats*, Guinness

— *Modern Combat Uniforms*, Brian Trodd Publishing

— *Tactics of Modern Warfare*, Brian Trodd Publishing

Loran, Pierre: *Secret Warfare, The Arms and Techniques of the Resistance*, Orbis

Lucas, James: *Kommando, German Special Forces of World War II*, Arms & Armour Press

— *Storming Eagles, German Airborne Forces*, Arms & Armour Press

Macdonald, Peter: *Soldiers of Fortune: The Twentieth Century Mercenary*, Admiral

— *US Special Forces*, Bison Group

— *The Special Forces*, Viscount

Macdonald, Brigadier Peter: *Giap, The Victor in Vietnam*, The Fourth Estate

McNab, Andy: *Bravo Two Zero*, Bantam Press

Melton, H. Keith: *CIA Special Weapons & Equipment*, Sterling Publishing Company

— *OSS Special Weapons & Equipment*, Sterling Publishing Company

Miller, Douglas: *The Landsknechts*, Osprey

— *The Swiss at War 1300-1500*, Osprey

Myatt, Major Frederick, MC: *Modern Small Arms*, Salamander

Nadel, Joel; Wright J. R.: *Special Men and Special Missions*, Greenhill Books

Nicolle, David: *Attila and the Nomad Hordes*, Osprey

— *The Armies of Islam 7th-11th Centuries*, Osprey

Palmer, A. W.: *A Dictionary of Modern Europe*, Penguin

Paschall, Rod: *LIC 2010: Special Operations and Unconventional Warfare in the Next Century*, Brassey's UK

Pimlott, John; Badsey, Stephen: *The Gulf War Assessed*, Arms & Armour Press

Pitt, Barrie: *Special Boat Squadron*, Century

Prebble, John: *Culloden*, Penguin

Quarrie, Bruce: *Special Forces*, Guild Publishing

Robinson, Mike: *Fighting Skills of the SAS*, Sidgwick & Jackson

RUSI: *Internal Security Review 1993/4*, Brasseys

Simpson, Jacqueline: *The Viking World*, B. T. Batfield Ltd

Strawson, John: *A History of the SAS Regiment*, Guild Publishing

Thompson, Julian: *No Picnic*, Secker & Warburg Ltd

Tickler, Peter: *The Modern Mercenary*, Guild Publishing

Bibliography

Urban, Mark: *Big Boys' Rules*, Faber & Faber

(Various): *The Military Balance*, Brasseys

Virgil: *The Aeneid*, Penguin

Watson Bruce W.; George, Bruce: *Military Lessons of the Gulf War*, Greenhill Books

Welham, Michael: *Combat Frogmen*, Patrick Stephens, Limited

West, Nigel: *The Story of SOE*, Hodder & Stoughton

White, Terry: *The Making of the World's Elite Forces*, Sidgwick & Jackson

— *Swords of Lightning*, Brasseys

Wilkinson-Latham, Robert: *The Royal Navy 1790-1970*, Osprey

Williams, Major Robert; Zuehlke, Arthur A.: *Unconventional Warfare Operations*

Winter J. M.: *World War I*, Hamlyn

Winter, Terence: *Medieval European Armies*, Osprey

— *Saxon, Viking and Norman*, Osprey

Wise, Terence: *Ancient Armies of the Middle East*, Osprey

Wood, Alan: *History of the World's Glider Forces*, Patrick Stephens Ltd

Young, John Robert: *The Dragon's Teeth: Inside China's Armed Forces*, Hutchinson

— *The French Foreign Legion*, Guild Publishing

Unattributed

Committee on Armed Services: *United States and Soviet Special Operations*

Department of Defense: *Soviet Military Power*

Marshall Cavendish: *Images of War*

Readers Digest: *The World at Arms*

Articles

Adams, Captain Tom: *Special Operations Forces of the Soviet Union*, Military Intelligence, October-December 1982

Armstrong, Major Richard: *Countering the Third Dimension*, Military Intelligence, January-March 1984

Evans, Michael: *Loss of Reluctant Heroes Undermines Nation's Fight Against Terrorism*, The Times

Leppard, David: *New Supremo in War Against IRA*, Sunday Times

McKittrick, David: *Dangers that Justified Gibraltar Killings*, Independent

—: *Security Forces Suffer Incalculable Loss*, Independent

Miller, Sergio: *Special Forces - A Future?*, RUSI Journal, August 1993

Mundy, General Carl E., US Marine Corps: *Soldiers of the Sea: Versatile Forces for an Uncertain Era*, JDW August 1994 Rados, Antonia: *War and the Power of Television*, RUSI Defence Yearbook, 1992

Rimington, Stella: *Security and Democracy - Is There a Conflict?*, BBC Education

Suvorov, Viktor: *Spetsnaz: The Soviet Union's Special Forces*, IDR9/1983

Abbreviations and Acronyms

ACE Allied Command Europe
ADC Aide de Camp
ARG Amphibious Ready Group (United States Special Forces)
ARRC ACE (Allied Command Europe) Rapid Reaction Corps
ASU Active Service Unit
AWACS Airborne Warning and Control Aircraft
AWADS Adverse Weather Airborne Delivery System
BAC Basic Airborne Course (US Army)
BATT British Army Training Team
BEF British Expeditionary Force
BEP Bataillon Etranger de Parachutistes (French Foreign Legion)
BSAP British South Africa Police (Southern Rhodesian Special Branch)
CAI Chinese Army in India (Lieut Gen Stilwell)
CAMFED Combined Amphibious Force, Mediterranean
CAWS Close Assault Weapon Systems
CENTCOM Central Command (Gulf Coalition Forces)
CIA Central Intelligence Agency
CinC Commander in Chief
CIDG Civilian Irregular Defense Group (Vietnam)
COBRA Cabinet Office Briefing Room
COIN Counter-Insurgency
COMINT Communications Intelligence
CQB Close Quarter Battle
CRAP Compagnies de Reconnaissance et d'Action Profondeur
CRW Counter Revolutionary Warfare
CT Communist Terrorist

DBLE Demi-Brigade de la Légion Etrangère
DEA Drug Enforcement Agency
DFLP Democratic Front for the Liberation of Palestine
DSF Director Special Forces
DZ Drop Zone
E & E Escape and Evasion
EPI Escadron de Protection et d'Intervention
EPL Peoples' Liberation Army (Colombia)
ETAP Ecole des Troupes Aeroportées
FAR Force d'Action Rapide
FANY First Aid Nursing Yeomanry
FARC Fuerzas Armadas Revelucionarias Colombianes
FBI Federal Bureau of Investigation
FIBUA Fighting In A Built Up Area
FIR Forza di Intervento Rapido
FLET Forward Line of Enemy Troops
FLN Front de Libération Nationale (Algeria)
FLOT Forward Line of Own Troops
FULRO Front Unifiée de Libération des Races Opprimées
GFCA Groupement Fusilier de l'Air (French Air Force)
GIGN Groupement d'Intervention de la Gendarmerie Nationale
GOC General Officer Commanding
GPMG General Purpose Machine-Gun
GRU Glavnoe Razvudyvatelnoe Upravenie
GSG-9 Grenzschutzgruppe-9
HUMINT Human Intelligence
HAHO High Altitude High Opening
HALO High Altitude Low Opening
HRU Hostage Rescue Unit

Abbreviations and Acronyms

ICCP Indo-Chinese Communist Party
IDF Israeli Defence Force
IGB Inner German Border
INLA Irish National Liberation Army
JOC Joint Operations Centre
JSOC Joint Special Operations Command
LCOCU Landing Craft Obstruction Clearance Unit
LRDG Long Range Desert Group
LRRP Long Range Reconnaissance Patrol
LSL Landing Ship Logistics
LZ Landing Zone
M-19 19 April Movement (Colombia)
MAAG Military Assistance Advisory Group
M&AW Mountain and Arctic Warfare Cadre
MACV Military Assistance Command Vietnam
MAU Marine Amphibious Unit
MEA Marine Einsatz Abteilung (Naval Assault Detachment)
MEF Marine Expeditionary Force (USMC)
MI5 Military Intelligence, Department 5
MI6 Military Intelligence, Department 6 (SIS)
MICV Mechanised Infantry Combat Vehicle
MRF Mobile Reconnaissance Force
NACA National Advisory Committee for Aeronautics
NATO North Atlantic Treaty O)rganisation
NCO Non-Commissioned Officer
NDRC National Defense Research Committee (OSS)
NEST Nuclear Energy Search Team
NIO Northern Ireland Office
NITAT Northern Ireland Training Advisory Team
NSA National Security Agency
NSWTU National Special Warfare Task Unit (United States Special Forces)
OCTU Officer Cadet Training Unit
ODF Operational Defence Force
OGBM Otdelnyy Guardeyskiy Batal'on (Red Army Guards Battalion of Miners)
OKH Oberkommando des Heeres (Second World War German Army Command)

OKW Oberkommando der Wehrmacht (overall German High Command)
OOA Out of Area (Operations)
OSRD Office of Scientific Research and Development
OSS Office of Strategic Studies
PDFLP Popular Democratic Front for the Liberation of Palestine
PIB Parachute (Infantry) Battalion - US Army
PIR Parachute (Infantry) Regiment - US Army
PIRA Provisional Irish Republican Army
PJI Parachute Jumping Instructor
PLA People's Liberation Army
PLO Palestine Liberation Organisation
PSI Permanent Staff Instructor
RAF Royal Air Force
RCMP Royal Canadian Mounted Police
RE Royal Engineers
REI Régiment Etranger d'Infanterie (French Foreign Legion)
REP Régiment Etranger de Parachutistes
RFC Royal Flying Corps
RFSU Regional Force Surveillance Unit (Australia)
RIP Ranger Indoctrination Programme
RLI Rhodesian Light Infantry
RM Royal Marines Commando
RMBPD Royal Marine Boom Patrol Detachment
RMLE Régiment de Marche de la Légion Etrangère
RPIMa Régiment Parachutistes d'Infanterie de Marine
RPM Rounds Per Minute
RTI Resistance to Interrogation
RTR Royal Tank Regiment
RTU Return to Unit
RUC Royal Ulster Constabulary
SAS Special Air Service
SASR Special Air Service Regiment (Australia)
SBS Special Boat Service (formerly Squadron)
SD Sicherheitsdienst (Security Service, SS)
SEAC South-East Asia Command
SEAL Sea Air and Land

SERE Survival Evasion Resistance and Escape
SF Special Forces
SFAS Special Forces Assessment and Selection
SFG Special Forces Group
SID Servizio Informazione Difesa (Italian secret police)
SIGINT Signals Intelligence
SMIU-NI Special Military Intelligence Unit - Northern Ireland
SIS Secret Intelligence Service (MI6)
SOE Special Operations Executive
SOS Special Operations Squadron (US Air Force)
SPF Special Purpose Forces
SSF Special Service Force
SVD Samozariyadniya Vintokvka Dragunova

TAB Tactical Advance to Battle (high-speed route march)
TAOR Tactical Area of Responsibility
TEL Transporter, Erector, Launcher
TELINT Telemetry Intelligence
UDA Ulster Defence Association
UDR Ulster Defence Regiment
UDT Underwater Demolition Team
UFF Ulster Freedom Fighters
USAF United States Air Force
USAAF United States Army Air Force
USARSOC United States Army Special Operations Command
USMC United States Marine Corps
UVF Ulster Volunteer Force
VC Victoria Cross
VSN Voiska Spetsialnogo Naznacheniya (Spetsnaz)

Roll-Call of Elite Forces

It is impossible in a work of this size to list every elite force. The following therefore is no more than a roll-call of a few of the most famous, now and in history:

82nd Airborne: 'All American' division formed in 1917 for service on the Western Front, reactivated in 1942, has seen action in every major campaign since, forms spearhead of US Rapid Deployment Force

101st Airborne: 'Screaming Eagles' division formed in 1942, deactivated after Korea but subsequently reformed as a helicopter air-mobile division in Vietnam

Air America: CIA private airline retained for non-attributable operations, particularly active in South-East Asia

Amrtaka: 'Immortals' in the service of the Persian emperors, Darius and Xerxes, 5th Century BC

Arstibara: the King's Spearbearers, an elite within the Amrtaka

Asthetairoi: elite brigades in the service of Alexander the Great

Athelings: princes of the blood who commanded Anglo-Saxon armies in the field

Auszug: corps of young Swiss pikemen of the 16th Century

BBE: Bizondere Bystand Eenheid, 'Different Circumstances Unit', an HRU elite within the Royal Netherlands Marine Corps

Brandenburger: German Second World War multilingual shock troops

Chindits: Special purpose force formed by Orde Wingate for service in Japanese-held Burma (1943-44), made two raids deep behind enemy lines

Cochran's Circus: RAF unit formed to support second Chindit raid

Companions: escort to Alexander the Great (c330BC)

Comsubin: Comando Subacquei Incursori, reformed in 1952 to undertake offensive and defensive underwater activities in the Mediterranean

Detachment Delta: US counter-terrorist unit formed in November 1977, its first operation ('Eagle Claw') a failure but has had successes since

Detachment Koch: formed for the attack on the fortress of Eben Emael, May 1940

Fallschirmjäger: German airborne troops first employed in 1939, after Crete fought as elite ground troops, disbanded after the war and reformed in 1956

Fallskarmsjagers: Swedish LRPS trained Parachute-Ranger Company

Garde Equipage: naval bodyguard to Russian Imperial family, defected to Bolsheviks in 1917

Gardes de Corps: Household troops in service of Louis XIV of France

GFCA: Groupement Fusilier Commandos de l'Air, formed to protect French air bases at home and abroad

Ghulams: freed slaves and horse-archers, ninth century bodyguards to the Caliph of Baghdad

GIGN: Groupement d'Intervention de la Gendarmerie Nationale, formed in France as police para-military elite in 1973

Green Berets: Special Operations Forces -

'Green Berets' - formed by Colonel Aaron Bank and based at Fort Bragg, saw considerable action (covert and overt) throughout South-East Asia, have been gradually run down since thawing in East-West relations

GRU: Glavnoe Razvedyvatelnoe Upravlenie, Soviet military intelligence responsible for intelligence gathering and in overall control of Spetsnaz operations

GSG-9: Grenzschutzgruppe-9, German hostage-rescue and anti-terrorist unit formed in September 1972 after the Munich Olympics massacre

Gurkhas: from Nepal have served the British since 1815, saw considerable action in the Second World War, and since then in Malaya, Borneo and the Falklands

Hastati: heavily armed shock-troops, c 300BC

Hatzanhanihim: Israeli paratroopers, were formed in May 1948, have fought in every Arab-Israeli conflict since

Hirds: Hearth troops, elite mobile units formed to combat Viking raids

Imperial Guard: Old and Young Guard, shock troops in the service of Napoleon

K-Verbande: Second World War German mini-submarine unit later redesignated Marine Einsatz Abteilung

Landsknechts: German, mainly pikemen, literally 'servants of the country', first formed in 1487

LCOCU: Landing Craft Obstruction Clearance Unit, formed to clear submerged obstacles prior to D-Day landings

Légion Etrangère: formed in 1831 of mainly foreign citizens in the service of France it remains one of the finest interventionist military forces in the world, it has seen service worldwide, most recently in the Gulf

M&AW Cadre: Mountain and Arctic Warfare Cadre, trained to undertake reconnaissance and intelligence gathering operations behind enemy lines, teaches mountain and arctic warfare skills to their fellow Royal Marines

Merrill's Marauders: formed by Lieutenant General Stilwell and originally designated the 5307th Composite Unit (Provisional), it operated throughout northern Burma in close cooperation with Chinese anti-nationalist forces. Badly trained and motivated, they suffered terrible losses before their ultimate withdrawal and disbandment

Moschin: 9th 'Colonel Moschin' Assault (Saboteur) Parachute Battalion, special forces unit within the Italian Folgore Brigade

Omon: Russian anti-terrorist unit, recently involved in a number of hostage rescue incidents

OSS: Office of Strategic Studies, Second World War US equivalent to SOE

Parachute Regiment: Formed in 1940 it first saw action in a raid against the Tragino Aqueduct; later deployed in North Africa, on D-Day, at Arnhem and in the Rhine crossing. Now a part of 5 (Airborne) Brigade

Paratroop-Grenadiers: Swiss para-trained elite, 17 Company formed in 1980 to undertake long-range recce and intelligence gathering missions

Praetorian Guard: bodyguards (not always loyal) to the Roman Emperors

Rangers: Based on British Commandos in 1942 they first saw action in Italy, they were reduced to cadre status after the Korean War and not reactivated for Vietnam. Two new battalions created in 1975, saw action in Grenada, third battalion formed in 1984

Recce Commandos: highly secretive former South African equivalent of the British SAS, specialists in reconnaissance and sabotage

Régiment Para-Commando: Belgian elite formed in 1952 but with origins going back to wartime SAS Brigade and Commandos

Régiments des Gardes Françaises: formed in 1691 as infantry element of Louis XIV's Household troops

RFSU: Regional Force Surveillance Units such as NORFORCE, Australian deep-reconnaissance specialists

Roll-Call of Elite Forces

Royal Marines Commando: formed as the Admiral's Regiment in 1664, became the Corps of Marines in 1755 and RM (Amphibious) Brigade in 1939. Nine commandos were formed throughout Second World War, now integral with 3 Commando Brigade

San Marco Marines: Italian airborne-trained marine unit, formed for service in NATO southern flank, recently saw service in Beirut

SAS: Special Air Service, formed by David Stirling for service in North Africa, expanded to incorporate French and Belgian units; disbanded in 1945, reformed, initially as a TA unit, in 1946

SASR: Special Air Service Regiment, Australian special force closely associated with British SAS, saw action in Borneo and Vietnam

Sayaret: parachute-trained Israeli reconnaissance units independent of conventional brigade structure

SEALs: US Navy Sea-Air-Land teams, origins go back to wartime Underwater Demolition Teams, operated well in Vietnam, the Gulf and Grenada but less successfully in Somalia

SBS: Royal Marines Special Boat Service (until recently Squadron) formed in Second World War and has since seen service (covert and overt) in Oman, Borneo, the Falklands and the Gulf

Select Fyrd: local, well paid regular elites retained to combat the Viking threat

SOE: Special Operations Executive, covert organisation formed to 'set Europe ablaze' in 1940

Spanish Foreign Legion: Tercio de Extranjeros, formed in 1920 it now has few foreigners in its ranks, has steadily declined since the death of Franco whom it helped to come to power, the Legion Special Operations Unit (OLEU) forms an internal commando elite

Spetsnaz: Voiska Spetsialnogo Naznacheniya, commonly known as Spetsnaz, until recently a highly secretive elite, part regular part conscript, took part in invasion of Czechoslovakia, saw extensive service in Afghanistan

Thegns: or huscarles, bodyguard to the Anglo-Saxon monarchs

Trabants: bodyguard to the Hapsburgs, remained loyal until the disintegration of Austria-Hungary in 1919

US Marine Corps: formed in 1798 and now the world's largest elite force, saw considerable Second World War action in the Pacific theatre and later in Vietnam, Grenada, the Gulf, Beirut and Panama

US Sharpshooters: formed by Hiram Berdan for service with the Union forces in 1961

VDV: Vozdushno-Desantaya Voyska, former Soviet airborne units, transferred from the Air Force to the Army in 1956, spearheaded invasion of Czechoslovakia, heavily involved in Afghanistan

Index

Index

Index

Index

Index

Index